D0919180

WOODROW WILSON CENTER SERIES

Industrial democracy in America

Other books in the series

Michael J. Lacey, editor, *Religion and Twentieth-Century American Intellectual Life*

Michael J. Lacey, editor, *The Truman Presidency*

Joseph Kruzel and Michael H. Haltzel, editors, *Between the Blocs: Problems and Prospects for Europe's Neutral and Nonaligned States*

William C. Brumfield, editor, *Reshaping Russian Architecture: Western Technology, Utopian Dreams*

Mark N. Katz, editor, *The USSR and Marxist Revolutions in the Third World*

Walter Reich, editor, *Origins of Terrorism: Psychologies, Ideologies, Theologies, States of Mind*

Mary O. Furner and Barry Supple, editors, *The State and Economic Knowledge: The American and British Experiences*

Michael J. Lacey and Knud Haakonssen, editors, *A Culture of Rights: The Bill of Rights in Philosophy, Politics, and Law—1791 and 1991*

Robert J. Donovan and Ray Scherer, *Unsilent Revolution: Television News and American Public Life, 1948–1991*

HD
5660
.U5
.I53

Industrial democracy in America

The ambiguous promise

Edited by
NELSON LICHTENSTEIN and HOWELL JOHN HARRIS

WOODROW WILSON CENTER PRESS

AND

 CAMBRIDGE
UNIVERSITY PRESS

SEP 4 1997

492522

Published by the Press Syndicate of the University of Cambridge
The Pitt Building, Trumpington Street, Cambridge CB2 1RP
40 West 20th Street, New York, NY 10011–4211, USA
10 Stamford Road, Oakleigh, Victoria 3166, Australia

© Woodrow Wilson International Center for Scholars 1993

First published 1993

Printed in the United States of America

Library of Congress Cataloging-in-Publication Data
Industrial democracy in America: the ambiguous promise / edited by
Nelson Lichtenstein and Howell John Harris.
p.   cm. — (Woodrow Wilson Center series)
Includes index.
ISBN 0-521-43121-2
1. Industrial management—United States—Employee participation—
History.   2. Industrial relations—United States—History.
I. Lichtenstein, Nelson.   II. Harris, Howell John, 1951–   .
III. Series.
HD5660.U5I53   1993
331′.01′12′0973—dc20   92-28462
                                                                              CIP

A catalog record for this book is available from the British Library

ISBN 0-521-43121-2 hardback

WOODROW WILSON INTERNATIONAL CENTER FOR SCHOLARS

BOARD OF TRUSTEES

William J. Baroody, Jr., Chairman; Dwayne O. Andreas, Vice Chairman; Robert McC. Adams; Lamar Alexander; J. Burchenal Ault; James A. Baker III; James H. Billington; Henry E. Catto; Lynne V. Cheney; Gertrude Himmelfarb; Carol Iannone; Eli Jacobs; John S. Reed; S. Dillon Ripley; William L. Saltonstall; Louis W. Sullivan; John H. Sununu; Robert H. Tuttle; Don W. Wilson

The Center is the "living memorial" of the United States of America to the nation's twenty-eighth president, Woodrow Wilson. The U.S. Congress established the Woodrow Wilson Center in 1968 as an international institute for advanced study, "symbolizing and strengthening the fruitful relationship between the world of learning and the world of public affairs." The Center opened in 1970 under its own presidentially appointed board of trustees.

In all its activities the Woodrow Wilson Center is a nonprofit, nonpartisan organization, supported financially by annual appropriations from the U.S. Congress, and by the contributions of foundations, corporations, and individuals. Conclusions or opinions expressed in Center publications and programs are those of the authors and speakers and do not necessarily reflect the views of the Center staff, fellows, trustees, advisory groups, or any individuals or organizations that provide financial support to the Center.

Woodrow Wilson International Center for Scholars
Smithsonian Institution Building
1000 Jefferson Drive, S.W.
Washington, D.C. 20560
(202) 357-2429

Contents

Foreword

This book is the result of a symposium organized by the Woodrow Wilson Center's Division of United States Studies, then called the Program on American Society and Politics. The project grew out of the daily life of the institution, in this instance out of conversations between the staff and the volume's editors that took place during a period in which both of the editors were in residence as fellows. In keeping with the scholarly aims of the program, the undertaking was conceived as a contribution to the growing stock of historically oriented knowledge on the relations between ideas and institutions in modern America.

Thanks are due to the authors of all the essays in this collection, and to many others as well who served at various points as critics and commentators. Among the latter, mention must be made of Douglas Fraser, former president of the United Auto Workers of America—a shrewd observer of the changing fortunes of the American labor movement—together with James Kloppenberg, Richard L. McCormick, James Gilbert, Alan Brinkley, Laura Kalman, W. Elliot Brownlee, Mancur Olson, Everett M. Kassalow, and Robert Wiebe. The Center also gratefully acknowledges the support received from the Ford Foundation, the Beirne Memorial Foundation of the Communications Workers of America, the Xerox Foundation, the Mobil Corporation, and the AFL-CIO.

MICHAEL J. LACEY
Director
Division of United States Studies
Woodrow Wilson International Center for Scholars

1

Introduction:
A century of industrial democracy in America

NELSON LICHTENSTEIN and HOWELL JOHN HARRIS

This collection of essays had its origins in a series of conversations between the two editors and Michael Lacey, director of the U.S. Studies
Division at the Woodrow Wilson International Center for Scholars. The
conversations centered on something that struck all three of us as anom-
alous, even paradoxical: that labor history was a flourishing subdiscipline
in the American academy, enjoying mutually stimulating relations with
business history, cultural studies, women's history, and the history of
law, but the contemporary labor movement was dying on its feet, politically and socially marginalized to a degree greater than at virtually any
other time in the twentieth century.

More was at issue here than two professional historians' concern that
they, like the institutions they studied, might be becoming irrelevant. The
United States had once been the world's most dynamic, rather than merely
still the largest, industrial society. Economic growth and transformation
were its defining characteristics, prosperity for an exceptionally large
fraction of the population its key promise. That productive system depended upon a vast blue-collar working class, a social group mid-century
contemporaries often referred to as the "armies of industry," concentrated in the construction, transportation, mining, and manufacturing
sectors.

That class of wage earners had numbers, it had a voice (indeed, many

The editors would like to thank Michael Lacey and the staff of the Woodrow Wilson
Center for the support they have given to this project. Our greatest thanks are reserved
for our contributors, for the quality and interest of what they have written, for their
readiness to make revisions and respond to our suggestions, and for their patience in
awaiting the appearance of this collection.

voices), it had votes, and it had its own leaders and organizations that projected its particular grievances, values, and aspirations. All these facts created what late nineteenth- and early twentieth-century observers referred to as the "labor problem"—a compound of overt industrial strife and a widespread perception of growing social injustice and dislocation—that troubled Americans between the great railroad strikes of the 1870s and the Great Depression.

It was in the context of discussions about the labor problem that the phrase "industrial democracy" came into use in the United States. At one level, the phrase is simply descriptive—the United States is an industrial society whose political culture and system are democratic. But as the term was actually used, it was freighted with hope—it referred to a variety of schemes involving the spread of producers' cooperatives and workers' control, or public ownership and the gradual socialization of the economy, or trade union recognition and collective bargaining, or simply the improvement of workers' participation in, and acceptance of, the organizational purposes of the firms where they worked.

Thus, in the decades when the labor problem stood near the top of the political agenda in the United States, that problem was often summed up as resulting from a lack of industrial democracy, or from its imperfect and incomplete realization within the sphere of work and market relations. Where would democratic values hold sway and where must efficiency and authority demand their prerogatives: in the workshop, the factory, the firm, the industry, or at the level of the entire economy? For the labor Left, a focus on "workers' control" at the shop-floor level has often complemented more general schemes of nationalization and regulation at the macroeconomic level. In contrast, reformers more interested in industrial order and efficiency have usually fixed their sights on the firm, where codified personnel policies, employee representation schemes, and collective bargaining have constituted the essence of industrial reform.

An exploration of the practical meanings Americans gave to the term "industrial democracy" may serve as a useful way of charting the long-run containment of the labor problem and the recurrent debate over what precisely constitutes a democratic and humane workplace. And that was one purpose of the conference at the Woodrow Wilson Center that grew out of our speculations, at which all of the essays contained in this volume, except Joseph McCartin's, were originally presented. But our objects were actually a bit larger than merely investigating the historical record and sketching in paths to the present because the issues raised in the long-running debate on industrial democracy seem to have acquired a renewed resonance. Contemplation of America's industrial decline has provoked a questioning, even within management circles, of the long-run viability of a work regime that does not respect or motivate its workers—that does not persuade them to identify themselves with the enterprises of which they are members, to take responsibility for themselves and their jobs, and to be and to feel that they are participants in a meaningful process of production.

So when we look at America in the 1990s we are struck by several related facts. First, industrial democracy no longer has any of the over-tones of radical social transformation it possessed seventy to a hundred years ago. Second, the system of legally established contract-oriented unionism and adversarial collective bargaining that Americans celebrated as the means to, or realization of, "democracy in industry" between the 1930s and the 1960s may well be in terminal crisis. Even so, the social critique developed in the long debate over the meaning of industrial democracy still appears to have a certain appeal, but now less in terms of its promise to transcend the inequities of American capitalism than in its program to make U.S. firms again competitive and dynamic leaders in a world market.

The structure of the conference, and of this book, was determined by what the editors and contributors perceive to have been a process of social construction and historical definition. Not unexpectedly, interest in industrial democracy has peaked when American capitalism has been most in flux, either challenged and transformed from within by the rise of giant corporations or radical social movements, or battered from without by new competitors that have called into question well-established production techniques and organizational structures.

So the present is hardly the first such moment of flux: indeed, we can identify two earlier eras when ideas about industrial democracy seemed to flourish. The term industrial democracy first came into use in both Great Britain and the United States in the 1890s during the great crisis of what many historians now call the second industrial revolution—the epoch of economic instability, great corporate mergers, and mass strikes in steel and coal and on the rails. At that time, native American working-class radicals—Eugene V. Debs is the outstanding example—still champ-pioned the egalitarian strain in the nineteenth-century tradition of working-class republicanism, with its call for extending basic civil and political rights into the realm of production and the sphere of the market. Meanwhile, socialists and syndicalists counterposed a fervently believed in, but vaguely defined, "cooperative commonwealth" to what they saw as the growing centralization and oppressiveness of a society dominated by big capital. Thus, to much of the labor movement and the Left, the idea of industrial democracy meant trade union power, even workers' control, at both the point of production and the nexus of ownership.[1]

The ideological challenge was not inconsiderable, especially in the reform years of the Progressive Era when the legitimacy of American capitalism, or of several of its more highly visible units, came under attack. Ludlow and Lawrence before the war, Seattle and Pittsburgh in 1919, marked the boundaries of a critical period in which immigrant risings, municipal general strikes, and mass industrial unionism suddenly appeared on the sociopolitical terrain. It was in this period, therefore, that many in the Progressive movement, including some elements of the business community, also came to see the "labor question" as of paramount importance. For many of these reformers, the idea of a well-planned industrial democracy represented a way to resolve the conflicts inherent in the emergent system of giant corporations and large factories that dominated the social and economic landscape. This progressive reform view took the large industrial enterprise for granted as the basic building block of the new society and looked for a solution to problems of authority, equality, motivation, and efficiency through its reorganization. To these reformers, industrial democracy certainly meant much more than mere collective bargaining, championed by the seemingly parochial and corrupt craft unions of that era.

World War I and the social turmoil of its immediate aftermath therefore generated a wave of experimentation that included government arbitration, works councils, company unions, producers' cooperatives, and profit-sharing and nationalization schemes for industry. Aware that democracy was being subjected to "tests of unprecedented severity throughout the world," the *New Republic* concluded that democracy's future "depends...upon the capacity of employers and workers to harmonize

[1] Nick Salvatore, *Eugene V. Debs: Citizen and Socialist* (Urbana: University of Illinois Press, 1982); Leon Fink, *Workingmen's Democracy: The Knights of Labor and American Politics* (Urbana: University of Illinois Press, 1982).

democratic ideals of freedom with the voluntary self-discipline essential to efficient production."[2]

In the hands of such reformers as Felix Frankfurter or such progressive managers as Otto Beyer, industrial democracy was intended as an answer to socialism, a remedy for industrial conflict, and a way of attaching workers to the firms employing them. A radical transformation of society might well take place, but it would be achieved in a gradual, peaceful fashion, by piecemeal activities of men and women of good will, of all social classes, sharing common concerns about the injustice and wastefulness of the social order. Many hard questions were left unanswered, but that was part of the attractiveness of the idea: it was a vision, a goal, an implicit ideal for focusing criticism of the existing order.

World War I has been called a dress rehearsal for the New Deal. But it was only a dress rehearsal, not the real thing. Had World War I lasted longer, or the Wilson administration been more resolute, or big capital less antagonistic, a model of industrial democracy generated during the Progressive Era might well have become hegemonic over the industrial landscape. But this complex and often contradictory Progressive Era conception of industrial democracy quickly faded once the United States put the sociopolitical crisis of the World War I mobilization era behind it. Thereafter, the socialists were increasingly marginalized, and the Protestant bourgeoisie grew less interested in ideas of evangelical social reconstruction. Insofar as some attention was still focused on means of increasing workers' participation in the everyday management of corporate America, the persons responsible were a handful of enlightened proprietors and a larger group of progressive engineers and corporate welfare workers. Their schemes, however, were but a branch of personnel management.[3]

The Great Depression brought an end to the first period of debate over the meaning of industrial democracy. That economic hurricane swept aside most of the welfare capitalist and employee representation

[2] Quoted in Steven Fraser, "The 'Labor Question' " in Steven Fraser and Gary Gerstle, *The Rise and Fall of the New Deal Order, 1930–1980* (Princeton: Princeton University Press, 1989), 58.
[3] Steven Fraser, "Dress Rehearsal for the New Deal: Shop-Floor Insurgents, Political Elites, and Industrial Democracy in the Amalgamated Clothing Workers," in Michael Frisch and Daniel Walkowitz, eds., *Working-Class America* (Champaign: University of Illinois Press, 1983); Sanford Jacoby, *Employing Bureaucracy* (New York: Columbia University Press, 1985); Lizabeth Cohen, *Making a New Deal* (Cambridge: Cambridge University Press, 1990).

plans that had been industrial reform's most substantial accomplishments. For almost two generations, from the 1930s to the 1970s, the debate over the reconstruction of the workplace would be confined to a more limited terrain. Liberal and laborite hopes for a more democratic society became increasingly identified with the idea that collective bargaining between unions and employers represented the sole model that governed the resolution of conflicts and the assertion of rights within the world of work. Indeed the very phrase "industrial democracy" went into eclipse, replaced by "collective bargaining" as the singular definition of, and means toward, democratic representation in industry.

Despite a flurry of corporatist experiments in the early Depression era, any broader conception was replaced by the idea, enshrined in the National Labor Relations Board's interpretation of the Wagner Act and ratified by the leadership of the labor movement, as well, that industrial democracy meant just one thing: collective bargaining between a legally recognized union and an employer over wages, hours, and working conditions. Other components of the early New Deal version of industrial democracy, such as national planning, industry councils, or a more direct and robust shop-floor unionism, were eliminated from the political and intellectual agenda as politics shifted rightward and the collective bargaining system became legally entrenched and institutionally routinized.[4]

But if collective bargaining now constituted the substance and method of an American industrial democracy, not all questions had been answered, by any means. To what extent had this new system "constitutionalized" workers' rights and employer prerogatives? Could a private system of industrial jurisprudence be created that would stand parallel to the constitutional system that governed civil society, or was there something inherent in the nature of a privately owned enterprise that forestalled the full deployment of the sort of workplace rule of law that would generate a rights-based work regime? What would happen if unions were undemocratic in character or corporations multinational in their structure?

---

[4]James Gross, *The Making of the National Labor Relations Board: A Study in Economics, Politics, and Law* (Albany: State University of New York Press, 1974); Howell Harris, "The Snares of Liberalism? Politicians, Bureaucrats, and the Shaping of Federal Labour Relations Policy in the United States, ca. 1915–1947," in Steven Tolliday and Jonathan Zeitlin, eds., *Shop Floor Bargaining and the State* (Cambridge: Cambridge University Press, 1985), 148–91; Christopher Tomlins, *The State and the Unions: Labor Relations, Law, and the Organized Labor Movement in America, 1880–1960* (Cambridge: Cambridge University Press, 1985).

As a method of class harmonization, collective bargaining had many difficulties, but the most fatal by far was its lack of universality. In the 1940s and 1950s, trade union growth, labor-liberal political power, and business accommodation to the standards set by the major unionized firms obscured the failure of the labor movement to recognize the essential fragility of a system of industrial democracy established on these uncertain foundations. Even within the context of its own limited ambitions, contract-oriented collective bargaining could only work when a substantial portion of the work force and a large proportion of all employers participated in the system. Under such conditions, the nonunion employers emulated the wage standards and grievance resolution techniques of the unionized firms, if only to forestall trade union organization themselves.

But the necessary high level of collective bargaining—80 percent in heavy manufacturing, 90 percent in mining, nearly 100 percent in utilities, newspaper publishing, and commercial construction—lasted for little more than a generation. In the American context—that is, where the state played but a relatively tepid role in providing legal and economic encouragement for mass unionization—such a system of essentially voluntary collective bargaining was bound to erode, as it did even before American industry was hit by a competitive international hurricane in the 1970s and 1980s. Once direct labor costs were again put into play as a competitive factor among firms foreign and domestic, a downward spiral of deunionization gripped industry after industry: airlines, mining, meat packing, steel, newspapers, and, with the invasion of the Japanese assembly plants, even the great American automobile industry, heretofore the classic example of private sector collective bargaining. By the last decade of the twentieth century, unionism outside the government sector stood at little more than 10 percent of the entire work force, making the model of industrial democracy once embodied in the collective bargaining regime an idea whose time seems to have passed.[5]

It remains to be seen if and when a new model of workplace governance, one embodying another set of values and standards, will become as widely adopted and emulated as that of union-management collective bargaining. But a glance at the business section of virtually any major

[5] Michael Goldfield, *The Decline of Organized Labor in the United States* (Ithaca: Cornell University Press, 1987); Kim Moody, *An Injury to All: The Decline of American Unionism* (London: Verso, 1988); Thomas Kochan, Robert McKersie, and Harry Katz, *The Transformation of American Industrial Relations* (Cambridge, Mass.: MIT Press, 1986).

newspaper indicates that in the last years of the twentieth century, the fate of U.S. capitalism and the structure of the American workplace are once more live subjects of discussion in this new era of uncertainty and exploration.

We are now living through a third period in the definition of an American industrial democracy, and one where, though analogies with the 1920s may be attractive to some, historians must admit themselves unable to guess what comes next. So we have brought into this volume contributors from the fields of management studies and labor activism to examine the contours of an emergent, enterprise-based, "cooperative" system of work and production in what is left of American manufacturing as it struggles for survival and renewal.

The essays in this collection fall into three sections, in line with the periodization identified above. The first four chapters, by David Montgomery, Howell Harris, Joseph McCartin, and Ronald Schatz, discuss the ideology and language of industrial democracy when it first burst upon the American scene in the years just before, during, and after World War I. The following section closely examines the collective bargaining system in the United States during its heyday, the mid-century years from the late 1930s until the early 1960s, with chapters by Nelson Lichtenstein, James Atleson, and David Brody. Finally, this volume concludes with chapters by Sanford Jacoby and Michael Parker that take a comparative look at the seemingly successful Japanese model to discuss the changing character of the industrial work regime in the United States during the current era of renewed experimentation and debate.

In addition to this chronological ordering, the chapters divide into two interpretative camps that provide divergent explanations for the relative failure of industrial democracy in U.S. industry. Harris, Schatz, Brody, and Jacoby explain the narrowly contractualist and firm-centered character of labor-capital engagement in America by emphasizing the broad social and political structures that have shaped public policy and private choice. They posit an overarching explanation for the embedded peculiarities of the American system: finding it in the power of liberal ideology, or the technical imperatives generated by the mass production system, or the particular history and timing of the industrialization surge in the United States. Their vision is one of institutional limits and ideological constraints, of an American exceptionalism that has systematically aborted union militancy and shop-floor activism, and tempered the idea of a labor voice in the governance of industrial America.

A different spirit infuses the work of many of the other contributors to this volume, who see historical contingency, ideological combat, and class struggle as playing far greater roles in generating the specific character of the American industrial relations system. The chapters by Montgomery, McCartin, Lichtenstein, Atleson, and Parker emphasize the specific historical context, the momentary sway of particular ideas, and the sheer power of capital to account for the impasse that has so often thwarted the growth of workers' rights, power, and participation. Although these authors largely reject the idea of an American exceptionalism in industry and politics, they eschew an explicitly comparative focus, especially notable in the work of Brody and Jacoby. Instead, they rely upon a close analysis of an episode or theme in order to keep in mind those roads not taken and those democratic impulses left unexplored.

The language of industrial democracy was never more widespread than during the era of social tension and political experimentation that reached its climax in 1919, and the industrial democracy idea became incorporated throughout the entire spectrum of Progressive Era reform thought. But, as David Montgomery, Joseph McCartin, and Howell Harris show, the meaning of this idea was never subject to a greater range of interpretations and structural reformulations. Both Montgomery and Harris find the initial usage of the term arising out of the effort by reformers and labor leaders to accommodate the spirit of nineteenth-century republicanism to the realities of a society widely believed to be dominated by giant corporations. Montgomery notes Henry Demarest Lloyd's comments to an 1893 AFL convention: "Democracy must and will rule wherever men coexist, in industry not less surely than in politics."[6]

Focusing his attention upon the workers' movement, David Montgomery finds that the use of the term quickly became a point of contention between Samuel Gompers and his socialist opponents inside the AFL. The phrase was conspicuously absent from the language of the Knights of Labor, of the AFL, and of the Socialists before the 1890s, but once introduced by the Left as a sort of code word for collective ownership—during the 1890s, when democracy itself seemed under attack—

[6]Henry Demarest Lloyd, "Men—The Workers" (New York, 1909), 14–15.

the phrase "industrial democracy" found itself quite useful indeed. Gompers and his circle of self-taught labor intellectuals adopted it as an argument for their brand of voluntaristic collective bargaining and as a bludgeon to deploy against union opponents. As both Harris and Montgomery note, this interpretation of industrial democracy emphasized the organic, evolutionary transformation of society. It was in keeping both with Spencerian laws of social evolution and with the then-fashionable Whiggish interpretation of the growth of democratic political institutions, especially as they seemed to have emerged from the centuries-long struggle in Great Britain between monarchy, parliament, and people to culminate in the reform bill of 1832 and a long era of constitutional stability.

But as Montgomery makes clear, even a "constitutionalized" collective bargaining regime failed to find a place for the radical, syndicalist spirit that many reformers and some union leaders disparaged as "primitive" trade unionism. Especially during World War I, when economic mobilization socialized all production, industrial struggles were infused with the ambitious political goals that echoed the democratic rhetoric of Lloyd, Debs, and Big Bill Heywood. Indeed, such primitive union democracy—most notably exemplified by the demand for workers' control that surged through the ranks of workers in the metal-working industry—was soon elevated into a new revolutionary doctrine of "direct action" that stimulated the growth of workshop organization in the World War I era.

Joseph McCartin examines directly the linguistic symbolism of that World War I moment of extraordinary mobilization. Like Montgomery and Harris, McCartin finds that the language of industrial democracy can serve many masters, but during the Great War for Democracy the rhetoric of industrial democracy spurred on a working-class insurgency that extended well beyond the confines of the union movement itself. The key phenomenon here was the legitimizing function of government-sponsored propaganda. The ideological impact of the war, encapsulated in such phrases as "Americanism," "industrial democracy," "self-determination," and "postwar reconstruction," generated a major shift in the subpolitical attitudes of masses of ordinary workers. Self-organization into shop committees and works councils sponsored by the wartime mobilization agencies now seemed patriotic and unproblematic, less a union response to management oppression than part of an American feeling appropriate to a war for democracy.

As McCartin points out, the language of industrial democracy proved both sweeping and flexible, appropriate to a working class enormously heterogeneous in its composition. Indeed, the discussion of "self-government in the workshop," or rhetoric attacking "Prussian management," proved even more inclusive and mobilizing than the language of traditional labor militancy, with its appeals to class solidarity and workers' control. For example, women who worked as semiskilled operatives could find in the vague term industrial democracy a legitimization for their aspirations that avoided a unionism too often identified with bitter strikes, craft pride, and male exclusiveness.

Of course, managers were not unaware of this troublesome liturgy, and after the armistice, they mobilized not only to transform government labor policy and corporate practice, but to turn the language of industrial democracy into a powerful weapon in their postwar counteroffensive. With Montgomery, McCartin finds World War I–era patriotic language Janus-faced, and in the months and years immediately after the conflict, employers such as General Electric and Goodyear successfully fought to conflate loyalty to the employer with loyalty to the country. The American Plan was indeed a well-chosen label for the open-shop drive of 1921 and 1922.

Harris looks well beyond the labor movement to the many worlds of liberal reform and progressive management to find the most vocal and influential proponents of industrial democracy in the World War I era. For liberals worried about social unrest or, even more expansively, about the promise of American life, industrial reform of a certain sort offered a broad, safe road into the future while it reasserted fundamental political beliefs of a recent past. But to these liberals, industrial democracy had taken on an instrumental cast: it was less an end in itself than a means to a somewhat different goal. Because of the very weakness of the American state, a democratization of the corporate order was essential, even more important than a democratic government itself because the former was now necessary to assure the continuing existence of the latter.

This instrumentalism is even more apparent when Harris turns his attention to the way in which employers and their technocratic servants projected their own highly influential definition of twentieth-century industrial democracy. From management's World War I–era perspective, the labor problem consisted less of an absence of democracy in the workplace than the inefficiency of a work force that was too often absent, alienated, and hostile to reasonable authority. In this context, a program of industrial democracy represented a psychologically sophisticated technique for the social integration of the work force with the enterprise.

Industrial democracy engendered that most precious commodity of the workaday world: informed and willing consent. It strengthened the legitimacy of managerial authority during a turbulent period. While such programs could sometimes take on a socially radical coloration, most such schemes of plant self-governance, such as the employee representation plans that flourished in the 1920s, were narrowly conceived and management-dominated. Howell Harris concludes that this reform impulse contained far more elite manipulation than democratic self-expression.

Ronald Schatz makes a similar point in Chapter 5, a study of industrial relations professionals who got their start, both as academic theorists and as result-oriented problem solvers, in the World War I era of organizational experimentation. It was a time, remembered the pioneering labor economist John R. Commons of the summer of 1919, when capitalists were throwing money at the fledgling profession in hopes that the professors might somehow solve their labor problem. In his analysis of the intellectual underpinnings of this very practical academic field, Ronald Schatz demonstrates the essentially corporatist vision of these industrial relations professionals, from Commons in the early twentieth century through Clark Kerr and John Dunlop in the post–World War II years.

Like so many other social theorists of the first half of the twentieth century who sought to resolve the explosive tensions inherent in a class society, the industrial relations professionals generated a theory of sociopolitical governance that departed sharply from nineteenth-century republican norms. Commons, who sought "to save capitalism by making it good," saw new forms of democracy created out of the negotiations that periodically took place among well-organized and soundly led constituent social blocs: labor, capital, agriculture, consumers, and government. By the late 1940s, industrial relations experts like John Dunlop, who had enjoyed considerable success resolving construction industry disputes in just such a World War II–era corporatist setting, hoped that postwar industry-wide bargaining would rapidly evolve into the kind of tripartite, quasi-governmental structures involving representatives of a moderate labor movement and a pragmatic business sector that governed economic life in countries like Austria and Sweden.

Of course, this corporatist vision held little room for a conception of industrial democracy that might have accommodated the more lively spirits of the Progressive Era. As Schatz points out, industrial relations professionals were committed to the existence of a strong union movement and to the institution of collective bargaining. But they envisioned a world in which capital clearly defined the limits of the contest, with such of its prerogatives as choice of product, general flow of production, and investment or disinvestment of capital outside the accepted realm of collective bargaining. Nor were they advocates of a democratic renewal within the unions themselves, for these corporatists often saw unmediated rank-and-file sentiment as disruptive to the process of elite accommodation and compromise that constituted the essence of collective bargaining and corporatist governance.

Industrial relations corporatism ultimately proved a dead end. To advance their social vision, these professionals assumed that large-scale capitalist economies virtually required the existence of a strong trade union movement. But the unexpected demise of the unions left these practical theorists stranded at the end of the twentieth century. Despite the influential posts in government and academy to which many industrial relations professionals had succeeded—several served as presidents of some of America's most important universities, and Dunlop himself worked as secretary of labor in the 1970s—their influence waned as the union movement shrank and as both neoclassical economics and left-wing social thought enjoyed a renaissance within the academy.

The enormous influence wielded by the industrial relations professors in the mid-century decades testifies to the extent to which collective bargaining had supplanted all other models of industrial democracy and become the institutionally dominant structure for the social and political reform of American industrial life. The possibilities and limits of such a collective bargaining regime constitute the subject of the chapters by Nelson Lichtenstein, James Atleson, and David Brody. In his discussion of the fate of an industrial jurisprudence in the 1930s and 1940s, Lichtenstein demonstrates the extent to which important industrial relations scholars like Sumner Slichter and William Leiserson continued to expect a constitutionalization of American industrial life, as the new industrial unions attempted to apply the rule-making, power-sharing collective bargaining model worked out in the needle trades and the highly skilled crafts a decade or two earlier. In these industries, a large number of highly competitive firms faced a relatively powerful and sophisticated trade union that saw the management of both production and labor relations as intrinsic to the continued health of the trade, and assumed, rightly, that the employers alone were not capable of looking after the industry's common interests. In hosiery and clothing, an expansive arbitration system, invariably presided over by a high-prestige industrial relations academic, proved the central institution in the movement to construct a viable industrial democracy.

But could such a system of grievance adjustment and production control take root in heavy industry, where the Congress of Industrial Organizations made such dramatic headway after 1936? The United Automobile Workers attempted to find out, once agreement was reached to establish an arbitration system at General Motors, then the world's largest industrial enterprise. Lichtenstein argues that the GM arbitration system, inspired directly by the experience of the Amalgamated Clothing Workers, embodied two seemingly irreconcilable goals: a mechanism for defusing shop-floor conflict and ensuring the maintenance of industrial discipline, that is, a system that mirrors Howell Harris's darker vision of Progressive Era industrial democracy; and a quasi-legal system that unionists expected would help them bring to the factory and mill the protections available to all citizens in civil society.

Lichtenstein's detailed examination of how the union challenged GM's authority in one region, the definition and application of seniority rules, demonstrates that the arbitration system did indeed institutionalize a system of industrial jurisprudence that served to advance the union's frontier of control. But unlike firms in the needle trades, huge General Motors—and other oligopolistically dominant firms—hardly had the same need for an arbitration system to help it maintain industrial discipline or facilitate more efficient production. And despite its militant reputation, the UAW had far less leverage in the auto industry than the Amalgamated Clothing Workers did in the men's suit and cloak trade.

Given this imbalance of power, not to mention the changing political configuration of labor-management relations in the immediate postwar era, General Motors soon regained the initiative and relegated the system of industrial rule making advanced by the union to an increasingly narrow and technical compass, one that clearly subordinated the institution's democratizing potential to the more pressing effort to find social mechanisms that could sustain GM's traditional definition of industrial discipline and efficient production.

James Atleson reaches parallel conclusions in Chapter 7, on labor law during World War II and the years immediately thereafter. Emphasizing the formative role played by the National War Labor Board, whose general philosophy latter-day legal scholars would characterize as one of "industrial pluralism," Atleson demonstrates the extent to which the decisions of this government agency were later formalized by the Supreme Court in the postwar era. Under pressure to maintain production and social order, the War Labor Board sought a rational, bureaucratic, and peaceful mechanism to resolve conflicts between managers and workers. It defined industrial democracy largely in terms of the process of dispute resolution rather than in terms of the character of the power held by the contending forces, or of the justice or fairness of the bargaining procedure's outcomes. Since its leading personalities were among the same individuals who had pioneered arbitration schemes in the garment trades and the auto industry, the WLB threw its considerable weight behind a vast elaboration of such arbitration mechanisms, which it saw as a necessary complement to the no-strike pledge that most unions honored during the war itself.

The judiciary greatly extended and distorted the logic of this quid pro quo after the war. In the 1960 *Lucas Flower* case, for example, the Supreme Court insisted that the mere presence of an arbitration clause in a union contract meant that the union had waived its otherwise statutorily protected right to strike over an arbitrable grievance. And in the *Boys Market* decision of 1970, the high court would make virtually all work stoppages illegal during the term of a contract, in the process legitimizing again labor injunctions of the sort that had once so crippled the union movement between the 1890s and the New Deal.

Atleson also argues that the War Labor Board proved decisive in defining the scope of collective bargaining in terms that sustained the essence of management's unilateral power: that is, those prerogatives of capital whose successful defense thwarted any possibility that the evolution of the contractual relationship might eventually result in the limited industrial democracy of a firm-centered co-management. The WLB did widen the scope of collective bargaining to cover fringe benefits, vacations, and the like, but drew the line at what it considered management functions inherently necessary to efficient production. The Supreme Court's 1964 *Fibreboard* decision formally incorporated this policy into the nation's basic industrial relations law by declaring outside the scope of collective bargaining those issues, such as production planning and investment decisions, that "lie at the core of entrepreneurial control."

The Lichtenstein-Atleson perspective, once considered a radical, New Left-ish challenge to the pluralist scholarship that held sway until the late 1970s, has now become part of the mainstream interpretation that explains the decline in collective bargaining's democratic potential. But their view is hardly uncontested, and in Chapter 8, David Brody reaches conclusions quite different from those of Atleson or Lichtenstein. Rejecting the idea that the late 1930s or the era of World War II represented some sort of a conservative turning point in the evolution of workplace power relations, Brody argues that in the core industries of the U.S. economy, workers themselves sought the rigidly defined system of work rules and seniority rights that, in the eyes of Lichtenstein and other like-minded historians, sharply circumscribed the promise of a more fluid and robust industrial democracy.

Indeed, from a shop-floor perspective, the new industrial unions underwent no management-inspired and legally sanctioned counterrevolution. Instead, Brody argues, along with Charles Sabel and Michael Piore, authors of the influential book, *The Second Industrial Divide,* that the logic of mass production generated demands, by workers themselves, for clearly demarcated job classifications, seniority rules, and lines of authority. These together constituted the workplace contractualism so negatively appraised not only by labor historians such as Lichtenstein, but by the school of critical legal scholars that includes Karl Klare and Katherine Van Wezel Stone as well as James Atleson.[7]

Brody buttresses his argument with a comparative look at other labor relations systems. After surveying labor law and union-management practice in several industrial democracies, Brody finds that "insofar as shop-floor struggles are about industrial justice, they take their meaning from and are understood within the terms of the larger political culture." And like so many other observers, Brody finds American political culture particularly litigious, which has further served to legitimize the workplace contractualism that he finds so pervasive on the U.S. scene. Finally, Brody concludes his argument with the enormously sympathetic story of Nick DiGaetano, a skilled metal polisher and veteran shop-floor activist, the very sort of early twentieth-century syndicalist that one might have expected to have bitterly resisted the contractualist web that came to circumscribe and define his workplace freedom. Yet DiGaetano welcomed the UAW contractual system that made it possible for his Italian co-workers to throw off their deferential attitude toward the foreman and

---

[7] See for example Karl Klare, "Judicial Deradicalization of the Wagner Act and the Origins of Modern Legal Consciousness, 1937–1941," *Minnesota Law Review* 62 (1978): 265–339; Katherine Van Wezel Stone, "The Post-war Paradigm in American Labor Law," *Yale Law Journal* 90 (1981): 1509–80; and James Atleson, *Values and Assumptions in American Labor Law* (Albany: State University of New York Press, 1983).

superintendent. Their worklife took on a more dignified meaning and the predictable rules and regulations under which they now worked gave to their factory existence a measure of bourgeois citizenship it had never held before.

Just as work rules and work rights are at the center of the debate over the origins and nature of workplace contractualism in the 1930s and 1940s, so too are they central to the contemporary exploration of new forms of work and authority. In Chapters 9 and 10, Sanford Jacoby and Michael Parker offer two very different but highly complementary analyses of the forces that are changing the work regime, both in Japan and in the United States. Jacoby's perspective is a broad, comparative overview of labor relations in Japan and the United States over the last century; Parker's is that from the shop-floor up, examining how Japanese management technique, with its promise of a more participatory, team-oriented workplace, is actually being deployed in the American automobile industry.

Jacoby argues that the differences and similarities between Japanese and American work regimes and internal labor markets are a product less of cultural uniqueness or government policy than of the timing and thrust of industrial growth in both nations. Despite a U.S. obsession with the uniqueness of Japan's labor relations system, Jacoby demonstrates that until the early 1930s, Japan and the United States had a great deal in common, especially when compared to European industrial societies. On both sides of the Pacific, large corporations, often deploying mass-production techniques, appeared relatively early in the twentieth century, before widespread unionization had struck deep roots among skilled workers. A wave of labor radicalism during World War I swept through both nations, but by the late 1920s, union densities remained below those in northwest Europe.

As a result of this historic union weakness, corporatism of the sort that emerged in Western Europe (and of the sort so fondly hoped for by so many American labor intellectuals) failed to appear in either Japan or the United States after World War II. Instead, collective bargaining remained both fragmentary and decentralized, reinforcing the hostility of most employers to independent unionism and industry-wide bargaining. But these similarities did not mean that the internal labor markets generated by Japanese and American firms would also run parallel. Indeed, the differences were quite striking between 1950 and 1980 when industrial relations in each nation moved along their own path.

In the United States, a weak welfare state and highly mobile work force have provided the context in which a decentralized union movement has sought income security rather than job security for its members in the face of periodic employer efforts to cut costs by slashing payrolls. As a consequence, internal labor markets in the United States, even among nonunion firms, are geared to a fluctuating employment level, which in turn generates a proliferation of seniority-based work rules designed to define jobs precisely, allocate workers, and protect their pay and position during layoffs. To a large extent, trade unions have merely ratified and extended the preexisting tendency of American management to generate such a work regime.

In Japan, by way of contrast, unions and employers have favored employment security over well-defined job definitions and income security. But the lifetime employment guarantees so famously implemented by Japan's largest firms are possible only under two conditions: a far greater degree of management flexibility than in the United states, involving unilateral employer control over job definitions and employee wages; and second, a vast dual economy heavily staffed by an unstable work force of lower-paid men and women. This Japanese system, concludes Jacoby, may represent the future of American industrial relations, especially given the contemporary near demise of the old industrial unions and the industries they inhabited, and the huge expansion of the temporary, contingent work force in the United States.

In the final chapter, Mike Parker examines what this brave new world actually looks like from the perspective of an American automobile factory. As in the era of World War I, language and symbolism are all-important, but in the fin de siècle United States, management has largely captured the rhetoric of work reform and humane production. Today American managers counterpose their Japanese-style system of team production and flexible work rules to traditional Taylorism and adversarial labor relations. They have seen the future, and it works; and it requires the scrapping of ideologies and institutions inherited from the American industrial past. This system marginalizes the role played by the union inside the plant, but a sizable slice of organized labor endorses the new work structure. The extent to which this outlook is a genuine conversion, not a tactical accommodation, remains an open question.

But just as the rhetoric of industrial democracy has often embodied contradictory impulses, so too does Mike Parker find both the ideology and the reality of this new shop-floor work regime highly problematic.

Indeed it hardly represents a new era of participatory management or democratic reorganization. Instead, he finds the team production regime now being installed in many U.S. factories one of "management by stress," which undercuts worker autonomy and reproduces many of the most egregious elements of the early twentieth-century drive system of punitive supervision. Parker emphasizes the way in which the erosion of negotiated work rules in heavy industry leads to a deterioration in the rights-based quality of factory worklife. In this respect, his analysis runs parallel to that of both Nelson Lichtenstein and David Brody. Their attention to the structural features and ideological impulses that favor a rule-bound system of workplace governance also stands in opposition to the idea that management-initiated tinkering with a firm's internal labor market can fundamentally eliminate the endemic conflict between workers and managers in twentieth-century factories, mills, and offices. The quest for an American industrial democracy thus remains an unfulfilled item on the nation's social agenda.

2

Industrial democracy or democracy in industry?: the theory and practice of the labor movement, 1870–1925

DAVID MONTGOMERY

Although *industrial democracy* has become, in Milton Derber's words, "One of the most widely used terms in the lexicon of individuals and groups concerned with industrial relations," since its appearance in the 1890s, it has had different and often contradictory meanings imputed to it by people with divergent social objectives.[1] Howell John Harris has traced this diversity as it appeared in the writings of middle-class reformers. The purpose of this chapter is to examine the term's historic origins and various meanings within the American labor movement before the 1920s. Contrary to the belief of Ray Stannard Baker that the trade union constituted at best "a blind but mighty impulse toward democracy,"[2] in need of interpretation and guidance by reformers like himself, it was activists within the labor movement who produced the earliest theoretical analyses of their own institutions. Although the antistatist conception of the union's role developed by the leadership of the American Federation of Labor provided the basis on which reformers like those of the National Civic Federation and the Wisconsin school of institutional economists erected their own image of industrial democracy, there were also many articulate dissenters from that vision not only in the Socialist party and the Industrial Workers of the World but also within the AFL itself. The diversity of ideas within the labor movement

[1] Milton Derber, *The American Idea of Industrial Democracy, 1865–1965* (Urbana, Ill., 1970), 111.
[2] Quoted in Howell John Harris, "Industrial Democracy and Liberal Capitalism, 1890–1925," p. 54, this volume.

was a product both of its own ideological heritage and of the very limited success of the AFL's pursuit of its own declared objectives during the first three decades of this century.

Workers of the 1860s, 1870s, and 1880s did not equate industrial democracy with work relations. In fact, they did not use the term industrial democracy at all. The first significant coupling of the words *democracy* and *industry* appeared in the 1890s, and then their joint use suggested collective ownership of the means of production. Nevertheless, union efforts to regulate work relations had by then paved the way for an alternative employment of the concept, much narrower in scope, which identified democracy in industry with collective bargaining (or, in the language of that day, with the trade agreement). Despite the sudden popularity of this notion in public discourse, its inadequacies were quite evident to employers and workers alike.

Most business executives were determined to keep their enterprises free of unions or other so-called outside interference, though their concern with worker productivity, turnover, and channels of communication within the firm had provoked by 1920 corporate experimentation with reforms of work relations that did not involve trade unions.

And, despite the growth of union membership, many activists in the labor movement remained keenly aware that trade agreements covered only a small minority of workers, that collective bargaining was not synonymous with workers' control, and that the question of democratizing economic life simply could not be limited to the changing of work relations. The dissenters looked to political mobilization or to direct action as strategies for social transformation that would supplement, or even replace, the trade agreement. The full employment and heady propaganda atmosphere of World War I increased the size and the aspirations of the trade unions, while the war's demonstration of the administrative capacity of the modern state encouraged efforts by labor activists to harness the government's coercive power to the service of workers' needs.

By the end of the postwar depression (1920–22), however, the union movement, while larger than it had been before the war, had few trade agreements other than those with relatively small employers who serviced localized markets. In this context, advocates of political action and workers' control were marginalized in small revolutionary parties or in the world of labor journalism and labor colleges, while the leadership of the AFL revitalized the contractualist and antistatist notion of industrial democracy that their organization had first developed in the 1890s. The limited and contracting scope of trade unionism in the 1920s imparted a peculiarly self-satisfied tone to their declarations.

LABOR REFORM AND ITS ADVOCATES

The message of post–Civil War labor reformers had been neatly summarized by Henry Demarest Lloyd, in a speech he delivered to a trade union picnic on 4 July 1889. "The labour movement," Lloyd argued, had "a definite, clearly defined mission."

> That mission on its constructive side is to extend into industry the brotherhood already recognized in politics and religion, and to teach men as workers the love and equality which they profess as citizens and worshippers. On its other side, the mission of the labour movement is to free mankind from the superstitions and sins of the market, and to abolish the poverty which is the fruit of those sins.[3]

Lloyd's exhortation developed two themes familiar to labor reformers of the late nineteenth century and often encapsulated by recent historians within the term *republicanism*. The first was the notion that all men and women were bound by moral obligations to each other's welfare. The task of labor reform was to saturate the new industrial life with commitment to the commonweal. Even the many freethinkers among labor activists recognized and often made rhetorical use of the Christian heritage through which this obligation had historically been expressed. Thus Massachusetts-born George E. McNeill assured his readers that the "Pilgrim leaven still works" and that in "this movement of laborers toward equity, we will find a new revelation of the old Gospel."[4] Similarly, Belgian-born Victor Drury, who had been prominent in both the First International and the Knights of Labor, after predicting that solidarity would become the bond attaching people "to society, to humanity, to truth, [and] to justice," added: "if we prefer the word, religion will be the pivot upon which all physical, intellectual and moral manifestations will turn." In a land where "religious liberty" existed, "what is there," he asked, "to prevent the in-

---

[3] Henry Demarest Lloyd, "Men—The Workers" (New York, 1909), 14–15.
[4] George E. McNeill, *The Labor Movement: The Problem of To-Day* (New York, 1887), 2. See Herbert G. Gutman, "Protestantism and the American Labor Movement: The Christian Spirit in the Gilded Age," in Gutman, *Work, Culture, and Society in Industrializing America: Essays in American Working-Class and Social History* (New York, 1976), 79–117. For a discussion of republicanism and its recent uses by historians, see Sean Wilentz, "Against Exceptionalism: Class Consciousness and the American Labor Movement, 1790–1920," *International Labor and Working-Class History* 26 (Fall 1984): 1–24.

dustrial school from establishing the religion of solidarity?"[5] The second theme was the belief that the revolution of the eighteenth century had endowed the inhabitants (or at least the male adults) of the United States with citizenship, that is to say, with active participation in determining their collective destiny and with a loyalty to the nation that transcended individual prosperity. That legacy had survived and been explicitly extended to black men by the Civil War. Labor activists repeatedly made citizenship the standard against which industrial society was measured and found wanting. Thus the declaration of principles approved by trade-union delegates to the Industrial Congress of 1874 and then adopted unchanged by the Knights of Labor four years later began:

WHEREAS, The recent alarming development and aggression of aggregated wealth, which, unless checked, will inevitably lead to the pauperization and hopeless degradation of the toiling masses, renders it imperative, if we desire to enjoy the blessings of the government bequeathed us by the founders of the Republic, that a check should be placed upon its power and unjust accumulation, and a system adopted that will secure to the laborer the fruits of his toil.[6]

The term industrial democracy was conspicuously absent from this movement rhetoric. Indeed, it would have been out of place. As Milton Derber has pointed out, in those rare instances in which the term appeared in print before the 1890s, it referred to some scheme of profit sharing, which was being proposed by liberal reformers to counteract the dangerous appeal of unions and labor legislation.[7] Such use of the term gave it a very narrow construction: workers' participation in sharing the fruits of the enterprise. Quite different was the discourse of Knights, Socialists, and trade unionists alike in the last half of the nineteenth century, which referred not just to alienating conditions of work and inequitable distribution of income, but also to the corruption of the commonwealth.

"The great mass of the people are dependent upon those who monopolize land and capital for the privilege of working," wrote the widely read Canadian Phillips Thompson. "What they receive for their labor bears no relation to the value of what they produce to the consumer."[8] Thus the benefits of economic growth accrued to "the selfish and arbitrary

[5] *Journal of United Labor,* 25 May 1886.
[6] *Workingman's Advocate,* 25 April 1874; McNeill, 151. The first academic study of the labor movement, Richard T. Ely, *The Labor Movement in America* (New York, 1886), was also devoted to the relationship between labor reform and Christian social ethics.
[7] Derber, 7; E. L. Godkin, "The Labor Crisis," *North American Review* 55 (July 1867): 177–213; George J. Holyoake, *Among the Americans* (London, 1881), 44–46.
[8] Phillips Thompson, "The Land Question," in Terence V. Powderly and A. W. Wright, eds., *Labor Day Annual* (n.p., 1893), 18–22. The quotations are on p. 20.

few," while the bulk of the population competed mercilessly with each other for jobs. "These extremes of wealth and poverty are threatening the existence of the government," proclaimed George McNeill, and he added his famous warning: "there is an inevitable and irresistible conflict between the wage-system of labor and the republican system of government—the wage-laborer attempting to save the government, and the capitalist class ignorantly attempting to subvert it."[9]

More intriguing is the fact that the word *democracy* itself rarely appeared in labor reformers' discourse. It was conspicuously absent from the vocabulary of Samuel Gompers until he identified democracy with the war aims of President Wilson, after which he inserted it into his almost every other sentence. An AFL appeal of 1888 had used vocabulary more familiar to the nineteenth-century labor movement, when it spoke of "the fast-coming grand struggle between Capital and Labor, involving the perpetuation of the *civilization* we have so laboriously evolved."[10]

One year later, George Gunton referred to democracy in a pamphlet written for the AFL, but he did so with specific reference to measures then being espoused for "imposing property, educational and other qualifications for voting, lengthening the terms and increasing the appointing powers of executive officers, making popular elections less frequent, ... taking public offices out of the reach of politics, etc." These measures, Gunton contended, were "simply attempts to whittle away our democratic institutions in order to sustain a pernicious industrial policy."[11]

It was Henry Demarest Lloyd's appeal for political action to secure collective ownership of the means of production that made democracy a clarion call to the 1893 AFL convention. Our "present aristocratic and monarchical government of industry stands a self-confessed failure," he argued.

It is by the people who do the work that the hours of labour, the conditions of employment, the division of the produce is to be determined. It is by them the captains of industry are to be chosen, and chosen to be servants, not masters. It is for the welfare of all that coordinated labour of all must be directed. Industry, like government, exists only by the cooperation of all, and like government, it must guarantee equal protection to all. This is democracy.[12]

[9]McNeill, 459.
[10]William Trant, *Trade Unions*, 3d ed. (New York, 1888), 48. Italics mine.
[11]George Gunton, *The Economic and Social Importance of the Eight-Hour Movement* (AFL Eight-Hour Series, No. 2, Washington, D.C., 1889), 23. Cf. Frank K. Foster's reference to "the rising wrath of American Democracy" as one of many current popular protests. Gutman, 87.
[12]Lloyd, 91.

A year later Gompers uncharacteristically inserted the word into a speech of his own. He did so in order to turn Lloyd's own rhetoric against Lloyd's call for political action:

> It is ridiculous to imagine that the wage-workers can be slaves in employment and yet achieve control at the polls. There never yet existed coincident with each other autocracy in the shop and democracy in political life.[13]

"THE NATURAL GROWTH OF NATURAL LAWS": THE TRADES UNIONS' RATIONALE

Gompers's response reveals the intensity of his opposition to the proposal for political action and the goal of collective ownership, which had been introduced into the AFL conventions of 1893 and 1894 with Lloyd's support. Gompers's remedy for "slavery" in employment was for workers to pull themselves up by their collective bootstraps by means of union organization. Through careful management of union dues they could insure each other against illness, funeral costs, and even unemployment. They could halt the ruinous competition of worker against worker by establishing standard wages for their crafts, below which no member would accept employment. They could drive greedy, tyrannical, or submissive behavior out of their workshops by enforcing the workers' own ethical codes of conduct toward each other and toward their bosses. In short, through unions they could act like citizens in industrial life.

Early trade unions often declared, as did the Sons of Vulcan in 1868, that in "upholding and advancing the principles of our own organization, we positively affirm that we have no disposition to deteriorate the just claims of capital."[14] In fact, such pronouncements were most likely to emanate from the strongest and most effective unions—those that had been able to impose their terms of conduct on many places of employment. The unions of skilled craftsworkers especially relied on the commitment and courage of their individual members to enforce both union wage rates and work codes that had been inscribed in the unions' bylaws. As Christopher Tomlins noted, trade-union pleas that their members' actions were "voluntary" provided an effective response to threats of

---

[13] *Report of the Proceedings of the Fourteenth Annual Convention of the American Federation of Labor held at Denver, Colorado, December 1894* (Bloomington, Ind., 1905), 14.
[14] *Vulcan Record* 1 (January 1868): 21.

prosecution as conspiracies, but they also reflected the obligations to which workers had committed themselves upon joining the unions.[15]

Nevertheless, the institutional role and discipline of unions grew increasingly important. Among other things, unions of coal miners, iron molders, bricklayers, and shoe workers during the late 1860s and early 1870s had tried to enforce uniform wage scales over larger and larger geographic regions in an effort to minimize the impact of wage competition on the behavior of both workers and employers. In anthracite coal, cotton spinning, and iron puddling unions often pegged their piece rates to employers' selling prices. Anthracite miners suspended work en masse in 1869 and 1870, when the price of coal received by their bosses fell too low to sustain the wages to which the miners had pledged themselves. By the 1880s, the timing of strikes in most industries revealed that union members had learned to retreat when conditions were bad, then seek improvements when their services were in high demand.

Written trade agreements, negotiated between a union and an employers' association and usually specifying little more than a scale of wages for specified crafts, had appeared by the late 1860s, and twenty years later they played a significant role in the lives of Chicago bricklayers, Ohio Valley iron mill "tonnage men," Philadelphia and Cincinnati shoe workers, and printers, hat finishers, cigar makers, and stove molders in various places. As Chris Evans of the coal miners wrote, "A labor organization . . . trains the mind of economic thought," resolving the "wide difference of opinion among its members" by intelligent discussion. His union's efforts to overcome the injury done to miners by competition in the coal industry, however, had also made Evans an administrator of trade agreements, as well as an organizer of struggles that sometimes covered large regions.[16]

Moreover, the larger industrial enterprises grew, the greater became their capacity to withstand strikes, replace obstreperous employees, punish those who adhered to union work rules rather than company com-

---

[15]Christopher L. Tomlins, *The State and the Unions: Labor Relations, Law, and the Organized Labor Movement in America, 1880–1960* (Cambridge and New York, 1985), 60–91.

[16]*American Federationist* 1 (September 1894): 144. On trade-union practice, see David Montgomery, *The Fall of the House of Labor: The Workplace, the State, and American Labor Activism, 1865–1925* (Cambridge and New York, 1987), 9–44, 180–213, 341–47; Stuart B. Kaufman, ed., *The Samuel Gompers Papers* (Urbana and Chicago, 1987), 1:337–51; John H. Griffin, *Strikes: A Study in Quantitative Economics* (New York, 1939); Harold W. Aurand, *From the Molly Maguires to the United Mine Workers: The Social Ecology of an Industrial Union, 1869–1897* (Philadelphia, 1971).

mands, and undermine union wage scales with subdivision of tasks, piecework, and inside contracting. Unions' efforts to counteract that power often took the form of the legislation by union conventions of increasingly draconic rules governing members' behavior on the job and sanctions against offenders. Delegates to the 1891 convention of the Amalgamated Association of Iron, Steel, and Tin Workers, for example, adopted rules ordering promotion within rolling mill crews by seniority, ostracizing inside contractors, reducing the amount of iron that could be puddled by a member in any one heat, and banning overtime turns where anyone was out of work. In practice, the unions' much-vaunted voluntarism was turning into majority rule by union conventions. Employers, in turn, were quick to assume the posture of defenders of workers' individual liberties against union tyranny.[17]

The growing importance of the trade union as an institution inspired a group of well-read and thoughtful autodidacts, who surrounded Gompers during those years, to work out a coherent theory of its role in modern society. David Kronburg, Edward King, Chris Evans, Gabriel Edmonston, Frank K. Foster, and Hugh McGregor were influenced by Karl Marx, but much more directly by Herbert Spencer and Auguste Comte. In 1877, Kronburg had denounced his contemporaries who tried to "plan for the redemption and regeneration of the world by passing resolutions," and summoned them instead to study "the waking realities of this work-a-day world," because "the present encloses the germ of the future."[18] The same 1888 appeal that had rallied workers to "the perpetuation of the civilization we have so laboriously evolved," also described trade unions as "the natural growth of natural laws"—a Spencerian phrase that was to become one of Gompers's favorite expressions.[19]

In the early 1890s, McGregor wrote a series of articles explaining history as a succession of ruling classes, each of which had come to power by methods appropriate to its own needs. As the "warrior class" had risen by force of arms, and "the trading class" through parliaments, so the working class was creating economic institutions that would bring it to power. After Gompers had decisively defeated the advocates of socialist political action within the AFL (1893–95), the pages of the *American Federationist* were filled with articles explaining the historic role of trade

[17] Montgomery, 32–37.
[18] Quoted in Stuart B. Kaufman, *Samuel Gompers and the Origins of the American Federation of Labor, 1848–1896* (Westport, Conn., 1973), 76.
[19] Trant, 48.

unions, as opposed to parliamentary activity. Among them was one by Henry C. Barter, secretary of the International Seamen's Union, who argued that, in contrast to Socialists who wished to expand the powers of "the old forms of representative government," the organic social growth represented by the trade unions was "sloughing off" representative government. Barter concluded:

You have got to get away from politics before any material progress can be achieved. . . . The representative form of government, as we know it to-day, stands for the past and [is] decaying; the trades union councils, and the organizations of merchants and manufacturers stand for the new order of things.[20]

In defiance of countless protests from other AFL activists, but with complete consistency, Gompers spurned all invitations to join antitrust coalitions, and he explained to his members that the consolidation of business ownership, like the rise of trade unions, was the inevitable product of economic development. "Experience will demonstrate," he wrote at the end of 1896, "that there is a power growing . . . which will prove more potent to deal with the trusts, or if the trusts possess any virtue at all that they shall be directed into channels for the public good. . . . And that power is the much despised labor movement. . . . Wait and see."[21]

TOWARD COLLECTIVE BARGAINING

This was the context in which the phrase industrial democracy entered public discourse in the United States. Its earliest usage came from the trade-union movement of the 1890s, where it was introduced first by Socialists, then by their foes. Thus A. Seaman (possibly a pseudonym for Barter), writing in 1896, resorted to the same contrast between democratic government and autocratic property rights as Lloyd had evoked, without reaching Lloyd's conclusion that industry should be collectivized: Trade unionism, he argued, "is the budding, growing industrial democracy—the conscious or unconscious effort on the part of the workers to extend into the industrial field the political democracy which we now have, as a result of the struggle of ages." The presence of union orga-

[20] George B. Cotkin, "The Spencerian and Comtian Nexus in Gompers' Labor Philosophy: The Impact of Non-Marxian Evolutionary Thought," *Labor History* 20 (Fall 1979): 510–23; *American Federationist* 3 (July 1896): 95. I am indebted to Shelton Stromquist for bringing this article by Barter to my attention.
[21] Quoted in Philip S. Foner, *History of the Labor Movement in the United States,* 9 vols. (New York, 1947–89), 2:372–73.

nization, he explained, "immediately says to the employer that 'the business' is not 'his business,' but 'our business'—his and ours."[22]

Five years later, however, the term was given a subtly modified definition and widespread circulation among public policymakers by the report of the U.S. Industrial Commission, which had been appointed by Congress and President McKinley in 1898. The commission approached with special caution the claims of trade unionists (and the protests of business) that "the very organization" of unions gave employees a share in the control of the enterprise.

"The entire character of the report," Richard T. Ely noted, showed "the constant guidance of the economist," and specifically of "the younger generation of American economists," such as John R. Commons.[23] The outlook of those young economists, in turn, had been heavily influenced by two recent books by Sidney and Beatrice Webb: *The History of Trade Unionism* (1894) and *Industrial Democracy* (1897). The point to be emphasized is that *Industrial Democracy* was an analysis of British trade-union practice. "In the Anglo-Saxon world of to-day," wrote the Webbs, "we find that Trade Unions are democracies; that is to say, their internal constitutions are all based on the principle of 'government of the people by the people for the people.' "[24] The book set out to study their "natural history" and found there an evolution from "primitive democracy" to "representative government," and the gradual codification of rules and standards formulated by those workers' self-governments to deal with work relations. The problem for public policy, in the Webbs' view, was how to fit workers' self-governments into the framework of a legal system based on notions of individual property rights and contractual relationships. And that was precisely the way the report of the U.S. Industrial Commission framed the question: how should the law and employers respond to "the growth of democratic government in their industries"?[25]

In the opinion of the commissioners and of the Webbs, carefully nurtured collective bargaining could replace the "primitive democracy" of

---

[22] A. Seaman, "Things to Shun," *American Federationist* 3 (August 1896): 107.
[23] *Report of the U.S. Industrial Commission*, 19 vols. (Washington, D.C., 1901), 1:834; Richard T. Ely, "A Government Investigation of Labor," in Robert M. La Follette, ed., *The Making of America*, vol. 8, *Labor* (Chicago, 1905), 24–45. The quotation is on p. 26.
[24] Sidney and Beatrice Webb, *Industrial Democracy* (London, 1897; 1920 edition reprinted in New York, 1965), v–vi.
[25] *Industrial Commission* 1:805.

standard wages and work rules, unilaterally adopted by groups of workers, with contractual agreements between elected union representatives and employers (or more often with associations of employers), which would become part of predictable market relationships and which would impinge upon the employers' discretion in managing the firm only insofar as was mutually acceptable to the two parties to the bargain. That formula proved to be easier to propose than to realize.

After 1899, the National Civic Federation (NCF) gathered together business, trade union, academic, and religious leaders to promote the goals identified in the commission's report. William H. Pfahler, a member of the NCF's executive board and president of the National Founders' Association, explained that he had found advantages as a business executive in dealing with "such organizations of workingmen as are conducted along reasonable lines and are led by representatives worthy of the best element composing the membership, who formulate their demands in harmony with known business conditions and control their movements within the lines of law and order." In prosperous times, he explained, employers were slow to adjust wages upward, and unions usually won strikes for higher pay. Under such circumstances, an amicable negotiation of wage increases was the best for all concerned. Moreover, the officers elected by union members were "in many cases far above the average of their craftsmen" and were more amenable to rational persuasion than a crowd of angry workers.

Two formidable obstacles had to be overcome, however, if industrial peace was to be established through trade agreements. The first Pfahler described as the employer's "refusal (usually sentimental) to recognize the union, and [his] determination to destroy it." The other arose from the very workplace solidarities and ethical codes that had nurtured unions. All too often, union members used the strength provided them by trade agreements "to enforce rules and methods in the conduct of the business without the consent or co-operation of the employer." That is to say, to succeed the collective bargaining agreement had to overrule primitive union democracy, and it could do so only with the help of professional guidance and carefully drafted legal restrictions. Only those work rules and practices to which the employers consented at the bargaining table and which were not forbidden by law were to be enforced.[26]

---

[26] William H. Pfahler, "Co-operation of Labor and Capital," in La Follette, 89–99. The quotations are on p. 97.

Although Pfahler's ideal of industrial relations had been rejected by most employers in the metal trades (including his own National Founders' Association in 1904) in favor of militant struggle for exclusion of unions, in the name of the "open shop," it was practiced in bituminous coal mining, on many railroads, where it had been institutionalized by the Erdman Act of 1898, and, in an odd way, in the construction industries of many cities. John R. Commons responded to charges by open shop advocates that unions were exclusive, coercive, and monopolistic by arguing that recent trade agreements did not provide for union control of hiring:

Agreements made in the stove industry, in bituminous coal mining, in three fourths of the team driving agreements, in railway machine shops, and many others, are plainly open shop agreements, where it is often even stipulated that the employer has the right to employ and discharge whomever he sees fit.[27]

Because the same wages had to be paid to all workers, whether union members or not, and any discharge for union membership could be arbitrated as a violation of the contract, such agreements did not undermine union strength, in Commons's opinion. Arbitration of grievances could eliminate minor and often unpredictable strikes. Furthermore, because the agreements were made with employers' associations, those companies that adhered to their terms had a vested interest in forcing their competitors to do the same, and even in contributing to the ability of the unions to strike effectively against violators. It was for this reason that the bituminous coal agreement of 1898 provided that the companies would withhold union dues from the miners' pay.

Moreover, trade agreements replaced unions' reliance on the courage and commitment of individual members to enforce their rules and standards with institutionalized authority. They also shifted the locus of decision making within unions toward the officers and away from membership meetings. Even though most union miners refused to work beside nonmembers, coal operators had found that their contractual relationship with the United Mine Workers had gradually reduced the impact of union rules and of miners' local pit committees on the daily operations of the mines. State legislation concerning mine safety, payment, and housing had been integrated into the trade agreements, and the union had even agreed to seek no new legislation that was not jointly agreed to by the

---

[27] John R. Commons, "Causes of the Open Shop Policy," in La Follette, 199–214. The quotation is on p. 202.

two parties. Correspondingly, when pit committees gave orders to miners in contradiction to those of the foremen, operators could call in officials of the union and the operators' association to resolve the controversies.[28]

Union officers, therefore, were not simply tribunes of the workers but also agents of an institution that was bound by contractual relationships to groups of employers. Adolph Strasser of the Cigar Makers advised union officials that their task was to "represent the interests of the International Union, regardless of the local instructions of the strike committee." Specifically, that meant

to bring about an amicable and honorable adjustment of the trouble as speedily as possible, thus saving the funds of the International Union, which would otherwise be wasted; and to maintain the honor and reputation of the International Union for fair dealing with union manufacturers.[29]

Although collective bargaining had thus become the formula through which the National Civic Federation and the "younger generation of American economists" in the Industrial Commission had sought to cope with the "growth of democratic government" within industry, that formula had by no means become the normal pattern of American work relations. Total union membership in 1913 embraced little more than 10 percent of those considered potential members by the National Bureau of Economic Research. The overwhelming majority of employees in the steel, automobile, meat packing, maritime, textile, and chemical industries worked under terms unilaterally established by their employers, as did most office clerks, sales personnel, and farm workers. Industrial enterprises often experimented with incentive pay schemes, time and motion study, new machinery, and even company welfare plans, all of which changed people's working lives and some of which aroused their covert resistance. Before the introduction of employee representation plans on the transit systems of Philadelphia (1910) and New York (1916), and the highly publicized Colorado Industrial Plan of 1915, however, few companies not involved in trade agreements made any pretense at democratic consultation of their employees.[30] Across the country, local em-

---

[28] John R. Commons, ed., *Trade Unionism and Labor Problems* (1st ser., Boston, 1905), 10–12; Montgomery, 342. Carter L. Goodrich depicted a revival of pit committee power by the aftermath of World War I. Goodrich, *The Miner's Freedom: A Study of the Working Life in a Changing Industry* (Boston, 1925).

[29] Quoted in G. M. Janes, *The Control of Strikes in American Trade Unions* (Baltimore, 1916), 118.

[30] As H. J. Harris points out in his essay in this volume, editor James C. Bayles of *Iron Age* had broached the idea of shop councils in 1886.

ployers' associations fought vigorously and successfully to keep their industries and their cities open shop and any bargaining with workers that did take place individualized.

Moreover, workers who were covered by trade agreements often opposed the restraints on their workplace power and initiative on which the contracts were predicated (at least from the employers' perspective). Their continued reliance on group solidarities and ostracism of "scabs," despite the self-restraining pledges made by their officers in negotiating trade agreements, provided boundless ammunition for charges by open shop advocates that trade unions tyrannized over individual workers and were inherently untrustworthy.

For example, building contractors' associations locked out all the union trades workers of Chicago in 1900 and New York in 1903 in efforts to force the unions to put an end to sympathetic strikes, discard union rules that limited output, dissolve building trades councils, and negotiate separate agreements by craft with provisions for arbitration of grievances. In both cases, the employers believed they had won—not by destroying the unions, but by forcing them to sign contracts on terms desired by the contractors. In both cities, however, the practices opposed by the contractors had returned to the building sites within three or four years of the lockouts as full of vitality as ever.[31]

In other industries, union members expected their officers to help them enforce their ethical codes on the job despite the terms of trade agreements. A minor, routine illustration is provided by the strike at the New Haven Iron and Steel Works, which was covered by a contract with the Amalgamated Association of Iron, Steel, and Tin Workers. The mill was shut down for two months in the summer of 1902. One of its employees had asked for a raise, been refused, and quit. When Tony Alto was assigned to the vacant job and learned why his predecessor had left it, he refused the work and was fired. One hundred fifty union members then struck in protest, forcing the company to lay off another 250 unorganized laborers. The local union stood by Alto, whose nineteenth-century code of honor had prevailed over twentieth-century contractualism. Only when Alto was reinstated did everyone else resume work, in accordance with the scales and rules of the local trade agreement.[32]

Most of the notorious injunctions that were hurled from judicial

---

[31] William Haber, *Industrial Relations in the Building Industry* (Cambridge, Mass., 1930), 346–99.
[32] *New Haven Daily Union,* 19 June, 28 June, 7 July, 15 July, 23 July, 7 August 1902.

benches at strikers and boycotters before the war (though by no means all of them) prohibited sympathetic strikes, workers' violations of contracts, and secondary boycotts. Although the National Civic Federation endorsed legislative proposals to exclude trade agreements and strikes from the purview of the Sherman Antitrust Act, its officers who were drawn from the ranks of business and the public shared the hostility of the militant open shop associations toward union actions that violated the sanctity of contracts.[33]

To even the most conservative of AFL leaders, however, all injunctions were anathema. It was not the democratic character of representative government in which they placed their hopes, but rather the civil liberties that gave trade unions the social space in which to develop their "organic" alternative to "archaic" parliamentary government. Judicial redefinitions of property rights that constricted that space directly threatened the AFL's basic project. The *American Federationist* denounced court orders prohibiting strikes as imposition of involuntary servitude in violation of the Thirteenth Amendment, and bans against boycotts and picketing as infringements on the First Amendment's protection of free speech. To obey an injunction that trampled on constitutional liberties was a dishonorable act, as Gompers and John Mitchell attested when they risked jail rather than obey a court order not to boycott the Bucks Stove and Range Company.[34]

In short, the contractualist, antistatist conception of industrial democracy developed by AFL leaders and nurtured by the Industrial Commission and the NCF met with vigorous and effective resistance from most business leaders and from the judiciary. That resistance, which had slowed the federation's growth to a virtual halt by 1909, also reinvigorated those very tendencies within the workers' movement that Gompers and his colleagues had labored so hard to suppress in the 1890s: political action and "primitive" union democracy.

BEYOND THE TRADE AGREEMENT: SOCIALISM, SYNDICALISM,
AND VISIONS OF A NEW ORDER, CIRCA 1905–1920

Despite the 1895 resolution declaring that "party politics" of any kind should "have no place" in the AFL, Gompers's controversial circular of

---

[33] Marguerite Green, *National Civic Federation and the American Labor Movement, 1900–1925* (Washington, D.C., 1956), 203–4; Pfahler, 98–99; Tomlins, 60–67.
[34] Tomlins, 64–67; Philip Taft, *The A.F. of L. in the Time of Gompers* (New York, 1957), 293–98.

1896 calling on its constituent unions "to vanquish the political intruder at the doors of our meeting rooms," and the subsequent barrage of articles in the federation's journal proclaiming representative government obsolete, local and international unions continued to offer support to candidates in hopes of obtaining desired legislation and a friendly reception in government offices. By 1908, the AFL's struggle against injunctions, which was indispensable to its antistatist policy, had led it to endorse a Democratic candidate in the presidential election and organize a nationwide solicitation of votes on his behalf.[35]

Although the federation maintained its thinly disguised alliance with the Democratic party until 1920, leaders of the machinists', ladies' garment workers', and brewery workers' unions, and of important districts of the United Mine Workers had affiliated with the Socialist party by 1912. The socialists not only kept alive Lloyd's dream that workers might use democratic government to bring industrial life under social direction, but also aspired to change the whole fabric of everyday human relationships, along with those of the workplace. In both respects, the Socialists repudiated the contractual image of industrial democracy espoused by the NCF, the Industrial Commission, and the leaders of the AFL.[36]

The experience of World War I strengthened the appeal of those AFL members who favored a quest for social democracy through political as well as workplace action. War mobilization showed workers what an impact the coercive authority of government could have on economic activity in general and on industrial relations in particular. On the one hand, the government's repressive apparatus had silenced critics of the war, marginalized Socialists within the union movement, and forced unions to operate within the space allowed by the state's war aims and policies. On the other hand, its economic mobilization had brought full employment, demonstrated that major industries could function well under public administration, established national standards for wages and hours, placed prominent feminists and other social reformers in positions of considerable authority over industrial activity, and incorporated trade unions into the administrative apparatus of the war machine.

---

[35] *American Federationist* 3 (August 1896): 106–7; Foner, 2:337; Robert Hunter, *Labor in Politics* (Chicago, 1915); William M. Dick, *Labor and Socialism in America: The Gompers Era* (Port Washington, N.Y., 1972); Marc Karson, *American Labor Unions and Politics, 1900–1918* (Carbondale, Ill., 1958).

[36] For studies of the Socialist party of America, see below, note 46.

One consequence of this experience was the emergence of a self-styled progressive bloc within the leadership of the growing unions, with special strength in the mining, machine-shop, garment, maritime, meat packing, and railroad workers' organizations. Its adherents sought to amalgamate related craft unions and to promote pacts of mutual assistance among unions, all with rather limited success. More effectively, they also raised political demands, which had been popularized in union circles by the wartime experience and were often incorporated into the official programs of major unions.

The infusion of industrial struggles with ambitious political and social goals was illustrated by resolutions adopted at the 1919 and 1920 conventions of the United Mine Workers of America. They endorsed nationalization of the coal mines, public ownership of the railroads through the Plumb Plan, legislation to make employer interference with the unionization of workers a criminal offense, a thirty-hour week, national health insurance, release of all political prisoners and the demilitarization of the United States, the creation of a labor party, and an international alliance with the labor movement of Great Britain.[37]

Although the Progressives lacked the cohesiveness and organization that Socialists had manifested in the prewar AFL and were decisively undermined by the postwar defeat of unions in mass production industries, during their hour of strength they had upheld a vision of industrial democracy in which government had a major role to play. That vision had been informed by earlier socialist influences, to be sure, but also and more immediately by the experience of war mobilization. By the time Frank Walsh had completed his work on the U.S. Commission on Industrial Relations, he had become a leading advocate of social reform through the state. He described to the 1916 convention of the mine workers the prospect of "every engine of production, every man and every instrumentality . . . hooked up into one co-operative drive . . . for the life of the people." What was then being done for destructive purposes of war could also be done in the future, "for love and life." This, he said, was the promise of "a democracy, industrious [*sic*] and political, based on enduring justice."[38]

---

[37]Montgomery, 370–410; *Seattle Union Record*, 25 January 1921, p. 3; Frank L. Warne, *The Workers at War* (New York, 1920), 210–11; Leo Wolman, *The American Labor Movement: A Syllabus for Study Classes* (New York, 1927), 20.

[38]United Mine Workers of America, *Proceedings of the Twenty-Fifth Consecutive and Second Biennial Convention*, 2 vols. (Indianapolis, Ind., 1916), 1:12–13.

The most thorough repudiation of the efforts of the Industrial Commission, AFL leaders, and the National Civic Federation to substitute collective bargaining for "primitive" union democracy, however, arose not from advocates of political action but from the Industrial Workers of the World. While the IWW discarded traditional craft unionism as obsolete, it also repudiated all attempts at contractual relations between workers and capitalists, declared that the two classes had "nothing in common," and summoned workers to organize direct action at the point of production, not only to improve earnings and conditions, but also eventually to "take possession of the earth and the machinery of production, and abolish the wage system."[39]

The gospel of direct action soon proved to be popular even among workers who belonged to the Socialist party and to the AFL. Because the International Ladies' Garment Workers' Union (ILGWU)–AFL was both a stronghold of Socialist party influence and a pioneer in the negotiation of elaborate trade agreements, support for direct action among its members threatened to disrupt not only the industry's famous Protocols of Peace but also the Socialist party itself. In the garment industry, debates over union strategies assumed a highly ideological coloration.

The protocols negotiated by New York's cloak makers (1910) and dress and waist makers (1913) were the most elaborate and the most famous of all attempts to subject work relations to collective agreements before World War I, but even they did not succeed in insulating contractual relationships from endemic workplace conflict or from governmental pressures. The joint boards and impartial arbitrators they authorized not only promised to end decades of industrial strife, but also admitted third parties and presumably objective standards of justice into the resolution of workplace disputes. Such hopes foundered quickly on conflicts over the routine fixing of piece rates.

Piecework ruled the workers' lives in this industry, as in many others. The prices per piece determined not only the workers' incomes, but also the intensity of their toil, the inducements to start work earlier or finish later than the scheduled hours, the repetitive or specialized character of their tasks, and even the significance of foremen's authority to assign jobs. In nonunion settings, the overseers usually fixed the prices, and there was little the individual worker could do about it. When workers

---

[39] Joyce L. Kornbluh, *Rebel Voices: An I.W.W. Anthology* (Ann Arbor, Mich., 1968), 12–13.

unionized, the shoe was on the other foot. The rate on each individual job could now be contested collectively.

The cloak makers' protocol authorized the fixing of prices "by a committee of the employees in each shop, and their employer," but manufacturers' spokesman Julius H. Cohen soon found there was "a veritable hell in the factory every time a price is to be set for a garment."[40] Although the dress and waist protocol created a wage board to establish "a scientific basis for the fixing of piece and week-work prices," the workers soon learned that speedy and favorable rulings were best won by going on strike.[41] Cohen complained that 141 strikes had been called against members of the dress and waist association in 1915 alone. "There are very few plants in which some workers do not take it upon themselves to run things as they see fit," protested *Women's Wear* in 1916. "To refuse to work is a common occurrence, the people laughing when the employer threatens to discharge them."[42]

Although industrial counselor Robert G. Valentine had praised the protocols in 1915 as "organized consent" that provided "the basis of a more efficient group,"[43] champions of this point of view within the union, like General Secretary J. A. Dyche, had been driven from office by more militant foes the previous year, and in the year Valentine published his remarks, the manufacturers' association tried to repudiate the agreement. The newly elected president of the ILGWU, Benjamin Schlesinger, denounced the manufacturers for frequent violations of their pledges in the agreement, while he supported his members' shop actions against employment of men and women who were not union members and against dismissals of allegedly inefficient workers at the start of new production seasons (both of which were allowed by the protocol). The success of the union in achieving a de facto closed shop reduced the employers' ability to rely on conservative workers in their enterprises, while it greatly strengthened militant workers' capacity to summon up the ethical codes and tactics of primitive union democracy. In a union where most officers were Socialists or anarchists, tactical disputes were readily translated into theoretical controversies over revolutionary strategies.[44]

[40] Jesse T. Carpenter, *Competition and Collective Bargaining in the Needle Trades, 1910–1967* (Ithaca, N.Y., 1972), 90, 270.
[41] Louis Lorwin, *The Women's Garment Workers: A History of the International Ladies' Garment Workers' Union* (New York, 1924), 299; Carpenter, 270–73.
[42] Carpenter, 263–64.
[43] Valentine, quoted in Chapter 3 of this volume.
[44] The best analysis of the protocol remains Lorwin, 196–319. See also Melvyn Dubofsky,

When J. A. Dyche declined to run for reelection as general secretary of the ILGWU at its 1914 convention, he denounced his more radical rivals for making "appeals to the galleries."

Our Syndicalists, [Dyche explained,] our so-called revolutionaries, the people who believe that we must apply the sacred principle of the "Class War" to our relations with the Manufacturers' Association have triumphed. The few men in the Organization who may believe in the possibility of cooperation and good will between the Employers' Association and the Union are afraid to open their mouths for fear of being accused of being agents of the Manufacturers' Association. The forces of primitive or "revolutionary" unionism are victorious.[45]

Dyche's words were carefully chosen to identify his union rivals with espousal of direct action and sabotage, which the Socialist party of America had banned since its convention of 1912. Indeed, controversies within the ILGWU over wildcat strikes in defiance of the protocols may have played a much larger role in the famous syndicalism debate among Socialists, which had culminated in the recall of William D. Haywood from the party executive and the resignation of thousands of party members, than most historians have recognized. So many participants on both sides of the debate over collective bargaining and direct action within the needle trades were Socialist party members that the controversy split the party itself.[46]

Contrary to Dyche's implications, the "primitive unionism" described by the Webbs was by no means the same as the "revolutionary unionism" espoused by the IWW. What his patently self-serving rhetoric reveals, however, is that by the second decade of the twentieth century, socialist and syndicalist influences had served to couple workers' discussion of trade agreements to controversies over how modern capitalism might be overthrown. Advocates of direct action also devoted increasing attention to the practical application of their doctrines—to the details of organizing workers inside the workplace for continuous exercise of control through direct action, as distinct from occasional strikes. During and after the war, their calls for the selection of shop delegates and councils of delegates

When Workers Organize: New York City in the Progressive Era (Amherst, Mass., 1968), 40–101.

[45] Quoted in Carpenter, 56. See also Lorwin, 308–9.

[46] For three different interpretations of the "sabotage" debate in the party, see Ira Kipnis, *The American Socialist Movement, 1897–1912* (New York and London, 1952), 402–8, 413–20; James Weinstein, *The Decline of Socialism in America, 1912–1925* (London, 1967), 34–45; Nick Salvatore, *Eugene V. Debs: Citizen and Socialist* (Urbana, Ill., 1982), 251–61.

to mobilize and coordinate struggles on the job often met with favorable responses among workers in electrical equipment, garment, and textile factories, as well as in lumber and harvest camps and shipyards. The large numbers of workers who were relatively unskilled and easily replaced and the arbitrary powers of foremen in those enterprises made a mockery of personal acts of courage and commitment to group ethics, while piecework and incentive pay frustrated union efforts to establish standard wages.

Many activists also considered workshop organization a practical step to circumvent the jurisdictional divisions of craft unionism. They hoped that the contractual standards negotiated by unions could be supplemented (if not replaced) by well-organized direct representation of the small work groups that were the strongest and most spontaneous source of bondings among workers. The way such bondings could be linked to revolutionary action was suggested by the advice offered by James Robertson of the One Big Union to his fellow boilermakers in 1919: Elect shop stewards in each work group and "deal 'directly' with the conditions under which you work." Safe working conditions, the abolition of "piece or contract work," and even the resolution of unions' "jurisdictional disputes," could best be secured by direct action. Moreover, he argued, such continuous mobilization of workers' power would "promote the discipline necessary to mass action."[47]

By 1919, however, the question that G. D. H. Cole had named "workshop organization" had engaged the attention of government policymakers, management consultants, and corporate executives in every industrialized country, as well as that of revolutionaries.[48] The subject of controversy had shifted from the trade agreement to the organized representation of workers on the job, and the different groups concerned with the question had different, even mutually exclusive, social objectives. The National War Labor Board had played an especially important role in developing shop committees elected by workers, with which employers were required to negotiate. Where shop committees encouraged union participation and allowed aggrieved workers to appeal to the government against their employers, they enabled workers to dispute the authority of the managers of their plants effectively. Consequently, use

---

[47] James Robertson, *Labor Unionism, Based upon the American Shop Steward System* (n.p., n.d.), 14.

[48] G. D. H. Cole, *Workshop Organization* (Oxford, 1923). See also Ernst Mandel, *Contrôle ouvrier, conseils ouvriers, autogestion. Anthologie* (Paris, 1970).

of the phrase *workers' control,* which came into vogue among social reformers at the war's end, was invariably coupled with discussion of workshop organization.

More than one employer shared the fear of former President William Howard Taft that "laborers have had their heads swelled with the power they have had during the war."[49] Some of them sought a remedy right where the threat to their authority seemed most acute: in workshop organization. Walter G. Merritt, an attorney for the antiunion League for Industrial Rights, agreed with the revolutionary industrial unionists that the factory, not the trade, "is the normal unit of economic self-interest for workers." Through properly instituted workplace organization, well insulated from "outside" intervention by unions or by government, he argued, it would be possible to cultivate "the workers' loyalty to the individual company ... to become stronger than his sense of class consciousness and class solidarity."[50]

Henri de Man put the issue in more general terms:

The actual producers' joy in their work, and, consequently, in great measure their effective productivity, will not be so much promoted by any centralist reform of the relations of ownership, as by a local reform of working conditions in respect of workshop technique and in respect of hierarchical workshop organization. The essential thing is the formation of a new group consciousness within the individual enterprise.[51]

In short, workshop organization, like workers' "participation," could have various and contradictory social meanings. As had been the case with the institution of collective bargaining in 1900, workshop organization twenty years later posed the question of who would guide its development and toward what ends. All contenders in the effort had adopted the word *democracy* as their own.

INDUSTRIAL DEMOCRACY'S AMBIGUOUS ORIGINS

The twentieth-century notion of industrial democracy, therefore, had originated in the theory of society's organic development proposed by trade-union thinkers who opposed socialism and political action. Their ideas were modified by middle-class reformers (and especially by the

[49] Quoted in Green, 452.
[50] Walter G. Merritt, *Factory Solidarity or Class Solidarity?* (2d ed.; reprinted from *Iron Age,* n.p., n.d.), 49.
[51] Henri de Man, *Joy in Work,* translated from German by Eden and Cedar Paul (London, 1929), 53.

"young economists" of the U.S. Industrial Commission) into a proposal for contractual relations between trade-union officers and employers' associations, which could adapt the "primitive" democracy of unions to the requirements of the marketplace and of efficient management, while obtaining the workers' organized consent to their conditions of employment and to the social order. The opposition of most manufacturers to unions in their enterprises restricted the influence of this proposal in practice, while the appeal of political action to labor activists increased, rather than diminished, during the century's second decade. Moreover, primitive union democracy was not extinguished by collective bargaining. In fact, it was elevated into a new revolutionary doctrine of "direct action" and stimulated the growth of workshop organization. Consequently, no single model of industrial democracy had triumphed in American economic life by the 1920s.

By the end of the 1920–22 depression, unions had been driven out of mass production industries, and whatever representation of workers existed there was that promoted by the corporations themselves. The AFL had not disappeared, however, but continued to bargain effectively with small employers facing localized markets. Its famous 1923 manifesto, "Industry's Manifest Duty," reaffirmed the AFL's antistatist vision of the 1890s in an updated vocabulary, which described trade unions as "the conscious organization of one of the most vital functional elements for enlightened participation in a democracy of industry whose purpose must be ... the enfranchisement of the producer as such, the rescue of industry from chaos, ... and the rescue of industry also from the domination of incompetent political bodies."[52]

Despite the grandiose rhetoric of the manifesto, it described rather well the secondary role in local power elites into which most union officers had settled during the 1920s. Its conception of industrial democracy was the craft union orthodoxy against which the founders of the CIO rebelled during the period of the New Deal.

[52] American Federation of Labor, *History, Encyclopedia, Reference Book*, 2 vols. (Washington, D.C., 1921, 1924), 2:99. On the role of the AFL in the 1920s, see David Montgomery, "Thinking about American Workers in the 1920s," *International Labor and Working-Class History* 32 (Fall 1987): 4–24.

3

Industrial democracy and liberal capitalism, 1890–1925

HOWELL JOHN HARRIS

Addressing the British Trades Union Congress in 1916, the chair spoke the then-conventional wisdom that "industrial democracy was the only condition of lasting industrial peace." Unfortunately for my purposes here, he did not specify what industrial democracy meant.

There was nothing unusual about his unhelpful reticence; according to one recent student of this term, with its associated ideas and institutions: "Industrial democracy emerged as the organizing principle and popular goal of labor relations reform in America at least as early as the 1890s, and by the eve of World War I, there was hardly anyone who didn't have a good word for it. [However, the] meaning of the concept ... varied enormously."[1]

My object is not to try to supply a single meaning for industrial democracy where contemporaries manifestly "failed," but to describe the range of meanings different people gave the term at the time and explain why they used it. This is a deceptively simple goal that I hope to make attainable by, first of all, concentrating my attention on certain kinds of "industrial democrats," and, second, treating this more as an exercise in the history of words than of acts.

My main focus will be on those members of the middle classes who made the words their own, who infused them with a variety of hopes, but who made very little impression on social reality with them. Like

---

[1] P. H. Kerr, "Labour and Industry," in John Hilton et al., *The Other War: Being Chapters ... on Some Causes of Class Misunderstanding* (London: George Allen and Unwin, 1917), 37; Howard Dickman, *Industrial Democracy in America: Ideological Origins of National Labor Relations Policy* (La Salle, Ill.: Open Court, 1987), 217.

many an investigation of turn-of-the-century liberal "reform," this must be a study in disappointment.

The chief subject of this chapter is liberals' attempts to expand their traditional ideals to encompass the dynamic new industrial order and to adapt that order to accommodate their traditional ideals. Industrial democracy was supposed to be reflective of old verities and constitutive of new realities. But it gained most of its ethical content and affective force from a memory of the past rather than a clear vision of the future it hoped to create. Accordingly, an examination of it must begin, not with the present the industrial democrats thought they were confronting but with the past, which had bequeathed them tools inadequate for the task.

EARLY CONCEPTS OF INDUSTRIAL DEMOCRACY

Industrial democracy had deep roots in popular American political thought in the nineteenth century, summed up by Ralph Gabriel as having assumed that "the dignity of human personality . . . could only be realized when the individual was free to express himself and to participate in decisions of vital import to him"; that "principles of universal validity underlie the common life of men in society, the application of which to affairs makes possible the realization of freedom and dignity"; and that the fate of the American national experiment and the furtherance of freedom were intimately bound up with one another.[2]

Leon Fink has brought us down from these heights of lofty abstraction to remind us that American workers, their spokespeople and sympathizers, "early and persistently collaborated, adopted, and identified with the charter of American liberty as the basis of their own ambitions." They "sought to identify their interests and actions directly with national governmental institutions and political principles." The labor movement built on this "connection to state-related values" and relied on the "tradition of individual 'rights'" as the basis of its claims to legality and recognition. "They looked confidently to the principles of the new nation itself to safeguard and justify their legitimate interests" by making "a claim on the central political culture."[3]

Accordingly, when friends of labor from the "adversary tradition,"

[2]Ralph H. Gabriel, *The Course of American Democratic Thought,* 2d ed. (New York: Ronald Press, 1956), 3.
[3]Leon Fink, "Labor, Liberty, and the Law: Trades Unionism and the Problem of the American Constitutional Order," *Journal of American History* 74 (1987): 904–25. The quotations are at pp. 905–9.

notably Henry Demarest Lloyd, and Social Gospelers who took up the workers' cause in the 1880s and 1890s, particularly Richard T. Ely, tried to make a case for labor's legitimacy in the aftermath of the "Great Upheaval," the Haymarket Affair, the Homestead and Pullman strikes, and in the midst of the developing judicial war against the unions, they had a widely resonant language ready to hand—the language of labor republicanism and popular "antimonopolist" radicalism.

The *Encyclopaedia of Social Reform* expressed the common faith, "modern democracy finds its first chief actual development in the United States." Brushing aside a growing conservative critique of democracy, the *Encyclopaedia* instead identified America's problem as a trend toward plutocracy—"with us corporations rule the Government." But this could be corrected by a return to first principles: "The masses of this country want not less democracy but more. They want . . . industrial democracy added to political democracy. Their problem is not how to limit the suffrage but how to save the political liberties of the people."

Lloyd and Ely helped introduce the concept of industrial democracy to the American public in the 1880s and 1890s and gave it much of its lasting meaning. Admittedly, their definitions were somewhat confused: Ely looked to the tradition of producers' cooperation as a practical demonstration of it or a way to realize it, and Lloyd did much the same, when he was not conflating industrial democracy with the achievement of a general welfare state through political action. But the rhetorical structures on which Lloyd rested his key statement of the case, before the Annual Convention of the American Federation of Labor in 1893, became the truisms of the most common sort of argument for industrial democracy for the next quarter century.[4]

However, this argument had a fatal weakness: itself a product of an egalitarian reading of the liberal-republican tradition, it was contradicted by an equally or more authentically American variant of the same tradition, whose implications were much more conservative.

Pioneer industrial democrats hoped to build a new society in the interests of underprivileged *groups* on an expansive interpretation of the members of those groups' *individual* civil rights; and they assumed that standards that held good in the public or political sphere should apply to their market relationships also. But the dominant American reading

---

[4] William D. P. Bliss, ed., *The Encyclopaedia of Social Reform* (New York: Funk and Wagnalls, 1897), "Democracy," 482–86.

of the liberal tradition centered on the "belief in the explicit separation of the 'private' economic and 'public' political spheres and an interpretation of liberal democracy in terms of the protection of the right of all to pursue individual interests according to the rules of economic competition and free exchange."[5]

The industrial democrats' syllogism—America is a democracy; but industrial America is not; therefore industry must be democratized—was countered by the conservative dualisms: that rights of individuals were one thing and rights of groups something else, and less; and that individuals' political rights and their rights in the marketplace as producers, consumers, and proprietors of their labor power and other goods were logically and necessarily separable. Modern rightist or "libertarian" critics such as Howard Dickman and Frank Tariello argue that the disease of collectivism has been gnawing away at America's vitals for the past century and that the pioneer industrial democrats were among the first and most important vectors. They suggest, in agreement with a rather passé, consensual liberal reading of American history but inverting its onward-and-upward optimism, that collectivism has won. We may be permitted to differ.[6]

By the mid-1890s, the pioneer industrial democrats had elaborated their egalitarian, ambiguously collectivist critique of American capitalism. Their arguments would resonate through the next two decades, gaining intellectual force and new adherents, but not much affecting the actual development of the industrial relations system. There, the rights of property and contract received valuable support from the courts, fresh advocates in the 1900s in the shape of the American Anti-Boycott Association, and other promoters of entrepreneurial liberty.

In response to this bourgeois onslaught, the *Iron Molders' Journal* editorialized in 1904 that the fundamental question in the industrial conflict was "the right of labor to have a voice in the industrial world. Political equality is not sufficient and unless the wage-earner possesses

[5] Margaret Kiloh, "Industrial Democracy," in David Held and Christopher Pollitt, eds., *New Forms of Democracy* (London and Beverly Hills: Sage Publications, 1986), 17. Kiloh deals with the liberal-democratic tradition in general; for the United States, cf. Fink, "Labor, Liberty, and the Law," 909.

[6] Dickman, *Industrial Democracy in America*; Tariello, *The Reconstruction of American Political Ideology: 1865–1897* (Charlottesville: University Press of Virginia, 1982); but see James Atleson, *Values and Assumptions in American Labor Law* (Amherst: University of Massachusetts Press, 1983); Christopher L. Tomlins, *The State and the Unions: Labor Relations, Law, and the Organized Labor Movement in America, 1880–1960* (Cambridge: Cambridge University Press, 1985), esp. chapters 2, 3.

an industrial equality that places him upon a par with his employer there can never exist that freedom and liberty of action which is necessary to the maintenance of a republican form of government."[7]

But the American Federation of Labor was by then more generally resting its claim to be counted among the accepted "going concerns" of an incorporated economy on new and much more utilitarian foundations than the old republican vision. These were, principally, its contributions to social peace, to the reduction of wage and price competition within industries, and to the equitable and efficient distribution of income and purchasing power.

By the 1900s, the true inheritors of the nineteenth-century ethical advocacy of labor's rights were to be found outside the labor movement, in the many worlds of liberal reform.

LIBERAL REFORMERS AND THE LABOR PROBLEM

The great merger movement, "The Discovery That Business Corrupts Politics," the spreading middle-class concern about corporate power and the transformation of American society, gave added force and wider resonance to traditional metaphors in the rhetoric of labor republican-ism—in particular, that industry was a sphere of anachronistic and un-American despotism. In his *Our Benevolent Feudalism* of 1902, W. J. Ghent "sought, by a satirical interpretation of the facts and tendencies of the time, to depict the not impossible return of a regime of lord, agent, and underling." By the time the third edition was published, Ghent was more optimistic: a way out was available, "the assertion of the democratic spirit and will, the conquest of the baronial regime and the transformation of the industrial system." For liberals worried about the "promise of American life," or, more prosaically, social unrest in the "Age of Indus-trial Violence," industrial democracy offered a broad, safe road into the future, at the same time as it reasserted the fundamental political beliefs of a receding past.[8]

Ghent's threateningly metaphorical language was representative of a common tendency in Progressive Era reflections on the political impli-cations of corporate capitalist employment practices. For a few contem-poraries, the *answer* to the problem involved a restoration of premodern

---

[7] *Iron Molders' Journal* 40 (1904): 750.
[8] W. J. Ghent, *Mass and Class: A Survey of Social Divisions* (New York: Macmillan, 1904), vi–vii.

social relations, "bringing the world nearer to the ideals of the Middle Ages" through an "approximation of the Catholic guild system" applied to modern industry.

But for most social commentators, speaking from within a Protestant and whiggish vision of history, the present industrial regime was described in terms reminiscent of the bad old days only to condemn it: as one Social Gospeler rumbled, "To-day, great financial and industrial power is concentrated in the hands of men nearly as independent of the public will as was Louis XIV of France or Catherine of Russia." The industrial editor of the *Survey* saw a "new stratification, without albeit the loyalties of the older feudal system," emerging. The industrial revolution, "whose unconscious drift has been towards servility instead of freedom," had reversed in part the political revolution toward liberal democracy since the eighteenth century. This was intolerable: "If self-government is right on the political field, self-government is right in industry, for the same arguments arise in each case."[9]

But we know that there was change as well as continuity in American social analysis in the first quarter of this century; that as well as an egalitarian ideal rooted in the American political creed and the Social Gospelers' complementary vision of the realization of the Kingdom of God on earth entailing recognition of the brotherhood and dignity of man, there were new and self-consciously modern elements in Progressive worldviews.[10]

The first and second threads in the web of arguments for industrial democracy outlined above correspond closely and relate to the first and second "clusters of ideas" or "social languages" Daniel Rodgers identifies within Progressivism—the antimonopolist tradition, and that which emphasized "social bonds and the social nature of human beings." But what of his third category, "the language of social efficiency"? What could industrial democracy come to mean in this new language and to the people who used it? And what would become of the ambiguous collectivism of the labor-republican tradition in an age that was half turning

[9] Joseph Husslein, S.J., *Democratic Industry: A Practical Study on Social History* (New York: P. J. Kenedy, 1919), 290–91; Frank T. Carlton, *The Industrial Situation: Its Effect Upon the Home, the School, the Wage Earner, and the Employer* (New York: Fleming H. Revell, 1914), 147; William L. Chenery, *Industry and Human Welfare* (New York: Macmillan, 1922), 156, 160.

[10] For Social Gospelers' adoption of the language of industrial democracy, see Samuel Z. Batten, *The New World Order* (Philadelphia: American Baptist Publication Society), esp. chapter 3; Harry F. Ward, *The Labor Movement from the Standpoint of Religious Values* (New York: Sturgis and Walton, 1917), esp. chapter 8.

its back on liberal individualism and embracing corporatist notions of the functional group as the basic building block of society?[11]

THE STATE'S ROLE

There was always something a little odd about the central axiom of industrial democratic thought, that industry had to be democratized because all social institutions had to be made to conform to a common standard of civic values, else the republic itself would be in peril. This was a state- or at least government-centered argument in a country with no "sense of the state" that the English social commentator H. G. Wells could discover at the time, which had "subordinated, in the name of Liberty, all the grave and ennobling affairs of statescraft to a middle-class freedom of commercial enterprise."

American public discourse might be obsessively political, but the state did not really matter very much or vitally affect its citizens' everyday experiences. America had "the feeblest, least accessible and most inefficient central government of any civilized nation in the world west of Russia." The collectivist Charles Steinmetz agreed with the Fabian Wells, that "our Governments, from the federal down to the municipal, are not organized for constructive activity, and thus their entrance in the field is largely inhibitory, liable to disorganize by interference."[12]

What did the state have to do with the drama of economic development and technological progress? Nothing much; and yet these were the real, material forces for social change. What happened to Americans in the parts of their lives lived in relation to the world of work and the corporate order began to seem increasingly important in comparison with their formal civil and political rights, which were taken for granted and somewhat depreciated.

Voluntarists and mainstream syndicalists within the American labor movement developed this theme. The grand chief of the Brotherhood of Locomotive Engineers and Firemen put it nicely in 1919: "We have a democratic form of government but an autocratic control of industry.

---

[11] Rodgers, "In Search of Progressivism," *Reviews in American History* 10 (1982): 113–32: James Gilbert, *Designing the Industrial State: The Intellectual Pursuit of Collectivism in America, 1880–1940* (Chicago: Quadrangle, 1972), esp. chapters 1–4; R. Jeffrey Lustig, *Corporate Liberalism: The Origins of Modern American Political Theory* (Berkeley: University of California Press, 1982).

[12] H. G. Wells, *The Future in America: A Search After Realities* (London: Chapman and Hall, 1906), 213, 137, 399; Charles P. Steinmetz, *America and the New Epoch* (New York: Harper, 1916), 126.

We exist under government, but by industry we live. Under such a system the majority of a democracy can, through their government, enjoy only such rights and privileges as an autocracy in industry permits them to receive."

The AFL's Reconstruction Program of 1918 amplified this point: "Two codes of rules and regulations affect the workers; the law upon the statute books and the rules within industry.... Both forms of law vitally affect the workers' opportunities in life and determine their standard of living. The rules, regulations, and conditions within industry in many instances affect them more than legislative enactments." The conclusion was inescapable: if representative government was desirable in one sphere, it was equally appropriate, and even more urgently necessary, in the other.[13]

To Charles Henderson, professor of sociology and Baptist minister, the political implication of the importance of workers' everyday experience for their quality of life was clear: "The manager of a great mill, factory or railway, determines the physical, moral and spiritual conditions under which human beings must toil all their days. Evidently such colossal power, inevitable under capitalist management, must be held responsible for what it does, or the world is enslaved."[14]

Henderson was concerned that one could not trust in the benevolence of autocracy. More secular progressives took a different tack, that what mattered was not so much the moral outcomes of one sort of industrial regime or another but ensuring citizens the right to meaningful participation in fundamental decisions affecting their lives. If the corporate order mattered more than the state, then democratizing the corporation must be the reformers' primary objective.

In the early teens, the two Walters, Weyl and Lippmann, those usual suspects any investigator of reformist thought is compelled to bring in for questioning, summed up this line of argument very neatly: "The democracy of tomorrow, being a real and not a merely formal democracy, does not content itself with the mere right to vote, with political immunities and generalizations about the rights of man.... Without democracy in industry, that is where it counts most, there is no such thing as democracy in America."[15]

---

[13] Cited in Frank J. Warne, *The Workers at War* (New York: Century, 1920), 211, 206.
[14] Charles R. Henderson, *Citizens in Industry* (New York: Appleton, 1915), 7.
[15] Walter Weyl, *The New Democracy: An Essay on Certain Political and Economic Tendencies in the United States* (New York: Harper Torchbook ed., 1964; originally published 1912), 164; Walter Lippmann, *Drift and Mastery* (1914), quoted in W. Jett Lauck,

This collectivist case for some version of industrial democracy, as a primary guarantor of social justice and the effective representation of people's fundamental interests, reflected a subtle shift in the arguments deployed in its favor. The old ones were neither forgotten nor abandoned, as the war period, in particular, showed. But the character of Progressive Era debates about industrial democracy moved away from the simple moralism and analogies from an idealized account of American political development of Ely or Lloyd, toward a much greater concern with the quality of working life and problems of industrial conflict and distributive justice in a corporate capitalist economy with a partly organized labor force.

Summing this up as a move from a "state-centered" to a "society-centered" mode of analysis is only partly true because the defense and realization of America's democratic civic values remained a basic concern throughout the period. So the debate on industrial democracy became even more confused as more voices, speaking with different accents but using the same idioms, joined in; and the old ones did not quit the chamber.

INDUSTRIAL DEMOCRACY AND THE "GOLDEN AGE OF THE TRADE AGREEMENT"

However, industrial democracy did acquire something approaching an agreed practical meaning to collectivist liberals at the turn of the century. In the 1890s, it had been mixed up with a variety of reform panaceas— government ownership, producers' cooperatives, labor copartnership, or even profit sharing initiated by enlightened proprietors. In the 1900s, it came to mean one thing only: the self-organization of workers into independent trades unions whose internal procedures and constitutions conformed to representative-democratic standards; the recognition of those unions by employers for purposes of collective bargaining over wages, hours, and working conditions; and the resulting "constitutionalizing" of industry, through the abolition of "arbitrary government" and the joint development of agreed rules and means for their quasi-judicial, or at any rate peaceful, enforcement.[16]

Political and Industrial Democracy 1776–1926 (New York: Funk and Wagnalls, 1926), 81.

[16] Sidney and Beatrice Webb, *Industrial Democracy* (London, 1897); Milton Derber, *The American Idea of Industrial Democracy, 1865–1965* (Urbana: University of Illinois Press, 1970), esp. chapters 1, 5.

This is the version of industrial democracy enshrined in Milton Derber's work as the American Idea; though of course it was neither distinctively nor originally American nor the sole contender for the title.
Still, it was clearly the most important after 1900, receiving influential
public endorsement from the U.S. Industrial Commission in 1902, from
the National Civic Federation and other public-spirited worthies, from
the first generation of American labor economists, from the U.S. Commission on Industrial Relations in 1916, the president's Mediation Commission in 1917, and in a host of secular and religious reconstruction
programs in the wake of the Great War.

This vision of industrial democracy received support for a number of
reasons. In places, it already existed and seemed to work quite well—in
the United Kingdom and in certain industries in the United States. It
could be described, approvingly, as a natural, an organic, an evolutionary
development, not an artificial system. It suited the voluntarist and antistatist proclivities of the English-speaking peoples; it replicated the forms
and even the processes of their political development. History, and the
record of contemporary regimes outside the singularly blessed Anglo-
Saxon nations, could be raked over in the search for pejorative metaphors
to describe unilateral employer control over workers. The unbroken,
optimistic course of English history, in which more educated Americans
were instructed as an integral part of their national story then than ever
since, could be used for very different purposes.[17]

England's past as then understood was progressive. The parallel histories of monarchical and elite concessions of "rights," of the growth of
the common law, and of the assertion of parliamentary sovereignty,
combined with the comparatively recent extension of the franchise, provided American industrial democrats with a useful range of analogies to
use in justifying and predicting the constitutionalizing of American industry. What they envisaged was not the imposition of a formal governmental structure from "outside" (for example, by legislation) but rather
the gradual, piecemeal, and above all *peaceful* development of jointly
agreed and adaptable rules by the parties themselves.

This was how John R. Commons visualized the workings of the trade
agreement system in the 1900s, after he had imbibed the Webbs' classic

---

[17] Bruce Russett, *Community and Contention: Britain and America in the Twentieth Century*
(Cambridge, Mass.: MIT Press, 1963), 131.

Industrial Democracy and come to think of the American coal operators' and miners' representatives at the Interstate Conference as rather like the House of Lords and the House of Commons respectively, legislating together for their industry.[18]

Twenty years later, after the "golden age of the trade agreement" (circa 1898–1902) had been terminated by the employers' open shop crusade and the hopes of pro-labor collectivists had been revived in the war period, only to be dashed by the great postwar reaction and the "American Plan," Commons's immigrant student William E. Leiserson was still using the same arguments for the same optimistic purposes. And the garment workers he served used the same historical language as their WASP contemporaries to describe their successful union-building project: "What was achieved in British political life many centuries ago the workers in the American clothing industry undertook to fight for in the twentieth century. We have finally written our industrial Magna Charta."[19]

Obviously there was more to this collectivist liberal identification "of the labor union 'with all its crudities' as the most promising instrument for workers' representation in the management of business," to borrow the *New Republic*'s formula, than the mere imitation of English schemes or the appeal of historical analogy. Labor unions and trade agreement systems were established facts before American reformers recognized their significance and potential; but it was their rapid growth in the turn-of-the-century boom that compelled middle-class Americans to reevaluate them, in the light of their concerns about corporate power and the future of the American social order.

Was the trade union a violator of property rights, a threat to class harmony and social peace, an irrelevance or distraction for the forces of reform, a political danger, a focus of irresponsible private power threatening a future of bilateral control of the economy by business and labor leaders indifferent to the public and consumer interest? This viewpoint had a long and respectable history and gained added support among the American middle class in the Progressive Era when and where rapidly

---

[18] John R. Commons, *Myself* (Madison: University of Wisconsin Press, 1964; originally published 1934), 71–73.

[19] William E. Leiserson, "Constitutional Government in American Industries," *American Economic Review* 12 (1922): 56–79; *Report of the General Executive Board to the Fourth Biennial Convention of the Amalgamated Clothing Workers of America* (Boston, Mass., 10–15 May 1920), 48. Cf. Earl D. Howard, comp., *The Hart Schaffner and Marx Labor Agreement: Industrial Law in the Clothing Industry* (Chicago: 1920), 7.

growing union power became an important public issue, as Michael Kazin's influential study of San Francisco has pointed out.[20]

But, in the 1900s, the established antilabor consensus was challenged. It was not overturned, but a countervailing opinion gained respectable support. Perhaps the trade union was instead "a blind but mighty impulse toward democracy and the equal rights of man . . . at once an expression of democracy and an education in democracy" that "teaches the workingman to lift his head, to be a man among men." Many early twentieth-century American liberals, unlike their late nineteenth-century counterparts, seem to have concluded, with Ray Stannard Baker, that on balance it was "with full knowledge of its stumbling organization, its pitiful mistakes, its excesses, and even its crimes."[21]

The trade union was a vehicle, perhaps the only one available, for functional representation of the workers' interests within the emerging corporate order. The less content one was with the legitimacy or the results of unchecked proprietorial and managerial power, the more attracted to a model of industrial democracy based on the trade union, as an agency of reform, one might become. Industrial democracy offered an alternative to statism or socialism, an antidote to industrial conflict, a means of social adjustment.

A synthesis between these two conflicting opinions was possible: that trade unions were a good thing, in theory, and industrial democracy, in the abstract, desirable, though nobody really knew what it meant; but that union power was in practice suspect whenever it showed itself. This ambivalence remained at the center of middle-class liberal attitudes toward the labor movement thereafter. So it was the continuing underdevelopment of union power in the United States in general that, ironically, created the space within which labor-liberal harmony could ineffectually flourish.

The collective bargaining model of industrial democracy, to be achieved through the independent trade union, had one final and enduring argument in its favor among many American liberals. In Great Britain, in comparison, middle-class socialists could take the organization of labor and its recognition by employers and the state for granted; and then they

---

[20] Michael Kazin, *Barons of Labor: The San Francisco Building Trades and Union Power in the Progressive Era* (Urbana: University of Illinois Press, 1987), esp. chapters 7–9.

[21] John E. Semonche, *Ray Stannard Baker: A Quest for Democracy in Modern America, 1870–1918* (Chapel Hill: University of North Carolina Press, 1969), 118. Cf. Charles W. Eliot, *The Future of Trade-Unionism and Capitalism in a Democracy* (New York: Putnam, 1910).

could move on, to contemplate state-socialist or guild-socialist futures. But in the United States, a legally secure labor movement, at least tolerated by employers, remained an unfulfilled hope.

The labor movement's continuing marginality for another generation is surely what fixed the understanding of industrial democracy within the mainstream of independent liberalism into the grooves carved out at the turn of the century. The basic questions of union recognition and collective bargaining remained firmly at the top of its agenda, as unfinished business, from the early 1900s to the mid-1930s. Partly as a result of the want of better alternatives, the trade union was the necessary instrument for the realization of important liberal corporatist or collectivist schemes. This view, quite surprising when first enunciated, acquired the status of dogma through the following decades of hopes deferred.

MANAGERIAL SUPPORT FOR INDUSTRIAL DEMOCRACY

The advocates of industrial democracy whose reference points were the trade unions belonged to or, more commonly, sympathized with the labor movement from their settings in academe, journalism, organized religion, or independent liberal politics. Many of the collectivists in the latter groups were fluent in at least two of Daniel Rodgers's "social languages" of Progressivism. But what could industrial democracy mean to those managerial professionals for whom the language of "social efficiency" was their mother tongue? And what strange uses might be made of it by more traditional, less technocratic, members of the owning and controlling elites who actually had power to determine whether their enterprises were to be used for purposes of social experimentation?

There is a history to managerial variations on the theme of industrial democracy that parallels its development in other middle-class circles sketched above. This is not surprising: their authors shared many of the same values, lived through the same times, reacted to the same big public events. But there is a difference: liberal managerialists who advocated participative, representative, or consultative approaches to people management as supplements to, or substitutes for, simple or technical control did so on the grounds that they worked, more than because they were "right."

Other reformist arguments for industrial democracy, of course, had system-sustaining rationales too, but the privately owned and controlled, hierarchically ordered, profit- and production-driven corporation was one part of the system they usually wished to transcend. Managerial reformers worked within it and just wanted to make it work better.

Managerial interest in the democratization of industry seems to have had two distinct purposes. One was the pursuit of higher productive efficiency through a more psychologically sophisticated social integration of the work force with the enterprise. The other was a strengthening of the legitimacy of managerial authority in what Aileen Kraditor aptly calls a "shake-up period."[22]

Pioneers in scientific and personnel management attempted to steer their less-enlightened peers toward a less authoritarian, more consultative or participatory style of leadership, with the best arguments they could muster: it worked, and it paid. As one advocate of the new approach wrote, "One chief objection to exploitation is that it does not get enough out of the workers. . . . Men cannot be treated like machines; they must be consulted." Another similarly argued that "No matter how close is the supervision of machines from above, the best results can not be had unless the men below also supervise."

The punitively overcontrolling organization could never be optimally productive, because as the liberal Taylorites H. B. Drury and Morris Cooke explained, "While it is possible under certain conditions to compel obedience, there is no possible way in which a man can be *compelled* to do his work willingly, and when he does it unwillingly he is very far from being efficient." "We want all along the line not only men who can do what they are told to do, but men who can do things we would never think of for ourselves." Finally, as personnel manager Neil Clark emphasized at the height of the postwar concern about the labor problem, workers who were not consulted, who did not consent, had other ways of getting their own back against their employers than just working ineffectively, or leaving for another job: they could revolt. "Labor is the product of sentient beings. It is a commodity with a kick."[23]

That we should find members of the scientific management movement

---

[22] Aileen Kraditor, *The Radical Persuasion 1890–1917* (Baton Rouge: Louisiana State University Press, 1981), esp. chapter 3.
[23] Henderson, *Citizens in Industry*, 49, 83; William R. Bassett, *When the Workmen Help You Manage* (New York: Century, 1919), 83; H. B. Drury, quoted in Morris Ll. Cooke, "Who Is Boss in Your Shop? Individual vs. Group Leadership, and Their Relation to Consent and the Ideals of Democracy," *Bulletin of the Taylor Society* 3 (August 1917): 3–10, at p. 7; Neil M. Clark, *Common Sense in Labor Management* (New York: Harper, 1919), 10.

in the vanguard of the army of the righteous working for what they called industrial democracy by the late teens may surprise those who remember that, for Frederick W. Taylor, democracy in industry meant little more than that all, managers and workers alike, should be equally compelled to accept the truths his expertise revealed. But if readers of this chapter are surprised, it can only be because they are ignorant of the work of Nadworny, Haber, Layton, Meiksins, and Stabile, which demonstrates how far and how fast the management movement developed after Taylor's death.[24]

Louis D. Brandeis, speaking at a memorial meeting of the Taylor Society to honor its late chief in 1915, set the course it would soon follow: "In a democratic community men who are to be affected by a proposed change of conditions should be consulted and the innovators must carry the burden of convincing others at each stage in the process of change that what is being done is right." Brandeis clearly supposed that convincing people must involve more than the early management movement's strident announcement that it had discovered the "one best way."[25]

Robert G. Valentine, pioneer industrial counselor and an associate of Brandeis in joint labor-management efforts to bring order out of chaos in the New York garment trades, amplified the argument: what was required was not just consultation but actual *informed consent* on the part of the work force: "a free man—a consenting man—is the more desirable worker. . . . [O]rganized consent as well as individual consent is the basis of a more efficient group."

How should one build such groups? On the basis of representation of group interests. "Representation is the oldest, the simplest, the most effective and the most neglected principle of organization, and it is most neglected where we need it most—at the very base of our producing and

---

[24] Milton J. Nadworny, *Scientific Management and the Unions 1900–1932: An Historical Analysis* (Cambridge, Mass.: Harvard University Press, 1955); Samuel Haber, *Efficiency and Uplift: Scientific Management in the Progressive Era 1890–1920* (Chicago: University of Chicago Press, 1964); Edwin T. Layton, Jr., *The Revolt of the Engineers: Social Responsibility and the American Engineering Profession* (Baltimore: Johns Hopkins University Press, 1971); Peter Meiksins, "The 'Revolt of the Engineers' Reconsidered," *Technology and Culture* 29 (1988): 219–46; Donald Stabile, *Prophets of Order: The Rise of the New Class and Socialism in America* (Boston: South End Publishers, 1984).

[25] Brandeis, "Efficiency by Consent: To Secure Its Active Cooperation Labor Must Be Consulted and Convinced in Regard to Changes," *Industrial Management* 55 (February 1918): 108–9.

consuming system.... [E]very interest existing where people work and deal together must be represented in organized and effective ways in the decisions made."[26]

Valentine, an inspirational friend to such liberal collectivists as Felix Frankfurter and the rest of the *New Republic* crowd, pointed a way toward an accommodation between their pursuit of social efficiency and their attachment to democratic norms. Valentine challenged the engineer's hubris and, even more, the conventional employer's or manager's unitary ideology by breaking with the common assumption that a leader-led hierarchy was technologically determined in the complex world of modern industry.

This did not mean, however, that he was advocating government from below, free of expert guidance. This was not what he meant by "democracy"—it was not "almost necessarily a mere crude expression of untrained information through votes"; it could acquire "a finer texture ...through self-training groups constantly growing in strength through the consideration of scientifically accurate data." Scientific managers, according to this vision, would both establish the institutions of organized cooperation and shape its results by the nominally apolitical process of agenda setting and supplying "technical" information.

All that was needed to fit trades unions into this blueprint was a confidence that, given the correct enlightened leader such as Sidney Hillman, they could be employed as scientific managers' chosen instruments for rationalization through representation; there was no need to invent new ones when the existing ones would serve.[27]

What was involved here was more than the effecting of a reconciliation between some scientific managers and some trades unions, whereby the former became advisors to and advocates of the latter. What was also involved was a redefinition of "democracy" to allow for inequalities of knowledge and expertise and to permit a technocratic elite to play an undisputed leading role.

The Taylorites were perhaps the most interesting, certainly the most

[26] Robert G. Valentine, "The Progressive Relation Between Efficiency and Consent," *Bulletin of the Society to Promote the Science of Management* 1:6 (December 1915): 26–30; "Representation," *New Republic* 3 (17 July 1915): 285–86.
[27] Felix Frankfurter, "General," in "Industrial Relations: I. Some Noteworthy Recent Developments," *Bulletin of the Taylor Society* 6:6 (December 1919); 12–31, at 12–16; "Democratic Control of Scientific Management," *The New Republic* 9 (23 December 1916): 204–5. Cf. William S. Graebner, *The Engineering of Consent: Democracy and Authority in Twentieth Century America* (Madison: University of Wisconsin Press, 1987).

articulate, managerial advocates of a less horny-handed approach to everyday industrial relations in the teens and twenties. In the readiness some of them showed to work with and through existing trade unions and to integrate them into their plans for maximizing enterprise-level efficiency and pursuing interfirm rationalization and industry planning, they were unique.

But they were not the first service intellectuals of the corporate order to see the advantages of the consultative approach. James Bayles, editor of *The Iron Age,* had recognized it during the "Great Upheaval" in 1886: the shop council system he envisaged was not necessarily an antiunion device, but was intended to be a means of rapid, direct, and relatively informal grievance settlement through "constant and intimate conference between employers and employed" within the enterprise. This plan anticipated the central feature of the most successful "unionesque" employee representation schemes of thirty to fifty years later.[28]

The shop council's business was to be prevention, the elimination of minor disagreements within the industrial family before they exploded into open conflict. Management consultant H. J. F. Porter, a former collaborator of Taylor's at Bethlehem Steel whose final solution to the labor problem could not have been more different from his more famous colleague's, went a step further in the early 1900s, making the working of a suggestion program focused on production problems the central purpose of the representative councils he installed in middle-size failing companies, to help turn them around.[29]

These two pioneering proposals concentrated on the individual plant and on mutual problem solving. They were innocent of formal psychological or quasi-political theorizing. In that respect, they seem more important in retrospect than they did at the time, because their very modesty meant that they represented a method with a future. The Taylorites' approach, in contrast, came to presuppose a collaboration between enlightened technocrats and formally recognized, equally enlightened trade unions. Despite well-publicized successes in some railroad workshops and in the garment trades in the 1920s, and rebirth in the form of the "Scanlon Plan" in the 1940s and 1950s, the Taylor idea was actually at odds with the sort of job-related collective bargaining that was the chief object and

---

[28] James C. Bayles, *The Shop Council* (New York: Society for Political Education, 1886), 20.
[29] K. H. Condit, "Solving the Labor Problem," *American Machinist* 51:7 (14 August 1919): 301–4.

eventual achievement of most liberal, pro-labor reformers from the 1900s onward. It also offered more of a challenge to managerial assumptions and standard operating procedures. As a result, the Taylorites neither won friends nor influenced people who mattered.

If we are examining the past for the origins of the present, we must conclude that the Taylorites' reconciliation of expertise and democracy, interesting though it may be as an incident in the history of ideas, is actually less significant than these humbler and generally overlooked experiments. Together with Robert B. Wolf's more self-consciously "scientific" program of what we would now call worker involvement and job enrichment, they point toward Douglas MacGregor's "Theory Y" and contemporary proposals for building an informed, involved work force.[30]

What was most "modern" about them was that they had no larger political purpose. Their focus was the firm, their goal production and, to achieve that, a contented, well-adjusted labor force. The Taylorites could see that certain managerial styles and techniques were appropriate to a nation with a democratic civic culture, and they made connections between their programs for industry and their visions of a reconstructed society. These other pioneers had no such vision; in this respect, they look quite like most of us.

MANAGEMENT-INITIATED EMPLOYEE REPRESENTATION PROGRAMS

The approaches to the democratizing of management outlined above made precious little headway at the time. What made much more contemporary impact was a style of employee representation plan initiated by managements for a variety of different reasons. Some schemes were paternalist attempts to reconstitute proprietary firms as "little commonwealths" clothed with pseudodemocratic forms; others were obvious union-avoidance ploys; many were directly created by the National War Labor Board of 1918–19 or inspired by its example.

The war and reconstruction period was the seedtime of most of these schemes. Many of them were examples of managerial faddishness and imitativeness, curious by-products of a fusion of the wartime vogue for "democracy" and alarmism at industrial conflict at home, Bolshevism abroad. Some had more substance and durability—particularly those

---

[30] Douglas McGregor, *The Human Side of Enterprise* (New York: McGraw-Hill, 1960).

associated with the very large firms that banded together into the Special Conference Committee—and saw their employee representation plans or company unions as integral parts of comprehensive programs of personnel management and welfare capitalism.[31]

These plans have been adequately studied. Few of them lasted more than a handful of years; they never affected more than a small minority of the industrial work force; very few of them survived the Depression, the challenge of organized labor, or the impact of the Wagner Act. So why bother with them here, apart from considerations of completeness?

The fact is that employer-initiated employee representation schemes reflected a degree of realism about the limitations of the applicability of political forms and language to capitalistic employment relations that was lacking in most of the independent liberal advocacy of industrial democracy. They recognized that speaking metaphorically about the firm as a political entity had its attractions and its uses, particularly for a management concerned to make its authority more legitimate and more effective. But they were very clear that the adoption of quasi-democratic forms had everything to do with these purposes and nothing much to do with limiting the prerogatives of ownership and management or altering the essential purposes of the enterprise.[32]

Even when proprietors and managers came closest to a political analysis of industry's problems, the solutions they recommended differed from the liberal industrial democrats' in one key particular: they were homegrown. They did not display the affection for models and metaphors drawing on England's political history of the pro-labor collectivists; they were not persuaded that British institutions—collective bargaining or "Whitley Councils" for industry-wide joint consultation—could or should be imported wholesale.

When they wanted to constitutionalize industry, they thought in terms of American political history, in terms of enshrining due process and

[31] For employee representation, see Howard M. Gitelman, *Legacy of the Ludlow Massacre: A Chapter in American Industrial Relations* (Philadelphia: University of Pennsylvania Press, 1988); Sanford M. Jacoby, *Employing Bureaucracy: Managers, Unions, and the Transformation of Work in American Industry, 1900–1945* (New York: Columbia University Press, 1985); and Daniel Nelson, "The Company Union Movement, 1900–1937: A Reexamination," *Business History Review* 56 (1982): 335–57.

[32] Clark, *Common Sense in Labor Management*, chapter 2; Fred H. Colvin, *Labor Turnover, Loyalty and Output: A Consideration of the Trend of the Times as Shown by the Results of War Activities in the Machine Shops and Elsewhere* (New York: McGraw-Hill, 1919), chapter 3; Edward S. Cowdrick, "Progress and Tendencies in Works Councils," *The American Review* 3 (1925): 443–50; Walter G. Merritt, *Factory Solidarity or Class Solidarity* (pamphlet, n.p., n.d., reprint from *The Iron Age*), esp. 31–34.

establishing an industrial *republic,* a "government of laws not of men," which recognized from the outset certain limitations on majority will. Citizenship in such a republic implied duties as well as rights and was not something acquired simply by virtue of employment. In an age of 100 percent Americanism confronting a heavily alien working class and of massive labor turnover, industrial citizenship often had language, nationality, and "residence" (i.e., job tenure) limitations placed upon it.

Constitutionalizing of industry under these terms did not imply giving labor a voice in management, except on certain minor job-related matters. It had much more to do with domesticating and stabilizing the labor force, with encouraging long-service, relatively skilled and senior, American or Americanized employees to identify their personal interests with the company they worked for, to feel they belonged, that they had a "stake." It was mostly a confidence-, trust-, or morale-building exercise, which might involve attempting to draw on workers' initiative and suggestions but aimed principally at making them more contented with their subordination.[33]

The narrow version of industrial democracy seen in the employee representation movement used the forms and language of democratic government for strictly managerial purposes. It thought itself peculiarly well adapted to American conditions because, as John D. Rockefeller, Jr., pointed out, it was "constructed from the bottom up" among a people "committed by our individualistic philosophy and make-up to a policy of de-centralized experiments." It argued that the firm, not the industry or the class, was the proper basis for functional representation. The state had no role to play; trade unions might or might not. In theory, they were not excluded totally or for all time; but they certainly did not enjoy the status the AFL claimed, and its liberal allies allowed, of being not just a preferred but the only vehicle for the genuine democratization of industry.

The horizons of the employee representation movement of the 1920s were determined by the structures and interests of the existing corporate order. It depended strictly on managerial initiative and commitment for its very existence. This unilateral-corporatist, vehemently antistatist in-

[33] O. F. Carpenter, chapters 7, 8, and 22 in John R. Commons et al., *Industrial Government* (New York: Macmillan, 1921); John Leitch, *Man to Man: The Story of Industrial Democracy* (London: Putnam, 1920); Paul W. Litchfield, *The Industrial Republic: Reflections of an Industrial Lieutenant* (Cleveland: Corday and Gross, 1946; originally published 1919), esp. book 1.

dustrial relations strategy was a distinctively new, but became an enduringly important, component of "American exceptionalism." Even after the New Deal had outlawed 1920s-style company unionism, and more firms had seen their representation plans used as foundations on which workers erected their own unions than were able to steer them toward formal independence, corporate America's attachment to its own peculiar version of corporatism would remain, though it had to find expression in different forms—the "human relations" school of management, the construction of private welfare states through the proliferation of fringe benefits in the 1940s and 1950s, "team building" in firms with strong "company cultures" like IBM and Xerox, and most recently, the vogues for positive human resource management and the "Japanization" of employer-employee relations.[34]

After all the rhetoric and hyperbole of the war and reconversion years, all the expectations of a new social order or a "new industrial day," this was all that the various movements for industrial democracy had accomplished:

1. A substantial degree of independent liberal and middle-class support for the American labor movement and its institutional objectives. Progressive Taylorites thought that movement's functions ought not to be confined to mere collective bargaining; they should expand to include some voice in the management of the productive enterprise and the cooperative planning of the industry. But, through the 1920s, there was hardly any constituency even within the labor movement itself for such a radical program. Labor's plans centered on the wage-and-effort bargain, on working conditions, and on the firm.

The AFL's conservatism did not reflect much lowering of labor's sights, for there is precious little evidence they were ever raised any higher; collective bargaining on job-related issues was a sufficiently ambitious objective, difficult enough to attain before the late 1930s. What is more significant is the adjustment of liberal friends of labor to the same comparatively modest hopes. Trimming the meaning of industrial democracy to fit existing realities was part of the general deflation of American ideals

[34] John D. Rockefeller, Jr., "Representation in Industry." Address before the War and Reconversion Conference of the Chamber of Commerce of the United States, privately printed, 1918, 20; Sam A. Lewisohn, "Recent Tendencies in Bringing About Improved Relations between Employer and Employee in Industry," reprinted from *The Economic World* (New York, 1921), 6. For post–New Deal versions of unitary corporatist ideology and practice, see Stephen P. Waring, *Taylorism Transformed: Scientific Management Theory since 1945* (Chapel Hill: University of North Carolina Press, 1991).

to cope with the disillusionment of the early 1920s, and the decline of the habit of moralistic argument and millenarian prophecy that had afflicted confessedly evangelical and nominally secular Progressives throughout the previous generation.[35]

2. A number of employer-initiated plans that involved some degree of sharing by workers in ownership and control, which sometimes worked with and through trades unions, and which were obviously sincere attempts to deal with the ethical problems of hierarchical and inegalitarian employment relations. Such schemes were confined to relatively small, generally personally or family-owned firms, the only locales where such well-meaning but quixotic quests for community could be attempted. The most common motivation behind such plans was their initiators' religious convictions, which might include some species of Social Gospel Protestantism or individualistic, esoteric blends of a "religion of democracy" with a nominally secular humanism. What these plans illustrated was the cultural conservatism of idiosyncratic small-business people and their freedom to do what they liked with their own property, including giving it away.[36]

3. The mature, consolidated employee representation movement, pruned of the schemes that had reflected transient managerial concern about industrial conflict and the threat of Bolshevism, pruned too of some of the quasi-governmental rhetoric and forms that had reflected employers' search for reassurance and legitimacy by clothing their authority in the trappings of the American constitutional order.

This formative period in American business's unitary-corporatist industrial relations strategies had profound and lasting consequences, deepening managers' commitment to antiunionism and widening the array of tactics at their disposal for the maintenance or, after the 1940s, the restoration of a union-free environment. Experience of the company union era also soured organized labor's leaders and friends on the possibilities of cooperative industrial relations policies, and alerted them to its dangers, which included the subversion or crowding out of independent working-class organizations. As a consequence of this unhappy experience, the legal framework for the extension of trade union power

[35] Samuel Gompers, *Collective Bargaining: Labor's Proposal to Insure Greater Industrial Peace with Questions and Answers Explaining the Principle* (Washington: American Federation of Labor, 1920).

[36] See, for example, James Myers, *Representative Government in Industry* (New York: George H. Doran, 1924); Paul H. Douglas, *The Columbia Conserve Company: A Unique Experiment in Industrial Democracy* (Chicago: University of Chicago Press, 1925).

that labor's friends erected in the 1930s was designed, in good part, to insulate individual workers and their unions against employer influence. To the extent that it outlawed old-style iron-fisted antiunionism, as well as 1920s-style company unionism, it certainly succeeded.

Ironically, therefore, the apparent success of the employee representation movement in the New Era helped guarantee its destruction in the different political climate of the Depression. And the Wagner Act, which did so much to hasten its demise, in its turn helped make sure that the relationship of employers and organized labor in the future must be carried on at arm's length. Protective distance maintained American labor's independence of overt managerial control; but it also, as later contributors in this volume will argue, entrenched its marginality.

Historians are not at their best when getting into the business of counter-factual hypothesizing, but one may plausibly suggest that the lessons business and labor leaders and makers of public policy learned from the company union era of the 1920s helped foreclose the possibility of an alternative corporatist future. That future might have involved a Northern European-style "codetermination model" of cooperative rather than adversarial, firm- or industry-level labor relations—an option that attracts some observers of the American industrial present, beset by problems of managerial competency, worker commitment, and international competitiveness. But more than half a century of divergent institutional development, as well as the deeper societal and cultural predispositions at the center of David Brody's analysis, renders any such future highly improbable.

A MODERN CORPORATE ORDER AND THE DECLINE OF DEMOCRATIC REFORM

If we can borrow Aileen Kraditor's insightful organizing concept of the long Progressive Era as a "shake-up period," it is clear that by the 1920s the American corporate order had shaken down into more stable, recognizably modern forms. Managers' claims to legitimate control based on traditional arguments (property rights, the obedience due those of superior status, the necessity of preserving an ordered society) had been reinforced—by technocratic arguments emphasizing their professionalism, public-spiritedness, and strategic vision, and by general welfare arguments that asserted that managerial capitalism guaranteed economic progress and an ever more equitable distribution of the opportunity to live in secure affluence. In the emerging "culture of consumption," industrial democracy's assumption that work, not leisure, was the "central life interest" of an alienated and oppressed majority seemed out of place.

When we shift our attention from ideology to practice, we find another explanation for the declining appeal of proposals for the "democratic" reform of work relations. Quite simply, they proved to be unnecessary. Workers' willing effort did not, after all, *need* to be courted through the institution of formal representative machinery. There were other ways: Most important, the fear of losing a job regained its power in the early and late 1920s, and strict supervision and technical control still seemed to work in producing obedience and adequate performance, if not willing compliance, which might be nice to have, but which could be done without.

And even where managers moved from coercion to manipulation as their favored control strategy, they could do so without giving their subordinates the right to an independent voice. In a minority of managerially progressive firms, personnel management satisfied some workers' demands for more equity and predictability in the employment relationship, indicating that a sufficiently intelligent and efficient bureaucracy did not need the assistance of an organized, internal "loyal opposition." Welfare capitalism attempted to turn some corporations into real communities organizing their workers' nonwork lives, at the same time offering individual workers and their families the promise of improved security in return for loyalty. Industrial psychology promised managers new ways of predicting and encouraging the individual worker's commitment to the goals of the enterprise, making industrial democracy's presumptions about the free will, rationality, and virtuous independence of spirit of the worker appear positively unscientific and rather old hat.

All the talk about industrial democracy looks, in retrospect, to have been nothing more than a symptom of liberal capitalism's crisis of confidence at the turn of the century. It illustrates very well that all kinds of citizens of the same state can use the same language, share what appears to be a common public discourse, all the while meaning entirely different things and ending up meaning very little at all.

4

"An American feeling": workers, managers, and
the struggle over industrial democracy in the
World War I era

JOSEPH A. McCARTIN

When a General Electric worker who helped organize a union in his plant
in 1918 was asked by friendly government officials whether he had to
hide his union sympathies on the job, his answer surprised them. "In a
way, I didn't have any [union sympathies]," he replied, "only—I might
say I had an American feeling, that is all. . . . I didn't have much thought
in the matter . . . of union stuff."[1] Upon further questioning, the examiners
found that indeed this employee saw his union work as but an extension
of the war effort that he loyally supported. That response signified something important about the industrial battle that rocked the United States
in 1919, just months after this interview.

Heretofore, most historians have looked at the labor conflict of 1919
largely as a battle waged by employers seeking to push back wartime
union gains and restore the open shop—what employers came to call
the American Plan. With the notable exception of Gary Gerstle's study
of Rhode Island textile workers and their attempts to forge a "working-
class Americanism" following the war, most interpretations of postwar
labor struggle have been institutional in approach, focusing on the fate

Although none of them bears responsibility for the arguments made here, the author would
like to acknowledge gratefully the insights of Melvyn Dubofsky, Alice Kessler-Harris,
Howell Harris, Mike McCartin, Jennifer Miller, Mary Nolan, and Thom Wermuth, all of
whom immeasurably enriched this essay.

[1] "Transcript of Proceedings," casefile 231, p. 775, Records of the National War Labor
Board, National Archives, Record Group 2 (hereinafter cited as RG 2, NA).

of workers' organizations.[2] But by examining 1919 in this way, historians have neglected an important feature of the upheaval: the battle between labor and capital over the ideological legacy of the war. We know too little about the struggle of employers to take back from trade unionism the "American feeling" that had suffused wartime union organizing. Yet this was at the heart of the conflict between labor and capital over postwar reconstruction.

This chapter argues that labor conflict of 1919 in the United States was in part a battle for legitimacy that was waged over language as well as over union organization.[3] There is perhaps no clearer evidence that managers and workers battled over language in 1919 than the controversy that raged over *industrial democracy,* a term that, as historian David

[2] Gary Gerstle's work has had an important influence upon this author. In part, this essay may be seen as an attempt to uncover the roots of the "working-class Americanism" that Gerstle found among Rhode Island textile workers in the 1930s. While he argued that the ideology of Woonsocket textile workers had its origins in "the dramatic changes in American politics and culture World War I brought to a head," Gerstle's study focused on the postwar era and did not fully explore the impact of the war in shaping their language of Americanism. Nonetheless, his study provides an important point of departure for this essay. See Gerstle, *Working-Class Americanism: The Politics of Labor in a Textile City, 1914–1960* (New York, 1989), 1, 5–15. Institutional studies of postwar labor struggle would include David Brody, *Labor in Crisis: The Steel Strike of 1919* (Philadelphia, 1965); Philip Foner, *Postwar Struggles, 1918–1920: History of the Labor Movement in the United States,* vol. 8 (New York, 1988); Alan Wakstein, "The Origins of the Open Shop Movement, 1919–1920," *Journal of American History* 51 (1964): 460–75. Although it emphasizes different points than those taken up in this essay (or in Gary Gerstle's work for that matter), another study that examines postwar conflict through the lens of ideology is Haggai Hurvitz, "The Meaning of Industrial Conflict in Some Ideologies of the Early 1920s" (Ph.D. diss., Columbia University, 1971).

[3] Recently, a number of historians have begun to show the important role that language plays in social conflict and accommodation. Many of these historians have made fruitful use of the deconstructionist methods employed by literary theorists. Since I consciously avoid employing this method in this essay, a word of explanation is in order. To employ deconstructionist analysis or to deploy other theoretical constructs here would, I believe, detract from the purpose of this chapter, which is to examine the material struggle between employers and workers that made language—and specifically the term *industrial democracy*—a contested terrain in the World War I era. To shift my focus to the *terrain* of language itself at the expense of analyzing the *contest* over power in the workplace (and the way language was used in this contest) would, I believe, only reify the language of industrial democracy, which was both fluid and historically specific. Nonetheless, I am greatly indebted to the growing literature on language and social history. See Gareth Stedman Jones, *Languages of Class: Studies in English Working Class History, 1832–1932* (New York, 1983); William Sewell, *Work and Revolution in France: The Language of Labor from the Old Regime to 1848* (New York, 1980); Joan W. Scott, "On Language, Gender, and Working-Class History," *International Labor and Working-Class History* 31 (Spring 1987): 1–13; John Foster, "The Declassing of Language," *New Left Review* 150 (March-April 1985); Bryan D. Palmer, "Response to Joan Scott," *International Labor and Working-Class History* 31 (Spring 1987): 14–23; and Bryan D. Palmer, *Descent into Discourse: The Reification of Language and the Writing of Social History* (Philadelphia, 1990).

Brody points out, had become a "national byword" by the end of World War I.[4] In developing their postwar American Plan attack, and in making their own version of industrial democracy an important feature of that plan, employers were not only trying to roll back trade unionism; they were attempting to reconstruct their legitimacy by incorporating the rallying cry of the wartime union upsurge into their managerial lexicon. For during the war, American labor militants had rallied behind industrial democracy—previously popularized by wartime government reformers—and successfully roused their followers with patriotic language. In doing so, militants cloaked labor protest—even demands that deeply challenged managerial authority—in a protective "American feeling." In 1919, the tasks of neutralizing that troublesome phrase, industrial democracy, and taking back the mantle of Americanism to which labor militants had laid claim, were integral to U.S. employers' counteroffensive against trade unionism. It is that neglected aspect of the postwar upheaval that this chapter addresses.

Paraphrasing E. P. Thompson, historian David Alan Corbin has observed that the "ideological impact of war propaganda on American workers may have been 'one of those facts so big,'...that it is easily overlooked,...and yet it indicates a major shift in the...'subpolitical' attitudes of the masses."[5] If the language of the wartime union movement is any indication, such a shift in attitudes indeed occurred in the United States during the era of the Great War. An important measure of that shift was the popularity of the slogan "industrial democracy," which, by the end of the war, was on the tongues of millions of American workers. While industrial democracy was not a new phrase—it had been used in the United States as early as the 1880s—wartime government labor reforms had given the term a new legitimacy, incorporated it into wartime propaganda, and spread it to virtually every corner of industry.[6]

[4]David Brody, *Workers in Industrial America: Essays on the Twentieth Century Struggle* (New York, 1980), 56.
[5]David Alan Corbin, *Life, Work and Rebellion in the Coal Fields: The Southern West Virginia Miners, 1880–1922* (Urbana, 1981), 177; E. P. Thompson, *The Making of the English Working Class* (New York, 1964), 78.
[6]Lyman Abbott of the *Christian Union* used the term "industrial democracy" in the 1880s. Henry Demarest Lloyd had also used the term in the 1890s. English Fabians Sidney and Beatrice Webb adopted it, and several progressive reformers had used it prior to World War I. The war, however, both popularized the term and invested it with enormous prestige as government reformers began to call for industrial democracy at home while American troops were fighting to "make the world safe for democracy abroad." See Daniel T. Rodgers, *The Work Ethic in Industrial America, 1850–1920* (Chicago, 1974), 57–58; Howell John Harris, "Industrial Democracy and Liberal Capitalism, 1890–1925," Chapter

The federal government's role in spreading the industrial democracy slogan during the war derived from the Wilson administration's efforts to foster labor peace. Most historians agree that World War I constituted an important turning point in the relationship between American trade unionism and the state. Prior to the war, a hostile judiciary armed with the power of injunction offered American workers only what Christopher Tomlins in another context called a "counterfeit liberty."[7] The massive strike wave of 1917 and the "inadequacy of the existent agencies for dealing with the industrial strife," however, pushed the Wilson administration toward important breakthroughs in the protection of trade union rights.[8] These culminated with the creation by presidential authority of a powerful new agency, the National War Labor Board, in April 1918.[9]

Set up as a kind of industrial court, the NWLB was chaired by William Howard Taft and labor attorney Frank P. Walsh and composed of an equal number of employers and AFL unionists. It adopted a set of progressive principles to serve as a bench mark in settling wartime labor disputes. These principles acknowledged the right to join a union, the duty to bargain collectively, and the impropriety of antiunion tactics. As a concession to open shop industry, the NWLB did not require employers to recognize unions if they had not done so prior to the war. In such cases, collective bargaining was to be accomplished through worker-elected shop committees. The installation of these shop committees may have been the most important policy the NWLB pursued.

Altogether the NWLB program represented a great leap forward for U.S. trade unionism. Intervening in over one thousand strikes before the war ended and applying its principles on a broad basis, the NWLB sharply limited the arbitrary power of employers. In his typically enthusiastic language, the NWLB's cochair, Frank P. Walsh, announced that the board

---

3 in this volume; Sidney Webb and Beatrice Webb, *Industrial Democracy* (London, 1898); Charles Forcey, *The Crossroads of Liberalism: Croly, Weyl, Lippmann, and the Progressive Era, 1900–1925* (New York, 1961); Milton Derber, *The American Idea of Industrial Democracy* (Urbana, 1970).

[7] Christopher Tomlins, *The State and the Unions: Labor Relations, Law, and the Organized Labor Movement in America, 1880–1960* (New York, 1985), 328.

[8] Dallas Lee Jones, "Organized Labor and the Wilson Administration" (Ph.D. diss., Cornell University, 1954), 346. An astounding 438 strikes occurred in May 1917 alone. Meanwhile over six million workdays were lost to labor strife in the first six months of war. *Monthly Labor Review* 8 (June 1919): 308; National Industrial Conference Board, *Strikes in American Industry in Wartime: April 6 to October 6, 1917* (Boston, 1918), 3–5.

[9] Valerie Jean Conner, *The National War Labor Board: Stability, Social Justice and the Voluntary State in World War I* (Chapel Hill, 1983), 18–34.

was creating "a new deal for American labor."[10] Trade-union membership figures support Walsh's assessment. Under the board's protection, union membership grew by nearly one million by the war's end. As one autoworker put it, "For once every citizen, no matter how humble, was made to realize that the government was a real thing and that it wielded power, enormous power."[11]

Some scholars argue that the AFL's cooperation with the war effort and its submission to the NWLB's mediation undermined the AFL's militancy and independence. To be sure, the AFL's participation in the government's program helped legitimize the brutal suppression of the "disloyal" Industrial Workers of the World and Socialist party. However, to argue, as one scholar has done, that working with the NWLB "practically meant the transformation of the AFL from an independent trade union center to a government department which assumed the duty of preventing strikes and if necessary breaking them," is to overlook a central reality of the war for labor: the importance of language, symbolism, and ideology.[12] When one examines the influence of the NWLB on the language of working-class militancy during the war, it becomes clear that the war had far more complex implications for labor than these critics have understood.

In promoting its program, the NWLB helped to popularize the slogan industrial democracy. That phrase fit the board's purposes well. Its mission was, as the president defined it, to end undemocratic management practices at home while troops ended autocracy overseas. No one did more to link the board's mission to the establishment of industrial democracy at home than its cochair Frank Walsh. "Political Democracy is an illusion," Walsh was fond of saying in his numerous speeches on behalf of the NWLB, "unless builded upon and guaranteed by a free and virile Industrial Democracy."[13] He aimed to use the board to achieve such a vision, and Walsh firmly believed "the process of democratization [initiated by the NWLB] will continue until there remains not one single

[10] Ibid., 33.
[11] *The Auto Worker* 1:1 (May 1919): 3–4. Business leaders tended to concur in this assessment. Justice Elbert Gary confided that "no one can tell what is going to happen with respect to the labor question, because the Government is very powerful." Quoted in David Brody, *Steelworkers in America: The Non-Union Era* (Cambridge, Mass., 1960), 204.
[12] John Steuben, *Labor in Wartime* (New York, 1940), 67. Similar arguments may be found in Simeon Larson, *Labor and Foreign Policy: Gompers, the AFL, and the First World War* (Rutherford, N.J., 1975); Philip Foner, *Labor in World War I, 1914–1918: History of the Labor Movement in the United States,* vol. 7 (New York, 1987).
[13] *Bridgeport Labor Leader,* 29 August 1918.

wage-earner in the country deprived of his voice in determining the conditions of his job and consequently his life."[14]

Undoubtedly, official speeches about industrial democracy were often motivated by utilitarian concerns. The slogan was used along with a remarkable cult of the flag—including daily flag ceremonies at factories and workshops draped with hundreds of flags—to arouse maximum output. The word in many shops was: "Not Just Hats Off to the Flag, But Sleeves up for It." War production was the key. But by so closely linking work to patriotism, the government endowed labor with a new prestige, as when one official speaker told a group of Cleveland steelworkers: "Your greasy overalls ... are as much a badge of service and honor in ... the eyes of your country today as the uniform of the army or navy."[15]

Such powerful rhetoric—which became increasingly common throughout 1918—had manifold implications. On the one hand, it served to chasten employers who were determined to persist in antiunion practices. On the other it reassured the AFL leaders who cooperated with the government that their loyalty was well placed. But at the same time, it evoked in millions of workers skyrocketing hopes for substantial change in their lives. Many came to believe that " 'Making the world safe for democracy' [would] go a long way toward lifting the burden of social and economic oppression" from their shoulders.[16] The AFL's Matthew Woll later declared that as a result of the government's labor policy, "Men and Women came to think of democracy as they had never thought of it before. Democracy became the great, flaming religion of mankind."[17] It was in this hopeful context that workers embraced the government's promised industrial democracy.

Historian David Montgomery has contended that during the World War I era, "the phrase 'workers' control,' seldom heard before that time, became a popular catchword throughout the labor movement." The evidence contained in the records of wartime labor disputes that elicited government mediation supports a different view.[18] Rather than "workers'

[14] Machinists Monthly Journal (October 1918): 902–3.
[15] Quoted in Brody, Steelworkers in America, 195.
[16] Norfolk Journal and Guide, 24 September 1917.
[17] Matthew Woll, "The Policy of Organized Labor," in Lyman P. Powell, ed., The Social Unrest: Capital, Labor, and the Public in Turmoil (New York, 1919), 581.
[18] See Montgomery, Workers' Control in America: Studies in the History of Work, Technology, and Labor Struggles (New York, 1979), 99; Joseph A. McCartin, "Labor's 'Great War': Workers, Unions, and the State, 1916–1920" (Ph.D. diss., State University of New York at Binghamton, 1990), xxii–xxviii.

control," this evidence suggests, most U.S. workers demanded industrial democracy. The latter was a much vaguer slogan to be sure and one that enjoyed the imprimatur of the government, but these were precisely the attributes that made it attractive—even to working-class militants and radicals.

By allowing workers to connect democracy in industry to democracy in Europe, the federal program had the effect of offering a potent vocabulary to labor militants who had little trouble in seizing it to attack the authority of employers. If the NWLB implied that employers who opposed collective bargaining were subverting the war effort, on the shop floor union militants made the implication explicit, equating obstinate managers with the autocratic enemy. In the era when sauerkraut became "liberty cabbage," Bridgeport, Connecticut, machinists began referring to Remington Arms as "The American Junkers."[19] The steelworkers of Birmingham, Alabama, called the Tennessee Coal and Iron Company the "Kaiser of Industrial America." "The American Hohenzollerns" was another favorite appellation. Most common of all, however, were the terms "prussian" and "autocratic."[20] Indeed, the German "kultur," excoriated by George Creel's Committee on Public Information, seemed to offer a perfect analogy to industrial management and so bossism became "Kaiserism" in the language of union activists. By using this kind of language, the labor movement portrayed itself as demanding the "de-kaisering of industry," rather than merely seeking higher wages and shorter hours.[21] Indeed, such language cast the labor movement as the agent of industrial democracy, making unionizing a patriotic act. Thus a machinists' leaflet used in Akron tire factories did not mention the union but only organizing for "democracy in industry":

Wake Up! Machine Shop Workers, Wake Up! Uncle Sam proclaimed to the World that the freedom and democracy we are fighting for shall be practiced in the Industries of America.

Workers who did not organize, the leaflet went on to say, were nothing more than "industrial slackers."[22]

Portrayed in this way, union organizing was as much an act of good

---

[19] *Bridgeport Labor Leader*, 21 November 1918.
[20] For an example of the use of "prussian" as a pejorative term directed at antiunion management, see "Record of Proceedings of Mass Meeting of Employees," 2 May 1918, casefile 18, RG 2, NA.
[21] Quoted in *Pennsylvania Labor Herald*, 22 November 1918.
[22] IAM leaflet, casefile 172, RG 2, NA.

citizenship as an act of self- or class-interest and workers could defend it as such. This gave activists a valuable ideological shield. When her foreman demanded to know whether Mrs. C. W. Brooks, an operative in the magazine department of a Colt firearms factory, had been attending union meetings, Mrs. Brooks could simply reply: "Yes, and as a free American citizen I have a right to go if I want to."[23] For many labor militants it was a short step from identifying union organization as a citizen's right to defining it as a citizen's responsibility. The Machinists' organizing cry in Bridgeport was "Wake Up! Be Real Citizens!"[24] With admonitions such as these sprinkling wartime union drives, it is little wonder that the GE activist mentioned above could claim that his union sympathies were really "an American feeling."

This "feeling," as the Wilson administration (and the AFL leadership for that matter) found, had many implications. It could be used by the union movement to ward off slanderous accusations that legitimate strikes were financed by the Kaiser's gold. Indeed, unions began to defend strikes as actions taken in defense of democracy at home and hence as *supportive* of the war effort. Thus, strikers at one electrical plant informed President Wilson that their walkout was "the only course of action that true Americans [could] pursue."[25] But this same reasoning enabled militants to clothe in patriotic garments demands that challenged managerial authority; industrial democracy, militants proved, could serve subversive ends.[26] Perhaps nothing illustrated this truth more clearly than the response of workers to the NWLB's shop committees.

While some government officials initially felt that shop committee

---

[23] "Report of the Discharge of Mrs. C. W. Brooks from the Magazine Department," 9 October 1918, casefile 217, RG 2, NA.
[24] *Bridgeport Labor Leader*, 22 August 1918.
[25] Casefile 231, RG 2, NA; *Lynn Daily Evening Item*, 15 July 1918.
[26] The leadership of the AFL similarly found that anti-autocracy propaganda could be turned against them by rank-and-file militants as easily as it was turned against employers. "The American workers are getting sick and tired of [labor's] Grand Dukes," wrote some dissident auto workers. "The workers want DEMOCRACY in the labor movement as well as in Politics and Industry." Thus the "flaming religion" provided a rationale for what historian Philip Taft described as an increasing "dissatisfaction with traditional policies [that] spread through [labor's] ranks" during the war. The International Association of Machinists, the United Textile Workers, and the United Mine Workers were just a few of the unions that witnessed growing rank-and-file unrest during the war. *The Auto Worker* 1:3 (July 1919): 1; Philip Taft, *The AFL in the Time of Gompers*, 362. For a discussion of the increasing rank-and-file militancy which was often directed at union leaders during the war, see McCartin, "Labor's 'Great War,'" 36–38, 107–23, 217–36, 282–99, 451–61; Montgomery, *Workers' Control*, 96; Sylvia Kopald, *Rebellion in the Labor Unions* (New York, 1924).

representation "might help in getting hold of some [workers]," such was rarely the case.[27] In practice, the shop committees came to represent a new covenant, the inauguration of "democracy in the shop." Thus, evidence indicates that shop committees encouraged rising expectations among the workers in the more than 125 factories where the NWLB installed them. Most workers apparently agreed that, as one put it, the creation of shop committees was "the most important thing the Board did."[28] Government investigators confirmed this sense. "The interest of the employees [in the shop committee] was so great as to strike me as almost pathetic," reported one federal investigator about shop committee elections in munitions plants. "They appeared to see in it something of hope and betterment beyond anything they have heretofore had."[29] His counterpart at Bethlehem Steel agreed that shop committee elections put workers "in a mood of great hope."[30]

In many shops, militants found it easy to translate these hopes into aggressive shop-floor organizations that sought to erode managerial prerogatives under the banner of industrial democracy. Union delegates swept the slates in almost all shop-committee elections held by the NWLB. And in many—particularly in the metal trades—radicals dominated the committees. In such cases, NWLB-created shop committees became major headaches to employers. Committee delegates "spent most of their time going from department to department and keeping things generally upset," groused one manager. His complaint found many echoes.[31] In some shops—such as the GE plant in Lynn, Massachusetts—workers embraced the committee system as a mechanism to roll back the authority of the foreman and achieve greater autonomy in the workplace. The chief vehicles of the NWLB's promised industrial democracy, then, sometimes became the staging grounds for militant shop-floor organizations that did indeed demand something like Montgomery's "workers' control." But, it is important to remember, even when this occurred, workers tended to call it not "workers' control" but "self-government in the

---

[27] Curtis N. Mitchell to William Hale Brown, 21 November 1917, Records of the President's Mediation Commission (microfilm, University Publications of America, reel 3).
[28] Quoted in William Leavitt Stoddard, *The Shop Committee: A Handbook for the Employer and Employee* (New York, 1919), 88.
[29] Hugh McCabe to Basil Manly, 24 March 1919, "Shop Committee File," entry 15, box 53, RG 2, NA.
[30] Russell to Lauck, 16 October 1918, casefile 22, RG 2, NA.
[31] Quoted in National Industrial Conference Board, *Experience with Work Councils in the United States*, Research Report Number 50 (New York, 1922), 22.

workshop . . . part of the democracy for which our armies are fighting in France."[32]

Nor should this surprise us. For the industrial democracy slogan and the rhetoric attacking "prussian" management provided a language both sweeping and flexible enough to accommodate the interests of semiskilled operatives as well as artisan radicals. Workers whose shop-floor experience and worldviews were not conducive to the development of a "workers' control" consciousness—women who worked as semiskilled operatives for example—could still find in the vague term industrial democracy legitimation for their desires for dignity on the job. Thus federal investigators found that women who were "afraid of the term unionism" were still "anxious to take advantage of committee representation" promised by the industrial democracy crusade.[33]

Far from suppressing labor unrest, then, the rhetoric of the government's program empowered the workers' movement in ways no one could have foreseen. The spread of aggressive shop committees, the talk of industrial democracy, the hard-hitting attacks on "prussian management," it can be argued, helped shift the "sub-political" attitudes of American workers, igniting Woll's "flaming religion." By the end of the war, more workers were flooding into union ranks than served in the American Expeditionary Force in Europe.[34] Many were simply swept up

[32] "Statement on Behalf of the Striking Cigar Makers from the Offterdinger Factory," casefile 1, box 19, RG 2, NA. Many workers, it should be noted, desired government ownership of their industries in the postwar era. New England Telephone operators joined other workers in equating industrial democracy with state ownership. "We believe in government ownership," they said, "and we know it is not inconsistent with representative government in industry." Such demands were also raised by workers at General Electric, Wagner Electric, and Remington Arms, who were among those who also called for the government to take over their factories. Many of those workers hoped that the introduction of shop committees would be a step in that direction. Telephone operators quoted in Ethel Smith, "Government Control and Industrial Rights," *Life and Labor* (April 1919): 86; for evidence on demands for government ownership by other workers, see McCartin, "Labor's 'Great War'," 119–22.

[33] Evidence from the records of the NWLB indicates that women responded even more enthusiastically to the board's representation program. Indications are that they voted in higher percentages than their male counterparts in shop committee elections. At the same time, once NWLB protection was extended to them a number of women stepped from the ranks to become ad hoc organizers. For example, Laura Cannon, who worked at Fort Wayne's GE plant, was credited with singlehandedly recruiting one thousand women during 1918. See "Report of Robert M. Buck," 30 January 1919, casefile 130; "Memorandum on Shop Committee System, General Electric Company, Pittsfield, Mass." 7 February 1919, casefile 19; "Brief for Women Workers in the Case of Employees v. the Colt's Patent Fire Arms Co.," n.d.; Mildred Rankin to Lauck, 15 October 1918; "Brief of Fort Wayne General Electric Workers," 8 January 1919, casefile 1011, RG 2, NA.

[34] More than a million workers joined unions in the United States during the eighteen months the nation was at war, pushing overall membership figures to roughly 3.3 million

in the "pentecostal" mood that saw the lines between trade unionism and "American citizenship" blurred.[35] The mood was illustrated by an episode that occurred to Machinists' organizer Robert Corley. While sitting in a hotel lobby in Kokomo, Indiana, one evening in 1918, Corley reported, a stranger ran up to him. "Can you help me out tonight?" he said. "There is a bunch of men . . . and they have crowded the carpenters completely out of [their] hall . . . and they want to be organized." As in Corley's case, organizers often had difficulty keeping up with workers clamoring for organization.[36]

By the time the Armistice was signed, not only were an increasing number of U.S. workers joining unions, they were doing so believing, as a Minneapolis trade-union paper put it, that "the dream of industrial democracy [was] coming true."[37] Moreover, they looked to the postwar Reconstruction era, as most people termed it, for the fulfillment of that dream. As one steelworker told a Reading, Pennsylvania, throng during a celebration of the peace treaty, "You have been fighting for democracy, [but] there can be no peace until you have obtained . . . industrial democracy."[38] Those kinds of statements led a contemporary observer, John Graham Brooks, to conclude that workers had "learned the troublesome liturgy about 'self-determination' " and were determined to have "something of it for themselves."[39]

It was this "troublesome liturgy" as much as the growth of union organization that employers sought to reverse following the war. The

by the end of 1918. Leo Wolman, *The Growth of American Trade Unions, 1880–1925* (New York, 1924), 33.

[35] Bruce Nelson argues that in the 1930s, the waterfront workers' movement experienced a "pentecostal" rebirth. That analogy would work just as well during the World War I period, when garment union leader Sidney Hillman believed "Messiah is arriving. Labor will rule and the world will be free." Bruce Nelson, *Workers on the Waterfront* (Urbana, 1988); Steven Fraser, *Labor Will Rule: Sidney Hillman and the Rise of American Labor* (New York, 1991), 144; Matthew Josephson, *Sidney Hillman: Statesman of American Labor* (Garden City, N.Y., 1952), 193.

[36] "Transcript of Proceedings," 3 December 1918, pp. 163–65, casefile 619, RG 2, NA.

[37] *Minneapolis Labor Review*, 20 September 1918.

[38] *Amalgamated Journal*, 14 November 1918.

[39] John Graham Brooks, *Labor's Challenge to the Social Order: Democracy Its Own Critic and Educator* (New York, 1920), 278. W. L. MacKenzie King, the Canadian labor relations consultant, put it slightly differently. In a confidential memo to General Electric, King argued that government intervention in labor disputes had the same effect on workers "which comes from 'once tasting blood.' " W. L. M. King, "Confidential Memorandum Respecting Employees' Committees in the Works of General Electric Company," 5 August 1918, W. L. M. King Papers, file 196, Canadian National Archive. For background on King's role in shaping the company union movement, see H. M. Gitelman, *Legacy of the Ludlow Massacre: A Chapter in American Industrial Relations* (Philadelphia, 1988).

task must have initially seemed awesome to them. So widespread had become the wartime demands for industrial democracy that reformers of many stripes, church groups, and trade-union leaders alike had adopted the term in their calls for "social Reconstruction" after the war.[40] By 1919, industrial democracy had become, as one journalist at the time observed, a national "fetish," "the most ecumenically satisfying phrase now at large."[41] Employers ignored the demand at their own peril.

But what had been labor's strength during the war turned out to be its weakness in peacetime. Industrial democracy provided an attractive organizing principle as long as the federal government—and specifically the NWLB—continued to play an active mediating role in labor conflict. While the government played that role, militants could even exploit its stance to advance a brand of radical workplace politics under the banner of industrial democracy. In effect, militants had labored in the ideological free space inadvertently created by Wilsonian labor reform. Following the war, however, the government's stance dramatically shifted toward demobilization, powerful labor allies—including Frank Walsh and Felix Frankfurter who headed the War Labor Policies Board—left government service, and as a result the free space within which workers had begun to organize was radically constricted.[42]

Several factors account for this shift. First, the entire war labor administration had been created by emergency presidential initiative and lacked a solid legislative basis. Any hopes that the NWLB would be put upon sturdy legal footing after the war were quickly dispelled by the 1918 congressional elections that swept into office conservative legislators bent on hastily dismantling the war labor administration. At the same time, employers' hostility to wartime interference in their affairs by "petty government officials and shop committees" had coalesced into a powerful

[40] See Ordway Tead, "Labor and Reconstruction"; John A. Ryan, *Social Reconstruction* (New York, 1920); Glenn E. Plumb and William G. Roylance, *Industrial Democracy: A Plan for Its Achievement* (New York, 1923); Frederick A. Cleveland and Joseph Schafer, eds., *Democracy in Reconstruction* (Boston, 1919); John R. Commons, *Industrial Goodwill* (New York, 1919); Samuel Gompers, *Labor and the Employer* (New York, 1920); Felix Frankfurter, "New Labor Ideas Taught by the War," in Edwin Wildman, ed., *Reconstructing America* (Boston, 1919); W. Jett Lauck, *Political and Industrial Democracy, 1776–1926* (New York, 1926).

[41] Samuel Crowther, "The Fetish of Industrial Democracy," *World's Work* 39 (November 1919): 23.

[42] An informative account of the shifting personalities and political philosophies within the Wilsonian war labor administration during the war is contained in Bruce I. Bustard, "The Human Factor: Labor Administration and Industrial Manpower Mobilization during World War I" (Ph.D. diss., University of Iowa, 1984).

lobby for labor deregulation.[43] But perhaps most importantly, President Wilson and his advisors concluded that postwar union demands would fuel spiraling inflation. Consequently, the administration set itself against postwar wage demands, using the remaining federal labor boards to block the unions (particularly in the railroad and mining industries) rather than defend them as they had done during the war crisis. Wilson thus threw the moral authority of the government against not "autocratic" employers but "unreasonable" unions.[44]

That the shifting stance of the state was the crucial factor in American labor's defeat in 1919 is widely recognized. The impact of this shift on the language that workers had used during the wartime upheaval, however, has not been fully explored and is thus deserving of attention.

Labor's call for industrial democracy in 1918 was indeed a powerful rallying cry. But it was powerful partly because it was such an amorphous concept: to government administrators it promised greater war production; to AFL leaders it meant the acceptance of trade unionism; to rank-and-file militants it often symbolized "self-government in the shop." Indeed, it was the flexibility of the term that struck journalist Samuel Crowther in 1919. Crowther found that people across the political spectrum, from "the craziest and most violent radical yelling and waving a red flag" to the "most staid . . . hidebound employer," all advocated something called industrial democracy. What made the term acceptable to all of them, Crowther concluded, was that each applied to it a different definition of democracy.[45] In the absence of state support, labor found it impossible to prevent employers from applying a denuded definition of democracy to industrial democracy and then using that very phrase to battle trade unionism.

One employer put the postwar objectives of his class this way: "With

---

[43] William H. Barr, president of the National Founders Association, quoted in *The Iron Age* 14 (November 1918): 1208.

[44] Moreover, Wilson was moved by political considerations, taking the advice of those like Joseph Tumulty who felt that the administration had already done more than enough for labor. See David Montgomery, "Thinking About American Workers in the 1920s," *International Labor and Working-Class History* 32 (Fall 1987): 7–8; John Morton Blum, *Joe Tumulty and the Wilson Era* (New York, 1969), 148–49; Melvyn Dubofsky, "Abortive Reform: The Wilson Administration and Organized Labor, 1913–1920," in James E. Cronin and Carmen Sirianni, eds., *Work, Community and Power* (Philadelphia, 1983), 214.

[45] Crowther, "The Fetish of Industrial Democracy," 23. Historian James Gilbert's discussion of the ambiguity of industrial democracy during the era of World War I is informative on this question. See Gilbert, *Designing the Industrial State: The Intellectual Pursuit of Collectivism in America, 1880–1940* (Chicago, 1972), 97–100.

labor crying for democracy," he wrote, "capital must go part way, or face revolution."[46] Many employers had grasped this inevitability even before the war ended. As early as the ninth Yama conference of the National Industrial Conference Board, held in October 1918, there was evidence that an increasing number of employers were willing to go "part way." At that meeting, employers discussed demands for industrial democracy and debated possible counter strategies. Although conferees arrived at no consensus, many delegates returned to their respective companies to begin implementing representation plans or company unions like those pioneered by Midvale Steel and the Colorado Fuel and Iron Company in order to head off the demand for democracy in their shops.[47] Soon the famous Special Conference Committee that included the executives of America's largest corporations was busily coordinating the spread of Employee Representation Plans (ERPs), the employers' alternative to shop committees and "self-government in the shop."

With the role of the state in guaranteeing workplace representation receding quickly, employers moved to implement ERPs "with a maximum of publicity and a minimum of interference."[48] In doing so, employers played an important part in shaping what historian William Graebner has aptly characterized as a "new and profound appreciation for democratic modes of social control" in postwar America.[49] Before 1919 was six months old, William Leiserson of the Labor Department reported that "a deluge of shop committees and employee representation plans [was] flooding the country."[50] While such schemes bowed in the direction

[46] C. P. Marshall, of the Plymouth Cordage Company, quoted in Stuart D. Brandes, *American Welfare Capitalism, 1880–1940* (Chicago, 1976), 27.

[47] The Colorado Fuel and Iron—or "Rockefeller union"—plan had been installed prior to the war; the Midvale plan was installed in September 1918 in order to head off an NWLB shop committee election. On the first plan, see Ben M. Selekman, *Employee Representation in Steel Works* (New York, 1924); on the second, see Gerald Eggert, *Steelmasters and Labor Reform, 1886–1923* (Pittsburgh, 1981). On the Yama conference, see H. M. Gitelman, "Being of Two Minds: American Employers Confront the Labor Question, 1915–1919," *Labor History* 25 (Spring 1984): 214–15.

[48] David Montgomery, *The Fall of the House of Labor: The Workplace, the State, and American Labor Activism, 1865–1925* (Cambridge, 1987), 412.

[49] William Graebner, *The Engineering of Consent: Democracy and Authority in Twentieth-Century America* (Madison, Wis., 1987), 46.

[50] W. M. Leiserson, "Employee Management, Employee Representation and Industrial Democracy" (Address before the National Association of Employment Managers, 23 May 1919, Department of Labor, Working Conditions Service, Washington, D.C., 1919). Quoted in Gary Dean Best, "President Wilson's Second Industrial Conference, 1919–20," *Labor History* 16:4 (Fall 1975): 513. For figures on the spread of employee representation plans, see National Industrial Conference Board, *Works Councils in the United States*, Research Report 21 (Boston, 1919), 2, 11; Daniel Nelson, "The Company Union

of democracy, they did so, as one of their proponents put it, "without surrendering any final authority" to the workers represented.[51] Their purpose, the manager of a GE factory frankly acknowledged, was to "transmit the personality and character of the management to the men most effectively."[52] Unions resisted the introduction of employee representation schemes, the hated "Rockefeller unions" that intended to "bunco...employees into thinking that they are getting a real taste of industrial democracy."[53] When they were skillfully introduced, however, as at the Lynn plant of GE where nonradical AFL unionists were even encouraged to serve as delegates, the ERPs did gain approval from workers.[54] In all, workers were in a poor position to resist the spread of ERPs in the industries where unions had secured only a tentative foothold before the war ended. By 1921, over seven hundred thousand workers labored in plants with this truncated version of shop committee representation.[55]

The story of management's postwar representation movement has been well documented. Less thoroughly understood is the attempt by employers to capture the patriotic terminology that labor insurgents had used during the war. Yet this too was an important thrust of the postwar managerial counteroffensive; indeed, it was one of the factors that underlay the success of the employers' strategy. Following the war, employers proved that the patriotic language around which workers had built their movement could indeed be Janus-faced. If workers had begun to equate unionism with "an American feeling" during the war, employers

Movement, 1900–1937: A Reexamination," *Business History Review* 56:3 (Autumn 1982): 338. Additional contemporary reports on the spread of the employee representation idea may be found in *The Iron Age* (24 July 1919): 239; Samuel Crowther, "When They Get Together," *World's Work* 39 (December 1919): 185–94.

[51] *The Iron Age* (11 September 1919): 728.

[52] R. H. Rice to E. W. Rice, 16 May 1920, in box labeled "G.E. Labor Policy," Owen D. Young Papers, Van Hornesville, N.Y.

[53] Quote from the *New Majority*, 22 March 1919. The AFL's 1919 convention approved a strong resolution opposing management-designed shop committees, and union leaders complained that the industrial democracy plans being circulated by employers in 1919 were bogus. See Lewis L. Lorwin, *The American Federation of Labor: History, Policies, and Prospects* (Washington, D.C. 1933), 174–5; John Golden, "Editorial," *The Textile Worker* (October 1919): 308–9, (December 1919): 404.

[54] David Montgomery, *The Fall of the House of Labor*, 454–57; Brody, *Workers in Industrial America*, 48–78; Gerald Zahavi, *Workers, Managers, and Welfare Capitalism: The Shoe Workers and Tanners of Endicott Johnson* (Urbana, 1988); McCartin, "Labor's 'Great War'," chapter 10.

[55] Rodgers, *The Work Ethic in Industrial America*, 59. By 1927, there were 430 companies using some sort of representation plan. See Robert W. Dunn, *The Americanization of Labor: The Employers' Offensive Against Trade Unions* (New York, 1927), 128–29.

made it their task to Americanize their version of employee representation. Thus their open shop movement became the American Plan. According to the propaganda of the open shop associations, their plan embodied "the spirit of the Declaration of Independence"; it constituted "a perfect manifestation of the American spirit."[56]

Perhaps the most striking evidence of employers' attempts to capture the language of the wartime mobilization concerns their conscious use of the industrial democracy rhetoric that workers had used against them only months before. The employers' success in neutralizing or co-opting that rhetoric following the war revealed the fundamental ambiguity inherent in the language labor had used to articulate its wartime demands. During the war, the notion of industrial democracy had served as an instrument for both unions and employers. On the one hand, by linking war production and democracy it served as a tool for getting more work and greater loyalty out of workers. On the other hand, workers and unions used it to their own purposes. In this trade-off, employers had gotten more work at the cost of investing workers with new conceptions of citizenship; unions recruited more members at the cost of phrasing their demands in a language less working-class than American. During the war, labor had gained more than it lost in embracing industrial democracy; following the war, the tables were turned. In the language of industrial democracy, patriotism, citizenship, and Americanism were more at issue than class solidarity. Thus the phrase could be used with as much facility by employers following the war as it had been by labor militants during the war—a factor that helped to undermine labor's defense against the postwar open shop drive.

To be sure, this is not to suggest that the success of the employers' American Plan turned solely—or even largely—around the question of language. As David Montgomery reminds us, and as other historians have made clear, "ubiquitous repression by local, state, and federal police and above all the mounting toll of unemployment" played significant roles in labor's defeat.[57] But to ignore the importance of the postwar

---

[56] Seattle employers were among the first to use the term American Plan to describe the open shop; they did so in March 1919. Foner, *Postwar Struggles, 1918–1920*, 173; Wakstein, "The Origins of the Open Shop Movement, 1919–1920," 460–75.

[57] Montgomery, *The Fall of the House of Labor*, 453. To Montgomery's argument about the role of unemployment and repression in the postwar defeat of labor should be added the role played by ethnic, racial, and geographic divisions within the working class. See Lizabeth Cohen, *Making a New Deal: Industrial Workers in Chicago, 1919–1939* (New York, 1990), 13–52.

struggle over language—and employers' efforts to capture the industrial democracy slogan thus denying workers an effective language with which to both conceptualize and rally their movement—is to miss a central theme in the story of the employers' counteroffensive.

Employers themselves were surprisingly frank in their efforts to make the language of industrial democracy their own following the war. John Leitch, a theorist of the ERP movement, argued before the 1919 convention of the National Association of Manufacturers that employers could not afford to "let labor think that industrial democracy means anything like Bolshevism as it is run in Russia." Management's task, as Leitch understood it, was to make sure that the definition of democracy, implied by the term industrial democracy, did not challenge managerial prerogatives.[58]

One way employers could ensure that industrial democracy would no longer connote a threat to management's power was to call their own ERPs "Industrial Democracy plans," as many of them did following the war. The plans devised by John Leitch, for example, took this name. They consisted of elaborate bicameral shop committees organized as houses of representatives and senates. Among the companies that created their own versions of "Industrial Democracy plans," was the Dan River cotton mills.[59] Other employers improvised a bit. The plan implemented by the Goodyear Tire and Rubber was called an Industrial Assembly.[60]

Whether called an Industrial Democracy or an Industrial Assembly or simply a conference committee or employee representation committee, postwar ERPs all attempted to redefine the notion of industrial citizenship that union militants had attempted to construct during the war. While union organizers had rallied their followers with the cry "Wake Up! Be Real Citizens!" in 1919, employers introduced a new "citizenship theory of labor relations," as GE's Gerard Swope described it.[61] If Americanism could serve as a language with which to unite workers during the war,

[58] *Proceedings of the Twenty-Fourth Annual Convention of the National Association of Manufacturers* (New York, 1919), 342.
[59] Leitch developed his ideas while working as manager of an envelope plant. He defined industrial democracy as "the organization of any factory or other business institution into a little democratic state, with a representative government which shall have both its legislative and executive phases." See John Leitch, *Man to Man: The Story of Industrial Democracy* (New York, 1919), 140.
[60] Paul Litchfield, *The Industrial Republic: Reflections of an Industrial Lieutenant* (Cleveland, 1946).
[61] Brody, *Workers in Industrial America*, 59. On the notion of "industrial citizenship" as a method of repressing labor conflict, see Michael Burawoy, *Manufacturing Consent: Changes in the Labor Process Under Monopoly Capitalism* (Chicago, 1979), 113–14.

it could also be wielded by employers seeking to foster division among workers after the Armistice. In 1919, steel mill owners circulated hand-bills that read: "WAKE UP AMERICANS!! ITALIAN LABORERS... have been told by labor agitators that if they would join the union they would get American jobs."[62] If during the war workers challenged managerial authority by appealing to a higher loyalty—the nation's war effort—in peacetime, the government's antistrike stand allowed employers to claim that the country demanded loyalty to the company. Goodyear's Industrial Assembly drove home this point. "I want you to consider this company," Goodyear vice-president Paul Litchfield told his workers, "the same way as you would consider the United States." Litchfield aimed, he said, to create "a citizenship of the right type."[63]

The Goodyear program, in fact, represented perhaps the most fully articulated effort by a corporation to clothe itself in the rhetoric and symbolism popularized by the war.[64] Those who served as representatives in the Industrial Assembly took an oath of office that reinforced the dual loyalty to company and country Goodyear hoped to foster: they pledged to defend "the Constitution and laws of the United States and...the Industrial Representation Plan of the Goodyear Factory." "Loyal" employees earned the right to vote in Industrial Assembly elections. Significantly, however, while the NWLB allowed all workers to participate in shop committee elections, companies like Goodyear sharply restricted the franchise. Goodyear required voters to have been employed by the company for six months, to have obtained U.S. citizenship, and to have a command of the English language. In order to serve as Industrial Assembly delegates, longer tenure with the company was required.[65] Those who could meet the requirements of Goodyear "citizenship" earned a new sobriquet designed by the company to describe its loyal employees: Goodyear called them "industrians."[66] Goodyear "industrians," of course, enjoyed only a pale imitation of the "self-government in the

[62] Quoted in Cohen, *Making a New Deal,* 41.
[63] Litchfield, *The Industrial Republic,* 33.
[64] For a brief review of Goodyear's strategy and its impact upon other rubber companies, see Daniel Nelson, *American Rubber Workers and Organized Labor, 1900–1941* (Princeton, 1988), 57–60.
[65] See *Industrial Representation Plan of the Goodyear Tire and Rubber Company* pamphlet (Akron, 1919), 8. The Bloedel Donovan Lumber Mill of Bellingham, Washington, was similarly selective in granting employee "citizenship." See Bloedel Donovan Mills, *Shop Committee Plans and Standard Practice Rules* pamphlet (Bellingham, Wash., [1923?]). Both of these pamphlets are contained in the imprints collection of the Hagley Museum and Library, Wilmington, Delaware.
[66] *Industrial Representation Plan of the Goodyear Tire and Rubber Company.*

shops" that the militant wartime industrial democracy movement had advocated.

The efforts of Goodyear and publicists like John Leitch to redefine industrial citizenship after the war direct our attention toward the importance employers placed on neutralizing the language and symbolism that served the wartime union upheaval. These efforts also indicate that U.S. labor's reversal between 1919 and 1922 was a more complex defeat than historians may have heretofore understood. For in that defeat, workers saw employers attack not only their organizations but the words and concepts upon which they had built them. The importance of this dimension of the conflict was not lost on the labor militants of that era. As employers laid their own claims to the language of the wartime upheaval, words such as industrial democracy and reconstruction that had fortified the wartime workers' movement left a bitter taste in the mouths of those who had once used them. Thus a textile union leader railed against the "57 varieties . . . of definitions of industrial democracy" that undermined labor's message. Meanwhile the leader of perhaps the most militant of the wartime union drives, Sam Lavit, a Bridgeport munitions worker, wrote in 1919:

For months [reconstruction] spelled a new world to me. For months it suggested better things for all mankind, a new deal all around, a square deal all around. But now I see my mistake. The people who use that word most are simply trying to "reconstruct" things so they will be just as they were before the war. They don't want anything different. . . . Reconstruction used to be the slogan of progress. Now it is the watchword of reaction.[67]

Labor militants did not abandon their claims to industrial democracy or their dreams of reconstruction after the war. Indeed, the wartime upheaval had in some ways permanently altered the language with which labor militants articulated their vision. Erstwhile labor radical turned scholar Frank Tannenbaum, for example, still hoped in 1921 for "the displacement of the capitalist system by industrial democracy." Railroad unions advocated the Plumb Plan under the banner of industrial democracy and the influential Intercollegiate Socialist Society rechristened itself the League for Industrial Democracy after the war.[68] Industrial democ-

[67] United Textile Workers' President John Golden, quoted in *The Textile Worker* (October 1919): 308–9; Sam Lavit, quoted in *Bridgeport Labor Leader*, 27 March 1919.
[68] Frank Tannenbaum, *The Labor Movement: Its Conservative Functions and Social Consequences* (New York, 1921), 44; Glenn Plumb, *Industrial Democracy* (Washington, D.C., 1921); Plumb and Roylance, *Industrial Democracy: A Plan for Its Achievement*; Lauck, *Political and Industrial Democracy*; League for Industrial Democracy, *Twenty*

racy thus remained a contested term even in the midst of postwar managerial ascendancy. The labor movement, however, would not soon be able to challenge successfully the definition of the phrase that American employers deployed in 1919. In the final analysis, that fact, as much as the trade-union defeats of that eventful year, defined the bitter legacy of the "Great War" for American workers.

Years of Social Pioneering: The League for Industrial Democracy Celebrates Its Twentieth Anniversary (New York, 1926).

5

From Commons to Dunlop: rethinking the field and theory of industrial relations

RONALD W. SCHATZ

College professors, more than any other group, have been responsible for defining the concept of industrial democracy in the United States. Taking off from the British Fabian Socialists Sidney and Beatrice Webb, University of Wisconsin professor John R. Commons, his protégés, and their successors have consulted with union, business, and government officials; headed government agencies created at their own urging; served as mediators and arbitrators in industry; and written histories of organized labor. In doing so, they popularized the idea of industrial democracy, assisted mightily in the shaping of labor and welfare law, and helped legitimate unions in an often unfriendly culture. After World War II, the most outstanding of the Industrial Relations professionals—as these academics came to call themselves—went even farther. Serving in effect as general "social fixers" for the United States, they represented the nation in world affairs (for instance, the president of the Industrial Relations Research Association for 1968, George P. Shultz, went on to serve as U.S. secretary of labor, secretary of the treasury and, finally, secretary of state), attempted to steer top universities through troubled waters (for example, Clark Kerr, Shultz's predecessor as IRRA president in 1954, served as chancellor of the University of California during the 1960s and as director of the Carnegie Commission on Higher Education from 1967 to 1973) and even defended the United States Constitution against a possibly criminal president (Watergate prosecutor Archibald Cox had

I thank Donald W. Rogers, Nelson Lichtenstein, and Thomas Kochan for their suggestions and Marc Casper for his research assistance.

published highly influential articles on industrial relations twenty-five years before).[1]

But during the past quarter century, relations between unions, business, and government have been thoroughly disturbed, and in the process, the industrial relations profession has been deeply challenged too. Union membership in nonagricultural industries has fallen by half since the end of the Korean War (from 32.5 percent of the work force in 1952 to 16.4 percent in 1989), and the decline has been accelerating sharply since the mid-1970s.[2] Pattern bargaining and industry-wide collective bargaining, concepts central to mid-twentieth century industrial relations thinking, have disappeared from many industries, and morale among union organizers—especially in the private sector—is dismal. For the moment, the United States seems to be moving toward an "enterprise-based" system of industrial relations in private industry in which unions negotiate not with corporations, let alone across industries, as before, but in separate workplaces within single firms. Under such conditions, neither industrial democracy nor industrial stability, at least as conceived by Commons and his successors, is possible. Indeed, these developments have gone so far as to cause some members of the Industrial Relations Research Association, the field's professional association, to worry publicly about whether they have become "dinosaurs," while Professor Michael Piore of MIT, a prominent younger labor economist originally trained in the industrial relations tradition, has declared the field "dead."[3] Piore may be mistaken, but just for that reason the profession's history demands examination.

The history of the industrial relations profession falls into three generations. The first, consisting of Professor Richard T. Ely, John R. Commons, and their students at the University of Wisconsin in the first quarter of the twentieth century, had both contemporary and historical concerns.

[1] Milton Derber, *The American Idea of Industrial Democracy, 1865–1965* (Urbana: University of Illinois Press, 1970), 6–9. For contributions by Archibald Cox, see his articles on regulation of collective bargaining by the National Labor Relations Board, written jointly with John T. Dunlop, "The Duty to Bargain Collectively During the Term of an Existing Agreement," *Harvard Law Review* 63 (May 1950):1097–1133; "Regulation of Collective Bargaining by the National Labor Relations Board," ibid. (January 1950):389–433.

[2] Henry S. Farber, "The Recent Decline of Unionization in the United States," *Science* 238 (13 November 1987):915–20; U.S. Bureau of the Census, *Statistical Abstract of the United States: 1991* (111th edition), Washington, D.C.: 1991, p. 425.

[3] Comments made from the floor at conference on "Historical Perspectives on American Labor: An Interdisciplinary Approach," New York State School of Industrial and Labor Relations, Cornell University, April 21–24, 1988.

On the one hand, they documented the history of the American labor movement and developed an interpretation of labor history that dominated the field completely until the 1960s and haunts its critics still. On the other hand, they worked closely with trade-union officials, liberal members of the business community, and representatives in the state capital, planning a workers' compensation system, unemployment agencies, mediation bureaus, and other state agencies to regulate labor relations. Originating in Wisconsin, institutions and systems such as these spread to the large majority of highly industrialized cities and states and were incorporated into the federal government—first on a temporary basis during World War I and then permanently during the Great Depression.[4]

Between the world wars, the industrial relations profession became more diffuse. On the one hand, there were some remarkably accomplished students of Commons—for example, Selig Perlman, the theorist and historian of labor history; William Leiserson, mediator and arbitrator; and Edwin E. Witte, author of *The Government in Labor Disputes* (1932) and the primary staff member behind the Social Security law.[5] On the other hand, there were academicians like Paul S. Taylor of the University of California at Berkeley, the renowned student of Mexican labor conditions in the United States, or the University of Chicago's Paul H. Douglas, the principal scholarly authority on working-class standards of living in the early twentieth century and later, of course, a distinguished United States senator. While both these academicians were concerned with industrial relations, very broadly defined, neither fit into the Commons mold, with its stress on institutions.[6]

[4]For the Wisconsin group's historical and theoretical work, see John R. Commons and Associates, *A Documentary History of American Industrial Society,* vol. 10 (Cleveland: A. H. Clark, 1910–11); John R. Commons, "The American Shoemakers, 1648–1895," chapter 14 in Commons, *Labor and Administration* (New York: Macmillan, 1913). The dispersion of Wisconsin-style agencies is suggested in John R. Commons and John B. Andrews, *Principles of Labor Legislation,* 2d ed. (New York: Harper and Brothers, 1920), 136–49, 172–74, 465ff; and Melvyn Dubofsky, "Abortive Reform: The Wilson Administration and Organized Labor, 1913–1920," in James E. Cronin and Carmen Sirianni, eds., *Work, Community and Power: The Experience of Labor in Europe and America, 1900–1925* (Philadelphia: Temple University Press, 1983), 197–220.
[5]Selig Perlman, *A Theory of the Labor Movement* (New York: Macmillan, 1928); J. Michael Eisner, *William Morris Leiserson: A Biography* (Madison: University of Wisconsin Press, 1967); "Witte, Edwin Emil," *The National Cyclopaedia of American Biography,* vol. 45 (New York: James T. White, 1962), 162–63; Edwin Emil Witte, *The Government in Labor Disputes* (London: McGraw-Hill, 1932).
[6]Paul S. Taylor, *Mexican Labor in the United States* (Berkeley: University of California

Then, with the coming of the New Deal, competitors in the industrial relations field emerged from the left—figures such as National Labor Relations Board member Edwin S. Smith, board general counsel Nathan Witt, and assistant counsel Thomas Emerson. Such attorneys were not necessarily members of the Communist party or fellow travelers, as right-wing members of the Senate charged during the late 1930s. Even if they had been, it is striking that left-wing attorneys never developed full-fledged alternatives to the Commons group's vision of industrial relations. Until the late 1960s at least, radicals in general tended to accept the Wisconsin construct, but in jurisdictional disputes definitely favored Congress of Industrial Organizations unions, with their industrial, seemingly more militant approach, over the older American Federation of Labor. In the process, left-wing members of government labor boards were giving their counterparts in the unions room to flourish.[7]

The truly radical challenge to the Commons group during the interwar years came not from the Left but the Right, from the group centered around Professor Elton Mayo of the Harvard School of Business Administration. An Australian born into a family of affluent professionals, Mayo had been educated in medicine, psychology, and philosophy, as opposed to economics, like most other seminal figures in industrial relations. After World War I, he had worked intensely with shell-shocked veterans. This experience, along with his education, had led Mayo to think of industrial questions in terms of mental disturbances. He came to the United States in 1922, shortly after the defeat of the massive postwar strikes in steel, textile, and coal and the onset of a decade of industrial peace. It was under these conditions that Mayo and his associates began a series of studies of workers in unorganized, technologically advanced factories.[8]

The most significant were the Hawthorne experiments, named for a factory operated by the Western Electric Corporation in Chicago. Through experiments of their own, company officials had discovered that

Press, 1928–34); Paul H. Douglas, *Real Wages in the United States, 1890–1926* (Boston: Houghton Mifflin, 1930).

[7] For discussion of 1930s left-wing labor board advocates, see Peter H. Irons, *The New Deal Lawyers* (Princeton: Princeton University Press, 1982); James A. Gross, *The Reshaping of the National Labor Relations Board: National Labor Policy in Transition, 1937–1947* (Albany: State University of New York Press, 1981); Christopher H. Johnson, *Maurice Sugar: Law, Labor and the Left in Detroit* (Detroit: Wayne State University Press, 1988).

[8] "George Elton Mayo," *Dictionary of American Biography: Supplement Four, 1946–1950* (New York: Charles Scribner's Sons, 1974); Elton Mayo, "Civilization—The Perilous Adventure," *Harpers Magazine* 149 (June 1924):590–97.

workers' productivity rose whenever the lighting in the room was changed—either up *or* down. Asked to explain this strange phenomenon, Mayo suggested that the major variable was not the lighting but the attention that workers—normally ignored or dismissed by management—were receiving from the investigators.[9] This research, which ultimately lasted nearly two decades, led Mayo to conclude that economists, corporate and union officials, psychologists, and physiologists all had failed to understand workers' motivations. "The economist talks of wage rates and prices; the collective bargainers follow this lead and import lawyers into the discussion. The psychologist speaks of vocational guidance and tests. The physiologist thinks in terms of fatigue and nutrition," Mayo declared. "But none considers the group and its function in society as a constituent unit of its integrity. Yet the group has an impulse to self-preservation as strong as, or stronger than, that of the individual; and many strikes are actually symptomatic of the attempt of a group to hold together, however the so-called causes are stated," Mayo concluded.[10]

Like the Commons group, Mayo's Hawthorne group dismissed laissez-faire analyses of market and society. Similarly, both groups were deeply committed to the goal of peace between capital and labor. But while Wisconsinites believed that cooperation among national unions, business associations, and the state offered the best hope for resolving conflict, Mayo and his followers were strongly critical of state intervention and frowned on unions. The Hawthorne group looked instead to small, spontaneously formed factory groups coordinated by private industrial elites.

In Mayo's opinion, economic, scientific, and technological advances had broken down the bonds between people. Writing at the end of World War II, he warned: "There is not much time left us; society, within the nation and without it, is breaking down into groups that show an ever-increasing hostility to each other; irrational hates are taking the place of cooperation. This, historically, has been the precursor of downfall for many valiant civilizations. There is no reason to suppose that our own fate will be otherwise, if we do not at once state explicitly the problem and struggle to develop a better *élite* than we can at present show in public, private, or academic life." In practice this meant the development

[9] "The Fruitful Errors of Elton Mayo," *Fortune* 34:5 (November 1946):181ff.; Elton Mayo, *The Human Problems of an Industrial Civilization*, 2d ed. (Boston: Harvard University, Graduate School of Business Administration, Division of Research, 1946), chapters 3–5.
[10] "The Fruitful Errors of Elton Mayo," 242.

of new kinds of business managers able to discern quickly workers' needs and disturbances before they mushroomed into formal protest and organization.[11]

The third generation of industrial relations professionals—people such as Clark Kerr; John Dunlop of Harvard University; William H. McPherson and Milton Derber of the University of Illinois; Richard A. Lester and J. Douglas Brown of Princeton University; Charles Myers of MIT; Frederick H. Harbison of the University of Chicago; and Maurice Neufeld, Jean T. McKelvey, Alice H. Cook, William F. Whyte, and Vernon Jensen of the Industrial and Labor Relations School at Cornell University, to mention only the most prominent—were all products of World War II. Preliminary research suggests that a male member of this group typically received his education at one of the more prestigious universities in the United States during the early to mid–1930s, suggesting a middle-class family background at least. He then obtained a position at a university department of economics before the war, perhaps combining teaching with work for a New Deal economic agency. The female industrial relations professionals were more diverse and will require even more investigation. But some of these women were older than the men, active in middle-class labor-reform organizations like the Young Women's Christian Association or the National Women's Trade Union League during the 1920s. Others were quite young, having been recruited by labor-relations schools after World War II.[12]

World War II, of course, utterly transformed U.S. industrial relations, as vast new shipyards and factories were built, millions of people relocated, thousands of firms recognized unions for the first time, and union membership continued to rise from its 1932 nadir of 3 million to 14.3 million by 1945. Workers struck often, defying firm pledges made by their national union leaders. Indeed, strike levels were higher during the

---

[11] Elton Mayo, *The Social Problems of an Industrial Civilization* (Boston: Harvard University, Graduate School of Business Administration, Division of Research, 1945), 119. See also Mayo, *The Human Problems*, 169ff.

[12] These profiles are based on personal interviews with Milton Derber at the Convention of the Industrial Relations Research Association, 27 December 1987, and with Maurice F. Neufeld (10 November 1988), Alice H. Cook (12 and 19 July 1989), Milton Konitz (14 July 1989), William F. Whyte (16 July 1989), and John P. Windmuller (20 July 1989), all of the latter conducted at the New York State School of Industrial and Labor Relations, Cornell University; Faculty Biographies, NYSSILR Labor-Management Documentation Center; sketches of faculty published in Cornell's *I and LR News* from its founding in 1946 onward; and James L. Cochrane, *Industrialism and Industrial Man in Retrospect: A Critical Review of the Ford Foundation's Support for the Inter-University Study of Labor* (Ann Arbor, Mich.: Imprint Series–Ford Foundation, 1979), chapter 1.

war than ever before in U.S. history.[13] Moreover, federal war contracts put enormous inflationary pressure on wages and prices.

These conditions created great need and opportunities for professional economists. Excused from military service, professors were put on federal war boards, working full-time in an attempt to maintain peace between unions and management, hold down wages and prices, or track the movement of workers and direct them to the centers suffering most from shortages of labor. After the war, the professors—"relatively young" but with "ample practical experience... at very high levels of industry, labor and government decision-making," to quote economist John L. Cochrane[14]—returned to academia. There they founded or revived existing industrial relations schools or programs that taught economics, personnel management, and the history of American unions to young men and women, especially veterans, who aspired to work in business, unions, or government. The schools also brought foreign trade unionists to the United States to teach them American principles of industrial relations, the idea being that visiting students would set up comparable programs in their homelands.

Having set up institutes of education, leading young industrial relations professors established a professional organization—the Industrial Relations Research Association—which brought labor economists together with psychologists, sociologists, political scientists, and others especially interested in labor relations questions. Industrial relations professors commonly accepted jobs as mediators or arbitrators between big corporations and unions and from time to time took up assignments for the federal government. Finally, industrial relations professors wrote, both on current events in industrial relations and on long-term developments, and obtained foundation grants for larger scholarly projects in the field.

So for three generations, industrial relations professionals helped structure American public policy, labor relations, education, and intellectual life. But what principles underlay their work? Earlier historians describe John R. Commons and his colleagues and students as uniquely American, "pragmatic," progressive reformers.[15] But if we lift our eyes beyond the

[13] U.S. Department of Labor, Bureau of Labor Statistics, *Handbook of Labor Statistics, 1975: Reference Edition*, 390.
[14] Cochrane, *Industrialism and Industrial Man*, 14.
[15] See, for example, *John R. Commons: His Assault on Laissez-Faire* by Lafayette G. Harter, Jr. (Corvallis: Oregon State University Press, 1962), 25: "John R. Commons always sought answers to every problem he studied. Economics to him was not an intellectual exercise, but one that had very practical results. Although he conceded the value of the

coasts, the first group—the Wisconsinites—appear not merely as progressives who sought to use the instruments of government to improve the condition of working men and women, although that was the case, but as reformers whose programs, to the extent that they succeeded, would have pushed the United States in a "corporatist" direction as that concept has been defined by a considerable body of scholars concerned with political and economic affairs in twentieth-century Europe and Latin America.

As used here, the term "corporatist" refers not to the "corporate liberal" interpretations of U.S. history produced (not ironically) at the University of Wisconsin in the 1950s and the early 1960s,[16] but to more recent material written by political scientists such as Philipe Schmitter, Claus Offe, Leo Panitch, Wyn Grant, and Alan Cawson, and to a lesser extent, historians, especially Charles Maier and Ellis Hawley.[17] This burst of research arose in the 1970s in reaction to the turmoil experienced in highly industrialized Western nations following successive oil boycotts, back-to-back recessions, extraordinary inflations, and, in Britain and the

---

pure theorist, Commons preferred working on immediate problems requiring solutions. This was one of the attractions social reforms had for him. Commons' practical nature was reinforced by the intellectual currents swirling around him. America's anti-intellectualism, its pragmatism, and its empiricism, as expressed by Ely and others, suited his temperament and capabilities." See also Merle Curti, *The Growth of American Thought* (New York: Harper and Brothers, 1943), 592–93; and Richard Hofstadter, *The Age of Reform: From Bryan to F.D.R.* (New York: Vintage, 1955), 154, 165, 242.

[16] James Weinstein, *The Corporate Ideal in the Liberal State: 1900–1918* (Boston: Beacon Press, 1968); Ronald Radosh, "The Corporate Ideology of American Labor Leaders," in *For a New America: Essays in History and Politics from "Studies on the Left," 1959–1967*, ed. James Weinstein and David W. Eakins (New York: Vintage, 1970), 125–52; William Appleman Williams, *The Contours of American History* (Cleveland: World Publishing Company, 1961).

[17] Philippe C. Schmitter, "Still the Century of Corporatism?" in *Trends Toward Corporatist Intermediation*, ed. Philippe C. Schmitter and Gerhard Lehmbruch (Beverly Hills, Calif.: Sage Publications, 1982); idem, "Neo-Corporatism and the State," in *The Political Economy of Corporatism*, ed. Wyn Grant (New York: St. Martin's Press, 1983); Claus Offe, "The Attribution of Public Status to Interest Groups: Observations on the West German Case," in *Organizing Interests in Western Europe: Pluralism, Corporatism, and the Transformation of Politics*, ed. Suzanne Berger (Cambridge: Cambridge University Press, 1981); Wyn Grant, "Introduction," *The Political Economy of Corporatism*; "Introduction" and "Conclusion," *Organized Interests and the State*, ed. Alan Cawson (Beverly Hills, Calif.: Sage Publications, 1985); Charles S. Maier, *Recasting Bourgeois Europe: Stabilization in France, Germany and Italy in the Decade After World War I* (Princeton: Princeton University Press, 1975); idem, "The Two Postwar Eras and the Conditions for Stability in Twentieth-Century Western Europe," *American Historical Review* 86:2 (April 1981):327–52, 363–67; and Ellis W. Hawley, "Herbert Hoover, the Commerce Secretariat, and the Vision of an 'Associative State,' 1921–1928," *Journal of American History* 61:1 (June 1974):116–40; idem, "The Discovery and Study of a 'Corporate Liberalism,'" *Business History Review* 52:3 (Autumn 1978): 309–20.

United States, the election of avowedly antiunion governments. Ever since the end of the Second World War and the establishment of American intellectual preeminence in the social sciences in Western Europe, political scientists on both continents had tended to rely on the concept of pluralism as their principal means of interpreting relations between state and society. In pluralist models of political science, to simplify somewhat, every conceivable sort of interest group—not only economic but religious, educational, and cultural too—lobbies a passive government competitively, replicating in a fashion business competition in laissez-faire economies. Economic conflict of an intensity not known for a generation led academicians to think again about this American-born paradigm, itself an offshoot of the Cold War. As ligaments of industrial cooperation were torn apart, some asked: What had been holding economic groups together before?

Previously, it had been impolitic, even inconceivable, to think of interest group/state relations in the non-Communist world as "corporatist," for the idea had been indissolubly tied to prewar fascist or other highly repressive regimes—Mussolini in Italy, Salazar in Portugal, and others. But thirty years had passed since Mussolini was hanged, and the term had lost some of its odor. In the meanwhile, proposals that smacked of corporatism were being advanced in many quarters to cope with economic wrench. These included efforts conducted in Britain throughout the 1970s, by both Heath and Wilson governments, to establish cooperation between the Trades Union Congress and the Confederation of British Industry, Pope John Paul's encyclical *Laborem Exercens*, issued on the ninetieth anniversary of Pope Leo's renowned 1891 encyclical, *Rerum Novarum*, and, closer to home, the negotiations to save the credit of the New York City government. The latter, conducted in Manhattan between the heads of top investment banks, insurance companies, state governments, and municipal unions, produced the powerful Municipal Assistance Corporation (MAC), directed by financier Felix Rohatyn. Thus the 1970s and early 1980s saw a flurry of theories of "neo-corporatism," "quasi-corporatism," and "societal" (as opposed to "state") corporatism among social scientists, simultaneous with the birth of "neo-liberalism" and "neo-conservatism" in public circles.[18]

---

[18] Peter Jenkins, *Mrs. Thatcher's Revolution: The Ending of the Socialist Era* (Cambridge, Mass.: Harvard University Press, 1988), chapter 1; Charles R. Morris, *The Cost of Good Intentions: New York City and the Liberal Experiment, 1960–1975* (New York:

The recent theories of corporatism are diverse and often contradictory, as would only be appropriate given the confused political milieu prevailing in the United States and Great Britain in the mid- and latter 1970s, before the triumph of British Prime Minister Thatcher and President Reagan. But certain common themes can be discerned. At bottom, corporatist theories rely on the notion that society is like the human body, all parts of which depend on each other: like the arm, the leg, and the head, so businesspeople, farmers, and workers. Such reasoning, often associated with the Roman Catholic Church of the Middle Ages, was revived in Europe and Latin America during the interwar years in response to the Bolshevik Revolution and the Great Depression. Proponents argued that a corporatist state could, by creating and coordinating economic associations, forge a middle way between socialism and unregulated capital.

During the interwar years, corporatist movements were nearly all antidemocratic. After World War II, however, according to social scientists like Schmitter, some democratic nations hit upon systems of planned intergroup cooperation autonomously, without state orders. In other words, in theory, there can exist societies in which individual citizens possess a wide range of democratic freedoms while labor and business associations are nonetheless certified by the state as the official representatives of a given sector of the society. The states in such societies in turn delegate portions of their power to the various economic groups.

In liberal corporatist societies each economic association is said to be organized hierarchically, presenting a leader or small committee of leaders who possess the authority to speak for the whole. Compromises are then struck between the associations, the terms written into law, with each participating organization insisting that its members adhere to the contract. (At that point, the freedoms of individuals are surely compromised, although most of the theorists of corporatism are oblivious of that point.)

This process of quiet, even stately negotiation between heads of economic associations provides an alternative, albeit not fully democratic, to the haggling normally characteristic of politics in liberal societies. The end goal is to reduce or prevent the depressions, currency inflation, and domestic class conflict that have historically plagued capitalist economies. Under ideal circumstances, liberal corporatist arrangements would pre-

McGraw-Hill, 1981); Pope John Paul II, "Laborem Exercens," *National Catholic Reporter*, 25 September 1981.

serve the private property and individual freedom promised by capitalist systems without the evils that usually accompany them.[19]

The recent theories of corporatism are mainly ahistorical, although Charles Maier and Ellis Hawley provide great and welcome exceptions. These two scholars have emphasized the decades between the world wars, Maier working mainly on Western Europe, Hawley working with the United States. The political scientists, by contrast, offer ideal types—that is, they do not claim to be describing precise relations in any existing nation but rather an end toward which many nations have tended in the mid-twentieth century. Philippe Schmitter, Wyn Grant, Gerhard Lehmbruch, and others invariably single out Austria as the most corporatist of modern European nations, with Sweden, the Netherlands, and Belgium generally added. Corporatist trends are also identified in West Germany and other countries, sometimes at the national level, more often at middle levels of government, or in particular industries (meso-corporatism).

When considered at the macro level, the United States has without question been one of the most anticorporatist lands in the world.[20] Yet there have been times when, in retrospect, it seemed as if the nation as a whole had been driving in a corporatist direction—most obviously, during the era of the National Recovery Act. Not only that, but there unquestionably have been some important American industries organized for lengthy periods in a corporatist manner.[21] Finally, some American groups and individuals have consistently attempted to hurry American society along this way. Industrial relations reformers were most outstanding in this regard.

"I had much trouble in Wisconsin," Commons recalled in his autobiography, written amidst the NRA experiment. "I was charged with

---

[19] This summary is drawn from the sources cited in note 17, particularly Schmitter, Grant, and Cawson.

[20] Robert H. Salisbury, "Why No Corporatism in America," in *Trends*, ed. Schmitter, 213–30; Graham K. Wilson, "Why Is There No Corporatism in the United States," in *Patterns of Corporatist Policy-Making*, ed. Gerhard Lehmbruch and Philippe C. Schmitter (London: Sage Publications, 1982), 219–36; David Vogel, "Why Businessmen Distrust Their State: The Political Consciousness of American Corporate Executives," *British Journal of Political Science* 8:1 (January 1978): 45–78.

[21] See, for example, Professor Jesse Carpenter's comprehensive study of the needle trades, *Competition and Collective Bargaining in the Needle Trades, 1910–1967* (Ithaca: New York State School of Industrial and Labor Relations, Cornell University, 1972). William Serrin made a strong argument for the existence of a corporatist-style relationship in the auto industry in earlier years in his *The Company and the Union: The "Civilized Relationship" of the General Motors Corporation and the United Automobile Workers* (New York: Vintage, 1974).

being an anarchist, or socialist, or communist, or, by a leading employer, with being the 'most dangerous man in Wisconsin.' Again I was charged with being a reactionary, lining up with big capitalists. Yet what I was always trying to do, in my academic way, was to save Wisconsin and the nation from politics, socialism, or anarchism in dealing with the momentous conflict of 'capital and labor.' "[22]

"Class conflict may be growing, but it is not inevitable," Commons counseled conferences of economists and sociologists at the turn of the century. He assigned much of the blame to the scholars themselves for refusing to acknowledge that new economic classes had emerged in the United States that required a new form of political representation. Criticizing the president of the American Economic Association at its national meeting in December 1899, Commons asserted that "as long as class antagonisms really exist, they will assert themselves, and the only alternative is civil war and class domination or mutual concession." The way to avoid civil war was for economists, employers, and the state to allow labor organizations into the world of political representation. "We cannot get away from organization. These employees will organize, in one way or another. The real solution is, not to try to destroy the organizations ... but to give them official recognition, to give them a part in the administration of the department," Commons observed to members of the Women's Trade Union League in 1907, referring in this instance to organizations of public servants.[23]

If it were not for politicians, capital and labor could realize their common interests, Commons told the 1899 economists' assembly. He admitted that politicians worked out compromises, but these were "logrolling." "These are not true compromises. They are made by men who represent nothing, who have no convictions, no principles, and are simply usurpers who have by their cunning gotten possession of our electoral machinery. Their so-called compromises are only secret dickers." "The true leaders of a class must have two leading qualities: they must have tenacity of purpose, but they must also understand the claims of the opposing class. That is, they must be broad-minded and patriotic enough to see that civil war must be avoided, that other classes have rights.... These are the only kind of men that can permanently lead a class to

---

[22] *Myself: The Autobiography of John R. Commons* (1934; reprint, Madison: University of Wisconsin Press, 1963), 170.
[23] Commons, *Labor and Administration*, 82, 59, 115.

victories. Labor unions have just such men as their leaders, and so do capitalists."[24]

Commons's thoughts were paralleled in Italy, France, and Germany, as Charles Maier has shown. Referring to years between the First World War and the onset of depression, he saw a tendency for "displacement of power to devolve from elected representatives or a career bureaucracy to the major organized forces of . . . society and economy, sometimes exerting influence through a weakened parliament, and occasionally seeking advantage through new executive authority." Maier continued: "Most conspicuously, this evolution toward corporatism involved a decay of parliamentary influence. . . . Ultimately, the weakening of parliament also meant the undermining of older notions of a common good and a traditionally conceived citizenry of free individuals."[25]

Commons had anticipated this evolution. Having witnessed the first great instance of collective bargaining on a continental scale in America—the 1897 negotiations between coal operators and the United Mine Workers—Commons conceived of collective bargaining not only as the regular, routine form of economic activity it ultimately became but a potentially new form of governance of society. He often likened the system of labor-employer contracts emerging at the turn of the century to the United States Constitution. Both balanced competing forces. "But justice is not merely fair play between individuals, as our legal philosophy would have it—it is fair play between social classes," he admonished the American Sociological Association in December 1906.[26] In that form of representation, collective bargaining received Commons's highest marks.

In the early part of his career, Commons spoke in more or less openly corporatist terms. For example, standing before the 1899 national meeting of economists he dreamed of a Congress capable of resolving all industrial conflicts:

Let the labor unions, irrespective of locality, come together and elect their members of Congress just as they elect the presidents and secretaries of their unions. They would then elect to Congress such men as Gompers, Sargent, Arthur, Debs and the like. These would be the true representatives of the wage-earning class. Let the bankers elect their representatives by themselves. They would elect men

---

[24] Commons, *Labor and Administration*, 59–60. The Webbs had earlier expressed a strong appreciation of the development of authentic representatives for labor. See, for example, Sidney Webb and Beatrice Webb, *Industrial Democracy* (London: Longmans, Green, 1920), chapter 2, esp. pp. 43–44.

[25] Maier, *Recasting Bourgeois Europe*, 9.

[26] Commons, *Labor and Administration*, 104, 81–82.

like Gage, J. Pierpont Morgan. Let the trusts elect theirs. They would elect Rockefeller, Carnegie... or rather they would elect their great attorneys like... Joseph H. Coate. The railroads would elect Depew; the express companies would elect Platt. The Farmers' Grange would send its president, Aaron Jones... and so on. In such a congress these various interests might also send economists, like Gunton, Hadley, Taussig, on one side, and men like Bemis, Ely, Henry George, on the other.

"Such an assembly I should call representative in the original historical sense of the word," he argued. "It would not be exactly suited to modern conditions, because the suffrage has been given to many classes which are not yet organized. But it illustrates the principle of true representation. ...Such an assembly would throw a very different light upon the question of compromise." Commons concluded: "As long as an economist does not recognize the existence of classes, he will fail to see the need of this readjustment of electoral machinery, which shall represent classes."[27]

Commons felt that his vision had been realized, if only temporarily, during World War I. Instructed by President Wilson to set the price of wheat, U.S. Food Administrator Herbert Hoover called in various farmers' organizations: they were to represent wheat producers. Then he called in the leaders of the American Federation of Labor: they were supposed to represent wheat consumers. Hoover asked the two committees to strike a compromise. "This was representative democracy in industry," Commons wrote. "It was class struggle reconciled in the public interest. Mr. Hoover did not fix the price of wheat. President Wilson did not fix the price.... For the organized interests to fix it themselves under the expert advice of the nation's food administrator and his statisticians was the practical democratic way of doing it. It was the procedure of appealing to the harmony of interest of both classes for the public good."[28]

Here was the most prominent of industrial relations professors advancing a vision of industrial democracy in thoroughly corporatist terms. Commons's approach obviously could not survive without change for a half century afterward. Yet in some important respects, the programs and outlook of Commons's successors down through the third generation also can be clarified by a theory of corporatism.

To say this will run against the grain of these men, who made a point of asserting that they were devoid of theory. Clark Kerr described the

[27] Ibid., 58–60.
[28] Quoted in Maurice Isserman, " 'God Bless Our American Institutions': The Labor History of John R. Commons," *Labor History* 17:3 (Summer 1976): 318.

outlook of the cohort of industrial relations professionals who coalesced during World War II in part as follows:

A rejection of ideology. Marxists and anti-monopolists alike were rejected; and, though to a lesser extent, so were the Wisconsin [i.e., Commons et al.] and Human Relations [Elton Mayo] schools—the one pro-labor and the other pro-management. The field became more unified in outlook and more neutrally professional in approach....
     Workable policies were of central interest. What would work among the "bumps and grinds" of the real world; not what might work in the "best of all possible worlds."...
     Reality is more complex than theory or ideology once supposed.

"THE BOTTOM LINE THEY SEEK IS FIDELITY TO REALITY" is the bold caption beneath a photograph on the title page of a recent book celebrating the accomplishments of professors Dunlop and Kerr and two other eminent postwar industrial relations leaders, Richard Lester and Lloyd Reynolds.[29]
     But such feelings as well as a wish to shed conflict-laden interpretations of this country's domestic life, in the face first of Hitler and then of Stalin, were widespread among American intellectuals of the 1940s. This drive contributed to the creation of pluralist theory among political scientists, the founding of modernization theory among sociologists, the development of consensus interpretations of American history, even the breakthrough of abstract expressionism among painters previously committed to Marxism and realism. To say this is not to invalidate the insights of industrial relations writers or other postwar thinkers. "The fact that our thinking is determined by our social [or historical] position is not necessarily a source of error. On the contrary, it is often the path to political insight," wrote Karl Mannheim. However, it does help put the postwar industrial relations work into perspective.[30]
     The experience and views of John Dunlop, who, with Kerr, was probably the single most important figure in the industrial relations field since

---

[29] Clark Kerr, *Labor Markets and Wage Determination: The Balkanization of Labor Markets and Other Essays* (Berkeley: University of California Press, 1977), 3, 11; Bruce E. Kaufman, ed., *How Labor Markets Work: Reflections on Theory and Practice by John Dunlop, Clark Kerr, Richard Lester and Lloyd Reynolds* (Lexington, Mass.: Lexington Books, 1988).

[30] The suggestion about abstract expressionism comes from Serge Guildbaut, *How New York Stole the Idea of Modern Art* (Chicago: University of Chicago Press, 1983); Karl Mannheim, *Ideology and Utopia: An Introduction to the Sociology of Knowledge* (New York: Harcourt, Brace and World, 1936), 125.

World War II, illustrates the point. During the war, Dunlop served as public member on the construction industry's War Adjustment Board (WAB). The WAB was separated from other war production industries (the latter being placed under the supervision of a newly created National War Labor Board) and given extraordinary responsibilities—not only regulation of wages and hours in the building trades across the country, but recruiting and supervising the workers at Oak Ridge, Tennessee, and Hanford, Washington, who built the atomic bombs.

Every aspect of the War Adjustment Board work contributed to Dunlop's corporatist outlook. On the one hand, the unstable condition of employment in construction made this industry (like clothing manufacturing, another ground from which corporatist practice and leaders sprang) ripe for regulation—first by collective bargaining, then by government tripartite boards.[31] On the other hand, labor and business figures seated on the WAB represented entire associations, rather than particular firms. This was corporatism in practice, though Dunlop never uses that term in his work. Moreover, the fact that the board concentrated on a particular industry, as opposed to being forced to issue general dicta, enabled it to operate in a flexible manner, responding to specific needs and emergencies. The result, Dunlop argued, was that work was steadier in construction than in other industries while wages were lower and strikes comparatively few.[32]

Unlike the National War Labor Board, the WAB remained in existence for two years after the war's end. Dunlop experienced disappointment at its termination. Indeed, for a decade after its disbandment, he continued the same work privately, chairing a National Joint Board for Settlement of Jurisdictional Disputes in the building and construction industry; and ever since World War II, Professor Dunlop has advocated corporatist-style regulation of the U.S. economy as a whole. For example, in a session at the Industrial Relations Research Association in December 1948, thirty months after strikes in steel, auto, electrical manufacturing, rubber, railroad, and coal had rocked the nation and created a seemingly unstoppable wage-price spiral, Professor Dunlop declared:[33]

[31] John T. Dunlop and Arthur D. Hill, *The Wage Adjustment Board: Wartime Stabilization in the Building and Construction Industry* (Cambridge, Mass.: Harvard University Press, 1950), chapter 1; Steve Fraser, "Dress Rehearsal for the New Deal: Shop-Floor Insurgents, Political Elites, and Industrial Democracy in the Amalgamated Clothing Workers," in *Working-Class America: Essays in Labor, Community and American Society*, ed. Michael H. Frisch and Daniel J. Walkowitz (Urbana: University of Illinois Press, 1983), 212–55.
[32] Dunlop and Hill, *Wage Adjustment Board*, chapter 10.
[33] John T. Dunlop, "Discussion: Collective Bargaining, Wages, and the Price Level," in

There seems to me to be no escape from the conclusion that in a world of powerful economic groups—unions, managements, farmers—there must be an attempt at coordination of the interests of these groups. Political compromise ... is a requisite to economic stability. Economic stability during the war was built upon political compromise, and postwar inflation was erected upon a bitter postwar political struggle. . . .

One need not be optimistic ... yet political and economic stability requires the administration in power to take an active part in developing working compromises among these major interest groups. . . . Some advisory board to the President and to the Council of Economic Advisors is in order. . . .

Discussions . . . must recognize that wages and prices in the main are set with long-run time horizons ... [and require] the development of mechanisms for political and economic compromise among our major interest groups.

These views were perfectly understandable in context. After all, large industrial unions and collective bargaining were reality by that point, not a dream, as in Commons's day. Moreover, the National Recovery Administration of the Depression era and the National War Labor Board of the Second World War were corporatist-style forms of government that seemed to succeed in adjusting production, wages, and prices. Hence Governor Thomas Dewey of New York had good reason to be optimistic when in November 1945 he made a nationally broadcast radio address celebrating the founding of the New York State School of Industrial and Labor Relations at Cornell University.[34]

It is a school which denies the alien theory that there are classes in our society that must wage war against each other. This is a school dedicated to the common interest of employer and employee and of the whole of the American people. It is dedicated to the concept that when men understand each other and work together harmoniously, then and only then do they succeed.

The State of New York will here provide the equipment to abate the fevers which rise from claims and counter-claims which are now the language of industrial relations.

To achieve their goals of reconciliation, industrial relations professionals worked with both management and labor leaders. Yet while their ties with leaders of unions were long-lasting, inspired by goodwill, and valued by all involved, industrial relations work was premised on a profound respect for, and subordination to, representatives of capital and its rights in a way that seemed not to be true vis-à-vis labor.

Industrial Relations Research Association, *Proceedings of the First Annual Meeting, December 29–30, 1948,* ed. Milton Derber (1949), 53–54.

[34] "Governor Thomas E. Dewey at Convocation of New York State School of Industrial and Labor Relations ... November 12, 1945," in Founding Documents Collection, box 1, New York State School of Industrial and Labor Relations, Labor-Management Documentation Center, Cornell University.

To make this claim, it is necessary to be precise, however, for even Commons hardly respected *all* capitalists—such a stance would have been incompatible with his wholehearted backing of unionization. Rather, he looked toward the more liberal among employers: those who for various reasons paid higher wages than the rule, kept employees at work even in times of depression, and accepted, at least in principle, the idea of collective bargaining: "I was trying to save capitalism by making it good," Commons declared, in a frequently quoted but often not understood remark in his autobiography *Myself*. He explained: "It was because I admired, not 'capitalism' but great capitalists, as far beyond my own abilities, but wanted to make them as good as the best instead of negligent. Most of them thought, at first, that I was guilty of malpractice."[35]

There is no reason to believe that industrial relations figures systematically favored management over unions when they reached positions of decision-making power in industry—for example, when they became arbitrators. This was hardly the case. Had it been, why would Samuel Gompers and George Meany have maintained such high regard for Commons, in the first instance, or Dunlop, in the second? Industrial relations's subordination to capital was manifested more fundamentally, in the way they envisioned the scope of collective bargaining. Within given parameters—the right of workers to organize, length of the work week and day, methods and amounts of pay—industrial relations professionals defended workers' freedom without question. But industrial relations thinkers intentionally left huge areas of activity or potential activity outside the range of organized workers. The precise bounds of bargaining expanded or narrowed over the course of time but excluded choice of product, general flow of production, and investment or disinvestment of capital.[36] In this respect, industrial relations thinkers resembled theorists of scientific management.

The place of capital in industrial relations is partially explained by the problems researchers faced in obtaining financial backing. One can go as far back as the Webbs, who in 1897 sorely complained that while the British generally agreed that "that nation will achieve the

---

[35] Commons, *Myself*, 143.

[36] For an excellent discussion of this point in the case of William Leiserson, one of the most important figures in arbitration in America between 1920 and 1950, see Christopher L. Tomlins, *The State and the Unions: Labor Relations, Law, and the Organized Labor Movement in America, 1880–1960* (Cambridge: Cambridge University Press, 1985), 79–81.

greatest success in the world-struggle whose investigators discover the greatest body of scientific truth ... practically no provision exists in this country for the endowment or support from public funds for any kind of sociological investigation."[37] Attitudes soon changed, however, at least in the United States, with the Carnegie Foundation providing the backing for Commons's work, the Rockefeller family funding the competitive (in the sense that they were much cooler in their attitude toward unions) Industrial Relations Counselors in New York, and scores of businesses hiring so-called industrial relations experts to help their firms during the labor upheavals of 1919.[38]

"It is astonishing what easy marks many employers had become in the summer of 1919," Commons joked afterward. "One would think that the capitalistic system was crumbling, in that employers had lost the power of discipline. In some cases we found that they had actually turned the labor end of their businesses over to professors. Just what it all portended was a puzzle. Certainly the temporary scarcity of labor was a leading factor and employers began to regain their independence, to reduce wages and lay off the professors in 1920."[39]

This same pattern of anxious businesses funding industrial relations research only to close the checkbook once the threat had passed appeared after World War II.[40] However, if it sometimes seemed as if professors of industrial relations were jumping at business's command or developing their interpretations in ways that tended toward business, it was not that they necessarily lacked integrity. On the contrary, the industrial relations scholar-activists were, as a matter of principle, trying to forge a "middle way" between the battling contingents of capital and labor, to recall an expression used by corporatist figures active on both sides of the Atlantic during the interwar years. "Wisconsin, with two-and-a-half million people," Commons wrote in 1933, "has been a miniature for me of one-and-a-half billion people around the world, driving on to Communism, Fascism, Nazism. The state university and the state government, only a mile apart in a small city, have been a focus, unique among the states for instruction, research, extension, economics, class conflict and poli-

---

[37] Sidney Webb and Beatrice Webb, *Industrial Democracy*, xxxi–xxxii.
[38] Commons, *Myself*, 137; John R. Commons, *Industrial Government* (New York: Macmillan, 1921), viii.
[39] Commons, *Industrial Government*, viii.
[40] E. Wight Bakke, "The First Four Years: Report of the Director of the Yale Labor and Management Center to the President and Fellows of Yale University," 15 June 1949, in Yale University Library, Manuscript Collections, pp. 20ff.

tics."[41] But except in rare circumstances, capital held the upper hand in that world.

Subordination to the rights of capital? How could it have been otherwise for anyone trying to win peace in a capitalist economy?

That dedication to peace, furthermore, premised as it was on corporatist assumptions, goes a long way to explaining why, as time passed, industrial relations professors lost interest in industrial democracy, a subject of pressing concern to vast numbers of both working-class militants and scholar-reformers at the turn of this century. The problem was that if labor was bursting with democratic vitality, unions might not be able to maintain the signed commitments to business and government necessary to insure continuous production and rising productivity.

Consider a grant proposal idea floated in the fall of 1949 by William F. Whyte, a highly regarded sociologist and anthropologist at the New York State School of Industrial and Labor Relations. Whyte argued that while scholars had devoted much time to issues of union-management relations as well as problems within management, "practically no work at all has been done on problems of the internal organization of unions."

Yet, these are not matters of merely internal, local, union concern, Whyte maintained. "We often observe cases in which an international officer reaches a tentative agreement with management only to find that he is unable to carry along the local people. In times of national crisis"—and as he wrote U.S. government animosity toward the Soviet Union and the Chinese Communists was reaching its climax—"such cleavages are matters of grave concern. We cannot afford to count on settling key industrial disputes through simply urging the top union officers to be reasonable. We must have a thorough understanding of the problems they face within their own unions, and we should begin the job of providing them with the knowledge and skills they need in order to handle the human relations problems of their unions more effectively."

Whyte asked the dean of the school if he would support a foundation grant proposal to hire a staff of three researchers who would work with him for two years to investigate "relations between locals and international officers," "factors determining the morale of local unions," and "political ideology and union leadership."[42]

[41] Commons, *Myself*, 97.
[42] William F. Whyte, "Human Relations Research in Unions," proposal to the New York State School of Industrial and Labor Relations, unpublished document, School Archives,

Although later in his career Whyte departed from the mainstream in the profession and became quite concerned with these questions, nowhere in this 1949 document did Whyte express concern with industrial democracy, or at least not in a positive way.[43] This lack of concern with industrial democracy had become normal. As Milton Derber has noted, the words "industrial democracy"—commonplace in the first two decades of the twentieth century—dropped out of the vocabulary of industrial relations leaders by 1960 or, in fact, even in 1930.[44] The words seldom appear in the multitude of textbooks on industrial relations published in the late 1940s and 1950s, and in *Collective Bargaining: Principles and Cases* by Dunlop and James J. Healy, one text where it does, "democracy" is mentioned only momentarily and then as a method that allows working people to relieve their frustrations and thereby feel secure enough to work to the maximum.[45]

Professor Dunlop and his younger colleague at Harvard, Derek Bok, elaborated on this point in their 1970 work, *Labor and the American Community*. Writing under Rockefeller Brothers' Fund auspices at a time when the unionized proportion of the American labor force was already declining markedly and organized labor was under sharp criticism from businessmen and radical intellectuals, Bok and Dunlop posed the question, "Are unions worth having?" They answered positively, commenting in part as follows:

Even if unions do not have a strong, direct impact upon the real income of their members, their presence helps to gain general acceptance for the rates of pay and working conditions that prevail even in unorganized plants.... [T]he existence of unions, the opportunity to join such organizations, the ability to compare one's wages with the union scale—all of these things help to persuade the worker that the conditions under which he labors are tolerably fair. Without unions, this assurance could not be given and workers might easily demand government regulation as the only practical alternative to protect their interests. Our experience with wage controls in World War II and the Korean conflict suggests that this alternative would exact a heavy price in red tape and in a loss of flexibility for our firms and labor markets.[46]

Accession No. 3065, file labeled "Suggested Research Projects," NYSSILR, Labor-Management Documentation Center, Cornell University, pp. 2–3.

[43] Ibid.

[44] Derber, *The American Idea of Industrial Democracy*, 11ff.

[45] John T. Dunlop, *Collective Bargaining: Principles and Cases* (Chicago: Richard D. Irwin Inc., 1949), 33; Dunlop and James J. Healy, *Collective Bargaining: Principles and Cases*, rev. ed. (Homewood, Ill.: Richard D. Irwin Inc., 1953), 29–30.

[46] Derek C. Bok and John T. Dunlop, *Labor and the American Community* (New York: Simon and Schuster, 1970), 464.

There was one exception which at first glance might tend to discredit this hypothesis. That was the rise of talk about "trade-union democracy" which arose in the industrial relations field in the late 1930s and became vigorous during the 1950s. Yet further consideration actually strengthens the argument.

Note the distinction between the industrial democracy agitation of the 1910s and trade-union democracy talk of the 1950s. It is not trivial. Industrial democracy meant different things to different intellectuals and labor activists in the era between the late nineteenth century and the depression of 1920–21, but generally it was thought of it as a movement that in some way would give working people a greater voice or power in *industry*—that is, between corporations, unions, and, often, government. Calls for trade-union democracy, by contrast, meant something much narrower: an effort to give union members greater representation within their labor organizations. Thus, while the Webbs' 1897 *Industrial Democracy* addressed such subjects—to quote the table of contents—as "the methods of mutual insurance," "the method of collective bargaining," "arbitration," "the normal day," "sanitation and safety," and "new processes and machinery" as well as internal union governance, William M. Leiserson's 1959 *American Trade Union Democracy* was confined to "the union constitution," "the union convention," "the normal convention in operation," and "the judicial process within the unions."[47]

Complaints about lack of democracy in unions originated among employers, legislators representing their interests in Washington and the state capitals, and to judge by the comments of William Leiserson, some of the older industrial relations figures who felt that organized labor or Communist labor leaders were getting out of hand. The critics attacked John L. Lewis of the Mine Workers and, later, James Hoffa of the Teamsters as "labor dictators," conducted hearings on questions of corruption or Communism in unions, and studied union government. Without any doubt, serious problems regarding freedom of expression and representation existed in unions, and in the long run, the Landrum-Griffin Act of 1959, which was the principal result of the protests about union corruption, may contribute to democratization of organized labor. But in the short run, its sole effect was to intensify federal regulation of union activities and thereby help slow down union organization and vitality.

[47] The tables of contents for William M. Leiserson, *American Trade Union Democracy* (New York: Columbia University Press, 1959) and Webb and Webb, *Industrial Democracy.* See also Sumner Slichter's "Introduction" to *American Trade Union Democracy.*

The late 1950s, like nearly all American labor history since 1950, need much more study, but preliminary research indicates that the widespread worry about trade-union democracy that arose in the early years of the Cold War represented part of the long-term slide away *from* the movement for industrial democracy in the United States, rather than its opposite.[48]

After World War II, some industrial relations professors had hoped that America would develop into a tripartite form of industrial government along the lines of Austria or Sweden. They were disappointed, as Professor Dunlop made clear in his 1960 presidential address to the Industrial Relations Research Association. Economic planning of that sort requires, among other things, highly centralized labor organization and, while he used discreet language, Dunlop clearly believed that the AFL and the CIO were not working together well and, in fact, that their 1955 merger was a shotgun marriage. Similarly, while he was impressed by the efforts of managers to resolve staff-line problems caused by the institution of collective bargaining, he was dismayed by the failure of the National Association of Manufacturers and the Chamber of Commerce to change their public political stances regarding unions, even though more than half the members of the board of directors of the NAM came from firms engaged in collective bargaining. Dunlop's views of the impact of lawyers' and politicians' work were even more negative than Commons's. "The national policy encourages litigation rather than settlement," he declared. "The proceedings are highly technical, lawyers are involved in game playing rather than in the process of practical settlement and dispute settlement."

Despite this dismal assessment, Dunlop did not in any way question or qualify the wisdom of searching for a corporatist-style consensus in industry. "The method of consensus is admittedly difficult to apply," he conceded to the audience of industrial relations scholars, teachers, and practitioners. As he continued, he began to sound like a clergyman or missionary, which was understandable given that he had been raised in

---

[48] Ralph C. James and Estelle Dinerstein James, *Hoffa and the Teamsters: A Study of Union Power* (Princeton: O. Van Nostrand Company, 1965); Melvyn Dubofsky and Warren Van Tine, *John L. Lewis: A Biography* (New York: Quadrangle, The New York Times Book Company, 1977), 389–529; Robert F. Kennedy, *The Enemy Within* (New York: Harper, 1960); R. Alton Lee, *Eisenhower v. Landrum-Griffin: A Study in Labor-Management Politics* (Lexington: University Press of Kentucky, 1989); David Montgomery, *Workers' Control in America* (Cambridge: Cambridge University Press, 1979), 153–80.

the Philippines of missionary parents. "It is so much easier to pass another law, or issue another decision of another resolution," Dunlop intoned. "The achievement of consensus is often a frustrating process since it must triumph over inertia, suspicion, and the warpath. It is slow to build. But it is clearly the most satisfying and enduring solution to problems."[49]

Dunlop achieved his greatest public stature while serving as director of the Cost-of-Living Council in 1973–74 and as secretary of labor in 1975–76, but his efforts to move the nation in a corporatist direction during those years failed. In the former case, his effort to turn back inflation ran smack into the wall of the Organization of Petroleum Exporting Countries oil boycott, which pushed general consumer prices even higher. In the latter case, his committee of a dozen top leaders of American business and labor was undercut by the corporate heads, who helped fund an antiunion drive in Congress at the same time that they met with the union leaders, and by President Ford, who refused to back up his secretary when he needed help. Nonetheless, Dunlop remained implacable. "It is *not* a major new era and that I am willing to sign my name to," he told *Business Week* amidst the sharp recession of 1982, adding more recently in a meeting with a group of journalists, "Men are always convinced that their era is one of profound transformation."[50]

Younger, prominent industrial relations figures were nowhere near as confident. Thus, in their acclaimed *Transformation of American Industrial Relations* (1986), Thomas A. Kochan, Harry C. Katz, and Robert B. McKersie asked whether unions can survive in the face of new, popular Japanese-style management commonly labeled "human resources." Although they qualified their predictions, their basic conclusion was negative. At the same time, the new intensity of labor-management conflict, combined with the collapse of tripartite planning agreements and the rise to power of antilabor governments in Britain, America, and elsewhere, pushed younger political scientists to doubt the inevitability-of-corporatism theses posited by Schmitter and others just a few years before.[51]

---

[49] Dunlop, "Consensus and National Labor Policy," *Proceedings of the Thirteenth Annual Meeting, Industrial Relations Research Association, 1960* (Madison, Wis.: IRRA, 1961), 6–7, 9–10, 13–15.

[50] Quoted in Mike Davis, *Prisoners of the American Dream: Politics and Economy in the History of the U.S. Working Class* (London: Verso, 1986), 103; "Dunlop, Lovell Debate Impact of Change in U.S. Industrial Relations," *Daily Labor Report*, 30 November 1987 (Washington, D.C.: Bureau of National Affairs, 1987), A–6.

[51] Thomas A. Kochan, Harry C. Katz, and Robert B. McKersie, *The Transformation of American Industrial Relations* (New York: Basic Books, 1986), 250–53; Leo Panitch,

An even better indication of the decline of older industrial relations–style thinking is the revival of Elton Mayo–style approaches in industry. Labeled QWL (Quality of Work Life), these programs bring small groups of workers and lower-level supervisors together to discuss production problems and determine ways to increase productivity. Often the meetings result in new, more flexible job descriptions. By most accounts, workers in both organized and unorganized shops often respond positively to these programs, both because—as Mayo had commented sixty years ago—in QWL groups they received more respect from management and because, in an era of intense international economic competition, the shop-floor committees may help save their jobs. Consequently, large international unions such as the United Auto Workers have opted to participate, despite internal dissent. However, polls show that the effect of Mayo-style programs is to reduce workers' attachment to unions, a report echoed by organizers.[52]

But the fortieth-anniversary meeting of the Industrial Relations Research Association offered the sharpest illustration of the strains put on industrial relations theory and practitioners by the turn of the economic cycle. Recalling the time just after the war when the IRRA was founded, Clark Kerr has written: "It was an exciting time. New approaches were developed, new ideas brought forth and disputed. The study of industrial relations, as other fields of study before, experienced its greatest expansion.... The field now had a core."[53]

At the fortieth convention, however, Arnold R. Weber, the president of Northwestern University and the meeting's distinguished speaker, plunged a sword into that core. Weber was highly experienced in the field himself, having preceded John Dunlop as executive director of the Nixon administration's Cost-of-Living Council and, before that, having served as head of a series of presidential labor-management advisory committees. "While it is not my purpose to argue this issue here," Weber began, "I will state for the record that I believe that the trends that have been so dramatically manifested in the last decade or so define a sea

---

Working-Class Politics in Crisis: Essays on Labour and the State (London: Verso, 1986), 161, 166, 175ff.; Claus Offe, *Contradictions of the Welfare State* (Cambridge, Mass.: MIT Press, 1984), 190–91, 290–92.

[52] Ruth Needleman, "QWL from a Labor Perspective: A Review Essay on *Inside the Circle*," *Labor Research Review* 7 (Fall 1985): 99–106; John Russo, "Killing Jobs with 'Cooperation': the GM Memo," *Labor Research Review* 5 (Fall 1984):61–69; Leo Panitch, *Working-Class Politics in Crisis*, 166, 175ff.

[53] Kerr, *Labor Markets and Wage Determination*, 2–3.

change in the American industrial relations system and that there is almost no likelihood that the old order can be repaired." Weber then asked the tough question: "Why . . . were [we] unknowing in identifying the breadth and significance of these trends as they were bursting on the scene?"

To answer the question, Weber probed industrial relations thinking. "The study of industrial relations has, from the beginning, been intertwined with ideological controversies concerned with the role of labor in industrial society," he noted. "Many of these ideologies also have been teleological in nature, imputing some inherent process or design to the labor movement." Marxist theories have the "most robust" of these, he continued. But ideology was not a foreign commodity in the non-Marxist world, he observed. "At a less apocalyptic level, most of us have harbored the belief, if not the earnest hope, that labor relations can or will evolve from 'conflict' to 'cooperation.' That is why," he continued, "so many of us imputed virtue to 'stable' industry-wide bargaining structures, multiyear agreements, wage formulas based on productivity, and the other accoutrements of statesmanship." Such hopes, he suggested, led industrial relations scholar-practitioners to blind themselves to stresses put on managements from competition, both domestic and foreign.[54] In the meantime, industry-wide collective bargaining collapsed in steel, airlines, meatpacking, and other industries.

Arnold Weber has a reputation as a raconteur, but in his IRRA anniversary address, he never raised his head once, offered no humor, but instead delivered blunt assertions, one after another, against what he may well have assumed would not be a receptive audience. Despite the power of his remarks, there was no large, sustained applause afterward and scarcely a soul came to the podium to offer praise.

[54] Arnold R. Weber, "Understanding Change in Industrial Relations: A Second Look," in *Proceedings of the Fortieth Annual Meeting, December 28–30, 1987, Chicago,* ed. Barbara D. Dennis (1988), 12–13, 21.

6

Great expectations: the promise of industrial jurisprudence and its demise, 1930–1960

NELSON LICHTENSTEIN

SUMNER SLICHTER REVISES HIS BOOK

When the Brookings Institution published Sumner Slichter's comprehensive 1941 study of union policies and industrial management, the idea of an emerging "industrial jurisprudence" stood at the very core of the book. Slichter's study rested upon almost a quarter century of social investigation by the foremost labor economist of his day. Slichter, who had been trained by John Commons at Wisconsin, was not an enthusiast of the Congress of Industrial Organizations (CIO) and his work reflected virtually none of the experience of the new industrial unions. Instead, his broad survey summarized the practice of those industries in which a stable system of collective bargaining had emerged over the previous decades. These included the railroads, the printing trades and construction, and above all, the garment and hosiery industries.

Collective bargaining, wrote Slichter, is a method of "introducing civil rights into industry, that is, of requiring that management be conducted by rule rather than by arbitrary decision."[1] To Slichter and many of his generation, industrial democracy represented both a technique of conflict resolution and an effort to establish a new constitutional order in America's factories and mills. These two concepts were not always compatible, but they represented a vision of shop society toward which both the state and the unions, and even some in management, seemed to be moving. He wrote:

[1] Sumner H. Slichter, *Union Policies and Industrial Management* (Washington, D.C.: Brookings Institution, 1941), 1.

Through the institution of the state, men devise schemes of positive law, construct administrative procedures for carrying them out, and complement both statute law and administrative rule with a system of judicial review. Similarly, laboring men, through unions, formulate policies to which they give expression in the form of shop rules and practices which are embodied in agreements with employers or are accorded less formal recognition and assent by management; shop committees, grievance procedures, and other means are evolved for applying these rules and policies.... When labor and management deal with labor relations analytically and systematically after such a fashion, it is proper to refer to the system as industrial jurisprudence.[2]

Fewer than twenty years after the appearance of *Union Policies and Industrial Management,* the Brookings Institution invited Slichter to head up a team of industrial relations scholars who would revise his original work in the light of the enormous changes in labor-management relations that had taken place during World War II and the decade or so afterward. The contrasts between the first and second editions are remarkable. Although Slichter and his team of postwar researchers were fully cognizant of the enormous increase in union size and power, and they devoted much space to labor's influence on management decision making, the entire structure of the book was shifted toward a managerial perspective in which "industrial relations" represented a problem to be solved rather than a process of self-government. Most striking, the 1960 edition contains no mention of the term "industrial jurisprudence" nor any section devoted to the implementation of civil rights or a constitutional governance in industry. Instead, the postwar edition contains a long discussion of the nature of collective bargaining in the large multiplant industrial firms where the trade unions had their greatest strength. Here three chapters are devoted to grievance procedures and the case law that emerged out of the near universal deployment of arbitration systems in heavy industry, a subject unmentioned in the prewar edition.[3]

The 1941 volume also devoted 180 pages, almost a third of its bulk, to various programs of union-management cooperation and self-government, including many participation and profit-sharing schemes that had their origins in the industrial turmoil immediately following World War I. In 1960, this section had been reduced to but forty pages, much of it a description of union-sponsored programs, such as the Scan-

---

[2] Ibid.
[3] Sumner H. Slichter, James J. Healy, and E. Robert Livernash, *The Impact of Collective Bargaining on Management* (Washington, D.C.: Brookings Institution, 1960) 1–26, 692–806 passim.

lon Plan, designed to rationalize the wage structure in heavy industry. And to take one final example: in the 1941 edition, Slichter approaches the issue of craft union work rules in terms of the rights they secure for workers and the overall efficiency they bring to the industry, even if they might seem harmful to an individual firm. But in the second edition work rules are seen in more unfavorable terms, largely as an obstacle to efficient operation of the firm, and much discussion is devoted to ways in which they can be eliminated with the least possible social friction.[4]

The differences between the two Slichter volumes reflected both a changing industrial relations practice and, perhaps even more important, the changing perceptions of those who sought to structure the work regime in American industry. We can see here not so much a shift from Left to Right (for Slichter and his colleagues were hardly of the Left) as it was a movement away from a model of industrial relations in which a system of industrial rule making stood at the center of the process and toward one in which the effort to introduce certain democratic norms was subordinated to the seemingly more pressing effort to find social mechanisms that could both maintain industrial discipline and resolve economic conflict between the big unions and their management adversaries.

THE ORIGINS OF INDUSTRIAL JURISPRUDENCE

In recent years, many observers have also noted the enormous gap that has arisen between the reality of managerial power in postwar American society and the theory of industrial self-government that was enshrined in the Wagner Act and in the rhetoric of the labor law that has evolved over the last half century. As the American unions decline in power and influence, and as capital has become ever more global and mobile, the idea that collective bargaining represents the road to an industrial democracy seems increasingly implausible. This view has been most forcefully advanced by a new generation of historians and legal scholars who have found in the institutional history and legal tradition associated with postwar labor relations a dramatic departure from the effort that even so conservative a labor economist as Sumner Slichter saw as the road to a genuine "industrial jurisprudence" that would mirror the laws govern-

---

[4]Slichter, *Union Policies*, 393–571, 164–200; Slichter et al., *Impact of Collective Bargaining*, 841–78, 317–41.

ing civil society.[5] As legal scholar Katherine Stone put it in 1981: "The premises of industrial pluralism [her term for the ideology of postwar industrial self-government] do not correspond to the reality of the industrial world. At bottom, the theory of industrial pluralism rests upon an assertion of equal power or potentially equal power between management and labor. Only if this assertion is true can the 'legislative process' of collective bargaining be said to produce industrial democracy."[6]

Stone and other critics have helped historians decode the labor law and get at the premises usually hidden behind the pluralist ideology of a generation of labor lawyers and industrial relations practitioners. But in demolishing, or at least substantially undermining this pluralist model of industrial relations, these important critics have been less than persuasive in explaining why for so many years scholars and practitioners as sober-minded as Sumner Slichter or as learned as Ivy League law professors Harry Shulman and Archibald Cox might think that a uniform system of industrial jurisprudence would come to govern the workings of the mid-twentieth-century factory and mill. What was it that made the power of this model of industrial democracy, now a shambles, so attractive for so long? To look for an answer we must probe somewhat more deeply into the social and economic origins of this notion and briefly sketch the fate of this idea as it was translated, in the actual tumult of union formation and management resistance, into the late New Deal system of grievance handling and arbitration that became such a powerful legal and ideological touchstone for the postwar system of industrial governance.

The idea that a system of genuinely pluralistic and democratic industrial self-government might emerge out of the bargaining relationships of the late 1930s was based heavily upon the arrangements worked out earlier in the needle trades and hosiery industries. First in the men's clothing industry, and then in the full-fashioned hosiery shops centered

[5] Ronald Schatz, "Into the Twilight Zone—The Law and the American Industrial Relations System since the New Deal," *International Labor and Working-Class History* 36 (Fall 1989): 51–60. And see especially Karl Klare, "Judicial Deradicalization of the Wagner Act and the Origins of Modern Legal Consciousness, 1937–1941," *Minnesota Law Review* 62 (1978): 265–339; Christopher Tomlins, *The State and the Unions, Labor Relations, Law, and the Organized Labor Movement in America, 1880–1960* (Cambridge: Cambridge University Press, 1985); Katherine Van Wezel Stone, "The Post-War Paradigm in American Labor Law," *Yale Law Journal* 90 (June 1981): 1509–80; and see the articles by Klare, Staughton Lynd, and Melvyn Dubofsky in *Industrial Relations Law Journal* 4 (1981): 450–502.
[6] Stone, "Post-war Paradigm," 1577; see also James Atleson's chapter in this volume.

in Philadelphia, a socialist-oriented union leadership reached an accommodation with the managers of a highly competitive, partly unionized, labor intensive-industry heretofore characterized by a tradition of ethno-political shop-floor militancy, periodic mass strikes, and acute economic instability. In both clothing and hosiery, the greatest threat to the stability of the union came far more from the expansion of nonunion sectors of the industry than from the employers themselves. The key features of this new system of industrial democracy were employer recognition of union strength and permanency, a union commitment to industrial self-discipline, including a program of wage rationalization and moderation, and the establishment of a quasi-judicial umpire system that would resolve any outstanding disputes between the parties. By the 1920s, the Amalgamated Clothing Workers had interpenetrated industry decision making at virtually every level. Its representatives jointly set piece rates, influenced the appointment of foremen, bailed out bankrupt firms, set the terms for the introduction of new technology, and in several instances helped managers even of the largest clothing firms plan and market new product lines. "The dominant factor in collective bargaining has been the Amalgamated," concluded two contemporary observers. "Far surpassing the employers, whose inability to form a strong national organization has limited their effectiveness, the union now determines the industry's major policies. Its chief adversary is the stubborn nature of the trade."[7]

This new model unionism proved exceptionally attractive in establishing the ideological and social framework through which a cohort of Progressive Era reformers and economists would grapple with the labor question during the first third of the twentieth century. As Howell Harris has shown in this volume, many reformers were taken with the idea of "constitutionalizing" industry, through the abolition of "arbitrary government" and the joint development of procedures for the quasi-judicial, peaceful resolution of conflict. All this fit remarkably well with the reigning Whiggery of the Anglo-American reform tradition, to wit, the evolution of political and social institutions embodied a steady advance of liberty and order. Such optimism could not last forever, least of all in the industrial world, but to the extent that this worldview did make contact with social reality, it came in these light manufacturing industries

---

[7] Robert J. Myers and Joseph Bloch, "Men's Clothing," in Harry Millis, ed., *How Collective Bargaining Works* (New York: Twentieth Century Fund, 1942), 444.

where trade unions of the interwar period had such a large economic and ideological impact.

Here grievance procedures, arbitration, union-management negotiations over piece rates, wages, and work processes promised the order and stability long sought by managers and the industrial citizenship demanded by many workers. As Sidney Hillman himself put it in 1914, "To see these people, only a few years ago from lands where factories are unknown, meeting to discuss problems of the rights and wrongs of shop discipline, of changing prices, of the rightfulness of discharge is a thing to fill one with the hope for the future of democracy."[8] And William Leiserson, himself an East European immigrant and clothing industry arbitrator, who would later play a key role in the development of National Labor Relations Board policy, saw the Amalgamated's collective bargaining arrangements as the kernel of a new order in industry. Here the "joint meetings of employers and union representatives, like the parliament of England, are at the same time constitutional conventions and statute making legislatures." Disputes over the interpretation or administration of the agreement were naturally subject to judicial review, embodied in the operation of the impartial umpireship system that had been established in all the major clothing production centers. Leiserson saw this constitutional schema as essential to any system of industrial order that might be substituted for private capitalism: "For however the form of ownership may change, there will ever be if not wage earners, at least workers who must obey orders and directors or managers with authority to issue orders."[9]

Labor-management collaboration and impartial adjudication of disputes began somewhat later in the hosiery industry than in men's clothing, but the system established in Philadelphia proved even more influential than the ACWA Chicago experience in establishing the pattern of arbitration and mediation that would later be advanced by the War Labor Board and adopted by heavy industry during the early 1940s. Although the production facilities were somewhat larger than in clothing, the full-

[8] Quoted in Steven Fraser, "Dress Rehearsal for the New Deal: Shop-Floor Insurgents, Political Elites, and Industrial Democracy in the Amalgamated Clothing Workers Union," in Michael Frisch and Daniel Walkowitz, eds., *Working-Class America: Essays on Labor, Community, and American Society* (Champaign: University of Illinois Press, 1983), 212–55. For a great deal more and a most penetrating interpretation of Hillman's remarkable career, see Steven Fraser, *Labor Will Rule: Sidney Hillman and the Rise of American Labor* (New York: The Free Press, 1991).
[9] William Leiserson, "Constitutional Government in American Industries," *American Economic Review* 12 (March 1922): 62.

fashioned hosiery industry presented an even more chaotic and intensely competitive social and economic terrain than did men's clothing. Because the work was highly skilled and localized, hosiery manufacture was a well paid occupation, almost a "profession" according to many of its long service workers. Work rules and piecework wage scales were exceedingly complex but largely under the control of shop committees powerful enough to prevent work on new hosiery styles until agreement had been reached on the new rates that would go with them.[10]

But the migration of the industry to rural Pennsylvania and to the South proved devastating during the 1920s. Among the four hundred hosiery plants scattered up and down the East Coast, union organization dropped from greater than 90 percent just after World War I to about 25 percent in 1929. Piece rates were slashed by a quarter and total wages, which peaked in 1927, declined by more than 60 percent over the next six years. Such grim statistics might well forecast the destruction of the union, but the Full Fashioned Hosiery Workers turned this economic and organizational catastrophe into a well-managed retreat. The key to their policy was collaboration with unionized hosiery firms and a program of wage reductions that would assure the competitiveness of the organized sector of the industry. Thus even before the inauguration of the National Recovery Administration and its stabilizing industry codes, the unionized hosiery workers had begun to make a comeback.[11]

The central institution in the union's program was the hosiery industry's impartial chairmanship, for many years presided over by George Taylor, the University of Pennsylvania professor who might well be considered the founder of modern grievance arbitration. Taylor's powers were exceptionally broad and his task exceedingly complex. He sat in on all collective bargaining sessions, reviewed preliminary contract language, made economic surveys of the industry, and proposed reforms in the wage structure. He worked out many of the key principles that have come to govern industrial arbitration disputes: dismissal for "due cause," the necessity for uninterrupted production, the importance of seniority

---

[10]Thomas Kennedy, *Effective Labor Arbitration: The Impartial Chairmanship of the Full-Fashioned Hosiery Industry* (Philadelphia: University of Pennsylvania Press, 1948), 4–19; George W. Taylor, "Hosiery," in Millis, ed., *How Collective Bargaining Works*, 450–72.

[11]Taylor, "Hosiery," 473–507; Kennedy, *Effective Labor Arbitration*, 20–25. For an excellent survey of the economic conditions and ideological mind-set that gave rise to collaborations such as those in hosiery, see Sanford Jacoby, "Union-Management Cooperation in the United States: Lessons from the 1920s," *Industrial and Labor Relations Review* 57 (October 1983): 18–33.

in layoffs and promotions. However, his most difficult task involved implementation of a program of labor cost reduction and equalization designed to make union firms once again competitive. The program generated much rank-and-file resistance and a number of bitter factional disputes. Although a majority of this exceedingly democratic union favored the policy of wage concessions, its leaders feared that if any particular reduction were put to a vote it would surely be defeated.

Taylor's exhaustive knowledge of the industry's structure, his great social prestige, and the informal manner in which he presided as impartial umpire were therefore crucial to the success of his office and the union program. In 1938, for example, Taylor facilitated a broad wage cut in return for employer installation of new equipment. But in undertaking this reduction, Taylor sought to sustain individual employee earnings. Therefore his work balanced a firm's productivity, piece rate schedule and competitive position with the speed and quality of its work force.[12] "Wage setting was not solely an economic problem," asserted Taylor, "but one in psychological reactions as well."[13]

By the mid-1930s, the collective bargaining systems in hosiery and men's clothing were well known throughout labor relations circles. The relative power of the unions there and the importance of arbitration in all aspects of industry governance gave this model of industrial democracy a social and ideological weight that cannot be overestimated. The collaborative arrangements that had taken root in these unstable industries offered to the unions an institutional security and to individual workers a species of due process, but all within a context that assured that these rights could exist only so long as they were subordinated to the always fragile economic health of the industry. Self-discipline therefore seemed the only road to industrial democracy. For the pioneering generation of industrial relations practitioners, for William Leiserson, Sumner Slichter, Harry Millis, and George Taylor, this was an idea that could hardly be overstated.[14]

Much that would come to characterize the postwar system of industrial

[12] Edward Shils et al., *Industrial Peacemaker: George W. Taylor's Contribution to Collective Bargaining* (Philadelphia: University of Pennsylvania Press, 1979), 30–34; George Heliker, "Grievance Arbitration in the Automobile Industry: A Comparative Analysis of Its History and Results in the Big Three" (Ph.D. diss., University of Michigan, 1954), 65–73; Clare McDermott interview with G. Allan Dash, Jr., in National Academy of Arbitrators, *Oral History Project* (Washington, D.C.: National Academy of Arbitrators, 1982), 3–6.
[13] Kennedy, *Effective Labor Arbitration*, 49.
[14] Christopher Tomlins, "The New Deal, Collective Bargaining, and the Triumph of Industrial Pluralism," *Industrial and Labor Relations Review* 39 (October 1985): 19–35.

relations arose out of the effort to transfer elements of the clothing and hosiery industry patterns onto the very different structures characteristic of American heavy industry. The most ambitious effort came in the steel industry where the Steel Workers Organizing Committee made an effort to collaborate with many of the industry's smaller, relatively inefficient firms during the Roosevelt recession of 1937–39. The key figure here was Clinton Golden, a former Socialist, Amalgamated organizer, and Brookwood Labor College instructor then serving as an assistant to SWOC president Philip Murray. While working in Philadelphia, Golden had not only observed the start of union-management collaboration in the hosiery industry but had worked closely with the pioneering industrial psychologist Elton Mayo in a study of human relations among textile workers.[15]

Once the SWOC had won a beachhead in the steel industry, Golden and his colleagues seemed to confront many of the same problems that had plagued textiles and clothing: nonunion competition, overproduction, wildcat strikes, union instability, and large differentials in the productivity of individual firms. If anything, the new steelworkers union was a far more fragile institution than the unions in the needle and hosiery trades. No major steel company was prepared to offer SWOC the security of a union shop contract. Moreover, steelworkers were a heterogeneous lot, with fewer traditions of shop-floor combativeness than needle trades workers, and they still faced the militantly antiunion Little Steel group.

With other staff intellectuals, including research director Harold Ruttenberg and Joseph Scanlon, the head of SWOC's new industrial engineering department, Golden sought to build something of the same kind of relationship with the steel industry that the unions in hoisery and clothing enjoyed with the needle trades firms. Focusing first on the marginal steel companies, Golden collaborated with Ruttenberg to write "Production Problems"—a widely distributed SWOC pamphlet that outlined how workers could help these companies stay in business by increasing productivity, reducing operating costs, and, in extreme situations, lowering their wage bill. Of course, the price of this support was the union shop, which SWOC leadership saw as company recognition that the union was a permanent institution in the industry, and thus partially responsible for the efficient operation of the mill.[16]

[15] Thomas R. Brooks, *Clint: A Biography of a Labor Intellectual* (New York: Atheneum, 1978), 65–107 passim.
[16] Clinton Golden and Harold Ruttenberg, *The Dynamics of Industrial Democracy* (New York: Harper and Brothers, 1942), 190–230; SWOC, "Production Problems" (Pitts-

Most steel firms resisted such "participation" schemes, and they fought tenaciously against the union shop, but such industry intransigence did not prevent Golden and other high steelworker officials from advancing the argument that union-management collaboration was essential to the overall economic health of the industry. At Golden's instigation, the Left-Taylorite Morris Cooke wrote *Organized Labor and Production*, which he "coauthored" with SWOC president Philip Murray in 1940. Then two years later, Golden and Ruttenberg put together the influential *Dynamics of Industrial Democracy*. Both books represented a sustained argument in favor of the union shop, with Cooke emphasizing the extent to which such security would facilitate technological efficiencies in the industry's production process, and Ruttenberg and Golden pointing out that only a self-confident union leadership could take the difficult measures sometimes necessary to discipline shop-floor radicals.[17]

These publications also made explicit another theme of growing importance in CIO–New Deal circles: the quasi-corporatist need for industry-wide bargaining as a device to eliminate wage competition and begin the politically difficult process, analogous to that undertaken in hosiery, of reducing some of the enormous wage differentials that had distorted the steel industry cost structure. Golden and Ruttenberg thought that only such industry-wide bargaining could prepare the way for a more general accommodation by labor and management along lines already pioneered in Sweden and advocated in the United States by Slichter, Taylor, and Leiserson. This accommodation could in turn make possible a Keynesian high wage–high demand program essential to the "application of democratic methods in the settlement of grievances and adjustment of wage rates."[18]

CIVIL SOCIETY AT GENERAL MOTORS

Although the idea of an industrial jurisprudence had been pioneered in the clothing industry and its meaning given a politically astute formulation by steel union staff intellectuals, it was in the auto industry that

burgh: SWOC, 1938), 4; Paul F. Clark, Peter Gottlieb, and Donald Kennedy, *Forging a Union of Steel: Philip Murray, SWOC, and the United Steelworkers* (Ithaca: ILR Press, 1987), 118–30.

[17] Morris Cooke and Philip Murray, *Organized Labor and Production: The Next Steps in Industrial Democracy* (New York: Harper and Brothers, 1940); Golden and Ruttenberg, *Dynamics of Industrial Democracy*, 168–202; Brooks, *Clint*, 197–98.

[18] Golden and Ruttenberg, *Dynamics of Industrial Democracy*, 317–18.

this construct would have its most pattern-setting and thorough elaboration. Indeed, it was in General Motors, the largest corporation in the world, where a widely admired and imitated system of grievance arbitration was first installed, largely at the prompting and with the guidance of those labor leaders and industrial relations practitioners who had been most influenced by the hosiery and clothing industry experiments. But as we shall see, General Motors provided a very different economic and political environment in which to evolve a system of industrial jurisprudence, one which substantially altered the meaning of the concept.

Elsewhere in this volume, David Brody has argued that such a system, which he calls "workplace contractualism," was the product of the logic of twentieth-century industrial production itself. Moreover, far from being imposed upon a feisty group of workers by a cohort of sophisticated managers, nascent union bureaucrats, and government-connected professors, the system arose organically out of the sometimes militant struggle for industrial unionism. Its early manifestations were in evidence long before passage of the Wagner Act, the formation of the CIO, or the elaboration of a dense legal-administrative apparatus in the years after 1940. Indeed, workers' efforts to construct a system of justice, of rules that might govern the factory work regime in place of the unilaterally imposed regulations of management or the seemingly capricious power of the foreman, constituted the essence of the unionism for which so many fought.

But this does not tell the whole story, for as we shall see, the content of this workplace contractualism is fluid and contingent. The scope of the contract, the character of its enforcement, the prerogatives of workers and managers were passionately and genuinely contested issues, nowhere fought out with greater consequences than at America's premier industrial corporation. The work rules, wage patterns, and grievance procedures established at GM were the product of the conflicts and compromises available to the contestants at a uniquely formative historical moment, one in which the terrain of struggle had begun to tilt toward the proponents of order, routine, and industrial bureaucracy.

The GM sit-down strike has been rightfully accorded an exceptional place in the history of U.S. labor. Its success opened the door to the organization of much of America's heavy industry and made certain that the CIO would play a major role in reshaping the politics of the late Depression years. But the great strike did remarkably little to set the terms of the bargaining relationship between the new United Automobile

Workers (UAW) and the giant corporation. One might well argue that its impact was as great in Washington and Pittsburgh as in Flint and Saginaw. GM did recognize the UAW as the sole representative of the workers in its plants, but the actual relationship between the union's shop-floor activists and the lower reaches of GM management had hardly been finalized. The first UAW-GM contract was a short, ambiguous document largely given over to assurances that the company would respect seniority and no longer discriminate against union members.

In contrast to several other heavy industry firms, including Chrysler, Allis Chalmers, Studebaker, and Goodyear, General Motors fought hard and successfully to retain control over work relations in its shops. To a degree quite rare in heavy industry, it kept most foremen loyal to a management vision of how the plants should be run, and GM managers succeeded in keeping the steward system built by UAW militants after the strike largely on the defensive and without formal company recognition. The UAW and GM established a multistep grievance procedure, but the only union representatives that GM formally recognized were the shop committee members, whose numbers were restricted to about one for every 250 workers. In contrast, at Chrysler and Studebaker, the new union forced their respective managements to recognize the group leadership and grievance processing authority of a dense system of working shop stewards whose numbers approximated those of their foreman counterparts. At Chrysler, a bitter, two-month-long strike in the fall of 1939 had won the several hundred "blue button" stewards there semiofficial recognition, which in turn enabled them to set production goals jointly and reorganize seniority lines. At Studebaker, it became standard practice for shop stewards to meet every morning to plan their approach to the day's work and to monitor the composition of work groups. They exercised effective control over the company's piece rate pay system, and as a consequence, recalled a local union officer, the foremen were "just clerks."[19]

GM's relative success had two sources. First, the Sloanist system of

---

[19] Steve Jefferys, *Management and Managed: Fifty Years of Crisis at Chrysler* (Cambridge: Cambridge University Press, 1986), 68–87; Stephen Amberg, "The Triumph of Industrial Orthodoxy: The Failure of Studebaker Corporation," in Nelson Lichtenstein and Steve Meyer, eds., *On the Line: Essays in the History of Auto Work* (Urbana: University of Illinois Press, 1988), 190–218; Stephen Meyer, "Rituals of Power: Workers, Shop Stewards and Control at Allis-Chalmers in the 1930s and 1940s," unpublished paper in author's possession; Frederick Harbison and Robert Dubin, *Patterns of Union-Management Relations* (Chicago: Science Research Associates, 1947), 19–26.

decentralized operations deployed by the corporation in the 1920s and 1930s meant that top management had already implemented a systematic labor relations policy long before the emergence of the UAW. A sophisticated recruitment and education program for foremen engendered "company mindedness" among this crucial stratum and succeeded in keeping General Motors virtually free of the movement toward foreman unionism that was sweeping much of the auto industry in the late 1930s and early 1940s. Even before the sit-down strikes, foremen were kept systematically informed of top management's labor relations program, put on salary, and assured of a 20–25 percent wage differential between themselves and the hourly payroll. Plant superintendents and department heads were held directly responsible for labor discipline, and unlike their counterparts at more highly centralized firms such as Chrysler and Allis-Chalmers, were seldom overruled by high company officials anxious to resume full production during strikes or slowdowns. GM managers were expected to "take a strike" in order to sustain discipline and maintain a consistent corporate labor policy.[20]

Second, GM had eschewed company unionism during the pre-UAW era. This meant that the UAW had had to build its shop-floor organization from scratch, without the system of departmental representation that unionists at Goodyear, Allis-Chalmers, and Chrysler had used to construct an even more far-reaching shop steward structure. The absence of a strong shop-floor organization largely explains the extent to which the 1937 GM strike was of necessity orchestrated by a determined cadre of "outside" organizers backed up by a few hundred sit-downers. Compared to the great Chrysler sit-down strike in April 1937, in which more than a quarter of all workers participated, the GM sit-down strike was not itself a mass movement. In Flint and elsewhere, most GM facilities continued in operation, which meant that when the newly unionized auto workers confronted GM plant superintendents and foremen in the spring of that year, they were less well organized and their company adversaries less demoralized than in Chrysler and many other heavy industry plants.[21]

More than 150,000 GM workers flooded into the UAW in the months

[20] Nelson Lichtenstein, " 'The Man in the Middle': A Social History of Automobile Industry Foremen," in Lichtenstein and Meyer, eds., *On the Line,* 153–89; Doug Reynolds, "Foremen on the Line: Management and Labor at General Motors, 1925–1937," unpublished manuscript in author's possession.
[21] Jefferys, *Management and Managed,* 59–67; Stephen Meyer, "The State and the Workplace: New Deal Labor Policy, the UAW, and Allis-Chalmers in the 1930s and 1940s," unpublished paper in author's possession.

immediately following the sit-down strikes, but the company was determined to resist what it called "joint management" with the new union. GM insisted that managers resist the enormous social and organizational pressures that could be generated by a new, highly politicized trade union and, according to one close observer, management's slogan might well have been: "Be tough, but fair, and don't deviate from the letter of the 'little grey book.' "[22] Not unexpectedly there were hundreds of short work stoppages—GM reported 235 in 1937—largely over management efforts to discipline those it considered the ringleaders of these episodes. From GM's point of view, the situation was untenable, and in midsummer, when CIO defeat in the Little Steel strike had restored a certain self-confidence in business circles, the company took the offensive against the UAW, demanding that the union sign a contract supplement that gave to management an unfettered right to discipline those workers responsible for wildcat work stoppages.[23]

All wings of the UAW also condemned these unauthorized quickie stoppages, but most active unionists insisted that industrial justice first demanded that the union carve a series of rights—substantive and procedural—out of the insecurity that had long characterized the work culture of the GM shops. Most workers did not mow their foreman's lawns or paint his house in order to keep their jobs: GM itself proscribed such bribes in the mid-1930s, but these apocryphal and widely repeated stories clearly conveyed some sense of the deferential relationship unionists were now determined to eliminate. GM workers wanted to inject onto the shop floor the legal norms and procedural safeguards found in civil society. As one Chevy worker put it in late 1937: "I want to ask this body of men and women here whether we, as organized people, will give the right to the company to accuse and judge, convict and sentence one of our members for an unauthorized strike . . . before the national [UAW] or the local, or the operators can pass sentence on any one of our members, we should be allowed as members of the organized union to give our evidence."[24]

UAW efforts to work out such a system of shop governance with GM

[22] Harbison and Dubin, *Patterns of Union-Management Relations*, 80.
[23] Archie Robinson, "Showdown on Outlaw Strikes Expected as UAW Board Meets," *Detroit News*, 20 June 1937; Bert Cochran, *Labor and Communism: The Conflict That Shaped American Unions* (Princeton: Princeton University Press, 1977), 129–40.
[24] Transcript, General Motors Delegate Conference, Detroit, 13 November 1937, box 3, Henry Kraus Collection, Archives of Labor History and Urban Affairs, Wayne State University (ALHUA), p. 79.

were made far more difficult by the bitter factionalism that engulfed and almost destroyed the union in 1938 and 1939. This complex and bizarre internal conflict had many sources: ethnocultural conflict, anti-Communism, and sheer personal opportunism. But the major substantive question over which the factionalists clashed involved GM's efforts to shape the new system of workplace collective bargaining to its advantage. From the moment the company signed its contract with the UAW in February 1937, GM wanted to limit the authority of the union's shop stewards, fire wildcat strikers, and enlist the union leadership as its disciplinary agent in the plants. Its hand was greatly strengthened in 1938 when the "Roosevelt recession" cut auto production by more than half.[25]

Moreover, GM did not relinquish, certainly in principle and often in practice, management authority to set the pace of production or the extent of the discipline it meted out to those who defied the corporation's own definition of appropriate shop-floor routine. In 1938, GM forced the UAW to agree to a reduction in the hours during which committeemen could handle grievances, a curb on in-plant dues collections, and the exclusion of national level UAW officials from grievance handling during the first twenty-four hours of the dispute. GM also insisted that an employee had to first sign his grievance before calling in the committeeman, a procedure that would not only intimidate most workers, but also give the foreman first crack at resolving the problem.[26]

By early 1939, therefore, the UAW held an extremely tenuous position at GM. The company no longer recognized the UAW-CIO, dues payments had practically ceased, a kind of civil war raged in Flint and Detroit. The *New York Times* and *Business Week* speculated that the UAW's days were numbered as a national union.[27] At this point, CIO leaders Sidney Hillman and Philip Murray stepped in. The union would collapse unless company-wide bargaining relationships with the major producers were restored and unless order was rebuilt in the industry. Hillman and Murray virtually dic-

[25] William Genske, "Dual Unionism: Group Format in the United Auto Workers," 3 December 1970, unpublished manuscript in author's possession; Roger Keeran, *The Communist Party and the Auto Workers Unions* (Bloomington: Indiana University Press, 1980); author's interview with Larry Jones, former vice-president UAW Local 659, 26 October 1987, Flint, Michigan; author's interview with Victor Reuther, 20 June 1986, Washington, D.C.
[26] Wyndam Mortimer to Homer Martin, 10 March 1938, box 12, file UAW-CIO Correspondence, Henry Kraus Collection, ALHWSU; Edward Levinson, "Martin Men Lose as Auto Workers Ballot in Locals," *New York Post,* 12 March 1938.
[27] Louis Stark, "Auto Union Holds Rival Conventions," *New York Times,* 27 February 1939; "UAW Break Now in the Open," *Business Week,* 1 March 1939.

tated the composition of a new slate of UAW officers at the union's March 1939 convention, in the process facilitating Walter Reuther's promotion to director of the all-important GM department of the union.

ARBITRATION AT GENERAL MOTORS

Under Reuther's energetic direction, the UAW refounded itself at the giant corporation. In the factionalism that followed the GM sit-down strike, Reuther sided with those in the union who favored aggressive efforts to defend the steward system and put "teeth" into the "machinery" of shop grievance handling "to make them realize we still have some fight in the old union." But he also recognized that a union is an institution that cannot always be mobilized for combat, an especially important idea in 1939 when Reuther and his colleagues faced widespread disaffection generated by the recession and the union's division into two warring camps. Here Reuther functioned in near classic form as the "manager of discontent" famously described by C. Wright Mills, a union leader who skillfully gauges the strength of his organization and the temper of his constituents in order to win the maximum possible gains without pushing so far as to threaten his union's destruction.[28]

Understanding the weakness of the UAW as against the financial and organizational strength of GM, Reuther successfully avoided a full-scale test of strength with the giant automaker. Under Reuther's leadership, the UAW rewon bargaining rights during the 1939 summer retooling season with a strike by the uniquely union-conscious skilled trades workers; but he then postponed for almost a year an NLRB election at the corporation that would test the loyalty of the far less resolute production workers. Only after impressive UAW victories in other sections of the industry had prepared the way did the union fully reestablish itself at GM in the spring of 1940. With this mandate, Reuther could finally negotiate a collective bargaining contract, in June 1940, that set forth in unprecedented detail mechanisms for resolving shop-floor disputes in the company's sixty-three UAW-organized plants.[29]

[28] Ternstedt and Fleetwood Divisions Instructions to Delegates, 13 November 1937, box 18, file 6, Walter Reuther Collection, ALHUA; C. Wright Mills, *The New Men of Power* (New York: Random House, 1948), 6.
[29] Frank Cormier and William Eaton, *Reuther* (Englewood Cliffs: Prentice-Hall, 1970), 152–64; John Barnard, "Rebirth of the United Automobile Workers: The General Motors Tool and Diemakers' Strike of 1939," *Labor History* 27 (Spring 1986): 165–87; author's interview with Larry Jones.

The key feature of the 1940 UAW-GM contract was the establishment of a permanent umpire who would rule on those disputes unresolved in the first four steps of the grievance procedure. The UAW had sought an arbitration device as a result of several long discussions Reuther had held with Sidney Hillman and other needle trades union leaders, and indeed, the first two umpires under the new UAW-GM agreement were Harry Millis, who had long experience as an arbitrator for the Amalgamated Clothing Workers in the Chicago cloak and suit industry, and George Taylor, the permanent umpire in the Philadelphia hosiery industry.[30]

Despite its needle trades antecedents, the UAW-GM arbitration experiment was a remarkable innovation, for it represented the very first such permanent mechanism established in heavy industry, and as such would go a long way in defining the character of the industrial jurisprudence that would evolve in the core sectors of the U.S. economy. Only 10 percent of all union contracts contained an arbitration clause at this time, and there were no permanent umpires in heavy industry. At its most immediate and crudely political level, Reuther and other union officials wanted an umpire system in order to protect the leadership from the consequences of undisciplined shop-floor militancy. GM department representatives had found their days and nights consumed with stopping these wildcat stoppages. "You cannot strike General Motors plants on individual grievances," Reuther told a meeting of autoworkers; "One plant going down will affect the 60 other plants."[31] Citing the experience of the clothing workers in Chicago, Reuther convinced the corps of sometimes wary GM local officers that this new institution would protect them from corporate reprisals and inner union factionalism that were so often the product of unconstrained shop-floor militancy. In later years, manipulation of the grievance procedure shielded many a local union officer from rank-and-file anger. "Out of the frying pan and into the umpire" was the catchphrase coined by GM unionists to describe the new system's conflict displacement properties.[32]

But it would be a mistake to see the umpire system as simply a mechanism designed to displace shop-floor conflict and protect the existing

[30] Heliker, "Grievance Arbitration," 96–108; Gabriel Alexander, "The General Motors-UAW Experience," in Jean McKelvey, ed., *Arbitration and the Law: Proceedings of the Twelfth Annual Meeting National Academy of Arbitrators* (Washington, D.C.: BNA Incorporated, 1959), 111–12.
[31] Alexander, "The General Motors–UAW Experience," 113.
[32] Transcript, National Defense Mediation Board, 5 May 1941, RG 202, National Archives, p. 520.

union leadership, for unionists like Walter Reuther saw in the new arrangements a bold effort "to substitute civil procedure for war in this industry."[33] They understood that the effort to build a system of industrial
jurisprudence, while not divorced from the shop-floor struggle over management power and steward rights, nevertheless contained a certain autonomous dynamic that could be turned to the advantage of the union.
UAW-GM arbitrators were full-time jurists, paid $20,000 a year, who ran
a kind of "court" in which the top officials of the corporate industrial relations staff battled it out with written briefs and oral arguments against
equally well-prepared unionists. Of the tens of thousands of grievances
that made their way upward to this court, between one hundred and two
hundred reached the arbitration stage and a definitive "umpire
decision."[34]

The UAW clearly hoped that it could use a combination of well-
organized pressure, grievance bargaining, and umpire decisions to build
a system of democratic, rule-bound governance on the shop floor. "Before
organization came into the plant, foremen were little tin gods in their
own departments," declared a 1941 UAW steward's handbook. "With
the coming of the union, the foreman finds his whole world turned upside
down. His small time dictatorship has been overthrown, and he must be
adjusted to a democratic system of shop government."[35] UAW strategists
thought that effective grievance handling could build up an advantageous
system of quasi-legal contract precedents. "The contract is your constitution, and the settlements of grievances under it are the decisions of an
industrial supreme court. *A complete record of such decisions is sometimes more important than the contract itself* [italics in the original]."
Moreover, UAW stewards were to function in a tradition akin to that
advocated by some legal realists: "Lawyers have been able to use a
Constitution written over 150 years ago to cover the complex issues of
modern life. A bright steward should be able to do just about as well
with his contract."[36]

Like other unionists of socialist or social democratic origins, Reuther
saw collective bargaining as an evolutionary process through which democratic norms would gradually spread. "Management has no divine

[33]Transcript, National Defense Mediation Board, 6 May 1941, RG 202, NA, p. 636.
[34]Clare McDermott interview with G. Allan Dash, 13 February 1978, in National Academy
   of Arbitrators, *Oral History Project* (Washington, D.C.: mimeo, 1982), 3–15.
[35]International Education Department, UAW-CIO, *How to Win for the Union: A Discussion for UAW Stewards and Committeemen* (Detroit, 1940), 8.
[36]Ibid., 8, 14.

rights," Reuther declared after the war. "Management has only functions, which it performs well or poorly. The only prerogatives which management has lost turned out to be usurpations of power and privilege to which no group of men have exclusive right in a democratic nation."[37]

Of course, General Motors had a very different conception of how the grievance system and umpire machinery might function. The company, which had closely observed the way in which Taylor handled disputes in the hosiery industry, wanted to avoid the freewheeling, all-inclusive style pioneered there. The largest corporation in the world had no need for the kind of economic tutelage so often meted out by those industrial relations "fixers" who had pioneered in the economically chaotic clothing trade. GM therefore insisted that the umpire be called an "umpire," and not an "impartial chairman" (as in the clothing trades) or arbitrator, because his job was merely to "call the balls and strikes," not "add to, subtract from, or modify" the collective bargaining agreement. Contrary to the traditions common in the clothing industry, the umpire was to refrain from asserting his own ideas on good labor relations policy.[38]

Most importantly, GM saw the umpire almost exclusively in terms of his ability to facilitate the company's disciplinary regime. Vice-President Donaldson Brown, one of the most reactionary of the DuPont executives on the GM board of directors, nevertheless endorsed the grievance arbitration system as a vehicle to dispose of those disputes that might otherwise be the "cause of continuing friction and annoyance." This was even more the view of Charles Wilson, the new GM president, who had assimilated many of the ideas of progressive personnel management when he worked at Westinghouse and Delco-Remy in the 1920s. Wilson further recognized that the maintenance of industrial discipline demanded a measure of employee consent. He accommodated the UAW demand for an umpire because he wanted to establish the legitimacy of "a new kind of thing in social relations, and that is an industrial crime" whose punishment would be seen as just not only by plant supervision, but by union officials and fellow workers alike.[39]

---

[37] "Management's Future in Labor Relations," UAW Research Department Collection, box 23, file "Walter Reuther—Unused Articles, 1948," ALHWSU.
[38] Heliker, "Grievance Arbitration," 172; McDermott interview with Dash, *Oral History Project,* 4.
[39] Donaldson Brown to William Harrington, 7 January 1941, box 35, Accession 1813 (Harrington Collection), Hagley Museum and Library; Transcript, National Defense Mediation Board, 6 May 1941, RG 202, NA, p. 629; E. Bruce Geelhoed, "Charles Erwin

Finally, some issues that the company saw as central to the maintenance of discipline or economic efficiency would simply not be subject
to umpire review. These included disputes over the speed of operations
or wage payments fixed in the collective bargaining agreement. The adjustment of piece rates and the determination of work norms had been
central to the umpire's duties in clothing, but at GM, disputes over these
issues could only be resolved by strike action authorized by the union.[40]

The grievance arbitration system at GM, and at the thousands of other
companies that would follow, therefore embodied two seemingly irreconcilable goals: a mechanism for defusing shop-floor conflict and ensuring the maintenance of industrial discipline, and a quasi-legal system that
unionists hoped would bring to the factory and mill the protections
available to citizens in civil society. The extent to which either of these
goals would be realized ultimately depended upon the general balance
of class forces in the larger society as well as upon the particularities of
the union-management and foreman-worker relationship at General Motors itself. But this did not mean that the grievance-arbitration setup at
GM had no impact on the system of industrial jurisprudence that emerged
at that corporation in the 1940s. In his *Whigs and Hunters*, E. P. Thompson argued that the "law mediated . . . class relations through legal forms,
which imposed, again and again, inhibitions upon the actions of the
rulers." Something of the same dynamic was at work in these GM shops,
for the system of arbitration-made case law served, again in Thompson's
words, as "a genuine forum within which certain kinds of class conflict
were fought out."[41] Thus the effort to structure the shop-floor struggle
into a system of quasi-legal rights and obligations had a powerful, and
initially quite advantageous, impact on the way many unionists conducted
their conflict with foremen and plant managers.

There were three reasons for this. First, any effort that forced management to codify a series of work rules curbed the capriciousness of
foremen and other management elements. Clear rules established a guide-
line by which well-organized workers could easily put plant officials on
the defensive. Second, the early auto industry umpires—Harry Millis and
George Taylor at GM, Harry Shulman at Ford, and Lloyd Garrison at
Allis-Chalmers—were men of high professional prestige and governmen-

Wilson," in George S. May, *The Automobile Industry, 1920–1980* (New York: Facts on
File, Inc., 1989), 481–490.
[40] Millis, ed., *How Collective Bargaining Works*, 607.
[41] E. P. Thompson, *Whigs and Hunters: The Origins of the Black Act* (New York: Oxford
University Press, 1975), 262, 265; see also Melvyn Dubofsky, "Legal Theory and Workers'
Rights: A Historian's Critique," *Industrial Relations Law Journal* 4 (1981): 496–502.

tal connections who came to their work with a good deal of the media-tionist and antijudicial social outlook they had deployed in needle trades labor relations. This was especially true of the Yale Law School's Harry Shulman. His brand of informal dispute resolution was particularly suited to the Ford Motor Company, whose highly factionalized work force and underdeveloped labor relations department made the kind of quasi-legal procedures practiced at GM impossible.[42] Finally, the wartime labor shortages, the need for uninterrupted production, and in the UAW, the intense competition for political advantage within the leadership, gave to many organized workers a considerable element of extracontractual shop-floor power. The sheer unpredictability of shop conflict, which grievance handling and arbitration schemes were in part designed to temper, helped create the environment that made the resultant set of newly minted work rules tilt against management's frontier of control.[43]

Starting in the fall of 1940, umpires Millis and Taylor both extended the web of rules governing the relationship between workers and foremen and simultaneously bent them in directions that union workers de-manded. Thus in one of his first rulings, Millis chipped away at what the UAW had long charged was GM's "remote control bargaining" strat-egy by forcing foremen to sign employee grievance slips, thus making it more difficult for them either to ignore these disputes or to pass the buck to higher levels of plant management. Shortly thereafter, Taylor criticized the "ineptitude of certain supervisors" and insisted GM executives make them adhere to the contract. Both Millis and Taylor ruled that manage-ment had no right to abrogate unilaterally "past work practices" if they had long been an uncontested part of the factory work routine. These early arbitrators also strengthened, in the name of what they considered good labor relations practice, the priority employment rights of shop committee members during layoffs; and in a later series of decisions, George Taylor demonstrated the unworkability of GM's harsh discipli-nary code, thereby forcing the company to cede to the umpire consid-erable discretion in assigning layoff penalties.[44]

[42] Slichter et al., *Impact of Collective Bargaining,* 777–81; Heliker, "Grievance Arbitration," 118–30. Millis was chair of the NLRB, Taylor and Garrison served on the WLB, and Shulman spent eleven years as umpire at Ford, where he became the nation's best known and most influential arbitrator.

[43] Lichtenstein, *Labor's War at Home: The CIO in World War II* (Cambridge: Cambridge University Press, 1983); see also Mike Davis, *Prisoners of the American Dream* (New York: Verso, 1986), 82–101.

[44] Harry Millis, General Motors Decision A–2, 28 October 1940, Decision A–6, 15 No-vember 1940, Decision A–7, 22 November 1940; George Taylor, General Motors De-cision A–13, 7 February 1941, Decision B–52, 22 June 1941, all in UAW-GM Decisions,

SENIORITY AND SHOP SOCIETY

The seniority question proved the most important shop-floor issue "litigated" through the grievance arbitration system. In the absence of a strong steward system at General Motors, the early UAW was determined to extend and codify the seniority principle, both to protect union activists from corporate discrimination during layoffs and to establish the principle that long-service workers had earned the moral right to keep their job or move up to a better one in their department or skill classification. Seniority was a key facet in the moral economy of American automobile workers. Both as an antidote against arbitrary personnel decisions and as a claim that long service gave workers a kind of property right in their job, seniority was a key index to union status and the reach of worker rights. Thus, in the March 1937 UAW-GM agreement seniority provisions took up fully 35 percent of the six-page text.[45]

General Motors conceded that seniority should cover the layoff and recall of workers during the annual model change: Such guidelines had been seen as an integral part of good personnel management even during the pre-union years. But the corporation was determined to limit the extent to which seniority governed the promotion or transfer of workers already on the job. Early UAW contracts at GM contained no guidelines that might cover such movement of workers from one job to another. But in the decade after 1940, this issue would be fought over and over again in every contract negotiation and in many special conferences and arbitrations. GM argued that if seniority determined who got higher-paying or more pleasant jobs as they came open, demoralization would set in among lower-level supervisors, and management would lose the "flexibility" needed to run the shop. Management insisted, in the language of the 1940 contract, that seniority must remain "secondary" to the "merit, ability or capacity" of an employee. GM would try to accommodate an employee's wishes in the administration of its promotion and transfer policy, but as to management's prerogative to assign work, "when the chips are down in a given situation, one of the parties either has a right or does not have it. There is no middle ground."[46]

NDMB, box 21, RG 202, NA; see also Heliker, "Grievance Arbitration," 156–64, 301–303.

[45] Carl Gersuny and Gladis Kaufman, "Seniority and the Moral Economy of the U.S. Automobile Workers, 1934–1946," *Journal of Social History* 18 (Spring 1985): 467.

[46] "GM Presentation on Paragraph 63," in Negotiations with the UAW–1955, Vertical File, General Motors Institute, Flint, Michigan.

But unionists were equally convinced that all of GM's talk about the need for individual initiative and flexibility was just a cover for the company's determination to restore the foreman's pre-union power to intimidate his work crew and reward pro-company workers with the best job assignments. When the National Defense Mediation Board reviewed the UAW-GM contract in the spring of 1941, it recognized that "the transferring of employees is the sole responsibility of management"; but in the case of permanent promotions to new, usually higher paid jobs, "when ability, merit and capacity are equal, employees with the longest seniority will be given preference."[47]

UAW committeemen took this language and used it to protest every time a foreman promoted any worker out of the line of strict seniority. Wildcat strikes and job actions are often seen as characteristic of wartime militancy, but these were the years when an extraordinarily large number of grievances were also filed: more than one hundred thousand annually of which about one thousand reached the umpire.[48] By pressing thousands of grievances on this issue and presenting scores of arbitration cases, the union gradually reshaped the meaning of this ambiguous language. In an important decision, umpire George Taylor declared that the company had to prove that an individual was "head and shoulders" above all others before he could be promoted out of line of seniority. This effectively shifted the burden of proof from the union to the company, made seniority the norm in most promotions, and established a new work rule at GM that was destined to last for many years.[49]

But before one is left with the impression that vigorous grievance bargaining was capable of an unlimited shift in the frontier of shop-floor job control, we must explore even further the union's effort to define and expand seniority rights. The UAW wanted seniority to govern not only promotions to new job classifications but the transfer of employees to new assignments within an existing department or classification. The distinction was crucial, for it struck at the heart of management authority in the workplace. Promotions to new job classifications were relatively infrequent, but foremen transferred workers from one job assignment to another scores of times, sometimes on an hourly or daily basis. GM felt

---

[47] Ralph Seward, *Decisions of the Impartial Umpire Under the March 19, 1946, Agreement Between GM and the UAW* (Detroit: UAW, 1950), 93–94.
[48] Transcript, National War Labor Board Panel, UAW-GM Case No. 111–4665-D, 4 January 1944, 235, RG 202, NA, p. 235.
[49] McDermott interview with Dash, *Oral History Project,* 15; Heliker, "Grievance Arbitration," 174.

its foremen must remain unconstrained in their ability to shift workers about; while UAW committee members and higher UAW officials were just as determined to make this authority subject to seniority guidelines as well. Reuther made this clear in 1944 when he told a War Labor Board panel: "We know that unless you have rules to govern the relationship of people, both Labor and Management, on the lower levels in the Agreement, unless these rules are explicit, you will revert back to where they pick this guy, not because he has potential, but because he lets the foreman run over him."[50]

Aside from the issue of company discipline against wildcat strikers, the question of seniority rights in promotions and transfers proved the single most contentious shop issue in the UAW-GM relationship during the 1940s. The dispute may well have held up settlement of the great 1945–46 GM strike for as much as a month; an only slightly modified version of the paragraph covering this issue was finally slipped into the contract at 2:25 A.M., just hours before negotiators announced a national strike settlement on March 13.[51]

But the question of what constituted a transfer remained unresolved. GM wanted transfers defined as only those changes that involved the movement of an employee from one department or wage classification to another; but the union argued that a transfer covered any basic change in an employee's job assignment and that employees might not only apply for vacancies in other wage classifications or departments but also for vacancies on specific machines or operations in their own classification. The distinction was important because a worker had job bidding rights if the change of work involved a transfer, but if he or she merely sought a change of job assignment within an already established classification, the employee was subject to the foreman's authority. To the outsider, such distinctions might seem esoteric, but for many GM workers, they constituted the difference between "freedom and servility."[52]

In early 1947, an important series of umpire rulings essentially confirmed General Motors' interpretation of this crucial distinction, and although the UAW made a vigorous effort to expand seniority rights in

[50]Transcript, National War Labor Board, 4 January 1944, UAW-GM Case No. 111–4665-D, pp. 291–92.
[51]Ed Lahey, "One Issue Bars GM Peace," *Detroit Free Press,* 18 February 1946; "Paragraph 63," box 23, file 11, Walter Reuther Collection, ALHWSU.
[52]Seward, *Decisions of the Impartial Umpire,* 93–94; author's interview with Irving Bluestone, former UAW vice-president, 25 October 1987, Detroit.

the 1948, 1950, and 1955 negotiations, the union got nowhere.[53] The rightward drift of American politics, the gradual routinization of labor-capital conflict, and the firm-centered character of postwar collective bargaining ensured that the decade-long erosion of GM's "right to manage" would turn into a stalemate on the seniority issue, as on so many others involving distribution of power and right in the early postwar era. As an element in an emerging system of industrial jurisprudence, the shop-floor balance between the seniority rights of workers and the prerogatives of foremen remained frozen for a quarter century and more, until the management effort to reorganize the auto factory work regime in the 1980s once again put the seniority question in contention.[54]

THE POSTWAR STALEMATE

This stalemate had important structural consequences both for the union and for the industry. Within the UAW, Reuther and other officers began to manage directly the grievance arbitration process, initially because of the sheer volume of umpire decisions, but later in order to make sure that the union lost no cases of potentially unfavorable consequence. During the war, the UAW set up a board of high union officials to review all fourth-step grievance cases, determining which should be dropped and which should be appealed to the umpire. The board eliminated those grievances—often more than half—whose rejection by the umpire might set an adverse precedent, but this new administrative apparatus was also a highly effective bureaucratic filter that generated even greater distance between American automobile workers and the world of industrial justice they sought to win. The review board and the union's arbitration staff soon became a lightning rod for rank-and-file discontent, and on at least one occasion, Reuther fired a top official to accommodate the complaints from below.[55]

The result was a kind of dehydration of the dispute-resolution machinery. The number of arbitration decisions handled by the GM umpire declined dramatically, from more than two hundred a year in the mid-

---

[53] "General Motors Reply to Union Demand to Amend Paragraph 63 on Transfers," in UAW-GM 1955 Negotiations, Vertical File, General Motors Institute, Flint, Michigan.
[54] See generally Howell Harris, *The Right to Manage: Industrial Relations Policies of American Business in the 1940s* (Madison: University of Wisconsin Press, 1982); and Harry Katz, *Shifting Gears: Changing Labor Relations in the U.S. Automobile Industry* (Cambridge, Mass.: MIT Press, 1985).
[55] George Heliker interview with Thomas A. Johnstone, 19 February 1954, ACC 940.5, Ford Archives, Dearborn, Mich.; Lichtenstein interview with Irving Bluestone.

1940s to about forty annually in the late 1950s. Although the volume of grievance activity increased about tenfold between 1947 and 1980, the proportion of grievances that ended up at the umpire stage declined by more than 96 percent. The precedents had all been set, and shop disputes were now handled at the lowest step of the grievance procedure, the level of foreman-worker interaction. The proportion of grievances settled by the UAW's local bargaining committees and the plant management, or by higher-level union officials and the corporate personnel department, declined rather dramatically after the mid-1950s.[56]

These patterns reflected the high level of shop-floor tension that existed during the relatively prosperous epoch that spanned the twenty-five years after the end of World War II. This became quite clear in two membership surveys that the UAW authorized in 1961 and 1967. In general, autoworkers held a strongly favorable impression of their union, and they backed the UAW's then-current efforts to secure higher wages and fringe benefits and greater protection against layoffs and short workweeks. They valued the UAW International as a wage-setting and welfare institution. However, when it came to an assessment of the union on the local level, workers were far more critical. While two-thirds of all production workers held a favorable impression of the International, only about half thought the same of their local union or their shop committee representative. When asked if they thought their committeeman was a "stand up guy who protects the workers," only about 16 percent answered in the affirmative in 1967. Workers approved of strikes called over work loads and local issues to a greater degree than those called over the national contract, but they were also more likely to think the handling of such strikes "only fair" or "poor."[57]

The stalemate that enveloped grievance bargaining at General Motors also had important long-range consequences for the rest of the auto industry and the labor relations that evolved there. Because of its sheer market dominance, as well as the systematic elaboration of its labor relations program, General Motors seemed the model upon which others in heavy industry must either mold their internal work regime or face extinction. A number of smaller firms, whose system of shop governance retained much of the flavor of the late 1930s, either went out of business

[56] Alexander, "The General Motors–UAW Experience," 117–33; author's interview with Irving Bluestone.
[57] Oliver Quayle and Co., "A Study in Depth of the Rank and File of the UAW: May 1967," box 147, Walter Reuther Collection, ALHWSU.

or merged with larger firms in the 1950s when competitive conditions returned to the auto industry in that decade. A strong shop steward structure and a flexible system of shop governance had continued at Studebaker, Packard, Kaiser-Fraser, Murray Body, Graham-Paige, and Briggs well into the postwar years, but none of these firms survived the 1950s as an independent entity.[58]

Ford, Chrysler, and Allis-Chalmers remained intact, but all three of these big firms brought their system of industrial jurisprudence more closely into line with that of GM. In a bitter eleven-month strike in the aftermath of World War II, Allis-Chalmers directly confronted its twelve thousand member work force, broke the local union, and destroyed the shop steward system. Ford and Chrysler traveled something of the same road but in a less dramatically confrontational fashion. The management of both companies copied GM's labor relations program, Ford in the late 1940s and Chrysler a decade later. In several instances, they hired GM managers away from the giant automaker to implement this program.

For its part, the leadership of the UAW saw little alternative to the transformation of all auto industry labor relations so that they followed GM's "firm but fair" standard. Throughout the 1950s and early 1960s, the union fostered a subtle brand of concession bargaining at many of GM's competitors. Wages and benefits were usually sustained at the Big Three pattern, but the UAW thought economic collapse of these rivals could best be avoided if the work rules and grievance-handling traditions embedded in the factory work regime were made more uniform with those at cost-efficient GM. Thus when Studebaker and Chrysler sought a radical transformation of their work rules and a reduction in the power of the shop stewards, Reuther and other top UAW leaders acquiesced, although this policy sometimes brought political tensions between locals at these companies and the International to the boiling point.[59]

CONCLUSION

This exploration of automobile industry union-management relations may offer some insight into why the idea of an emerging industrial jur-

---

[58] Robert McDonald, *Collective Bargaining in the Automobile Industry: A Study in Wage Structure and Competitive Relations* (New Haven: Yale University Press, 1963), 143–239 passim; Amberg, "The Triumph of Industrial Orthodoxy."

[59] Jefferys, *Management and Managed,* 127–45; McDonald, *Collective Bargaining,* 276–88; Katz, *Shifting Gears,* 14–38.

isprudence found no place in Summer Slichter's 1960 survey of American industrial relations. By then, grievance arbitration was an exceedingly well-entrenched and near-universal institution, and at that very moment, was being given an elaborate judicial codification. But the hope that such a system would have the capacity to generate a new and universally accepted set of workplace rights had foundered upon the inequitable structures of power that governed the relationship between managers and workers in postwar America. To Slichter and his colleagues, General Motors seemed to represent a solid, stable future upon which the whole industrial world would eventually remold itself. Meanwhile, the experimentation of the interwar period was long forgotten. The unionized hosiery industry had virtually collapsed, the needle trades were in a slow decline, and the big industrial unions captured public attention only when one of their periodic strikes established a new and higher pattern wage scale for the core sectors of the economy.

The industrial stability of those postwar years is now well behind us. To the extent that an industrial jurisprudence exists today, in the form of laws banning racial and sex discrimination and ordaining workplace health and safety standards, it is being advanced by state mandate, not private contract. Increasingly, large sectors of the economy have come to resemble those unstable, intensely competitive industries that were once thought anachronistic in the modern industrial economy. And the decline of U.S. unionism has proved collective bargaining a far more contingent social phenomenon than any observer in the 1960s might have expected.

Yet rigid, hierarchical managerial structures have never been in greater disrepute, less because of the challenge from below than as a consequence of the powerful competitive threat from abroad. The willing participation of American workers, if not their unions, in the renaissance of American productivity is a central concern of management thought. Thus, the language of participation, teamwork, and even industrial democracy has again achieved a common currency, even if much contemporary rhetoric has an ersatz quality.[60] Still, the ideological complacency and organizational stolidity that did so much to subvert the promise inherent in the

---

[60]Steven Fraser, "Industrial Democracy in the 1980s," *Socialist Review* 74 (1983): 99–122; Mike Parker and Jane Slaughter, *Choosing Sides: Unions and the Team Concept* (Boston: South End Press, 1988); and see Parker's chapter in this volume.

idea of an industrial jurisprudence have been shattered; in this we may find some hope that the rights-conscious citizenship that was the most valuable legacy of early twentieth-century conceptions of American industrial democracy may yet be rediscovered.

7

Wartime labor regulation, the industrial
pluralists, and the law of collective bargaining

JAMES B. ATLESON

Since the end of World War II, labor relations theory and the law of
collective bargaining have been closely intertwined. Both systems are
premised upon the stabilizing influence of unions, collective bargaining,
and arbitration. Yet, as Ronald Schatz notes in this volume, the industrial
and economic convolutions of the past decade have created a crisis in
the once unchallenged orthodoxy that has until recently constituted industrial relations thought.

A loose-knit group of postwar scholars and practitioners, who might
well be characterized as "industrial pluralists," are largely responsible
for the body of rules regulating collective bargaining, as well as the
supportive vision of industrial relations.[1] This group developed a set of
assumptions about the necessary legal structure of collective bargaining,
its regulation, and the appropriate forms of dispute resolution, which
has been clearly reflected in the Supreme Court decisions of the late 1950s
and 1960s. In this period, the federal judiciary for the first time defined

The preparation of this chapter has been supported by a fellowship from the National
Endowment for the Humanities and a research grant from the State University of New
York at Buffalo. I thank the many who read and commented on various drafts, especially
Fred Konefsky, Nelson Lichtenstein, Katherine Stone, and Clyde Summers. I also wish to
express heartfelt appreciation to David Woods, class of 1988, and to Joyce Farrell for their
assistance.

[1]See Katherine Von Wezel Stone, "The Post-War Paradigm in American Labor Law," *Yale
Law Journal* 90 (1981): 1509–80; Staughton Lynd, "Government Without Rights: The
Labor Law Vision of Archibald Cox," *Industrial Relations Law Journal* 4 (1981): 483;
Howell John Harris, "The Snares of Liberalism? Politicians, Bureaucrats, and the Shaping
of Federal Labour Relations Policy in the United States, ca. 1915–1947," in Steven Tolliday
and Jonathan Zeitlin, eds., *Shop Floor Bargaining and the State* (Cambridge: Cambridge
University Press, 1985).

the legal structure of collective bargaining, creating a system dominated by the promotion of arbitral settlement of contract disputes and the discouragement of collective action.[2]

Industrial pluralist thought had much in common with consensus theories in other disciplines in the 1940s and 1950s, combining a search for peaceful dispute resolution mechanisms with a reluctance to discuss existing imbalances in power or issues of class. The industrial pluralists focused upon the creation of legal rules and administrative processes to resolve workplace conflicts. The predominant device, however, was to be arbitration, a private mechanism that could supplant self-help, judicial intervention, or administrative regulation. The pluralists desired to humanize and regularize the workplace, transforming "the anarchy of the marketplace, which exploited workers, into the harmony of a 'modern' cooperative capitalism, which protected workers."[3] The views of the pluralists themselves can perhaps be traced to the Wisconsin school and John Commons and also to prewar theories of efficient, administrative resolution of industrial relations problems.[4]

Many of the pluralists were in government positions during World War II, a period in which it was critical to find efficient systems for the resolution of labor disputes that would serve as alternatives to strikes. Labor lawyers and economists, often very young and sometimes just out

[2] The Supreme Court in *Textile Workers v. Lincoln Mills,* for instance, cites Archibald Cox, "Grievance Arbitration in the Federal Courts," *Harvard Law Review* 67 (1954): 602–4, to support its conclusion that the Norris-LaGuardia Act does not bar specific enforcement of the arbitration clause. In the famous trilogy of arbitration decisions in 1960, Cox is cited in two cases and Harry Shulman is cited in *United Steelworkers v. Warrior and Gulf Navigation,* 363 U.S. 574, 578–9, 579 n. 6, 581, 583 n. 7 (1960). See also, *United Steelworkers v. American Manufacturing,* 363 U.S. 564, 568 n. 6 (1960).

[3] Melvyn Dubofsky, "Legal Theory and Workers' Rights: A Historian's Critique," *Industrial Relations Law Journal* 4 (1981): 497. The pluralists' relationship to the government-liberal tradition embodied by Senator Robert Wagner has not been studied. Both groups believed in a government framework for private action, although the Wagner Act focused upon bargaining, not contract administration. See Daniel Sipe, "A Moment of the State: The Enactment of the National Labor Relations Act, 1935" (Ph.D. diss., University of Pennsylvania, 1981); Stanley Vittoz, *New Deal Labor Policy and the American Industrial Economy* (Chapel Hill: University of North Carolina Press, 1987); Theda Skocpol, "Political Response to Capitalist Crises: Neo-Marxist Theories of the State and the Case of the New Deal," *Politics and Society* 10 (1980): 155–201; Peter Irons, *The New Deal Lawyers* (Princeton: Princeton University Press, 1982).

[4] As Steven Fraser has shown, the current system looks very much like that created by Sidney Hillman's garment workers' union in the 1920s, except for the present supportive legal apparatus. Steven Fraser, "Dress Rehearsal for the New Deal: Shop-Floor Insurgents, Political Elites, and Industrial Democracy in the Amalgamated Clothing Workers," in Michael Frisch and Daniel Walkowitz, eds., *Working-Class America* (Champaign: University of Illinois Press, 1983), 212.

of college, supplied the demand for wartime specialists. The first public members of agencies such as the National War Labor Board were skilled in mediation and arbitration. As characterized by Howell Harris:

> They were liberal pluralists, committed to the development of a labor relations system in which the triple objectives of efficiency, order, and representative democracy could be reconciled. They believed in the Wagner Act's legislative philosophy, and in strong, responsible unions as agents for its implementation. They preferred to see industrial disputes settled in decentralized, voluntarist negotiations between the parties rather than on terms imposed by the state from the center, or unilaterally determined by employers.[5]

One of the War Labor Board's most important and enduring contributions was the development of a group of experienced arbitrators who profoundly affected postwar labor law and practice. As Edwin Witte noted in 1952, the "great majority of the labor arbitrators of the present day gained their first direct experience in service on the staff of the War Labor Board or on its disputes panels."[6] With much justification, a speaker at an early meeting of the National Academy of Arbitrators greeted his audience as the "War Labor Board Alumni Association."[7]

The academy's first president, Ralph T. Seward, for instance, had been executive secretary of the National Defense Mediation Board and a public member of its successor, the War Labor Board. In 1944, he became the impartial umpire for General Motors and the UAW. William Simkin, one of the academy's vice-presidents, had been chair of the Shipbuilding Commission and associate member of the War Labor Board. The academy's original Board of Governors was also filled with veterans of wartime Washington. Although not active in the formation of the National Academy of Arbitrators, George W. Taylor often spoke at early meetings and helped draft the code of ethics eventually accepted by the academy as well as the American Arbitration Association and the Federal Mediation and Conciliation Service.

Other influential scholars and writers who gained experience in the wartime agency were Benjamin Aaron, David L. Cole, G. Allan Dash, Alex Elson, Nathan E. Finesinger, Jesse Freidin, Alexander H. Frey, Sylvester S. Garrett, Jr., Lloyd Garrison, Lewis M. Gill, James J. Healy,

---

[5] Howell Harris, *The Right to Manage: Industrial Relations Policies of American Business in the 1940s* (Madison: University of Wisconsin Press, 1982), 49.
[6] Edwin Witte, quoted in Roger Abrams and Dennis Nolan, "American Labor Arbitration: The Maturing Years," *Florida Law Review* 35 (1983): 577.
[7] Charles Killingsworth, "The Chronicle," *Journal of the National Academy of Arbitrators* (February 1988): 5.

Theodore W. Kheel, Thomas E. Larkin, Eli Rock, Peter Seitz, Ralph T. Seward, Harry Shulman, William E. Simkin, George W. Taylor, and W. Willard Wirtz. In addition, WLB staff positions were filled with people who would become influential in labor history, economics, and labor relations, such as E. Wright Bakke, Douglas V. Brown, John T. Dunlop, George H. Hildebrand, Louis Jaffe, Vernon H. Jenson, Clark Kerr, Richard Lester, E. Robert Livernash, Lester B. Orfield, Sumner H. Slichter, Edwin H. Witte, and Dale Yoder.[8]

Their government experience during the war stressed productivity and the critical need for labor peace, profoundly shaping their views on arbitration and collective bargaining. This group, who would become influential postwar writers and practitioners of labor law and labor relations as well as arbitrators, is the crucial link that explains why the current law of collective bargaining mirrors the web of rules created by the War Labor Board.

This essay focuses on two areas of War Labor Board jurisprudence and their current parallels. The first area concerns the administration and enforcement of collective agreements; the second deals with the range of subjects falling within the scope of mandatory bargaining under the National Labor Relations Act. Prior to the Taft-Hartley Act of 1947, there was little federal law defining collective bargaining or the means by which agreements could be enforced.[9] The Wagner Act of 1935 required employers to bargain in good faith, and the Supreme Court had made collective agreements predominant over individual contracts of employment.[10] The Wagner Act, however, did not focus on dispute resolution,

---

[8] These individuals are listed in the *National War Labor Board Termination Report*, vol. 1 (Washington, D.C.: Government Printing Office, 1947):2–46; *War Labor Reports* 6 (1943): 24; *War Labor Reports* 7 (1943): 26. This listing omits those who served with other wartime agencies such as the Office of Price Administration and the War Production Board.

[9] The 1937–41 period was too brief for a significant body of NLRA law to develop. In one significant case, however, the Supreme Court had held that strikes in breach of contract would be unprotected by NLRA Section 7, but the Court assumed it had the power to interpret the agreement. See *NLRB v. Sands Manufacturing Co.*, 306 U.S. 332 (1939); Karl Klare, "Judicial Deradicalization of the Wagner Act and the Origins of Modern Legal Consciousness, 1937–1941," *Minnesota Law Review* 62 (1978): 303. The union had sought to enforce its interpretation of the agreement, announcing that employees would not work unless this view was upheld. The Court interpreted the agreement to favor the employer's contractual position; thus, the workers "were irrevocably committed not to work in accordance with their contract" (306 U.S. at 344). Such a "repudiation" by employees of the agreement was deemed a severance of their employment. The decision suggests that the Court would be no less hostile to self-help when an arbitration procedure was present.

[10] *J. I. Case Co. v. NLRB*, 321 U.S. 332 (1944).

and certainly not on arbitration, except for its general encouragement of collective bargaining. The administration and enforcement of collective agreements were necessarily left to the vagaries of state law.

State courts, however, had initially encountered difficulty envisioning collective bargaining agreements as enforceable contracts or unions as proper vindicators of employment rights. Although some courts began to enforce agreements against employers in the 1920s and 1930s, belatedly paralleling the traditional willingness to enjoin breaches of contract by unions or to enjoin strikes, promises to arbitrate were not enforceable in most states.[11] Since the enactment of the Taft-Hartley Act in 1947, however, one of the most creative and vital areas of federal labor policy has concerned the contractual relationship of employers and unions, and the views of the judiciary have been profoundly affected by the writings of the pluralists. Section 301 of this statute permits unions and employers, and employees as well, to bring actions in federal court to enforce collective agreements. To find the statute constitutional, the Supreme Court was moved to hold that federal courts were empowered to create substantive law, that is, judicially created policies that would define the nature of "mature" collective bargaining agreements, their methods of enforcement, and the remedies for breach.[12]

At the same time, the War Labor Board would adopt a restrictive view of the scope of mandatory bargaining, that is, the subjects upon which employers were legally compelled to bargain. Although the postwar National Labor Relations Board would adopt a less limited view of such bargaining, the notion that a vague zone of managerial exclusivity existed stems from several key War Labor Board decisions.

THE WAR LABOR BOARD

American entry into the war made necessary a major expansion of the federal role in labor-management relations. Six days after the Japanese attack on Pearl Harbor, President Roosevelt issued a call for a conference of representatives of labor and management. In issuing the proclamation convening the conference, the president declared that he desired speed,

[11]See, generally, James Atleson, "The Circle of *Boys Market*: A Comment on Judicial Inventiveness," *Industrial Relations Law Journal* 7 (1985): 88; Katherine Stone, "The Post-war Paradigm," 1518–21.
[12]Federal courts under Article 2 of the Constitution only have authority to enforce rights under federal statutes and the Constitution. Generally, federal courts cannot be given jurisdiction to enforce rights that do not arise from these sources.

a complete agreement that all wartime disputes would be settled peacefully, and a no-strike pledge.[13] The conference responded by recommending the creation of a war labor board having jurisdiction over all issues, although no agreement was reached on the politically charged union security issue.[14]

Union leaders independently acted to grant no-strike promises. Immediately after Pearl Harbor, for instance, William Green called a special session of the American Federation of Labor's executive council, which determined "that a 'no-strike' policy shall be applied in all war and defense material production industries." A meeting of representatives from all the AFL unions endorsed the statement, urging that no repressive legislation should be passed and, ironically, that the right to strike as a last resort weapon be safeguarded. Similarly, the Congress of Industrial Organizations pledged its assistance in achieving "all-out production for the national defense," but cautioned that it would defend the "material interests of the working people and their democratic rights."[15] Theoretically a voluntary surrender of labor's most important right, the no-strike pledge was deemed compulsory by the government, even for unions that were not represented at the 1941 labor-management conference.[16]

The National War Labor Board was formally created on 12 January 1942, in a tersely worded Executive Order 9017.[17] The board was to be composed of twelve members, of whom four each would represent respectively labor, management, and the public. William Davis, the former chair of the National Defense Mediation Board, was named chair of the National War Labor Board. The other public members were George W. Taylor, Frank P. Graham, and Wayne L. Morse.

If a dispute threatened to interrupt work related to war production,

---

[13] Fred Witney, *Wartime Experiences of the National Labor Relations Board* (Urbana: University of Illinois Press, 1949), 118.

[14] The president accepted the conference's agreement and short-circuited the issue by interpreting the conference report as meaning that "all disputes," including the union shop controversy, were within the jurisdiction of the National War Labor Board. Witney, *Wartime Experiences of the National Labor Relations Board*, 118–19; Joel Seidman, *American Labor from Defense to Reconversion* (Chicago: University of Chicago Press, 1953), 80–81.

[15] *CIO News*, 15 December 1941; Seidman, *American Labor from Defense to Reconversion*, 78–79.

[16] Harris, *The Right to Manage*, 47. According to Martin Glaberman, no union consulted its membership in advance or after. M. Glaberman, *Wartime Strikes: The Struggle against the No-Strike Pledge in the UAW During World War II* (Detroit: Bewick Editions, 1980), 4–5.

[17] See *NWLB Termination Report* 2:49.

the Department of Labor could certify the case to the War Labor Board if it could not be resolved by its own conciliation service.[18] Once the board assumed jurisdiction, its powers were all-encompassing. The board was empowered to reach a final settlement of any labor dispute that might interrupt work that "contributes to the effective prosecution of the war." Unlike the National Labor Relations Board, the War Labor Board's responsibility extended to the actual settlement of disputes by "mediation, voluntary arbitration, or arbitration." Under the 1943 War Labor Disputes Act, for instance, the War Labor Board had the power "to decide the dispute and provide by order the wages and hours and all other terms and conditions (customarily included in collective bargaining agreements) governing the relations between the parties" and to "provide for terms and conditions to govern relations between the parties which are to be fair and equitable between an employer and an employee under all the circumstances of the case."[19]

Thus, the National War Labor Board largely determined the wartime terms of employment in American industry. In its first three years, the WLB decided fourteen thousand dispute cases, affecting a majority of the organized workers in the country. There were twenty-five occasions when government seizure was invoked to enforce compliance. In thirty-one cases, the board called on the president for enforcement action; seventeen involved union defiance and fourteen employer refusal. In four cases, the workers backed down; in one, the employer retreated before the president acted.[20] Not only was a firm foundation created for the CIO, but wartime regulation had permanent consequences for mass production unionism. As historian Nelson Lichtenstein has noted, "It was the specific social and political context of World War II that created the institutional framework for the kind of collective bargaining that evolved in the decade or so after the war."[21] The National War Labor Board helped in setting industry-wide wage patterns, legitimized fringe-benefit bargaining, encouraged arbitration as a method of resolving contractual disputes, and influenced the internal structure and role of new unions, primarily through the grant of union security clauses.

[18] Executive Order 9017, 3 C.F.R. 1075 (1938–43 compilation).
[19] Public Law No. 89, 59 Stat. 163 (1943). The statute was commonly referred to as the Smith-Connally Act.
[20] See Aaron Levenstein, *Labor Today and Tomorrow* (New York: A. Knopf, 1946), 53, 102.
[21] Nelson Lichtenstein, "Industrial Democracy, Contract Unionism and the National War Labor Board," *Labor Law Journal* (August 1982): 524.

World War II required unprecedented efforts to maintain and stimulate production. The War Labor Board believed:

Maximum production during the war is a duty; the duty is not discharged when production is impaired by lowered morale or strikes caused by the failure to settle grievances. The duty to achieve and maintain production implies, therefore, the establishment of grievance procedures and the prompt settlement of grievances according to that procedure.[22]

Labor arbitration, backed by federal support, required stable unions, both to effectuate such procedures and to contain rank-and-file militance. World War II, therefore, provided a rational basis for stressing bureaucratic dispute resolution, the restriction of midterm strikes, and union control over rank-and-file action. More broadly, the war itself affected the way Americans viewed labor, and those images remained after the war. After the emergency ended, the "needs of the peacetime economy" replaced the requirements of war, and federal policy continued to be based upon increased and continuous production and the stability of labor relations as well as unions.

The underlying themes of contemporary law were not, of course, exclusively created in wartime, for many of the underlying values in American labor law long predate federal statutes.[23] The war, however, helped to create, encourage, or cement visions of the proper labor-management system and the appropriate role of the state. The War Labor Board helped advance a definition of industrial democracy exclusively in process terms—outcomes or fairness were to be irrelevant. Postwar labor law has proceeded in a similar fashion.[24] In addition, the Supreme Court in the postwar period has, like the War Labor Board, repeatedly demonstrated its opposition to collective action or self-help in the resolution of labor disputes.[25] This concern is especially reflected in cases where "private" and "peaceful" avenues of resolution, such as arbitration, exist. The result is a set of rules that protects the "integrity" of arbitration, permitting the institution to carry out federal policy and making the

[22] "Instructions to Regional War Labor Boards: Importance of Grievance Machinery," *War Labor Reports* 9 (1944): 24–25 (National War Labor Board Memorandum Release, issued 24 July 1943).
[23] See, generally, James Atleson, *Values and Assumptions in American Labor Law* (Amherst: University of Massachusetts Press, 1983).
[24] Karl Klare, "Labor Law and Liberal Political Imagination," in David Kairys, ed., *The Politics of Law* (New York: Pantheon, 1982), 60–61.
[25] Ibid., 51; Atleson, *Values and Assumptions in American Labor Law*, chapter 3.

intentions of parties less important than the language of contractualism might initially suggest.

THE WAR LABOR BOARD AND
THE POSTWAR LAW OF ARBITRATION

Although grievance procedures and arbitration clauses were included in some prewar collective bargaining agreements,[26] and may well have flourished even without the strong encouragement of the War Labor Board, "it was left to the War Labor Board to convince American industry and labor that here was an indispensable tool to 'make collective bargaining work.' "[27] As the WLB *Termination Report* put it in 1947:

> The basis for the national war labor policy in America today is still the voluntary agreement between the responsible leaders of labor and industry that there be no strikes or lockouts for the duration of the war. All labor disputes, including grievances, therefore, must be settled by peaceful means.[28]

The War Labor Board stressed the indispensable value of this dispute-resolution process, refined its structure and scope, forced the system on unwilling employers, and provided rules for legal enforcement that would eventually be adopted by the Supreme Court almost twenty years later.

Even without government encouragement, grievance procedures provided advantages for unions and employers. Although employers generally resisted arbitration both before and during the war, arbitral systems provided an orderly means to resolve contractual disputes, discouraging strikes or other job actions, and they also served to enforce a system of rules for both employees and managerial personnel. A system of rules was important for unions as well because employees have historically objected to arbitrary supervisory behavior. Unions also found it valuable to have a means that avoided the constant need to consider strikes over every dispute. As Sidney Lens so persuasively argued forty years ago, arbitration procedures were not necessarily reflective of a loss of union power. Unions could not strike over every dispute, and a grievance pro-

---

[26] Sylvester Garrett, "Resolving the Tension: Arbitration Confronts the External Legal System," *Case Western Reserve Law Review* 39 (1988–89): 557; Dennis Nolan and Roger Abrams, "American Labor Arbitration: The Maturing Years," *University of Florida Law Review* 35 (1983): 575–77.

[27] Paul Fisher, "The National War Labor Board and Post-War Industrial Relations," *Quarterly Journal of Economics* 59 (August 1945): 505. See also, Benjamin Aaron, "Catalyst: The National War Labor Board of World War II," *Case Western Reserve Law Review* 39 (1988–89): 519.

[28] *NWLB Termination Report* 1 (1947): 65.

cedure offered an "opportunity for realignment of forces, for fencing, minor skirmishing, for strengthening of positions." A well-operating and effective grievance procedure, therefore, continued membership support during the life of a contract. "The grievance procedure in actual practice is used as a weapon . . . as a way to muster strength for class warfare."[29] The existence of arbitration procedures also could shield union leadership from the constant pressure to take or support workplace action, a consideration that helped explain the support for arbitration by unions such as the UAW even before the war.

Grievance procedures also tend to centralize dispute resolution in the union hierarchy, not in the affected work group, and the union generally controls the decision to initiate grievances and how far to pursue them.[30] Indeed, the multitiered grievance process exactly mirrors the hierarchies of both employer and union. Unions, however, defended institutional control as democratic because the representative of the employees controlled the dispute, and arbitration would serve as a judicial-like restraint upon managerial excess. This argument nicely meshes with the view of industrial democracy held by the War Labor Board and the postwar Supreme Court, focusing less on worker participation and influence than on routine and peaceful processing of grievances.[31] Notions of hierarchy and control were embedded in this view of industrial democracy, since, given the policies of international officials, independent rank-and-file action or wildcat strikes could be seen as undemocratic.[32]

It is difficult to plot precisely the development of the War Labor Board's views on arbitration, and perhaps it is misleading to try to rationalize its actions based upon the random flow of cases. From the beginning, the board set up arbitration panels to decide specific cases, generally appointing the arbitrator.[33] Early decisions merely encouraged

---

[29] Sidney Lens, "Meaning of the Grievance Procedure," *Harvard Business Review* 26 (1948): 713.

[30] The board permitted individuals to file grievances at the first step, but after that, the union was to participate in the settlement. *NWLB Termination Report* 1:113–45.

[31] Thus, as Nelson Lichtenstein notes, the United Steelworkers of America would be called "democratic" by the War Labor Board despite its top-down form of organization, primarily because it was cooperative with the policies of the administration. Nelson Lichtenstein, *Labor's War at Home* (Cambridge: Cambridge University Press, 1982), 181.

[32] The board sometimes instructed international officials to investigate local officials and impose fines on wildcatters. Chrysler Corp., *War Labor Reports* 10 (1943): 553. See also, Lichtenstein, *Labor's War at Home*, 180–82.

[33] See, for example, New York Telephone Co. *War Labor Reports* 1 (1942): 259; Willamette Valley Lumber Operators, 1 *War Labor Reports* 151 (1942); Steel Drop Forge Group, *War Labor Reports* 1 (1942): 22.

the parties to accept voluntarily arbitration clauses for future disputes.[34]
Unions that had voluntarily surrendered the right to strike had an especially critical need to find a means to hold employers to their promises
and, after 1943, the board often imposed arbitration clauses[35] because
outsiders would decide matters within the proper control of management.
The board's public members noted that "grievance procedures without
eventual arbitration is a one-sided affair." The absence of arbitration
systems "does not assure the employees of any settlement except on the
company's terms and in that respect it invites labor trouble."[36]

The structure of arbitration advocated by the War Labor Board
strongly resembled arbitral systems established in the hosiery and clothing
industry by the Amalgamated Clothing Workers union in the 1920s.
George W. Taylor, the vice-chair of the War Labor Board, had been
heavily influenced by the experience of the needle trades.[37] In a chronically
unstable industry, the union and larger manufacturers strove to control
the anarchy caused by both the market and the mass of small entrepre-
neurs by instituting procedures that would permit advanced planning.
The hosiery experience was influential in a variety of ways. For instance,
a General Motors representative observed hosiery arbitrations prior to
the creation of the General Motors–United Automobile Workers arbitral
arrangement. General Motors, however, insisted upon a more restrictive
umpireship, in which decisions were to be based upon evidence submitted
in a formal hearing and on the basis of contractual language. Its first
umpire in 1941 was George Taylor. Thus, Taylor had experience with
both the more fluid hosiery system and the more legalistic process in the
auto industry.

The War Labor Board's own experience served to confirm the value
of arbitration, and the situation at Chrysler, where arbitration was imposed upon a vigorous shop steward system, is instructive. At Chrysler's
Dodge Main plant in Detroit, the very first collective agreement provided
that both the elected plantwide bargaining committee and the chief stewards could confer with foremen or other management representatives

[34] Acmeline Manufacturing Co., *War Labor Reports* 9 (1943): 524.
[35] Chrysler Corp., *War Labor Reports* 10 (1943): 551; Champlin Refining Co., *War Labor Reports* 3 (1942): 155; Nolan and Abrams, "American Labor Arbitration: The Maturing Years," 571–73; Lichtenstein, "Industrial Democracy, Contract Unionism and the National War Labor Board," 524.
[36] Niles-Bement-Pond Co., *War Labor Reports* 5 (1943): 489.
[37] From 1931–41 Taylor served as the second impartial chair of the Full-Fashioned Hosiery Manufactures and the American Federation of Hosiery Workers, and in 1934, became the chair of the Philadelphia Men's Clothing Arbitration Board.

during working hours. As historian Steve Jefferys notes, the agreement provided for "two parallel systems of plant bargaining."[38] After a crucial 45-day strike in 1939, Local 3 altered its constitution, establishing the "primacy of the steward over the plant committee on departmental issues" and rank-and-file control over the chief shop steward. Deputy stewards were to be provided for every twenty employees. What is most fascinating about this development is that it occurred solely within the union's own internal legal system and not via collective bargaining.

By 1943, many activists at Dodge Main, as at many other industrial plants, had been dispersed to other locations or to the armed services; but a core remained, one sufficient to instruct the newly hired war workers on issues of job control. Like other companies in 1943, Chrysler attempted to tighten workplace discipline, refusing to deal with stewards and referring issues to the seriously backlogged War Labor Board. A walkout followed by firings led to a widespread sympathy strike in all of Chrysler's Detroit plants, at the very moment when the War Labor Board was holding hearings on the failure of the UAW and Chrysler to reach a new agreement. The board viewed its duty as resolving "the problems of which the industrial unrest is a symptom," noting that there had been sixty-six strikes at Chrysler between 23 December 1941 and 8 January 1943. To that end, the board insisted on an arbitration procedure similar to the system created at General Motors in 1940 and at Ford in 1941. At both firms, the UAW had advocated a grievance procedure that terminated in final arbitration by a permanent arbitrator or umpire. The existing grievance procedure involved a board consisting of two representatives of labor and management. The grievance would remain unresolved should the parties fail to agree, a system the board viewed as "obsolete." Instead, the board appointed an "impartial chairman."[39] The board's action in *Chrysler,* therefore, meshed with national UAW policy.

Within a year of the board's creation, the basic contours and rules of labor arbitration were established. Decisions in 1943 reflected the board's support for a formalized, multistep grievance process that would ultimately end in adjudication by a neutral arbitrator, a pattern that has

[38] Steve Jefferys, *Management and Managed: Fifty Years of Crisis at Chrysler* (Cambridge: Cambridge University Press, 1986), 74–75.
[39] Chrysler Corp., *War Labor Reports* 10 (1943): 551. In 1942 the board had refused to order arbitration of new wage rates, although it did approve arbitration of differential rates paid to men and women performing comparable work. Chrysler Corp., *War Labor Reports* 3 (1942): 447.

long since become commonplace.[40] The Supreme Court in the 1960s would adopt the basic design set by the War Labor Board, albeit without attribution.[41] The War Labor Board's structure of rules, although explainable by wartime exigencies, would also be consistent with the themes of industrial pluralism in the postwar period. More broadly, these themes were congruent with contractualist notions long present in American legal thought. Thus, for instance, the jurisdiction of the arbitrator would be restricted to the settlement of questions concerning the interpretation or application of the terms of collective bargaining agreements.[42] Arbitration fit a voluntarist, contractual model of industrial relations in which disputes could be settled without apparent government involvement.[43]

The contractualist vision extended beyond the scope of arbitration. If the parties had an arbitration agreement, for instance, the War Labor Board would order arbitration despite an employer objection that the grievance lacked merit.[44] Moreover, once an award was rendered, the board held that "every reasonable presumption is made in favor of such an award," and that awards would be upheld if there was no proof "of fraud, misconduct or other equally valid objection."[45] Thus the refusal to comply with an award was treated as a refusal to comply with an order of the War Labor Board.[46] Moreover, the War Labor Board affirmed arbitration awards despite an employer's contention that compliance would not be "in the interests of full production." As the board noted in one decision, "labor and industry generally throughout the country have come to regard arbitration as the wisest, fairest, and speediest method of settling industrial disputes, especially during wartime."[47]

[40] See, for example, Eclipse Fuel Engineering Co., *War Labor Reports* 6 (1943): 279.
[41] By 1960, the date of the Supreme Court's trilogy, arbitration clauses were found in over 90 percent of collective agreements. BLS Bull. No. 1425–1, "Grievance Procedures" (1964),1. The Supreme Court may have wished to support the arbitration process, but the War Labor Board had already accomplished that result over fifteen years earlier.
[42] Chrysler Corp., *War Labor Reports* 3 (1942): 447; *War Labor Reports* 10 (1943): 551.
[43] See, for example, *NWLB Termination Report* 1: 131; Realty Advisory Board, *War Labor Reports* 2 (1942): 183.
[44] Texoma Natural Gas Co., *War Labor Reports* 10 (1943): 438.
[45] See Sullivan Drydock and Repair Co., *War Labor Reports* 6 (1943): 467; Smith and Wesson, *War Labor Reports* 10 (1943): 148, 153; *Termination Report* 1:404–5. The board would refuse to review an award even though the arbitration agreement stipulated that either party could appeal to the WLB. Sullivan Drydock and Repair Co., *War Labor Reports* 6 (1943): 467. See also, "Statement of Policy Concerning Review of Arbitration Awards," *Termination Report* 2:694.
[46] *Termination Report* 1:411–12, 2:694–95.
[47] Alexander Milburn Co., *War Labor Reports* 5 (1942): 529.

This broad protection of arbitration awards would also be reflected in the Supreme Court's postwar jurisprudence.[48]

The state courts had generally been hostile to arbitral arrangements, apparently because they viewed arbitration as a threat to supplant the courts.[49] Many, therefore, refused to enforce such promises. Breaking from the common law view, the War Labor Board held that parties to an arbitration agreement must live up to their promises to arbitrate, and the board would enforce such awards.[50] In addition, the determinations of the War Labor Board would not be affected by any arbitration laws that might exist in various states.[51] Subsequently, the Supreme Court would also determine that collective bargaining law was exclusively federal, thereby preempting contrary state statutes and rules.

Despite the board's protection of arbitral systems, some revealing limitations were recognized, perhaps because of managerial concern that arbitrators would have "the final decision on all matters which the union may want to treat as grievances."[52] The board made clear in 1942 that arbitration would not involve matters of "managerial prerogative."[53] In

[48] In the famous arbitration trilogy of 1960, the Supreme Court held that courts should apply broad presumptions of coverage when questions arise about the scope of arbitration clauses and, second, that arbitration awards should be presumed valid unless their "words manifest an infidelity to the agreement." The arbitration trilogy involves three Supreme Court decisions decided on the same day in which the United Steelworkers successfully achieved broad protections for arbitration: *United Steelworkers of America v. American Manufacturing Co.*, 363 U.S. 564 (1960); *United Steelworkers of America v. Warrior and Gulf Navigation Co.*, 363 U.S. 574 (1960); and *United Steelworkers of America v. Enterprise Wheel and Car Corp.*, 363 U.S. 593 (1960). These conclusions not only mirrored the decisions of the War Labor Board, but they also flowed directly from concern by pluralists that courts would unduly enmesh themselves in the private dispute-resolution process unless they deferred to arbitration procedures.

These decisions made clear that arbitration was to be the primary vehicle for the resolution of industrial disputes involving the interpretation or application of collective bargaining agreements. In line with pluralist precepts, the courts would support the grievance and arbitration process while concurrently trying not to interfere with it, since the collective bargaining system was viewed as a form of private self-government. The emphasis upon enforcing the intentions of the parties masks the attempt to "civilize" industrial relations and restrain "jungle warfare."

[49] See, for example, *Gatliff Coal Co. v. Cox*, 142 F. 2d 876 (6th Cir. 1944); Charles Gregory and Richard Orlikoff, "The Enforcement of Labor Arbitration Agreements," *University of Chicago Law Review* 17 (1950): 233.

[50] See, for example, Smith and Wesson, *War Labor Reports* 10 (1943): 148. See, generally, Jessie Freidin and Francis J. Ulman, "Arbitration and the War Labor Board," *Harvard Law Review* 58 (1945): 315.

[51] Ibid.

[52] Montgomery Ward and Co., *War Labor Reports* 10 (1943): 415, 420.

[53] See, for example, Atlas Power Co., *War Labor Reports* 5 (1942): 371. (Denial of extension of arbitration to cover transfer and promotion disputes where hazardous nature of op-

the highly publicized *Montgomery Ward* decision in 1942 in which management prerogatives were an issue, the board ordered a contractual
definition of a "grievance" that would exclude "changes in business
practice, the opening and closing of new units, the choice of personnel
(subject, however, to the seniority provision), the choice of merchandise
to be sold, or other business questions of a like nature not having to do
directly and primarily with the day-to-day life of the employees and their
relations with supervisors."[54]

Managerial authority was also recognized in areas clearly within arbitral jurisdiction. The board had no difficulty in holding that disciplinary
matters were subject to arbitration, especially given the high incidence of
clauses in collective bargaining agreements preventing discipline or discharge without "just cause." But the board nevertheless strongly supported management's authority to take prompt action, including
suspending or removing an employee from a job pending investigation or a
hearing, subject to the right of the employee or the union to grieve. As War
Labor Board public members Jesse Freidin and Francis Ulman confidently
stated in 1945, "Arrangements have never been directed whereby the
union's approval must be secured before discipline can be meted out." Indeed, the authors noted that a contractual requirement of union approval
had existed at Brewster Aeronautical Corporation, but it was "changed by
the parties in conferences in which a Board representative participated, so
as to restore to management its initial power to discipline. The Board approved the changes."[55] Thus, the now common notion that the employer
acts and the employee or union can only grieve is not so much designed to
avoid the possibility that employees will otherwise engage in self-help or
because it is a necessary requirement of the grievance process as would be
argued after the war. Instead, it is based upon the board's assumption that
such a concept was an incident of managerial prerogative protecting hierarchy and aiding continued production.[56]

Yale Law School's Harry Shulman helped propound these views in a
most forceful manner.[57] Shulman, who became umpire for the Ford Mo-

erations necessitates complete control by company.) See also, Harris, *The Right to Manage*, 55–56.

[54] Montgomery Ward and Co., *War Labor Reports* 4 (1942): 277, 280.

[55] Freidin and Ulman, "Arbitration and the War Labor Board," 355–56.

[56] See, for instance, Brewster Aeronautical Corp., *War Labor Reports* 12 (1943): 40; Norge
Machine Products Division of Borg-Warner Corp., *War Labor Reports* 15 (1944): 651;
Briggs Manufacturing Co., *War Labor Reports* 5 (1942): 340.

[57] Harry Shulman's 1955 Holmes lecture, "Reason, Contract and Law in Labor Relations,"
was printed both in *Harvard Law Review* 68 (1955): 999, and Jean McKelvey, ed.,

tor Company–UAW in 1943, recognized the role of law in protecting unions, but he stressed that the law left the conditions of work to the "autonomous determination" of employers and unions.[58] Like all the pluralists, Shulman recognized that employment was a conflictual relationship, a contention which must have been repeatedly highlighted by the contentious labor relations at Ford; but he believed conflict should be restricted due to the imperatives of production, and disputes "will be adjusted by the application of reason guided by the light of the contract, rather than by force or power."[59] Strikes, an "integral part of the system of collective bargaining," were referred to as a "cessation of production" rather than as a refusal to work. Although Shulman believed that litigation was unsuited to the enforcement of agreements, he stressed that it did not "follow that the alternative is jungle warfare" because arbitration

is an integral part of the system of self government. And the system is designed to aid management in its quest for efficiency, to assist union leadership in its participation in the enterprise, and to secure justice for the employees. It is a means of making collective bargaining work and thus preserving private enterprise in a free government.[60]

Grievance procedures to Shulman were not only an "orderly, effective and democratic way of adjusting such disputes," but the procedure also represented the substitution of "civilized collective bargaining for jungle warfare."[61] The repeated reference to "jungle warfare" is instructive for the notion apparently includes the concerted withdrawal of labor, the basic right underlying the NLRA. Note that Shulman's argument is not premised upon an explicit union promise to avoid strikes. Instead, the very existence of an arbitration procedure foreclosed strikes over matters that fell within the ambit of such clauses.

Shulman was the most influential arbitrator during the war and in the immediate postwar period, but many of his most cited decisions were reached in wartime. Thus, his statement that "while management and

---

Management Rights and the Arbitration Process, Proceedings of the Ninth Annual Meeting of the National Academy of Arbitrators (Washington, D.C.: BNA Inc., 1956), 169. It is probably the most widely quoted article in the area of arbitration and contract dispute settlement.
[58] Harry Shulman, "Reason, Contract and Law in Labor Relations," *Harvard Law Review* 68 (1955): 1000.
[59] Ibid., 1007.
[60] Ibid., 1024.
[61] *Opinions of the Umpire, Ford Motor Co. and UAW-CIO, 1943–1946,* Case No. A–116.

labor are in adverse bargaining positions, they are joint participants in the productive effort," flows smoothly from wartime needs,[62] as does his comment that "maintenance of efficient production is of vital importance ...to the community as a whole."

In perhaps his most well-known award, issued in 1944, Shulman stressed the requirement that employees follow the grievance procedure instead of resorting to self-help. Such behavior was "essential in order to avoid disruption of relations between the parties and anarchy in the operation of the plant." In one of his most famous phrases, he argued that an "industrial plant is not a debating society."[63] This sentiment, reflected in thousands of postwar arbitration awards, makes clear that contract rights of unions will be treated differently from the assertion of such rights by employers because "to refuse obedience because of a claimed contract violation would be to substitute individual action for collective bargaining and to replace the grievance procedure with extra-contractual methods." Self-help, therefore, was "extracontractual" where a grievance procedure was in existence. "When a controversy arises, production cannot wait for exhaustion of the grievance procedure. While that procedure is pursued, production must go on." A challenge to a managerial order interferes with the "authority to direct work," which, Shulman believed, is vested in supervision "because the responsibility for production is also vested there; and responsibility must be accompanied by authority." Shulman's concerns were not limited to enterprises run for profit; instead, "any enterprise in a capitalist or socialist economy requires persons of authority and responsibility to keep the enterprise going."[64]

The argument that arbitration tames the often unruly rank and file has been used both to criticize the institution and, by the postwar judiciary, to strengthen it. Few authorized strikes occurred during the war, but workers demonstrated their power through the large number of wild-cat strikes that did occur. It is not at all clear that arbitration procedures avert wildcat strikes, for arbitral resolution is not necessarily quick nor does the process always involve the workers actually affected. Indeed, the existence of arbitration and the War Labor Board seemed almost irrelevant to most wildcat strikers, except to the extent that frustration

---

[62] *Opinions of the Umpire, Ford Motor Co. and UAW-CIO, 1943–1946,* A–561.
[63] *Opinions of the Umpire,* A–116; also published as Matter of Ford Motor Co., 3 LA 779 (1944). See also, A–29.
[64] *Opinions of the Umpire,* A–116.

with War Labor Board delays and policies can be deemed to have been the partial cause of some wartime stoppages. Regulators might have believed in such a connection, however, and experience in the apparel industry earlier in the century suggested that rank-and-file militance can be moderated and, at least with time, replaced by a more bureaucratized system of dispute resolution.[65]

Even on this question, however, there was a long and heated postwar debate among arbitrators and labor scholars on the scope of the grievance process. To most of the pluralists, and with perhaps George Taylor and Harry Shulman in mind, arbitrators were believed to be superior to judges because they could be less rigid, less rule-oriented, as well as more informed of the "practices, assumptions, understandings, and aspirations of the going industrial concern."[66] Indeed, this confident view of the arbitrator's role and ability was used by the Supreme Court in 1960 to explain its broad deference given to arbitration: "Even the ablest judge cannot be expected to bring the same experience and competence to bear upon the determination of a grievance, because he cannot be similarly informed."[67]

The job of the arbitrator, however, was to do more than simply search for, or create, the "intentions of the parties." As Katherine Stone has effectively demonstrated, the pluralist approach also was based upon the assumption that arbitration can be used as part of a therapeutic effort

---

[65] Despite both contractual and legal restrictions on the right to strike, however, wildcats or strikes violating no-strike clauses have not disappeared. James Atleson, "Work Group Behavior and Wildcat Strikes: The Causes and Functions of Industrial Civil Disobedience," *Ohio State Law Journal* 34 (1973): 750; Alvin Gouldner, *Wildcat Strike* (New York: Harper and Row, 1954); George Sayles, "Wildcat Strikes," *Harvard Business Review* 43 (1954): 42; James Kuhn, *Bargaining in Grievance Settlement: The Power of Industrial Work Groups* (New York: Columbia University Press, 1961).

This suggests that such activity cannot be fully suppressed by contract, institutional pressure, or law. As David Brody has perceptively noted, the contractual regime cannot totally supplant the "core of informal shop-floor activity," but it does "narrow the scope of such activity" and increasingly designates noncontractual activity and prerogatives as "extralegal in character." Brody, *Workers in Industrial America*, 202.

[66] Archibald Cox, "Reflections Upon Labor Arbitration," *Harvard Law Review* 72 (1959): 1500.

[67] *United Steelworkers v. Warrior and Gulf Navigation Co.*, 363 U.S. 574 (1960). The opposing view, stated most forcefully by Professor Lon Fuller, was that the arbitrator had no "roving commission to straighten things out." The assumptions that arbitrators could "loosely" interpret the agreement, Fuller argued, could not be based upon any generally assumed intent of the parties. Lon Fuller, "Collective Bargaining and the Arbitrator," in Mark Kahn, ed., *Collective Bargaining and the Arbitrator's Role*, Proceedings of the Fifteenth Annual Meeting of the National Academy of Arbitrators (Washington, D.C.: BNA Inc., 1962), 8. See also, J. Noble Braden, "Problems in Labor Arbitration," *Missouri Law Review* 13 (1948): 143.

to lessen underlying tensions and discontent at the workplace.[68] It is doubtful whether most arbitrators actually decide cases on the basis of alleviating workplace tensions, but the assumption reveals the role arbitrators are theoretically to play in easing tensions, rather than simply interpreting the agreement. The War Labor Board, however, had more immediate concerns, and its arbitration and union security policies were basically in place before the wildcat strike wave of 1943 and 1944. Moreover, the board's common grant of arbitration clauses was not simply based upon the need to find a peaceful and effective means to resolve workplace conflicts but also to find a fair method to settle conflict in a situation in which unions had surrendered the right to strike.[69]

By war's end, the basic structure of today's common arbitral system was in place. Typically, contracts called for a multistep grievance process that had the effect of transferring authority from shop-floor leaders to the union hierarchy. Rights were no longer to be based upon tradition or custom but upon the contract and arbitral case law, a process thought to parallel the "rule of law" in society. Discharge or discipline could only be for "just cause," but supervisory orders had to be obeyed, that is, the grievance system would substitute for self-help. Such a process requires patience over militancy, substituting third-party resolution for the exercise of shop-floor power.[70]

Wayne Morse, one of the four public members of the War Labor Board, strongly believed the board should not resolve disputes while a strike was in progress. Previously dean of the Oregon Law School, Morse had extensive arbitral experience on the West Coast prior to joining the War Labor Board. Experience in the "bare-knuckle environment" of longshoring, said former WLB member Lewis Gill, "had doubtless convinced him that only a firm grip by the arbitrator, in a strictly judicial proceeding, could insure a reasonably orderly and workable *modus op-*

---

[68] Stone, "The Post-war Paradigm," 1559–73.

[69] Caterpillar Tractor Co., *War Labor Reports* 2 (1942): 75; Borg-Warner Corp., *War Labor Reports* 6 (1943): 233. An arbitration clause was imposed in one case where the prewar agreement contained a no-strike clause. Thirteen Jobbing Machine Shops, *War Labor Reports* 2 (1942): 423.

[70] The board's policies fostering the routinization of workplace disputes combined by late 1943 with a managerial counterattack on union power in the workplace. For a description of the centralization and bureaucratization of disciplinary power at Ford's Rouge plant, see Nelson Lichtenstein, "Life at the Rouge: A Cycle of Workers' Control," in Charles Stephenson and Robert Asher, eds., *Life and Labor: Dimensions of American Working Class History* (Albany: State University of New York Press, 1986), 248–51.

erandi."[71] As Morse stated in a 1944 law review article, "the effective prosecution of the war cannot wait until the leisure of the party litigants."[72] More broadly, the board would insist that strikes were improper even while disputes were being processed through the contractual grievance system. This notion would find favor long after, both in the Supreme Court and in arbitral decisions barring self-help where grievance systems existed.

Collective bargaining and the arbitration process were also thought to require a different kind of union leader. Golden and Ruttenberg noted in 1942 that "most militant local union leaders, who rise to the surface in the organizing stage of unions, fall by the side when the union moves into the state of constructive relations with management."[73] "Constructive" labor relations, therefore, requires responsible unions led by "cooperative" leaders.[74]

In addition to the supposed need to alter the kind of leaders needed, bargaining and arbitration tend to change the issues to be decided. A grievance process transforms disputes, which could be based upon concerns for personal integrity or moral and political issues, into narrower, more legalistic questions.[75] Indeed, over time, disputes become contractual or else they are improper. For as rights become more clearly based solely upon the contract, disputes over other matters are treated as irrelevant, unimportant or, at least, unjustifiable.

The move from a system of workplace confrontation to higher-level bargaining or arbitration, therefore, may alter the substance of bargaining, that is, the nature of the issues. Workplace conflict tended to deal

---

[71] Lewis Gill, "The Nature of Arbitration: The Blurred Line Between Mediatory and Judicial Arbitration Proceedings," *Case Western Reserve Law Review* 39 (1988–89): 546.

[72] Wayne Morse, "The National War Labor Board Puts Labor Law Theory into Action," *Iowa Law Review* 29 (1944): 181; Lee Wilkins, *Wayne Morse: A Bio-Bibliography* (Westport: Greenwood Press, 1985), 14–18.

[73] Clinton Golden and Harold Ruttenberg, *The Dynamics of Industrial Democracy* (New York: Harper and Brothers, 1942), 58. In Richard Lester's words, the successors of the founding leaders of a union tend to be not "crusading agitator[s]," but the "skillful political operator and level-headed administrator." Richard Lester, *As Unions Mature* (Princeton: Princeton University Press, 1958), 26.

[74] Although nonmilitant, "constructive" union officials were not the exclusive type of leader, but the pattern described does seem to parallel some revolutions in which militant leaders are forced out, killed, or shipped abroad to be replaced by more managerial, bureaucratic types.

[75] Lynn Mather and Barbara Yngvesson, "Language, Audience, and the Transformation of Disputes," *Law and Society Review* 15 (1981): 775.

with speed of production, discipline, or actions of foremen.[76] "Mature" collective bargaining, on the other hand, often deals with other issues. Thus, a change in focus of concern, in the definition of what is important, occurred, rather than simply a change in the location of and participants in dispute resolution. Although unions of the 1940s often declared their intention to invade hitherto sacred management preserves, and employers seemed to have believed that such threats were real,[77] the labor movement primarily sought involvement in major capital decisions, not the types of workplace issues that often seem of greater immediacy to workers. Nevertheless, the combination of legal restrictions on the scope of bargaining and the protection of arbitration tended to deprive workers of influence on both capital decisions and workplace conflicts.

MANAGERIAL PREROGATIVES: COLLECTIVE BARGAINING'S FORBIDDEN ZONE

At the end of the war, the primary fear of American employers was the union challenge to managerial control of the workplace. Executives focused this concern less upon strikes than upon "the serious and lasting limitations on their freedom of action resulting from the orderly collective bargaining achievements of bureaucratic unionism, assisted by the orders of arbitrators and the NWLB."[78] Managerial fears, however, must have been based primarily upon union bargaining power and workplace pressures because the wartime "law" was certainly sympathetic toward managerial prerogatives.[79]

---

[76] "Reported Work Stoppages in Automobile Plants in Dec. 1944, Jan., Feb. 1945," set out in Glaberman, *Wartime Strikes, 51–60.*

[77] Harris, *The Right to Manage.* Although unions seemed to de-emphasize such attempted incursions during the 1945–49 period, there were economic reasons for such behavior. The primary concern of unions during this period was job security and the protection against raging inflation concurrent with a vigorous managerial counterattack. See David Brody, *Workers in Industrial America* (New York: Oxford University Press, 1980), 173–214.

[78] Harris, *The Right to Manage,* 67. For an argument that managers had lost considerable power during the war years, see Robert M. C. Littler, "Managers Must Manage," *Harvard Business Review* 24 (1946): 366.

[79] Despite the wartime statements by some union officials expressing their interest in further influence in management, statements by unionists supporting the concept of managerial rights could also be found. Thus, Philip Murray and Morris Cooke stated in 1940: "To relieve the boss or the management of proper responsibility for making a success of the enterprise is about the last thing any group of employees—organized or unorganized— would consider workable or even desirable. The Unions are on record in numerous instances as recognizing that in the last analysis management has to manage, if any concern is to be a success financially or in any other way." Philip Murray and Morris Cooke,

The first National Labor Relations Board, created by executive order in 1934, had endorsed a broad reading of the duty to bargain, expanding interpretations from its predecessor, the National Labor Board. Employers had been ordered to bargain over a wide range of matters that had an impact on terms and conditions of employment, including changes in terms occasioned by plant relocation or the introduction of a new line of products.[80] Despite this history, the War Labor Board at an early date recognized an area of decision making it designated as "managerial prerogatives." The determination that a matter is solely a management function means, first, that the employer need not bargain about such a matter despite the union's request that it do so, nor would the War Labor Board restrict managerial authority in these areas. Second, and often most important, an employer may initiate action in these areas without first bargaining with the union and without subsequent arbitral challenge. Although the scope of bargaining would be a vital question under the NLRA, little litigation under that statute had occurred on these questions between the determination that the NLRA was constitutional in 1937 and the outbreak of war.[81] Thus, the War Labor Board's assumptions would become deeply embedded in NLRA jurisprudence after the war.[82]

In 1946, Ludwig Teller, prolific writer of labor law articles and treatises, was pleased to report that "the decisions of the War Labor Board in labor dispute cases did much to reinstate management confidence in business continuity, in the right to initiate business decisions."[83] Teller argued that when the war and the War Labor Board ended, there was "increasing reliance" on the decisions of the War Labor Board "because of the belief that its decisions are a source of guidance for desirable practices in the field of labor relations." As Teller perceptively noted in 1946, the War Labor Board's "decisions are the beginnings of a labor jurisprudence." Indeed, it is the War Labor Board, not the National Labor Relations Board, that institutionalized the notion that the scope of mandatory bargaining is restricted by certain inherent managerial rights.

When faced with a dispute over the terms of the collective bargaining

Organized Labor and Production (New York: Harper, 1940), 84. As David Montgomery and Howell Harris demonstrate in this volume, labor's lack of desire "to manage or to interfere in the least with the employee's affairs" is longstanding.
[80] Atleson, *Values and Assumptions in American Labor Law*, 118.
[81] Ibid., 115–22.
[82] See, generally, Atleson, *Values and Assumptions in American Labor Law*.
[83] Ludwig Teller, "The War Labor Board and Management Functions," *NYU Law Quarterly Review* 21 (1946): 365.

agreement, the board might be required to write much or all of the agreement for the parties. The board might be faced with a dispute concerning a right asserted by the employer or a practice that either the employer or the union wanted established or terminated. In either case, employers often contended that the exercise of a particular right should be or remain part of the employer's "reserved rights." These asserted "managerial prerogatives" often involved production matters as well as union proposals for health insurance, company-financed unemployment funds, sick leave, and medical, hospital, pregnancy, and maternity benefits.

The War Labor Board tended to be keenly protective of managerial rights, and it routinely denied union welfare proposals. The War Labor Board, it was said, was "hesitant about breaking new ground."[84] The War Labor Board, however, did grant unions a measure of participation in many matters previously thought to be exclusively managerial. For instance, the board supported automatic wage progression plans that affected employers' control of labor costs and the work force. In addition, board-ordered job classification plans and other work arrangements gave unions the right to be consulted in both the creation and the administration of such schemes.[85] Nevertheless, what is noteworthy about the board's rulings is the lack of any felt need to explain the nature or scope, or to even justify the existence, of managerial prerogatives.[86]

The board's clearest statement of its approach is probably to be found in its *Montgomery Ward* decision. Management functions were excluded from arbitration to the extent that they related to:

changes in the general business practice, the opening or closing of new units, the choice of personnel, the choice of merchandise to be sold, or other business questions of a like nature not having to do directly and primarily with the day-to-day life of the employees and their relations with their supervisors.[87]

The scope of bargaining, therefore, was to be narrowed to the "day-to-day" concerns of employees. As under the National Labor Relations Act,

[84] Constance Williams, "Note on Management Prerogatives," *NWLB Termination Report* 2:623.

[85] Timothy Willard, "Labor and the National War Labor Board 1942–1945: An Experiment in Corporatist Wage Stabilization" (Ph.D. diss., University of Toledo, 1984), 40.

[86] "One of the most remarkable features of the War Labor Board cases dealing with management functions is the failure to define at length the meaning of management function in a union relationship, or even to discuss its essential qualities as a guide to future policies." Teller, "The War Labor Board and Management Functions," 365.

[87] Montgomery Ward, *War Labor Reports* 10 (1943): 415.

it is the challenge to the employer's control of production and the state's unwillingness to sanction such challenges that seem to underlie these cases.

A good deal of labor's creativity in creating bargaining proposals arose from the fact that possible wage gains were strictly controlled by the board's Little Steel formula. Even matters clearly involving working conditions, however, were often avoided by the board. The board would not always explicitly rule that particular issues were improper subjects for bargaining; instead, the War Labor Board often sent such issues back to the parties for further negotiation, a resolution with foreseeable results given the no-strike pledge. As Aaron Levenstein, a strong critic of the WLB, noted:

[The board's] refusal to decide made it impossible for the unions to bargain on those matters altogether. Since the strike weapon had been put in cold storage, the issues remained an economic no man's land which the Board would not enter and which labor could not invade because it had no persuasive power. In this region of disputed issues, the employers' only obligation was to negotiate before saying no.[88]

The unions argued that the no-strike pledge obliged the board to rule on all issues. The "no-strike, no lockout agreement," they argued in vain, was conditioned on the submission of "all disputes" to the board. The board's position was essentially that its jurisdiction was narrower than the no-strike promise. Effectively, then, the no-strike obligation was unlimited, but the right to bargain was not.[89]

The United Auto Workers, for instance, demanded that General Motors create an employee security fund equal to the one it had already put aside for postwar business contingencies. The fund would purchase war bonds and, after the war, it would supplement unemployment insurance for workers who could not be provided with a forty-hour workweek. The board agreed with General Motors that the union's demand was essentially a "profit-sharing plan and is beyond the powers of the War Labor Board to adjudicate."[90] The public members of the board believed

---

[88] See Aaron Levenstein, *Labor Today and Tomorrow* (New York: A. Knopf, 1946), 102.
[89] Unions did broaden the scope of bargaining, however, despite the board's lack of support. The UMW developed the concept of a royalty for every ton of coal mined to be used to create a fund for medical service, hospitalization, rehabilitation, and general economic protection. Levenstein, *Labor Today and Tomorrow*, 103–4. Other unions like the International Ladies' Garment Workers' Union required employers to contribute to union health and vacation funds.
[90] General Motors Company, *War Labor Reports* 22 (1945): 484.

they should prevent the introduction of "sociological innovations" during the war. The powerful wartime interest in labor peace could have led to a broad, inclusive reading of the scope of bargaining, especially given the unions' no-strike pledge. Yet, the interest in co-option, or in the institutionalization of dispute resolution, was apparently weaker than the War Labor Board's preference for unrestricted managerial freedom over certain matters.

In the War Labor Board's first decision in which the issue was raised, *Arcade Malleable Iron Co.*, the board denied an employer's request for a clause that specifically listed various management functions. The board's denial was accompanied with the statement that "adequate protection is afforded the company by law and by the many decisions of the courts and of other tribunals concerned with the question."[91] Given the paucity of NLRA decisions dealing with the scope of bargaining, it is difficult to know what body of law the board had in mind. Even in this case, however, the board, without dissent from its labor representatives, agreed to insert a clause to the effect that "the functions of management are vested exclusively in the Company except as modified by the specific provisions of this agreement." The union was enjoined from interfering "in the rights of the management in the matter of hiring, transfer, or promotion of any employees and in the general management of the plant." The board's only objection was to the employer's proposed "long list" of exclusive management functions.

The basis for the decision became clear in the later *Banner Iron Works* case: "The rights are inherent in management anyhow."[92] Nevertheless, the board in 1942, often without comment, began to approve management requests to insert clauses into collective bargaining agreements which would protect specific management rights.[93] Inherent rights, apparently, were sometimes deemed worthy of clear expression. These clauses generally gave management, among other things, the exclusive power to hire, promote, fire for just cause, and to maintain and schedule production. Moreover, the clauses often explicitly acknowledged the employer's exclusive control over the products to be manufactured as well as the location of plants.[94]

[91] *In re* Arcade Malleable Iron Co., *War Labor Reports* 1 (1942): 153.
[92] *War Labor Reports* 15 (1944): 332, 335.
[93] Because of space limitations and my own interests, I have not discussed internal debates within the board. The emphasis here is on the board's orders and parallels in current law.
[94] Levenstein, *Labor Today and Tomorrow*, 109; *In re* Fulton County Glove Industry, *War*

Under the rubric of "plant operations," the WLB deferred to many aspects of management decision making. For instance, the board denied a union request to reestablish a six-day workweek instead of a five-day swing-shift week, stating that "this matter is a technical administrative problem, which should be left to management to decide, involving as it does the rearrangement of working schedules by large-scale transfers of personnel and changes in the entire system of the company's operations."[95] The War Labor Board also generally believed that restriction and arbitration of employee transfers would interfere with efficiency.[96]

Indeed, the board's decisions on the scope of managerial prerogatives were far broader than the positions of the postwar NLRB. For instance, the War Labor Board held that even the distribution of overtime work was within the exclusive prerogative of management. Thus, the board denied a union's request for an equal division of overtime work on the ground that the "ultimate decision as to who is qualified to perform specific overtime work should rest with management."[97] Other matters swept into the broad management prerogatives category were the initiation of technological changes, even if layoffs should occur, determination of the size of the work force, and the determination of supervisory members.[98] Subcontracting work was also generally regarded as a managerial prerogative despite a union's claim that the company had used subcontracting in the past to evade contractual provisions and wage rates.[99]

Nor were "management functions" to be subject to arbitration.[100] Thus, the board had occasion to exclude expressly from arbitration the transfer and promotion of employees, the adjustment of piece rates, the determination whether additional employees should be hired for certain

Labor Reports 4 (1942): 307; Teller, "The War Labor Board and Management Functions," 322 n. 11.

[95] Mead Corp., *War Labor Reports* 8 (1943): 471, 474; Towne Robertson Nut Co., *War Labor Reports* 3 (1942): 40.

[96] See, for example, Detroit Steel Products Co., *War Labor Reports* 6 (1943): 495.

[97] Bethlehem Steel, *War Labor Reports* 11 (1943): 190, 196.

[98] Riverside and Dan River Cotton Mills, Inc., *War Labor Reports* 8 (1943): 274. Western Union Telegraph Co., *War Labor Reports* 6 (1943): 133; Petroleum Specialties Co., *War Labor Reports* 24 (1945): 597. (The board refused the union request to remove a supervisor who had been convicted of assaulting employees.)

[99] Tinius Olsen Testing Machine Co., *War Labor Reports* 11 (1943): 301; Bethlehem Steel Co., *War Labor Reports* 6 (1943): 513. Yet, in one case the board approved a clause restricting subcontracting until all employees were fully employed and the full capacity of plants utilized. Fulton County Glove Industry, *War Labor Reports* 4 (1942): 307.

[100] Teller, "The War Labor Board and Management Functions," 329.

operations, the retention of probationary employees, and the determination of work schedules.[101]

The board's willingness to grant a detailed management prerogative clause, after its initial refusal to do so, actually reflects a more liberal approach to collective bargaining. The board initially may have believed that no explication of management rights was required because they were "inherent" in the relationship. This is a reflection of what could be referred to as the "Genesis" theory of collective bargaining, one often found in judicial decisions and especially in postwar arbitration awards. "In the beginning," the theory goes, there was light, and then there were inherent managerial powers over the direction of the enterprise. Such power obviously included unfettered control to direct production and the work force and to make all decisions involving these matters. Later there came statutes and collective bargaining, but employers nevertheless still possess all powers that have not been expressly restricted by statute or agreement. The inclusion of express managerial rights in collective agreements, however, weakens the argument that certain prerogatives are "inherent" in the relationship.

A more sophisticated argument, and one made by the conservative legal scholar Ludwig Teller, is that collective bargaining was a replacement rather than a supplement to common law theories of labor relations. Thus, collective bargaining was created to supplant "common law individualism" with "new conceptions suitable to problems and situations that did not exist when the common law molded its intensely individualistic structure." Teller was aware that having replaced the old order with the new, "organized labor is properly suspicious of efforts to give continued life to the old order through the medium of emphasis upon 'the common law rights of management.' " Moreover, as many observers of industrial relations recognized, there is no objective or rational way to determine what is or what is not a managerial prerogative.[102] A decision concerning which matters should be exclusively in the managerial domain is basically a determination of the area from which labor should be excluded. In addition, as David Montgomery's work has shown, the context of this issue involves those areas in which management/ownership

---

[101] Ibid., 339. See also, Bethlehem Steel Corp., *War Labor Reports* 11 (1943): 190. Similarly, the hazardous nature of the work was used to deny arbitral jurisdiction over transfer and promotion grievances, suggesting some lack of faith in both arbitrators and unions. Atlas Powder Co., *War Labor Reports* 5 (1942): 371.

[102] Teller, "The War Labor Board and Management Functions," 348–49; Atleson, *Values and Assumptions in American Labor Law*, chapter 9.

has taken power from employees as well as those areas in which collective employee action and statutes have restricted managerial control.

An explicit managerial prerogatives clause offers a number of other values, both real and symbolic. First, according to Teller, it "has certain value in teaching the contracting union to think in terms of the problems and rights of management."[103] More importantly, such a clause limits the scope of proper union concern, a serious matter in a period in which many unions were both developing and experiencing economic power. Thus, the board upheld the grant of a management functions clause by a regional board because:

the present union is a new union and the inclusion of the clause will serve to educate the union more definitely as to management functions, thus serving to reduce the areas of conflict between union and management without loss of protection of the union under the other terms of the contract and especially of the grievance machinery.[104]

In addition, the managerial functions clause creates a source of legitimation when management takes a particular action, a further reflection of the contractualization of labor-management relations.

The War Labor Board's recognition of a zone of managerial exclusivity would eventually be employed by the Supreme Court to narrow the scope of bargaining under the NLRA. The Supreme Court held in 1964, for instance, that subcontracting, at least in certain situations, was within the ambit of mandatory bargaining in *Fibreboard Paper Products v. NLRB*.[105] The opinion, typical of Warren Court opinions, began with broad statements of policy only to finish by narrowing the ruling to the precise and very limited facts of the case before it.[106] A concurring opinion by Justice Potter Stewart noted that not "every management decision which necessarily terminates an individual's employment is subject to the duty to bargain." Echoing *Montgomery Ward*, Stewart noted that even decisions clearly affecting "conditions of employment" are excluded because of the nature of the managerial action, listing, among others, decisions to invest in labor-saving machinery or decisions to liquidate assets

---

[103] Teller, "The War Labor Board and Management Functions," 349.
[104] United Aircraft Corp., *War Labor Reports* 18 (1944): 9.
[105] 379 U.S. 203 (1964).
[106] "We are thus not expanding the scope of mandatory bargaining to hold, as we do now, that the type of 'contracting' involved in this case—the replacement of employees in the existing bargaining unit with those of an independent contractor to do the same work under similar conditions of employment—is a statutory subject of collective bargaining under § 8(d)." Ibid., 223.

and go out of business. These decisions, Stewart argued, "lie at the core of entrepreneurial control." Stewart's explanation was that "decisions concerning the commitment of investment capital and the basic scope of the enterprise are not in themselves primarily about conditions of employment, though the effect of the decision may be necessary to terminate employment." Thus, excluded from the zone of mandatory bargaining are matters of capital investment and decisions "fundamental to the basic direction of a corporate enterprise."[107] Despite the union's victory in *Fibreboard*, Stewart's cautionary phrases were not significantly at variance with the majority's conclusion that mandatory bargaining in this instance would not "significantly abridge [the employer's] freedom to manage the business."

The Court's concern for the freedom to manage would subsequently become the basis for restrictive rulings of the Burger Court. In 1981, for instance, the Supreme Court held that a partial closing of the enterprise was not subject to mandatory bargaining.[108] The issue, said Justice Blackmun, is whether a decision to terminate "should be considered part of petitioner's retained freedom to manage its affairs unrelated to employment." Like the War Labor Board, Blackmun thus assumed that an inherent body of exclusive management functions existed, and "management must be free from the constraints of the bargaining process to the extent essential for the running of a profitable business." Congress, said the Court, "had no expectation that the elected union representative would become an equal partner in the running of the business enterprise in which the union's members are employed."[109]

CONCLUSION

Although there are negative aspects of contractualism and legalization, there are also clear advantages for unions. Institutionally, grievance procedures, like collective bargaining, centralize power in the hands of union officials, but there are gains for employees as well. Guarantees written into collective agreements cannot easily be taken away, and this becomes the basis for one of the unions' most powerful arguments for representative status. In light of labor's relative weakness, the constant and very

---

[107] 379 U.S. at 223 (Stewart, J., concurring).
[108] *First National Maintenance Corp. v. NLRB*, 452 U.S. 666 (1981).
[109] Ibid., 676 (1981).

real threat of hostile legislation throughout the war, and the erosion of public support due to wartime strikes, these gains are significant.[110]

The WLB strongly criticized strikes as early as mid-1942, and public member Wayne L. Morse, especially upset over union jurisdictional conflicts, warned that the laws against treason would be applied to strikers in such disputes. In the Seventy-seventh Congress alone, twenty-one bills were introduced dealing with wartime strikes, three of which sought to make strikes in defense plants treasonous and punishable by death. Employer groups, notably the National Association of Manufacturers, charged that strikes were damaging war production even though workdays lost due to strikes were very low. It was the successive miners' strikes of 1943 that made that year so exceptional, walkouts that led to the War Labor Disputes Act of 1943 and helped inflame public opinion against strikes.[111]

Nevertheless, despite the gains, the practices and law of arbitration also have negative effects on industrial democracy. First, arbitration focuses upon the written agreement as the exclusive source of employee rights. The agreement is the result of economic struggle and, thus, represents the balance or imbalance of economic power. Indeed, the reliance upon contractualism means that rights are based upon the very kinds of economic imbalance that the Wagner Act sought to ameliorate. Moreover, the relative power of the parties is itself affected by the interpretations of the NLRA, often not favorable to union interests, especially in periods when unions are perceived to be weak. Second, arbitration removes the conflict, and its resolution, from the workplace and its affected workers. Just as important, arbitration and centralized bargaining alter the kinds of issues that are thought to be important.

Finally, arbitration procedures reflect the hierarchical system of the plant, and the substantive rules indicate, despite the rhetoric, that no

[110]Strong pressures were applied to unions during both the mobilization period and the war to curb the rank and file and strikes in general. Indeed, proposals for outlawing strikes in defense plants were introduced as early as 1941. Seidman, *American Labor from Defense to Reconversion*, 43–46. Hatton W. Sumners, chair of the House Judiciary Committee, suggested that "If it is necessary to preserve this country, [the committee] would not hesitate one split second to enact legislation to send them to the electric chair." *New York Times*, 29 March 1941.

Four days later a bill was introduced to make strikes treasonable, providing for twenty-five years in prison as a minimum penalty and execution as the maximum sentence. Throughout the war period, unions would fear such legislation and such fear would explain a good deal of their behavior.
[111]Seidman, *American Labor from Defense to Reconversion*, 135–42; David Ziskind, "The Impact of the War on Labor Law," *Law and Contemporary Problems* 9 (1942): 385.

participatory democracy is to be created. The key rule of arbitration, that employees must obey work orders and grieve, makes it clear that management may act upon its interpretation of the agreement but the union may not. Arbitration becomes the device to maintain production and the only avenue to test the union's view of its contractual rights. Inherent in the rule itself is a choice of managerial hegemony and continued production over more participatory industrial self-government.

This is not to argue that legal rules necessarily reflect reality or substantially affect behavior. The argument is only that the very assumptions of, and tensions within, pluralist thought would affect the shape of postwar law and aid in creating restrictive rulings, especially when labor's power is perceived to wane. Pluralist thought, after all, was immeasurably aided by the appearance of relative equality in the postwar period. Alan Fox's perceptive analysis of labor relations in the United Kingdom in the early 1970s is also applicable to the experience of the United States to the 1970s. With few exceptions, labor accepted

as given those major structural features which are crucial for the power, status and rewards of the owners and controllers. It is because this condition is usually fulfilled that owners and controllers are rarely driven to call upon their reserves of power in any overt and public exercise. Only the margins of power are needed to cope with marginal adjustments. This, then, is what accounts for the illusion of a power balance. Labour often has to marshal all its resources to fight on these marginal adjustments; capital can, as it were, fight with one hand behind its back and still achieve in most situations a verdict that it finds tolerable.[112]

The generally superior power of capital has been unleashed in a period when reduced profit margins and international competition induced management to contest labor and working conditions, the one aspect of production over which it has historically had most control.

Arbitration is but a part, albeit perhaps a necessary part, of collective bargaining, and it is no more confining than bargaining itself. Bargaining, after all, is affected by relative economic power, and imbalances will be reflected in the resulting contracts that arbitrators are called upon to interpret. Perhaps the most important legacy of the War Labor Board is its view that the scope of bargaining is itself limited to only those matters not deemed critical to managerial efficiency and, especially, capital mobility. Such assumptions after the war became part of the underlying basis

---

[112]Alan Fox, *Beyond Contract: Work, Power and Trust Relations* (London: Faber and Faber 1974), 279–80.

of the NLRA, helping to render unions impotent when faced with the torrent of plant removals and closures in the 1970s and 1980s.

Pluralist premises rest upon substantially equal power because only then can collective bargaining be considered "industrial self-government." The current sharp decline in the labor movement, matched by a crisis in pluralist circles, reveals that equal power does not exist and that the bargaining system, both defined and limited by legal decisions, will not likely result in substantial equality. The seeds of the problem stem in part from the War Labor Board's recognition and protection of inherent managerial or property rights, concerns even the needs of wartime could not weaken. The recognition of managerial rights would lead the Supreme Court to hold in 1981 that the Wagner Act Congress "had no expectation that the elected representative would become an equal partner in the running of the business enterprise in which the union's members are employed."

The pluralists as well as the War Labor Board deferred to the rights of owners and managers to direct their enterprises, although they qualified the arbitrary exercise of such power by insisting that responsible unions have a voice in the determination of those conditions of employment that did not invade the protective zone of managerial prerogative. The conflict between the protection of management decision making and the encouragement of collective bargaining has never been resolved, either by the pluralists or the courts.[113] The language of pluralism reflected in the writings of scholars and arbitrators is proudly antitheoretical and ahistorical. The pluralist vision is seen as pragmatic, an emphasis on what worked. Thus, William P. Murphy, president of the National Academy of Arbitrators during its fortieth year, recently discussed the accomplishments and continued problems of arbitration. Some problems such as "reserved management rights, implied obligations, past practice," he noted, still remained unresolved. Murphy suggested "that the subject has no final definitive answer, that we are now burdened by over-analysis, and that the best a conscientious arbitrator can do is to be aware of and understand the various points of view and then do what seems right in the particular case."[114] Noteworthy are both the absence of any discus-

[113] Stone, "The Post-war Paradigm," 1544–58; Atleson, *Values and Assumptions in American Labor Law*, chapter 9.
[114] William Murphy, "The Presidential Address: The Academy at Forty," in Gladys Gruenberg, ed., *Arbitration 1987: The Academy at Forty*, Proceedings of the Fortieth Annual Meeting of the NAA (Washington, D.C.: BNA, 1987), 9.

sion of the profound changes in industrial structure and labor relations and the assumption that choices of the unresolved issues in arbitration do not involve choices in policy and theory. Another reaction in industrial relations circles is simple denial that fundamental changes have occurred in American industrial and labor relations.[115]

Collective bargaining in its decentralized American form has left the labor movement particularly dependent upon the success and viability of certain mass production industries. Their decline weakens the institutional strength of unions, but the unions' history provides no way to question current institutional arrangements or to propose transformative ideas. Union structure has tended to match that of the employers with whom they bargain, but locally based bargaining would appear to make little sense in relation to large, multiplant firms with typically centralized labor policy making. Moreover, the modern growth of conglomerates and multinational corporations drastically affects the power relationships of labor and capital. Unions find themselves increasingly dealing with firms that can easily weather economic struggles, conceal information, and transfer, or more credibly threaten to transfer, work to other locales or, indeed, other countries. This drastic change in corporate and capital structure mandates a rethinking of our labor laws.

Labor law reform, however, is unlikely so long as unions are perceived to be weak, for the system responds to the strong and the troublesome. Instead, unions are likely to participate more willingly in "non-adversarial" participation schemes, such as quality circles and team arrangements, generally more favored by employees than union officials. These arrangements, hearkening back to employee representation structures in the early part of the century,[116] will likely become the hallmark of unorganized employers as well. A 1982 survey found that at least a third of Fortune 500 companies, organized and unorganized, have some form of participative management or quality of worklife program and that such programs have generally resulted in improved employee morale and increased productivity.[117] Although these arrangements are some-

---

[115]See, for instance, John Dunlop, "Have the 1980's Changed U.S. Industrial Relations?" *Monthly Labor Review* 111:5 (May 1988): 29.

[116]Thomas Kohler, "Models of Worker Participation: The Uncertain Significance of Section 8 (a) (2)," *Boston College Law Review* 27 (1986): 519–27; Sanford M. Jacoby, *Employing Bureaucracy: Managers, Unions, and the Transformation of Work in American Industry, 1900–1945* (New York: Columbia University Press, 1985), 187–89; Reinhard Bendix, *Work and Authority in Industry* (Berkeley: University of California Press, 1956).

[117]Office of Economic Research, New York Stock Exchange, *People and Productivity: A*

times created to deter the possibility of union organization, they tend in organized workplaces to deal with matters not covered by collective bargaining. Indeed, participation plans in unionized workplaces generally restrict the jurisdiction of participatory arrangements to matters not covered by the collective agreement. These arrangements, therefore, actually recognize the failure of collective bargaining to deal with the full range of employee interests and to respond to employee concerns for integrity on the job.

Challenge to Corporate America (November 1982). See Michael J. Piore and Charles F. Sabel, *The Second Industrial Divide* (New York: Basic Books, 1984), 240–50.

8

Workplace contractualism
in comparative perspective

DAVID BRODY

There is no argument about the essential characteristics of the unionized
workplace regime that emerged out of the great New Deal organizing
era in the mass-production sector of American industry: that the shop-
floor rights of industrial workers would be specified rather than left open,
that specification would occur through the process of collective bargaining, and take contractual form, and that the contractual rights of workers
would be protected through a formal grievance procedure (itself specified
in the contract), with arbitration by a neutral third party normally as
the final and binding step. The historical boundaries of this regime, which
I will call workplace contractualism, are likewise clearly marked. First,
workplace contractualism lasted as a relatively unchallenged system
roughly from the late 1940s to the late 1960s; second, its locus was the
mass-production sector where, despite a certain amount of variation
between industries and among companies within industries, workplace
contractualism can be said to have been experienced in essentially the
same way.

Every generation of scholars defines afresh what it considers to be
worthy of study. For this generation of labor scholars, the shop floor
occupies a special place. The initiating work, Harry Braverman's *Labor
and Monopoly Capital: The Degradation of Work in the Twentieth Century,* appeared in 1974. In its wake, there followed a stream of notable
books and articles in economics, sociology, critical legal studies, and

For their critical readings of earlier versions of this essay, I thank (in chronological order,
since each reading forced a further revision) George Strauss, Jonathan Zeitlin, Gary Gerstle,
and Sandra Van Burkleo.

history in what might be called the rank-and-file school of labor scholarship.[1] Braverman himself drew on Marx's concept of work alienation in capitalist production, while many younger scholars were inspired by New Left visions of participatory democracy, in which, as the critical legal scholar Karl Klare has put it, "the struggle [is] to make the workplace a realm of free self-activity and expression."[2]

Why the workplace should be treated as a central subject has perhaps been most cogently stated by Charles F. Sabel. His book *Work and Politics* (1982) is about justice. Industrial workers in all societies, says Sabel, hold notions of what is right and honorable at the workplace. Rooted in diverse "world views" that they bring into the factory, and, as between craftworkers, semiskilled operatives, and peasant workers, linked to specific interests within the occupational structure, their sense of workplace justice can manifest itself in submerged and even divisive ways. But whatever its guises, the notion of justice is always at the core of how workers understand the treatment they receive at the hands of managers. What happens on the shop floor is not a secondary affair in the lives of working people. On the contrary, it engages their innermost sense of self-worth and honor.

In times of crisis, the division of labor (and the sectional notions of industrial justice it engenders) can suddenly be surmounted, and new, unifying conceptions of workplace justice can be forged. It is these transformative moments that occupy Sabel's attention. The paradigmatic event for him is the *autunno caldo* of 1969, when peasant migrants from the southern provinces and seasoned craftworkers rose up together and imposed an extraordinary degree of workers' control over Italy's factories. For America, the 1930s are to Sabel a comparable experience. During the unionizing struggle of that era, the division of labor in mass-production industry was surmounted, and workers began to demand industrial unionism, notwithstanding past ethno-racial divisiveness, contrary traditions of craft exclusiveness, and the unyielding opposition of the American Federation of Labor. Indeed, the meaning of industrial

---

[1] Key early works are: Michael Burawoy, *Manufacturing Consent: Changes in the Labor Process* (Chicago, 1979); Richard Edwards, *Contested Terrain: The Transformation of the Workplace in the 20th Century* (New York, 1979); Karl E. Klare, "Judicial Deradicalization of the Wagner Act and the Origins of Modern Legal Consciousness, 1937–1941," *Minnesota Law Review* 62 (March 1978): 265–339; David Montgomery, *Workers' Control in America* (New York, 1979). And for an early survey of works in the rank-and-file vein: Jeremy Brecher, "Uncovering the Hidden History of the American Workplace," *Review of Radical Political Economics* 10 (Winter 1978):1–23.
[2] Klare, 338–39.

unionism seems to me much better understood in Sabel's terms of rank-and-file transformation than as a trade-union dispute over the appropriate jurisdictional response to the mass-production sector. Industrial unionism won out not because it offered a more efficient way of dealing with General Motors or U.S. Steel, but because it expressed the solidarity of the mobilized industrial workers. In the course of that struggle, too, unilateral control by corporate employers over the workplace dissolved, and for the first time a measure of power passed into the hands of industrial workers.

And how was the promise of that "transformative moment" fulfilled? The emergent system of workplace contractualism, writes Lichtenstein, was "one in which the effort to introduce certain democratic norms was subordinated to the seemingly more pressing effort to find social mechanisms that could maintain industrial discipline and resolve economic conflict between the big unions and their management adversaries" (p. 115). Workplace contractualism "defined industrial democracy in process terms—outcomes or fairness were to be irrelevant," writes Atleson in his chapter. "Collective action or self-help in the resolution of labor disputes" is constrained, making "it difficult for employees to assert their individual contract rights when they seek to challenge an employer's action that the union fails to challenge or where the arbitration process is tainted in some way" (p. 149). For the rank and file, industrial justice has not been won. On the contrary, as Katherine Van Wezel Stone has argued in probably the most influential critique, workplace contractualism (or, more precisely in her argument, the ideology of "industrial pluralism" underlying it) "serves as a vehicle for the manipulation of employee discontent and for the legitimation of existing inequalities of power in the workplace."[3]

From this tragic disjuncture between promise and fulfillment, a compelling logic of historical causation follows. In Stone's analysis, workplace contractualism is the work of an identifiable group of actors. Without George W. Taylor, Harry Shulman, and other strategically placed industrial pluralists, the future could have been different. In parallel fashion, Lichtenstein assigns to wartime labor administration the responsibility for "creat[ing] the institutional framework for the kind of collective bargaining that evolved in the decade or so after the war." The National

[3]Katherine Van Wezel Stone, "The Post-war Paradigm in American Labor Law," *Yale Law Journal* 90 (June 1981): 1517.

War Labor Board, in particular, "was a powerful force in nationalizing a conception of routine and bureaucratic industrial relations," which included "fixing a system of industrial relations on the shop floor."[4] What Stone and Lichtenstein share is a sense of historical contingency: that is, a tendency to explain the outcome they are describing by the intervention of specific actors or events.

In the chapters in this volume, that logic is more ambiguously asserted. Atleson cautions us against concluding that he is arguing that contemporary law was exclusively created in wartime, for many of the underlying values in American labor law long predate the federal statutes. The war, however, "helped to create, encourage, or cement visions of the proper labor-management system and the appropriate role of the state." Lichtenstein's richly informed account of the evolution of workplace contractualism at General Motors is ambiguous in a somewhat different way. The evidence it marshals might well be cast against contingent explanation, but not the frame within which the chapter itself is set. By bracketing it with Sumner Slichter's landmark books of 1941 and 1960—the first celebrating the promise of industrial jurisprudence, the second fixed in the rigidities of workplace contractualism—Lichtenstein is posing the problem in a manner wholly characteristic of the rank-and-file school of labor scholarship.

If the transformative moment is seen as genuinely open, and in particular if the actual outcome outrages the historian's own sense of values, then he or she is powerfully impelled toward a logic of contingent explanation: it could have been otherwise.

Yet there is strong empirical evidence to the contrary. Signs of workplace contractualism can be found before the Congress of Industrial Organizations (CIO), before the Wagner Act, before the first contracts. In Flint, for example, workers were already demanding seniority based on length of service and an impartial grievance procedure in March 1934. "People were longing for some kind of security in their work," one Buick rank-and-file leader recalled. "We had seen so much discrimination... people who had a lot of service and had been laid off and friends and relatives kept on. It was easy to organize people." And expectations were clearly rising during the National Recovery Administration (NRA) period. Fear of layoffs kept workers on the truck assembly line at the

---

[4] Nelson Lichtenstein, "Industrial Democracy, Contract Unionism, and the National War Labor Board," *Labor Law Journal* 33 (August 1982): 524.

Chevrolet St. Louis plant quiet in 1935, remembered another rank-and-file leader. "I mean we were supposed to have seniority but they did not recognize it when it came to layoffs." From the very start of collective bargaining in 1936 and 1937, seniority was high on labor's agenda.[5] Everywhere at the local level a major preoccupation after recognition was the renegotiation of individual wage rates to conform to some standard of equity within the job classification structure. The first contracts with U.S. Steel and Jones and Laughlin called for the elimination of inequalities in pay rates and, since this turned on the comparability of jobs, quickly led to demands for the negotiation of rationalized job classification systems.[6]

Inherent in seniority and pay equity was a notion of a workplace rule of law whose corollary was an adjudicative approach to grievance settlement. The very first contracts established formal grievance procedures. Final-step arbitration soon followed, initially only with the consent of both parties, but increasingly as the required final step in the process. When General Motors accepted a permanent umpire in 1940, the model of the grievance-resolution structure was virtually complete.[7]

This adjudicative development in turn magnified the contractual responsibilities of the union. By 1941, agreements commonly contained clauses formally obligating the union to enforce compliance on its members. By specifying the numbers, duties, and rights of the shop stewards, moreover, the early agreements incorporated shop-floor representation into the contractual relationship between union and company. That shop-floor relations fell within their orbit was a claim enunciated by every

---

[5] Ronald Edsforth, *Class Conflict and Cultural Consensus* (New Brunswick, N.J., 1987), 158–59, 166; James F. Doherty Interview, Oral History Collection, Walter Reuther Archives of Labor and Urban Affairs, Detroit, p. 18; Carl Gersuny, "Origins of Seniority Provisions in Collective Bargaining," *Labor Law Journal* 33 (August 1982): 518–24; Gersuny, "Seniority and the Moral Economy of U.S. Automobile Workers, 1934–1936," *Journal of Social History* 18 (Spring 1985): 463–75.

[6] Frederick H. Harbison, "Steel," in Harry A. Millis, ed., *How Collective Bargaining Works* (New York, 1942), 553; *SWOC Handbook* (Pittsburgh, 1937), 15. For early UAW concern with job classification systems, see Press Release, 16 September 1937 [re demands at GM], and *Chrysler Demands* [March 1937], box 11, Henry Kraus Collection, Reuther Archives. The centrality of pay equity as a local bargaining issue at General Motors during 1939–41 is very apparent in the correspondence in box 1, series 1, UAW General Motors Department Collection, Reuther Archives.

[7] On Reuther's successful efforts at negotiating for an impartial umpire, see Reuther to GM locals, 2 and 18 June 1940, box 1, series 1, UAW-GM Department Collection. As early as mid–1938, the GM department was already advocating an impartial umpire. Homer Martin and William E. Dowell to GM locals, 15 June 1938. Box 1, Series 1, UAW General Motors Department Collection, Reuther Archives.

industrial union, although it took a highly centralized and well-financed union like the Steel Workers Organizing Committee (CIO) to put that claim fully into effect. The steel union made itself signatory to every agreement, specified plant grievance committees "designated by the Union," required the entry of national SWOC representatives at the fourth step, and dealt sternly with rebellious shop stewards and local unions. Altogether, conclude two industrial relations scholars after surveying four hundred contracts of the 1935–42 period, the contractual pattern was fixed very early. "Many 'modern' provisions in fact existed in the prewar period.... It is clear that the parties did not require the civilizing influence of the NWLB to invent these features."[8]

If the evidence marshaled here seems strong, however, it by no means makes an ironclad empirical case for the necessity of workplace contractualism. "In the later 1930s and early 1940s," Nelson Lichtenstein has written, "the institution of collective bargaining was but one of several elements that defined the relationship between workers and their employers. At the shop-floor level, day-to-day conflict over production standards and workplace discipline permeated the work structure and authority in the factory.... Shop-floor assemblies, slowdowns, and stoppages proliferated after the sit-down strikes of 1936 and 1937.... Direct shop-floor activity legitimized the union's presence for thousands of previously hesitant workers who now poured into the union ranks, and such job actions established a pattern of union influence and authority unrecognized in the early, sketchily written contracts."[9] Granting Lichtenstein's authority on these matters, there would seem to be as much empirically to justify his sense of unforeclosed possibilities as for the rival conception of a contractualist outcome already determined even in the heat of the shop-floor struggles of the New Deal era.

Which is the correct assessment? The conundrum of contingency versus necessity does not seem to me susceptible to empirical resolution. Much remains to be learned about the shop-floor history of the industrial-union period, of course, but a deeper reservoir of information will surely not flow in only one direction. And if we know that the war had an important impact, or that (as with Sidney Hillman's role in the installation of an

---

[8] David Brody, "The Origins of Modern Steel Unionism: The SWOC Era," in Peter F. Clark et al., eds., *Forging A Union of Steel* (Ithaca, N.Y., 1987), chapter 2; Sanford Jacoby and Daniel J. B. Mitchell, "Origins of the Union Contract," *Labor Law Journal* 33 (August 1982): 512–18.

[9] Lichtenstein, "Industrial Democracy," 525.

impartial umpire at GM) identifiable people of industrial-pluralist persuasion played a part, we have no empirical test of the determinative
power of either the war or of key individuals. To settle the fundamental
issue of causation, we need to shift the discussion to a different level of
inquiry and ask whether or not a larger logic existed calling forth those
choices that made for workplace contractualism.

To that end, I propose to engage in a certain amount of opportunistic
comparative analysis. The difficulties inherent in the comparative method
are always formidable, but in this instance they seem manageable. For
one thing, workplace relations are a well-bounded topic. Moreover, we
can be reasonably confident of holding things constant, since the period
under review was a time of notable stability within the industrial relations
systems of all the principal industrialized countries. This perhaps bears
emphasis: the comparisons I am making relate strictly to the postwar
quarter century before the onset of a new cycle of change in the late
1960s. For this stable period, finally, there is a rich and accessible descriptive literature on which to draw, thanks to the flourishing industrial
relations scholarship of that era.[10]

In 1966, the International Labour Organization (ILO) took up an
agenda item entitled "Examination of Grievances and Communications
within the Undertaking." Under ILO procedures, the secretariat prepares
a working document, which is circulated for comment to the member
countries. Their replies to the questionnaire on grievances make instructive reading.[11] Consider the following demurrers from the American responses to the ILO preliminary document. On the formal procedures
strongly favored by the United States: not in the Netherlands, where
collective agreements or works regulations generally made no provision
for grievance mechanisms. Instead, the Dutch relied on "the natural
facilities offered by the organization of the undertaking," with the op-

[10] Useful entry points are Walter Galenson, ed., *Comparative Labor Movements* (New York, 1952); Adolf Sturmthal, *Workers Councils* (Cambridge, Mass., 1964); and, for a sustained effort at comparative analysis, John T. Dunlop, *Industrial Relations Systems* (New York, 1958). For specific countries, see, e.g., George S. Bain, ed., *Industrial Relations in Britain* (Oxford, 1981); Robert E. Cole, *Japanese Blue Collar* (Berkeley, Calif., 1971); Andrew Gordon, *The Evolution of Labor Relations in Japan: Heavy Industry, 1853–1955* (Cambridge, Mass., 1985); Val R. Lorwin, *The French Labor Movement* (Cambridge, Mass., 1954); Wolfgang Streeck, *Industrial Relations in West Germany: A Case Study of the Car Industry* (New York, 1984); Kenneth F. Walker, *Australian Industrial Relations Systems* (Cambridge, Mass., 1970). Especially rewarding among journals for its comparative coverage is *The British Journal of Industrial Relations* (1962–).
[11] The responses are in International Labour Organization, *Examination of Grievances and Communications within the Undertaking* [Report 7] (Geneva, 1966), vol. 2.

portunity always available to appeal to an outside public authority. "In the Netherlands there is no need to draw up formal procedures at the level of the undertaking." On the question of granting a major role for trade unions in the grievance process: not in West Germany, where this would have been illegal under the Works Constitution Act (1952). The representation of workers within plants was by law the function of the works councils.

What about the distinction that U.S. and Canadian unions draw between grievances and "general claims," that is, in American parlance, between "rights" and "interests"? French unions rejected the rights/interests distinction because they did not rely on rights-creating works agreements or differentiate between grievances and collective claims. Workplace regulation in France, in fact, fell much more to a multiplicity of public agencies than within the realm of collective bargaining. Likewise, Australia's compulsory arbitration system rendered the rights/interests distinction inoperable. On matters covered by arbitration awards, the tribunals adjudicated all disputes, making no distinction between individual grievances and general claims. What the awards did not cover, which included almost everything touching the workplace, was left to informal resolution within the plants. As the Australian response delicately put it: "The formulation of an international instrument dealing exclusively and specifically with grievances, however defined, may therefore introduce unreal, in local terms, or inappropriate conceptual distinctions into the industrial relations systems of some countries."[12]

On the mechanisms for securing the grievance rights of workers, the ILO listed works regulations, collective agreements, arbitration awards, national laws or regulations, "or in such other manner consistent with national practice as may be appropriate under national conditions." No one could take exception to so ecumenical an approach, of course, but the United Kingdom did put a word in for informality and diversity, as indeed it consistently did in its responses. What this reflected was the ambiguous nature of the concept of a grievance system in contemporary British industrial relations. Industry-wide agreements did specify dispute-settlement procedures, but within the plants these were rendered essentially inoperable by the shop steward system, which relied on unwritten "custom and practice" enforced through an ongoing process of informal shop-floor negotiation and shop action. As the Donovan Commission

---

[12] Ibid., 12, 28, 31, 42, 96.

concluded two years later, collective bargaining had "become increasingly empty, while the practices of the informal system have come to exert an ever greater influence on the conduct of industrial relations...and... cannot be forced to comply with the formal system."[13]

The Japanese, although always assenting, were discreetly unresponsive to the ILO proposals. Their formal grievance systems, as in England, had little correspondence to the realities of Japanese industrial relations. For one thing, the distinction between labor and management was blurred. At Hitachi, for example, it was the foremen who routinely protested too high standards set by rate fixers, while union officials wore company overalls and considered themselves part of the company team.[14] Collective-bargaining agreements were drawn in terms so general and ambiguous as sometimes to be ruled by the courts as technically impossible to adjudicate. The formal dispute procedures were, in any case, rarely used. "Japanese industrial relations are not concerned with the exact definition of the rights of parties in a dispute," remarked the labor law scholar Tadashi Hanami, but turn rather on "a kinship type relationship within the enterprise-family," in which harmony is expected to prevail and differences are to be resolved through "emotional understanding." "Subordinates are not supposed to express disagreement or to state their grievances openly; they are expected to endure hardships in anticipation of the benevolent consideration of the superior."[15]

Given the remarkable diversity of workplace regimes thus revealed, it becomes hard to think of the American arrangements as in any sense "normal." That is surely the first step toward useful comparative analysis. The second is to identify the influences that best account for the significant variations among workplace regimes.

In the case of workplace contractualism, the most salient influences derive from the technical and structural characteristics of the American mass-production sector. To get our bearings here, we start with the enlightening historical analysis of mass production in Michael Piore and Charles Sabel's *The Second Industrial Divide* (1984). Piore and Sabel insist, first of all, on the historically contingent nature of technological development. At the first industrial "divide" in the nineteenth century, mass production emerged as the dominant system, but it was neither the only possibility

[13] Quoted in Bain, 139.
[14] Ronald Dore, *British Factory–Japanese Factory: The Origins of National Diversity in Industrial Relations* (Berkeley, Calif., 1973), 169–70.
[15] Tadashi Hanami, *Labor Relations in Japan Today* (Tokyo, 1979), 54, 57.

nor the inevitable victor. Other real alternatives existed, in particular, what Piore and Sabel call "flexible specialization," which relied on skilled workers using sophisticated general-purpose machinery to turn out a wide and constantly changing assortment of goods—this in contrast, of course, to rigid mass-production techniques based on special-purpose machinery making standardized products for extensive, stable markets. From this, Piore and Sabel derive a second key point—namely, a persisting technological diversity within the twentieth-century industrial order. Although perceived worldwide as the paradigmatic model, mass production actually took relatively complete hold only in the United States. In varying degrees and ways, craft production persisted in the manufacturing industries of Germany, Italy, France, Japan, and England. And it is within the resulting diversity of productive systems—with the United States as the baseline case of mass production—that the diversity of their shop-floor regimes flourished.[16]

British metal fabricating affords the most instructive comparison for our purposes. Spurred in the 1890s by intensifying foreign competition and by access to advanced American machine tools, British engineering firms formed a strong trade association and moved to break the hold of craft regulation over production. In the great lockout of 1897–98, the Amalgamated Society of Engineers was decisively defeated. In the United States, a remarkably similar struggle occurred at almost the same time, with very much the same outcome. But in England this did not lead to a major reorganization of the workshop. Instead, the victorious British employers chose to exert their power within the existing system of craft production. Payment by results was the key to their strategy, enabling them to contain labor costs and intensify effort norms without having to incur the heavy capital investment and accept the managerial responsibilities that were the preconditions for asserting direct control over the labor process. Following Frederick W. Taylor, of course, American metal-trades employers also favored piecework,[17] but where they treated it merely as an incentive mechanism within a larger scheme of managerial control, British engineering employers saw piecework as a solution in

---

[16] It need hardly be added, of course, that diversity could be found in the United States as well. For a detailed study of flexible specialization in the Philadelphia textile industry, e.g., see Philip Scranton, *Proprietary Capitalism: The Textile Manufacture at Philadelphia, 1800–1885* (New York, 1983).

[17] In 1928, 53 percent of all manufacturing workers were on piecework. Sanford Jacoby, *Employing Bureaucracy: Managers, Workers, and the Transformation of Work in American Industry, 1900–1945* (New York, 1985), 195.

itself. In the American metal trades, industrial warfare developed into a life-and-death struggle over control of the shop floor;[18] in England, it took the form of endless skirmishing over the price of work. What became the very heart of the informal shop steward system—individual bargaining over piece rates—had started as an employer demand during the crisis of the 1890s.

Initially, the Anglo-American divergence remained somewhat masked because in the engineering trades, notwithstanding the claims of Taylor's disciples, there were very considerable technical constraints on managerial control of the labor process. But in automobile manufacturing, Henry Ford's assembly-line innovations effectively removed those constraints. British manufacturers were, of course, keenly aware of what was happening in Detroit. After a certain amount of experimentation, as Wayne Lewchuk demonstrates in his important analysis, British car firms adopted much of the technology but opted against the flow methods and managerial control structures that characterized American-style mass production.[19]

Only after the almost simultaneous resurgence of union organization among auto workers on both sides of the Atlantic from the mid-1930s onward did the shop-floor consequences of this technical divergence fully emerge. In their spontaneous beginnings, their bent for direct action, and their reliance on rank-and-file support, the shop steward structures that sprang up in Coventry and Detroit seem on their face to have been much alike. But over the longer term, after the heady seizure of power, fundamental differences surface. The work groups operating on collective piecework at the Coventry firms expelled the "gangers"—the foremen who shared in the collective wage—and elected their own gang leaders who, in Jonathan Zeitlin's words, "became in practice shop stewards negotiating collective piece rates with management."[20] No structural change occurred; the basis for independent action was already in place; and, so Lewchuk concluded, as soon as labor conditions turned favorable,

[18] David Montgomery, *The Fall of the House of Labor* (New York, 1987), chapters 4–6.
[19] Wayne Lewchuk, *American Technology and the British Vehicle Industry* (Cambridge, 1987), 113 and passim; Jonathan Zeitlin, "The Labour Strategies of British Engineering Employers, 1890–1920," and Wayne Lewchuk, "Fordism and British Motor Car Employees, 1896–1932," both in Howard F. Gospel and Craig R. Littler, eds., *Managerial Strategies and Industrial Relations: An Historical and Comparative Study* (London, 1983), 25–54, 82–110.
[20] Jonathan Zeitlin, "The Emergence of Shop Steward Organization and Job Control in the British Car Industry: A Review Essay," *History Workshop Journal* (Autumn 1980): 123.

"this independence was formalised in the rise of shop stewards and shop stewards' committees."[21]

In American automobile plants, there was no such supervisory vacuum. At the outermost limits, shop stewards might achieve what Nelson Lichtenstein has described at the Ford River Rouge complex as "dual power."[22] But without being rooted in a technically determined and self-sustaining workplace autonomy, even this degree of seized authority could not be carried beyond the enabling periods of militant organizing or wartime advantage. Afterward, management moved to regain the initiative, to restore the weakened supervisory structures, and to deny to the shop stewards any shop-floor basis for autonomous authority. That campaign never wholly succeeded, of course. Informal work groups persisted. Even in automobile plants, not more than 20 percent of the labor force was on assembly-line work, and elsewhere, in rubber and electrical manufacturing, machine-paced control was much less of a factor. And where management relied heavily on piece-rate systems, as at International Harvester, shop-floor resistance was likely to be especially strong.[23] But the redesign of work and machinery was unrelenting, and, what was perhaps more important, so was the supervisory oversight that confined the power of informal work groups to marginal and covert forms.[24] The American shop steward system was ultimately sustained, not as in England by the organization of work on the shop floor, but by its validation

[21] Wayne Lewchuk, "The Motor Vehicle Industry: Roots of Decline," in Bernard Elbaum and William Lazonick, eds., *The Decline of the British Economy* (New York, 1986), 140.

[22] Lichtenstein, "Life at the Rouge: A Cycle of Workers' Control," in Charles Stephenson and Robert Asher, eds., *Life and Labor: Dimensions of American Working-Class History* (Albany, N.Y., 1986), 243.

[23] Nelson Lichtenstein, "Auto Worker Militancy and the Structure of Factory Life, 1937–1955," *Journal of American History* 67 (September 1980): 335–53; Daniel Nelson, "Origins of the Sit-Down Era: Worker Militancy and Innovation in the Rubber Industry," *Labor History* 23 (Spring 1982): 198–225; Ronald W. Schatz, *The Electrical Workers: A History of Labor at General Electric and Westinghouse, 1923–1960* (Urbana, Ill., 1983); Stephen Meyer, "Technology at the Workplace: Skilled and Production Workers at Allis-Chalmers, 1900–1941," *Technology and Culture* 29 (October 1988): 839–64. On the influence of union ideology, see Toni Gilpin, "The FE-UAW Conflict: The Ideological Content of Collective Bargaining in Postwar America," and Mark McCulloch, "The Shop Floor Dimension: The Case of Westinghouse" (Papers delivered at the North American Labor History Conference, 20–22 October 1988).

[24] See especially James W. Kuhn, *Bargaining in Grievance Settlement: The Power of Industrial Groups* (New York, 1961). For an argument that seeks to minimize Anglo-American shop-floor differences, see Steven Tolliday and Jonathan Zeitlin, "Shop-floor Bargaining, Contract Unionism and Job Control: An Anglo-American Comparison," in Tolliday and Zeitlin, eds., *The Automobile Industry and Its Workers: Between Fordism and Flexibility* (Oxford, 1986), 99–120.

as a useful representational mechanism within the larger contractual relationship between managements and unions.

How workers perceived shop-floor justice was likewise expressive of differing factory regimes. Where tasks were subdivided and precisely defined, as they were in American mass production, the notion of job classification could not be far behind. The Ford Motor Company was designing such a scheme even before it introduced the five-dollar day in 1914.[25] Within the large manufacturing firms, the hallmarks of an internal labor market began to emerge—personnel departments, internal job ladders, promotion from within, welfare and training programs, and some consideration of seniority in layoffs and job assignments. So that, if pay equity and seniority rights were immediate union demands, they were demands arising out of the logic of the mass-production enterprise itself.

Ironically, these became fighting issues because corporate employers themselves proved only imperfectly committed to their own creation. As the wartime labor crisis subsided in the 1920s, in fact, there was considerable backsliding from earlier movements for personnel reform, including a relaxation of efforts to rein in the foremen.[26] Even in progressive firms such as General Electric and Westinghouse, Ronald Schatz has remarked, workers "lived in a half-way house between arbitrary rule and systematic policy."[27] And with the Great Depression, the worker's stake in predictable, rule-bound treatment grew enormously. Favoritism and capriciousness came to seem so peculiarly reprehensible because such acts violated the very precepts of bureaucratic order by which the corporate enterprise itself lived. When the Chevrolet management in St. Louis fired two union workers in 1934 for violating Factory Rule #23 (prohibiting solicitation of workers on company premises), the AFL local charged that the action was "plainly discriminatory" because that rule and others had been "promiscuously broken" by foremen and company-union workers. The two unionists were not reinstated, but the management did announce that Rule #23 would henceforth be strictly and uniformly enforced.[28] In these ways, a quite precise meaning of industrial justice emerged from the factory environment.

[25]Stephen Meyer, *The Five Dollar Day: Labor, Management and Social Control in the Ford Motor Company, 1908–1921* (Albany, N.Y., 1981), chapter 4; David Gartman, *Auto Slavery: The Labor Process in the American Automobile Industry, 1897–1950* (New Brunswick, N.J., 1986), 213.
[26]Jacoby, *Employing Bureaucracy,* chapter 6.
[27]Quoted in Jacoby, 193.
[28]George S. Danner, FLU #18386, to P. E. Baugh, plant manager, 14 November 1934,

Prior to the New Deal, the workplace was a realm mostly beyond the direct reach of the state. Certain industries, it was true, had experienced some degree of public intrusion as, for example, coal, where state mining laws not only regulated safety conditions, but mandated checkweighmen, licensed miners, and in other ways influenced workplace relations. From the Erdman Act (1898) onward, too, the mediation of disputes and adjustment of grievances on the railroads became matters of federal provenance. And there were a number of specific public interventions in workplace relations—prohibiting the use of Taylorist methods in federal arsenals, for example, or granting workers the right to shop committees during World War I. But, on the whole, the direct impact of the state was essentially negative, serving mainly to underwrite and legitimate the unilateral rights of management at the workplace. In what was surely the emblematic event, the *Hitchman* decision (1917) upheld the yellow-dog contract as a "lawful agreement" issuing from "the constitutional rights of personal liberty and private property." With the Norris-LaGuardia Act (1932), the balance began to shift. Congress repudiated that fictitious contractual equality between employers and individual workers and curbed the antiunion powers of the federal courts. Only when the New Deal granted workers' rights to organize and engage in collective bargaining, however, did the state begin to bear down in a direct way on American shop-floor relations.

Section 7a of the National Industrial Recovery Act (1933) set in motion a remarkable process of experimentation and controversy. Corporate employers denied that, as written, Section 7a required them to recognize or contract with trade unions. The antidote was the employee representation plan (ERP), which had gained some currency among the welfare capitalists of the New Era, but was in 1933 seized on wholesale by open shop employers. According to the National Industrial Conference Board's guiding definition, employee representation was "a form of industrial organization under which the employees of an industrial establishment, through representatives by and from among themselves, share collectively in the adjustment of employment conditions in that establishment."[29] The ERPs were systems of workplace representation; they were, by de-

box 1, Homer Martin Collection, Reuther Archives. See also, e.g., David M. Gordon, Richard Edwards, and Michael Reich, *Segmented Work, Divided Workers: The Historical Transformation of Labor in the United States* (New York, 1982), chapter 6, which views industrial unionism as the "consolidation" of an earlier phase of corporate labor policy.
[29] Quoted in Session 1, GM Executive Training Program: Section G—Employee Relations (1933), box 16, Kraus Collection, Reuther Archives.

sign, not collective-bargaining agencies. The NRA battles over labor policy are best understood, in fact, as a competition between two rival conceptions of labor organization. And if we look at that competition for what it tells us about the development of workplace contractualism, events of very considerable magnitude suddenly come into focus.

First of all, the institutional structure of workplace contractualism began to take shape at this time. Even at their most pliant, the employee representation plans mark a kind of beginning for a grievance system. After seven months of operation, for example, the AC [Sparkplug] Employes' Association reported 148 "requests" to management, mostly involving lighting, ventilation, and toilets, to be sure, but also a scattering of issues—complaints about job classification, layoffs, speedup, scheduling—destined to be the main business of union grievance processing. Employee representation, moreover, could provide a framework for more aggressive activity. At the Dodge Main plant in Detroit, where an independent union led by Richard Frankensteen gained control of the works council by participating in proportional representation elections under the Automobile Labor Board, the plan became an increasingly robust advocate of the Dodge workers.[30]

The AFL unions themselves strenuously resisted the ERP system, rightly viewing it as a stratagem for denying them genuine collective bargaining. But, given their impotence, they had little choice but to channel their energies into workplace organization. Failing to gain bargaining rights, they concentrated on representing their members within the plant. How far this might lead was evident in the settlement of the bitter strike at the Chevrolet Toledo plant in April 1935: no signed agreement or wage increase, but a shop committee of five selected by and representing union members in the plant. The committeemen were authorized to present grievances and, if not resolved with the shop foremen, to carry them to a higher company official. Discharged or suspended workers could appeal to the superintendent through the shop committee or personally and, if they appealed within twenty-four hours, could expect a decision in their cases within three days.[31]

[30] AC Employes' Association, *A Report of Activities (From September 1933 to March 1934)*, box 16, Kraus Collection; "Automotive Industrial Workers' Association Members: We Swept the Primary Election for the Union!" box 16, Kraus Collection; Dodge Main Works Council Minutes, 1935–1937, passim, box 17, Kraus Collection.
[31] Proposed Agreement, FLU #18384, 11 May 1935; To the Officers and Members of UAW FLUs—F. J. Dillon, 17 May 1935; clipping, Toledo *Blade*, 14 May 1935, all in box 2, Martin Collection.

The sense of formal process inherent in these emerging workplace structures was fostered as well by the NRA's halting efforts at adjudicating violations of Section 7a. In appealing to the Automobile Labor Board or the regional labor boards, for example, local unionists were instructed to pay attention to board procedures, clear cases through the AFL Detroit office, and check "as best they can upon cases to be certain that only legitimate cases are presented for hearing."[32]

Consider next how seniority emerged as a formal issue. The right to organize under Section 7a implied the existence of a standard by which employer discrimination could be tested. The insidious power of this logic is best observed in the industry most strongly situated to resist Section 7a. In negotiating the auto code, industry representatives insisted on a clause reserving the "right to select, retain or advance employees on the basis of individual merit, without regard to their membership or nonmembership in any organization." The idea was to defend the open shop, but in fact the industry was conceding something quite fundamental—namely, that layoff and rehire of workers were not absolutely management prerogatives but subject to some objective test. Merit was not much of a standard, to be sure, but a standard it was, and from it came a remarkable provision in the president's auto settlement of 25 March 1934: in layoff and rehire, "such human relationships as married men with families shall come first and then seniority, individual skill and efficient service," and within these categories "no greater proportion of outside union employees similarly situated" were to be laid off than "other employees." The Automobile Labor Board, created by the terms of the settlement, then promulgated specific rules—among them, seniority—governing layoff and rehire in the industry. Invoked as a corollary of Section 7a rights, seniority almost at once took on a broader meaning. At Fisher Body in St. Louis in November 1934, for example, the AFL union was protesting "the laying off of men out of turn in the Receiving Department." Neither the Labor Board nor the industry in fact limited seniority claims to discrimination cases. From March 1934 onward, the documentary record fills up with talk of seniority, or, more precisely, with complaints about the weakness of the ALB provisions and/or about company violations.[33]

[32] "Duties of Union Officers," n.d., box 2, Martin Collection.
[33] Sidney Fine, *The Automobile under the Blue Eagle* (Ann Arbor, Mich., 1963), 68, 212, 251; Blanche Bernstein, "Hiring Policies in the Auto Industry," WPA Research Project

Within the framework of state regulation stemming from Section 7a there thus sprung up conceptions of workplace rights and organization that might well be characterized as proto-workplace contractualism. In the competition with collective bargaining, workplace representation initially had the edge. By putting the ERPs swiftly into place, management seized the field and for a time defined the terms of debate. The power balance was likewise in industry's favor. The AFL was never capable of mustering enough power on its own to impose collective bargaining on the major corporate employers. Nor was any basic challenge likely to come from within the New Deal, so long at least as it needed business cooperation for the industrial-recovery program. President Roosevelt was in fact sympathetic to the concept of workplace representation. This was the basis on which he had engineered the auto settlement of March 1934, from which he hoped might develop "a kind of works council in industry in which all groups of employees, whatever may be their choice of organization or form of representation, may participate in joint conferences with their employers."[34]

Had this line of thinking prevailed, some variant of the European works-council system (a notion not entirely discounted by sophisticated employers)[35] might well have issued from the competition between employee representation and collective bargaining of the early New Deal era. When the ALB sponsored representation elections under its own supervision, auto unionists charged that a form of "government" unionism was being imposed on the workers. The AFL boycott of the elections underscored the real nature of the challenge. But then open shop industry lost the initiative, and there followed a reversal of fortunes that was at once stunning and utterly decisive. With the National Labor Relations [Wagner] Act of 1935, the impact of the state on American workplace relations enters a second phase.

The Wagner Act signaled the triumph of collective bargaining over employee representation as the goal of New Deal labor policy. The law aimed, by its own blunt assertion (Sec.1), at the promotion of "actual liberty of contract" and the remedying of the "inequality of bargaining power" between employers and employees. Everything in the law's pro-

(1937), box 1, W. Ellison Chalmers Collection, Reuther Archives; Joseph R. Wood to Homer Martin, 14 November 1934, box 1, Martin Collection.

[34] Fine, *Blue Eagle*, 223–24.

[35] See, e.g., Session 1—GM Executive Training Program (1933), box 16, Kraus Collection; Arthur H. Young, "Lessons to be Drawn from Industrial Relations Experience Abroad," 20 September 1933, A. H. Young Collection, California Institute of Technology.

visions was keyed to promoting collective bargaining: majority rule in the selection of bargaining agents; exclusive representation by such certified agents; the obligation of good-faith bargaining imposed on employers; their interference in any way with the independence of labor organizations prohibited; labor's right to strike specifically assured; and, of course, the right to organize protected by a powerful, quasi-judicial National Labor Relations Board. But, massively intrusive as it was in these ways, the reach of the law was quite precisely circumscribed. It would set collective bargaining in motion and leave the process itself within the realm of contractual freedom. "The law does not compel agreements between employers and employees," asserted the landmark *Jones and Laughlin* decision (1937). "It does not compel any agreement whatever."

Where did this leave the workplace rights of workers? Excepting to be free of employer coercion in the exercise of their associational rights (and to be free as individuals to confer with and present grievances to employers [Sec. 8 (2), Sec. 9 (a)]), the law conferred no workplace rights. As the Supreme Court pointedly remarked in *Jones and Laughlin*, "the Act does not interfere with the normal exercise of the right of the employer to select its employees or to discharge them." Only by means of collective bargaining could the employer's power over employment be limited. And this held as well for the mechanisms for enforcing job rights. Nothing in the law demanded either a shop steward system or a formal grievance procedure. Workplace representation had become, so far as the state was concerned, the creature of collective bargaining.

Even so, the substance of what went into the first collective-bargaining agreements came directly out of the ERP period. In settling the Flint sitdown strike, for example, General Motors was bent on showing that it had not abandoned its established labor policy. The starting point in negotiating seniority was the ALB rules the corporation claimed it had been observing since 1934. Similarly, the company considered the new grievance procedure "in principle a revision of the procedure" already in place except that, as William Knudsen said, "it is more specific now. The steps are perfectly definite from top to bottom now."[36] And likewise on the question of shop-floor representation. General Motors refused to recognize the shop steward system that had sprung up during the strike;

---

[36] Flint *Journal,* 17 February, 13 March 1937, clippings, box 2, Flint Labor Collection, Reuther Archives; Sidney Fine, *Sitdown: The General Motors Strike of 1936–1937* (Ann Arbor, Mich., 1969), 306.

in fact, supplementary agreements explicitly denied to this structure any role in the grievance procedure. Instead, the contract lodged this function in committeemen, specified as to numbers and rights, along the lines of what GM had granted to AFL unions prior to 1936.

In one fundamental way, however, the corporation's claims to continuity were profoundly wrong. By signing a union contract, even one not conceding exclusive bargaining rights, GM undercut the very foundations of the employee representation system it had been fostering since 1933. In that sense, the 1937 settlement conformed to what New Deal labor policy would henceforth require: that workplace representation be the product of collective bargaining.

After the auto settlement, a wave of wildcat strikes and slowdowns hit GM's plants. The corporation's response revealed the watershed change: the grievance procedure was a matter of contract, and the UAW, as signatory, was obliged to enforce it or, so GM warned more than once, forfeit its contractual standing. The UAW's answer was no less telling: it agreed with GM's basic contention. The union accepted, indeed (in Walter Reuther's words), "contends staunchly that a disciplined and responsible organization must be maintained" and that "the Union is to be held responsible for its contractual responsibilities."[37] The ensuing history is entangled in the union's factional fights, in the machinations of a still unreconstructed corporation, and in endemic warfare on the shop floor. But the outcome is altogether clear and altogether assertive of the contractualist character of workplace representation. And, once the constitutionality of the Wagner Act was settled, this was what the law itself demanded. The paramount duty, as the Supreme Court said in the decisive *Sands* case (1939), was to abide by the contract: workers who did otherwise forfeited the protections of the Wagner Act.[38]

State influence on workplace contractualism thus occurred in two stages. In the formative NRA period, key internal characteristics emerged; and then, with the Wagner Act, this workplace regime became the creature of the labor contract. There next followed a third stage in which, as it tried to define its own responsibilities, the state conferred on workplace contractualism the imprimatur of legitimacy.

What was the legal standing of the labor agreement under the Wagner Act? Did contracts achieved under its provisions acquire a binding force

---

[37] "Review of the Situation in General Motors," n.d., 1939, 4, folder 12, box 4, Reuther Collection.
[38] For a treatment of the key cases, see Klare, "Judicial Deradicalization," 293–325.

not hitherto attached to collective bargaining agreements? The Wagner Act was silent on that score, but the affirmative drift of court decisions was at once evident.[39] The postwar labor crisis brought the issue to a head. Under the punitive atmosphere prevailing at the time, the Republican Congress moved to make the unions more "responsible." Section 301 of the Taft-Hartley Act made "suits for violation of contracts between an employer and a labor organization" actionable and granted jurisdiction to the federal district courts. The provision remained effectively a dead letter[40] until, in *Lincoln Mills* (1957), the Supreme Court directed the lower courts "to fashion a body of federal law for the enforcement of these collective bargaining agreements."

Faced by this formidable task, the courts did a remarkable thing. They shifted the responsibility to the privately created grievance and arbitration machinery. The logic turned on the linkage the courts found between the arbitration and no-strike clauses in labor agreements. Insofar as they abandoned the resort to force over disputed rights, the parties in effect accepted as binding and *legally enforceable* the processes of the grievance and arbitration machinery they had established. It was the function of the courts, the Supreme Court ruled in the *Steelworkers' Trilogy* (1960), only to enforce the contractual obligation to arbitrate and without review of (save where it was "apparent" that an award did not derive from the terms of the agreement) the decision of the arbitrator.

Thus the law swung behind this private arrangement of dispute settlement, elevating it to quasi-legal status, and, moreover, legitimating the larger system of workplace representation within which it rested. The collective agreement, pronounced the Supreme Court, is "more than a contract." It is "an effort to erect a system of industrial self-government" and call into being "a new common law—the common law of the particular industry or a particular shop." Within this industrial order, arbitration is "the means of solving the unforeseeable by molding a system of private law."[41]

---

[39] Phillip Selznick, *Law, Society, and Industrial Justice* (New York, 1969), chapter 4. On the earlier legal history of the labor contract, see Christopher L. Tomlins, *The State and the Unions: Labor Relations, Law, and the Organized Labor Movement in America, 1880–1960* (Cambridge, 1985), chapters 2–3.

[40] Except for its influence on collective bargaining: in exchange for release from legal liability, many unions accepted tough management rights clauses and greater responsibility for policing the contract.

[41] David E. Feller, "A General Theory of the Collective Bargaining Agreement," *California Law Review* 61 (May 1973): 686–90, 700–707; Robin W. Fleming, *The Labor Arbitration Process* (Urbana, Ill., 1965), chapter 1.

And what of the rights of the individual worker? If he or she was denied access to tort law, then a particularly heavy "duty of fair representation" fell to the unions. Under *Vaca v. Sipes* (1967), unions became liable for how they handled the grievances of their members. The sight of dissatisfied workers suing their unions for mishandling or rejecting their grievances must surely have struck foreign trade unionists as one of the more arresting oddities of the American labor scene.

From a comparative perspective, the legal configuration whose evolution I have described would seem just as specific to the United States as were the characteristics of the American mass-production regime. On the enforcement of the rights of workers, for example, it appears that no other country established precisely the public-private balance enunciated in the *Trilogy* doctrine, not even Canada. In the United States, arbitration in the grievance procedure was contractually determined, and only to the extent that the parties agreed to it—most contracts reserved some issues from final arbitration—did they invoke the enforcement powers of the courts. Canadian law, on the other hand, required labor agreements to contain no-strike, binding arbitration clauses. Elsewhere, especially in countries with works-council legislation, labor courts enforced the rights of workers, while, at the other extreme, in England, no legal standing was accorded to labor agreements. Australia offered a still different mix of state-enforced arbitration awards and informally determined workplace rights.[42] So it is not any wonder that the ILO encountered so much difficulty in fashioning a policy on worker grievances that would be acceptable to all the signatory countries.

"The proposed instrument should not be too detailed, but should leave a large measure of freedom to the practices and customs of the various countries." So went the Swiss response. "Regulations must take national peculiarities into account," said the West Germans.[43] And so on. The very concreteness of grievance handling as an issue prevented the usual evasions and brought forth these acknowledgments of national diversity. In its particularities, so the ILO episode implies, the law of workplace relations must ultimately be linked to characteristics embedded in the larger political environment.

---

[42] For an extended consideration of the relationship between the legal system and the private rule of law in which the unionized workplace of the 1960s is offered as an important example, see Selznick, *Law, Society, and Industrial Justice.* For a convenient survey, see Roger Lanpain, ed., *Comparative Labour Law and Industrial Relations* (Deventer, Holland, 1982).

[43] ILO, *Examination of Grievances*, 2:85, 94.

Consider, for example, the fate of American labor law in Japan. In the course of the democratization process of the postwar occupation, the Japanese accepted as their model the National Labor Relations Act. "Thus," observes William B. Gould in his illuminating comparative study, "to an extent unknown in the case of any two other industrialized countries in the world, a similar legal framework provides us with the opportunity to see how institutions offer different answers to the same legal questions in dissimilar cultural settings."[44]

The concept of the unfair labor practice, which is at the heart of the Wagner Act, underwent a transmutation in Japan. The term, literally translated in the 1945 law, made no sense as applied to labor-management relations. "It seems that the Japanese language lacks an appropriate word to express the concept of fairness or unfairness in personal relations," remarks Hanami.[45] The Trade Union Act of 1949 retranslated the term to mean "improper" labor practices. In patron/client relations, however, impropriety can characterize the acts only of the authority figure. So that, in a variety of ways, Japanese law and the courts took a much more permissive attitude toward the behavior of unions and workers than toward employers. Likewise, although the Taft-Hartley Act had just made American unions subject to unfair labor practices, such a step seemed inadmissible in Japan. And since impropriety was something to be assuaged and mitigated, the functions of the Labor Relations Commission—the counterpart of the NLRB—became more nearly mediatory than adjudicative in nature.

Given Japan as borrower, Gould's comparative legal analysis naturally throws its light on the peculiarities of the Japanese. But the process can be reversed so as to suggest what was American about the law from which the Japanese were borrowing. Our instance is the representation election. This was never adopted in Japan, partly because it had been overtaken by events. Japanese workers unionized before the right to organize went into effect, thereby rendering irrelevant the central premise of the American law, namely, that without state coercion the antiunion power of management could not be overcome. Moreover, representation elections might have disturbed an emergent trade-union structure with

---

[44] William B. Gould, *Japan's Reshaping of American Labor Law* (Cambridge, Mass., 1984), 19.
[45] Hanami, 81. For an astute historical analysis of the patron/client basis for Japanese labor relations, see Thomas C. Smith, "The Right to Benevolence: Dignity and Japanese Workers, 1890–1920," *Comparative Studies in History and Sociology* 26 (October 1984):587–613.

which the Japanese authorities did not want to tamper. But the representation election was not only a matter of expediency, either in Japan or the United States.

The point can perhaps be more fruitfully exploited by shifting the comparison to Australia. As in the United States since 1935, access to certain state mechanisms is crucial to Australian unions. They cannot function within the arbitration system without being registered, any more than can American unions engage in collective bargaining within the terms of the National Labor Relations Act without being certified. Certification is what a union gains when it wins a representation election under the rules of the NLRB. Registration under the Commonwealth Conciliation and Arbitration Act, comparably important for Australian unions, is likewise closely regulated, with internal union rules and jurisdictional lines closely scrutinized. But there is no provision for determining whether or not workers within that jurisdiction want to be so represented.[46]

That the Wagner Act should turn on the right to choose of course touches basic assumptions about the American working class. What is generally unarguable in other advanced industrial societies—that workers do act as a class and that trade unions are their natural representatives— are in the United States open questions. The Wagner Act is not about the rights of unions but about the rights of workers. And insofar as they choose to exercise those rights, the representatives they select as bargaining agents are defined not as trade unions—a term absent from the law—but as "labor organizations" in a broadly inclusive sense (Sec. 2[5]). The new law in fact contradicted historic premises of American trade unionism, a truth brought painfully into focus by the rise of the CIO. No longer was the Federation's authority to assign union jurisdiction paramount, nor were its affiliates absolutely free to enter agreements with employers. When it realized that these fundamentals of trade-union voluntarism had been lost, the AFL moved to have the law amended. But the AFL did not challenge what had caused this legal crisis, namely, the assertion of the workers' right to choose. Nor, despite its insistent

[46]Walker, *Australian Industrial Relations Systems*, chapter 1. Other countries, especially in the Caribbean and in Southeast Asia, have followed the U.S. model of representation elections, but only in response to the problem of union competition, which was of course not an issue for the original Wagner Act. For a survey, see Alan Gladstone and Muneto Ozaki, "Trade Union Recognition for Collective Bargaining Purposes," *International Labour Review* (August–September 1985):163–89. I am grateful to E. M. Kassalow for calling this article to my attention.

demands for labor law reform, does the AFL-CIO do so today. So compelling is the notion of free choice that, at least in this respect, there is no going back to the status quo ante 1935. Thus the 1988 settlement of the AFL-CIO boycott of Coors beer: The NLRB is to be excluded, but a representation election there would be, under the auspices of the American Arbitration Association.[47]

Insofar as it embodies the larger political culture, the law can give shape to the rank-and-file conceptions of industrial justice that animate shop-floor struggle. For most of the nineteenth century, the American labor movement had drawn its inspiration from the Declaration of Independence and the American Revolution. Artisan republicanism celebrated personal independence, citizenship, and equal rights. These principles oriented the labor movement toward fundamental, even radical, questions—over what the Preamble of the Knights of Labor took to be "an inevitable and irresistible conflict between the wage-system of labor and the republican system of government"—but they also defined industrial justice at the workplace and translated it readily, for example, into the ethical code that David Montgomery finds in nineteenth-century craft-controlled machine production.[48]

In the mass-production regime of the twentieth century, workers found a more appropriate political analogue in the legal/constitutional order. That was, indeed, what Sumner H. Slichter perceived in his pioneering survey of collective bargaining as practiced in the 1930s. *Union Policies and Industrial Management* (1941) took as its central theme what Slichter called "industrial jurisprudence," which he defined as "a method of introducing civil rights into industry, that is, of requiring that management be conducted by rule rather than by arbitrary decision." The rules, as Slichter was at great pains to demonstrate, varied enormously from union to union. For example: in coal mining, union agreements did not regulate layoffs; in the needle trades, work sharing prevailed; in printing and on the railroads, it was seniority; a few unions gave job preferences to members; and elsewhere various combinations existed. This diversity, Slichter remarked, most of all reflected "differences in conditions within industries." And he did not doubt—indeed, his book already demon-

---

[47] *New York Times Magazine*, 31 January 1988, 19ff.
[48] Montgomery, *Workers' Control*, chapter 1. On the transition from a republican to a constitutional orientation, see Leon Fink, "Labor, Liberty and the Law: Trade Unionism and the Problem of the American Constitutional Order," *Journal of American History* 74 (December 1987):904–25.

strated as much—that in the newly organized mass-production sector workplace representation would develop its own distinctive character, but also embody the tradition of industrial jurisprudence, because all modern American workers "expect management to be conducted in accordance with rules ... and to have an opportunity to appeal to a proper person when, in their judgment, the rule has not been observed."[49]

Nothing better reveals this rights consciousness than the booklet handed out by UAW Local 7 to new hires at the Chrysler Jefferson-Kercheval plants in Detroit in 1949: "If you think that justice is not being done you ... see your steward about it. ... The grievance structure functions like a court of appeals—an agency to which the worker can appeal his case when he feels an injustice has been done him." Among the submerged histories yet to be charted is how a diverse, largely immigrant labor force moved to a conception of industrial justice that subordinated ethnic networks and personal connections to equal treatment by workplace rule[50]—from a world in which "the fair-haired boys [in some cases] blood kin to the foremen, such as nephews and brothers-in-law ... got all the breaks" to a world in which "if you had the seniority you stayed on the job." Some opposition certainly came, so the Buick-Flint activist Norm Bully believed, from those who "thought they could do better or had been doing better by being friends with the boss or relatives to supervision." But once in place, the contractual system overwhelmed, or at least forced underground, that kind of thinking. UAW Local 174 emblazoned this message on its application card: "The other fellow is only interested in helping you protect your job if you help protect his. PLAY FAIR—DO YOUR SHARE." A quasi-legal idiom—"to substitute civil procedure for civil war in this industry"—suffused official

---

[49] Sumner H. Slichter, *Union Policies and Industrial Management* (Washington, D.C., 1941), 1–3 and, on layoffs, chapter 4, especially tables, pp. 105–7. Given the jurisprudential tradition described by Slichter, it was entirely predictable that the new industrial unions would draw on the experience of established trade unions. Richard Frankensteen, for example, claimed as his model for seniority the Brotherhood of Railway Trainmen ("whose seniority is reputedly and by application the best") in negotiating the first contract with Chrysler in April 1937; and Walter Reuther, when he became interested in revising the grievance system at General Motors, turned to Sidney Hillman for advice about how the garment trades had used impartial umpires. *UAW-Chrysler Agreement with Introduction* (April 1937), 6, file 2, box 3, Reuther Collection; Reuther to the Officers and Members of [GM] Locals, 3 October 1939, box 1, series 1, UAW-GM Department Collection, Reuther Archives.

[50] For an instance capturing this shift of consciousness in one textile town, see Gary Gerstle, *Working-Class Americanism: The Politics of Labor in a Textile City, 1914–1960* (New York, 1989), chapter 4.

UAW doctrine and reached down to the local unions. Thus the concluding words of Local 7's booklet for new hires: "*Remember! Your union is your best friend. It is that wonderful defense lawyer, at the point of production, that every worker needs and desires.*"[51]

Ought workplace contractualism to be explained as a historically contingent event? In the setting within which it arose from the mid–1930s onward, surely not. The proximate causes as I have explored them compel us to see workplace contractualism as determined by the contemporary mass-production and legal/political regimes.

Our difficulty in accepting that conclusion arises in some degree, certainly, from a failure of historical imagination. Nearly twenty years after celebrating the industrial jurisprudence of American union-management relations, Sumner H. Slichter and two colleagues published a massive sequel to *Union Policies and Industrial Management*. The second book, *The Impact of Collective Bargaining on Management* (1960), bears witness to the centrality of workplace contractualism in the industrial relations system of the Eisenhower era. Procedure has become of commanding importance. In the 1941 book, dispute-resolution machinery received only passing attention and, as Slichter (or his coauthors) notes sheepishly, arbitration is not even in that book's index.[52] In the 1960 book, however, the grievance procedure consumes over a hundred closely packed pages. And the dominating topics—seniority, a minor topic in 1941, and job classification issues, entirely absent from the 1941 book—are likewise treated essentially as complex procedural problems.

This was not perhaps what Slichter had hoped for. Labor-management cooperation, a major enthusiasm of his in 1941, can be of little account (and receives scant attention) in a book that takes General Motors as the model industrial enterprise. The central question of the first book— was it possible to square labor's quest for justice with management's

---

[51] J. A. Beni Interview (1963), 4–5, Norm Bully Interview (1961), 2, both in Reuther Archives; Local 174 application card [n.d., 1938?], file 46, box 1, Reuther Collection; "Welcome, Fellow Workers" [UAW Local 7, January 1949], 14–15, box 3, Nick Di-Gaetano Collection, Reuther Archives.

[52] Sumner H. Slichter, James J. Healy, and E. Robert Livernash, *The Impact of Collective Bargaining on Management* (Washington, D.C., 1960), 739 n. 2. It was a puzzling omission, explained by the authors by the lack of surveys "undoubtedly . . . due to the infrequent use of the process." But in fact arbitration was the established practice in coal, printing, the railroads, and all the clothing industries—i.e., in a substantial part of the older unionized sector. In 1941 the U.S. Conciliation Service reported arbitration clauses in 62 percent of the twelve hundred contracts in its files. Fleming, *The Labor Arbitration Process*, 13.

quest for efficiency?—has become much more problematic in the second. And if "the American workman is more richly endowed with self-determined rights than the workman of any other country," labor's quest for justice has perhaps succeeded too well.[53] Slichter's own perspective has grown overtly managerial, and his message is that employers must defend their prerogatives.

It is the Slichter of 1960, not 1941, who resonates in our own day. As the manufacturing sector has fallen on hard times, Slichter's misgivings have blown up into a generalized repudiation of workplace contractualism. "The American system of organizing and managing work is obsolete," says John P. Hoerr in his account of the collapse of American steel in the 1980s. "The problem...[is] rooted in forty years of poor management of people and a misdirected union-management relationship.... Those decades of adversary relations on the shop floor... created an atmosphere of suspicion and hostility."[54] A wider-ranging analysis by three leading scholars in the field posits a systemic shift of historic proportions in American industrial relations.

Over the course of the past half century union and nonunion systems traded positions as the innovative force in industrial relations.... An alternative human resources management system... gradually overtook collective bargaining and emerged as the pacesetter by emphasizing high employee involvement and commitment and flexibility in the utilization of individual employees.[55]

The force of this assault on workplace contractualism has converted even some within the labor movement to the cause of "employee involvement," "commitment," and "flexibility in the utilization of individual employees."

Criticism of workplace contractualism from the left has today been joined—odd bedfellows—by denunciation from the right and center.[56] It would probably be fair to say that workplace contractualism has nearly exhausted the official legitimacy it once enjoyed. The historian must therefore search doubly hard for a vantage point that recaptures what

[53] Slichter, Healy, and Livernash, 3. It will be obvious to the reader that my reading of Slichter differs from Lichtenstein's in this collection.

[54] John P. Hoerr, *And the Wolf Finally Came: The Decline of the American Steel Industry* (Pittsburgh, Pa., 1988), 14, 20.

[55] Thomas Kochan, Harry Katz, and Robert McKersie, *The Transformation of American Industrial Relations* (New York, 1986), 226–27.

[56] It may be worth noting that critics from the right/center also seem inclined toward contingent historical explanations for workplace contractualism, as, e.g, the theme of "the road not taken" in Hoerr, *And the Wolf Finally Came,* chapter 24 and passim.

Slichter had seen in 1941, that is, an emerging system congruent with past experience and congruent, too, with the New Deal environment.

So let me conclude by invoking the name of Nick DiGaetano. One of the first at the Chrysler Jefferson plant in Detroit to join the UAW-CIO in 1937, DiGaetano was afterward elected a chief shop steward and, except for one term out of office, he served continuously from 1940 as a committeeman and then as chief steward of the OK assembly line until he retired in 1958. A few months later, still fresh from the shop, he recorded his experiences. In his oral history, there is an authentic voice about workplace contractualism as the embodiment of industrial justice for the mass-production workers of his generation.

DiGaetano was no innocent at shop-floor representation. He was a skilled metal polisher—"I was pretty good at the wheel, not to brag about it"—and before going to Chrysler he had worked in a contract shop where every polisher and buffer belonged to Local 1 of the Metal Polishers' International Union. The jobs were strictly piecework, and while the company did not recognize the union—"we had our own recognition," says DiGaetano—the foreman was in practice obliged to bargain over the rate for each new job. For this purpose, the metal polishers elected two shop stewards. From 1925 to 1928, DiGaetano was one of the two. Informal bargaining continued after he and most of the others followed the foreman over to Chrysler, but now they bargained over production standards, since Chrysler paid on a group incentive basis, not a straight piece rate. "Among ourselves we said, 'Well, this is what we want, demand so much time on this job.' . . . We had the time-study men and . . . we argued about it, and we came to an agreement that so many pieces per hour, eight hours, were enough. That was all there was to it." What DiGaetano was describing was a system of informal bargaining not unlike that in British auto plants at the time, and, although little is known about it, probably widely practiced by an elite of American craft workers in many presumably open shop industries.[57]

The possibility of holding to that informal system seems not to have crossed his mind. But DiGaetano did weigh the old against the new. With

---

[57] For a highly revealing account of noncontractual bargaining in one industry, see Philip Scranton, *Figured Tapestry: Production, Markets and Power in Philadelphia, 1885–1941* (New York, 1989); and for its existence under militantly open shop conditions, Howell Harris, "Employers' Collective Action in the Open-Shop Era: The Metal Manufacturers' Association of Philadelphia, ca. 1903–1933," in Steven Tolliday and Jonathan Zeitlin, eds., *The Power to Manage?: Employers and Industrial Relations in Comparative-Historical Perspective* (London, 1991), 117–46.

the UAW, first of all, "we had the bargaining structure in the contract to follow." Informal bargaining had always been rushed, a few minutes snatched from the wheel, since, as pieceworkers, the committeemen were losing money every time they talked to the foreman. As a shop steward, DiGaetano was on company time, and he took as long as necessary—maybe longer—to handle a grievance.[58] Then there was the question of access. In the informal system, the foreman was the end of it. But the stewards could get to the top labor-relations executives, "the whole cheese to transact the business of labor.... He had to talk with the Shop Committee, and he had to talk to the shop steward when it came down to it." And much more was on the table than the piece rate. "When we talked to the foreman, we talked to the foreman on an equal basis: 'This work is too hard; this man can do the job; this man's got seniority; this man does not get enough pay for his classification; this man got a pay shortage.' " But what was gained went beyond this. "We did not have to stand up like the Italian boys," DiGaetano digresses at one point. "They tell me in Italy when they go to speak with management about conditions...they stand up with their hat in their hand." What Di-Gaetano meant becomes clear in his parting words:

I tell you this: the workers of my generation from the early days up to now had what you might call a labor insurrection in changing from a plain, humble, submissive creature into a man. The union made a man out of him.... I am not talking about the benefits.... I am talking about the working conditions and how they affected the men in the plant.... Before they were submissive. Today they are men.

Anyone who characterizes workplace contractualism "as a vehicle for the manipulation of employee discontent and for the legitimation of existing inequalities of power" will have to reckon with Nick DiGaetano. And lest he be too readily dismissed as just another victim of false consciousness, one further biographical fact might be entered into the record: DiGaetano was a veteran Wobbly. He had joined the Industrial Workers of the World (IWW) back in 1912 at the time of the Lawrence strike; he had participated in the Italian-language Propaganda League; he knew Ettor, Giovannetti, and Big Bill Haywood, and he remained an IWW

---

[58] The local's executive board minutes for 1940–41, in fact, contain regular notations of company letters complaining of too much time away from work by stewards. UAW Local 7 Collection, box 1, Reuther Archives. The GM agreement, on the other hand, limited shop committeemen to four hours of paid grievance time per day and then down to two hours in the 1938 agreement.

member until 1938. DiGaetano considered his small circle to be "the cream of the crop" of the working class, not like the mass of auto workers who "did not have any ideology."[59] If anyone understood that the class struggle took place at the point of production, it was Nick DiGaetano. And he likewise understood that workplace contractualism was, in its origins, a product of that struggle.

[59] Nick DiGaetano Interview (1959), Oral History Collection, Reuther Archives, quotations from pp. 14, 22–23, 48, 71–72, 73, 74. DiGaetano's grievance books as chief steward are in his own collection, box 1, in the Reuther Archives.

9

Pacific ties: industrial relations and employment
systems in Japan and the United States
since 1900

SANFORD M. JACOBY

As other contributors to this volume have observed, it is not easy to
define precisely what is meant by the term *industrial democracy*. But it
confuses matters even more when the struggles of American workers are
analyzed according to Anglo-European conceptions of the term. The
result is either that American workers are pronounced exceptional, which
is the traditional view, or that they are found to have been every bit as
militantly anticapitalist as their European counterparts, which is the re-
visionist view.[1]

The new revisionism is problematic in its downplaying of differences
between the United States and Europe. Socialism was weaker in America,
as was trade unionism. Except for brief moments, socialist and syndicalist
strains were comparatively mild within American unions, most of whose
energy was directed toward control of labor markets or of the firm and
its employment rules.

The exceptionalists are closer to the mark. Here a voluminous literature seeks to solve the conundrum: Why, despite similarities in so many
areas, was socialism (social democracy, trade unionism) so much less
popular in America as compared to Europe? A good question. But because

For their comments, I am grateful to Robert E. Cole, Matthew Finkin, Andrew Gordon,
Howell Harris, Alexander Keyssar, Nelson Lichtenstein, Mori Takashi, Michael Piore, and
Michael Storper.

[1] John H. M. Laslett and Seymour Martin Lipset, *Failure of a Dream?: Essays in the History
of American Socialism* (Garden City: Doubleday, 1974); Sean Wilentz, "Against Exceptionalism: Consciousness and the American Labor Movement, 1790–1920," *International
Labor and Working-Class History* 26 (Fall 1984): 1–24.

of the way that the question is framed, the literature overemphasizes the singularity of the American experience and thus gives too much weight to factors unique to it, such as mass immigration and rugged individualism. This chapter tries to shift the balance and asks instead, Why, despite differences in so many areas, were labor market and labor movement outcomes so similar in the United States and Japan?

There is a widespread tendency in America to view Japan as The Other, a society whose various features—whether seen as quasi-feudal or hypermodern—are suffused with a particularist spirit that makes Japan fundamentally different from the United States. Differences exist, to be sure, but there also were, and are, numerous similarities, especially in industrial and employment relations. As in the United States, Japanese unions tended to be conservative and enterprise-oriented, and in neither country did the unions become a mass movement until the 1930s and 1940s, long after the major European countries. Even then, however, Japanese and American unions lacked the political influence of their European counterparts, and state welfare provisions remained relatively meager. As for large Japanese and American firms, their employment practices developed in tandem, bore a strong resemblance to each other, and diverged from those of European industrial employers. This chapter argues that, because the United States and Japan had in common many of their allegedly "exceptional" or "particular" features, any explanation of those features cannot rely on cultural factors unique to either nation but instead must be based on shared patterns of economic and social development. It traces out those patterns and their consequences for industrial and employment relations in Japan and the United States.

In exploring parallels between Japan and the United States, it is striking to observe how long it took—in world-historical time—for mass unionism to emerge in each nation. When that finally happened, Japanese and American employers already had gone quite far in developing elaborate, internal employment systems. Labor's struggles shaped those systems, to be sure. But the new unions of the 1930s and 1940s found their options circumscribed by the situation that confronted them and by their own enterprise-oriented approach. As a result, industrial democracy in postwar America and Japan had different meanings than in other places and at other times.

Outcomes in the two societies were not always identical, however. At its pre-1930 peak, America's labor movement was larger and more craft-oriented than Japan's. And, as so often is noted (too often, perhaps), employment practices in Japan and the United States were infused with distinctive cultural norms. The consequences of these and other differences became most evident during the decades following World War II, when large unionized American firms followed a trajectory that increasingly distinguished their employment systems both from those of large Japanese firms and from large nonunion American companies at the same time.[2]

During the 1950s and 1960s, industrial relations scholars thought that the employment system found in large, unionized American firms would become the norm in Japan and elsewhere. But as growth rates slowed during the 1970s and 1980s, a different pattern emerged. In both nations, a decline occurred in the relative number of workers holding secure jobs in bureaucratic organizations. Meanwhile, unions shrank more rapidly in America and Japan than in other industrial nations. Finally, in the United States there is an ongoing shift away from the kind of employment system associated with unionized firms and toward the kinds found in Japan or in America's large nonunion firms. Thus after a hiatus of some forty years or so, Japanese and American employment systems again are evolving toward each other, although the distance between them remains great.

INDUSTRIAL RELATIONS: ATLANTIC AND PACIFIC, 1900–1935

During the first third of the twentieth century, the world's industrialized nations moved from the first industrial revolution of textiles and steel on to a second based on electricity, internal combustion engines, and chemicals. National transitions occurred at varying times and speeds and with differing product mixes. Each also varied in the degree to which its state sought to regulate the industrialization process and accompanying social unrest. Yet this unrest was a shared experience, for each nation's working class organized itself—with varying degrees of success—into labor unions and radical parties that came into repeated conflict with employers and the state. The issues were universal: raising the pay, security, and dignity of industrial employment. But the means varied— from moral suasion, legislation, and collective bargaining to general

---

[2] Until the recent sharp decline in private-sector unionism in the United States, the American industrial relations literature rarely distinguished between unionized and nonunion firms. Studies comparing the United States and Japan still typically use unionized American manufacturing firms as their base, thus overstating national differences.

strikes, factory occupations, and collective expropriation—as did the response from above. From these variations there emerged distinctive national industrial relations systems, which, at the risk of some oversimplification, may be combined into two major groups.[3]

The first consisted of northwestern European nations, including Britain, Germany, the Netherlands, Sweden, Denmark, and France. Here, strong craft traditions and rigid social divisions created an interlocking structure of trade unions and socialist parties that had support throughout the working class. On the employer side were numerous small- and medium-size firms specializing in skill-intensive, nonstandardized products.[4] The prevalence of these firms, often family owned, was due to several factors: small national markets, the development of modern industry on top of a thriving preindustrial base, and the resulting persistence of preindustrial craft traditions and craft control. Industrial and personnel management in these firms was less professionalized and less bureaucratic than in more sizable organizations.[5]

Yet European employers were not without protective strategies when faced with opposition from below. To enhance their control of the shop floor and to allay larger threats to the economic order, they formed associations that proffered union recognition and industry-level bargaining in return for union support of basic property rights, including those concerning enterprise management. As in the 1918 Stinnes-Legien agreement between German employers and unions, recognition was intended to incorporate the unions into the existing order and so defuse their radicalism. Industry-wide bargaining gave employers strength in numbers; but more than that, it displaced bargaining over shop-floor matters by concentrating on those issues—typically wages—that could be settled at industry levels. Employers generally retained formal authority over the

---

[3] On classification issues, in particular whether to lump syndicalist France and Italy together with other European nations, see S. M. Jacoby, "American Exceptionalism Revisited: The Importance of Management," in S. M. Jacoby, ed., *Masters to Managers: Historical and Comparative Perspectives on American Employers* (New York: Columbia University Press, 1991), 173–200.

[4] Michael Piore and Charles Sabel, *The Second Industrial Divide* (New York: Basic, 1984); Jonathan Zeitlin, "From Labor History to the History of Industrial Relations," *Economic History Review* 40 (May 1987): 159–84.

[5] Reinhard Bendix, *Work and Authority in Industry* (New York: Wiley, 1956), 214–17; Tony J. Watson, *The Personnel Managers: A Study in the Sociology of Work and Employment* (London: Routledge, Kegan Paul, 1977); F. T. Malm, "The Development of Personnel Administration in Western Europe," *California Management Review* 3 (Fall 1960): 69–83.

workplace, leaving enterprise disputes to be resolved through informal means or by integrative institutions such as works councils.

This result has widely been interpreted as a victory for European employers, but several caveats are in order.[6] First, in those places where craft unionism was most deeply entrenched (as in much of British industry), multiemployer bargaining was ineffectual in eroding craft control on the shop floor. Here dual bargaining systems developed: formal at the industry level and informal (shop stewards) at the enterprise level. Second, even when employers succeeded in displacing conflict to higher levels, that outcome was not inconsistent with socialist objectives.[7] Industrial bargaining, especially when combined with contract extension to unorganized workers, promoted worker solidarity. It also legitimated unions as peak associations, making it easier for them to bring pressure on the state and to promote social welfare programs. That bolstered a regulatory framework (strengthened after the Second World War) consisting of such provisions as unemployment insurance and old-age pensions, as well as laws prescribing substantive terms of employment, such as dismissal rules and vacation pay.

The situation in Japan and the United States was completely different. The industrial landscape in each nation was dotted with giant industrial corporations geared to large-scale production. Most of these large firms were either unorganized or dealt with unions confined to a single enterprise. Although each nation experienced a surge of radicalism and unionism during the First World War, union densities and left-wing voting remained below European levels.[8] In neither case was the wartime crisis

---

[6]Lloyd Ulman, "Who Wanted Collective Bargaining in the First Place?" *39th Annual Proceedings of the Industrial Relations Research Association, New Orleans, December 1986;* Keith Sisson, *The Management of Collective Bargaining: An International Comparison* (Oxford: Basil Blackwell, 1987).

[7]But not all of them: revolution was dropped from the agenda, much to the consternation of radical (and present-day academic) critics of corporatism. On comparative welfare policies, see Daniel Levine, *Poverty and Society: The Growth of the American Welfare State in International Comparison* (New Brunswick: Rutgers University Press, 1988); Ann S. Orloff, "The Political Origins of America's Belated Welfare State," in Margaret Weir, Ann S. Orloff, and Theda Skocpol, eds., *The Politics of Social Policy in the United States* (Princeton: Princeton University Press, 1988).

[8]Note that this essay is focused on large firms in heavy industry, firms that typically employed male workers in urbanized areas. Hence little mention is made of the Japanese textile industry, which employed more than half of Japanese industrial workers until the 1920s. Textile firms were predominantly found in small towns in rural areas and relied heavily on young female workers. Although France and Italy had lower union membership density levels than the United States in 1914, per capita income—a rough measure of

sufficiently threatening to force employers or the state to sanction collective bargaining; that came later, during a second crisis experienced in
the United States during the 1930s and in Japan during the 1940s. Finally,
labor regulations and social insurance were underdeveloped in Japan and
the United States as compared to Western Europe. Corporate paternalism,
however, was more prevalent.[9]

How are we to account for these shared differences? First and foremost
are matters of timing and sequence: Large, capital-intensive manufacturing firms developed in Japan and the United States before unionism
had a chance to sink strong roots. Firms were relatively large for a variety
of reasons, including the size of the American market and the Japanese
government's enthusiasm for large-scale operations, as well as the use in
both cases of technologies that depended on scale economies to make
them profitable. American and Japanese firms were inclined to adopt
these technologies because they both faced a working class with weak
craft traditions, relatively few skilled workers, and large skill differentials.
This gave Japanese and American employers the incentive to use standardized, predictable technologies that economized on skilled labor; the
absence of strong craft traditions made it easier for them to do so.[10] But
the realization that unions might someday gather mass strength brought
preemptive measures to secure worker loyalty, especially the loyalty of
skilled workers. On both sides of the Pacific those measures included
bureaucratic personnel management, company unions, and welfare corporatism. These private regulations and benefits, although rudimentary

industrialization—was lower in those countries and by a much greater factor than their
union density rates. That is, unionization in the United States was far lower than it
"should" have been, given the level of economic development. Gerald Friedman, "Politics
and Unions: Government, Ideology, and the Labor Movement in France and the U.S.,
1880–1914" (Ph.D. diss., Harvard University, 1985), 31.
[9] Robert E. Cole, *Work, Mobility and Participation: A Comparative Study of American
and Japanese Industry* (Berkeley: University of California Press, 1979), 247; Kazuo Koike,
"Internal Labor Markets: Workers in Large Firms," in Taishiro Shirai, ed., *Contemporary
Industrial Relations in Japan* (Madison: University of Wisconsin Press, 1983), 39; Ronald
Dore, *British Factory–Japanese Factory: The Origins of National Diversity in Industrial
Relations* (Berkeley: University of California Press, 1973), 377.
[10] For evidence that skill differentials were wider in the United States than in Europe in the
early twentieth century, see E. H. Phelps Brown and Margaret Browne, *A Century of
Pay: The Course of Pay and Production in Europe and the U.S.A.* (London: Macmillan,
1968); Peter Lindert and Jeffrey Williamson, *American Inequality: A Macroeconomic
History* (New York: Academic Press, 1980). On the scarcity of skilled labor in Japan,
see Koji Taira, *Economic Development and the Labor Market in Japan* (New York:
Columbia University Press, 1970).

and limited to an elite section of the working class, undermined tendencies toward industrial solidarity and made it difficult to form coalitions to press for a modern welfare state.[11]

Nevertheless, both Japanese and American Federation of Labor unions did become larger and more militant during the First World War. But this was a brief interlude, and the ensuing combination of repressive and preemptive personnel policies had the effect of holding down union density rates in both nations, particularly in large firms. The U.S. rate peaked in 1920 and then declined to its nadir of about 10 percent in 1933; the Japanese rate followed a different trend, peaking in 1931 at 8 percent and then shrinking steadily thereafter.[12] While repression was not uncommon in Europe, Japanese and American employers were more likely to stand and do battle. Their size gave them the economic and political resources to mount major offensives, such as occurred at Homestead in 1892 and 1919, or at Mitsubishi Kobe Shipyard in 1921. Moreover, in these years American and Japanese labor was neither strong nor radical enough to pose a threat to political stability of the sort that led European employers to favor recognition via industry-wide bargaining. That is, Japanese and American employers chose not to buy their unions out because there was little or nothing to be bought. Why was that?

Theorists of exceptionalism have tried to explain the conservative and job-conscious outlook of American workers and their unions. But Japanese labor shared this orientation, and for some similar reasons. Although Japan was hardly a nation of immigrants, it resembled the United States insofar as much of its working class and many of its industrial cities were entirely new. During the early twentieth century, there was little in Kawasaki or Calumet City that could compare to the complex and long-established craft traditions of cities like Paris, Stuttgart, or Milan. Moreover, the scale and strength of Japanese and American firms reinforced the relative weakness and conservatism of labor in each nation.

During the 1880s and 1890s, when the AFL was forming itself, its leaders repeatedly witnessed what they believed to be the disastrous con-

---

[11] Andrew Gordon, *The Evolution of Labor Relations in Japan: Heavy Industry, 1853–1955* (Cambridge, Mass.: Harvard University Press, 1985); Sanford M. Jacoby, *Employing Bureaucracy: Managers, Unions, and the Transformation of Work in American Industry, 1900–1945* (New York: Columbia University Press, 1985).

[12] Gordon, *Labor Relations*, 250; Leo Wolman, *Ebb and Flow in Trade Unionism* (New York: NBER, 1936); Kazuo Okochi, *Labor in Modern Japan* (Tokyo: Science Council of Japan, 1958), 65. After World War I, the AFL proposed joint conference boards—a step in the European direction—but the idea was rejected by employers.

sequences of radical unionism and mass strikes—at Haymarket, Homestead, Pullman, and elsewhere. To achieve even limited economic goals, Gompers thought that American unions would have to make themselves respectable, garnering the support of the middle class and avoiding repression from the government. Out of this came the AFL's conservative, pragmatic, and exclusive approach, as well as its distrust of government. The AFL made a strategic decision to adopt not only a philosophy— economistic voluntarism—but also a decentralized organizational form—job control unionism—that gave it the greatest chance of making headway in an unfriendly environment. With their rigid structures and working rules, the AFL unions made an easy target for critics from both poles of the ideological spectrum. But the logic of job control unionism was shaped less by ideology than by the need to create disciplined fighting organizations capable of winning strikes and of sustaining union membership during hard times.[13]

Yet even with all that, AFL unions were unable to penetrate large mass-production firms. Instead, they hunkered down in local industries where numerous small companies produced customized or batch products, often on a seasonal basis: machinery, construction, shoes, and furniture. In these settings, AFL members worked according to unilateral craft rules, supplemented by collective bargaining with local employers. Occasionally, however, AFL unions were found in medium- to large-sized firms in industries that operated on a year-round basis and produced more standardized commodities, including meatpacking, newspaper printing, steel, and railroads. Here the unions kept their craft controls but combined them with employment rules adapted to (or taken from) a particular employer, blending what Clark Kerr once called the "guild" and "manorial" forms of unionism. That is, union members played two roles: that of guild artisans adhering to craft traditions of shop-floor autonomy and market control, and that of incumbent employees in a continuing relationship with a given employer. Out of this grew such practices as promotion ladders governed by seniority as well as seniority-based layoff systems, codified in written agreements.[14] This form of

---

[13] Jacoby, "American Exceptionalism." As in the United States, new Japanese towns regularly were incorporated in growing industrial areas, especially in the decades after World War I. Thomas O. Wilkinson, *The Urbanization of Japanese Labor* (Amherst: University of Massachusetts Press, 1965), 48.

[14] Clark Kerr, "The Balkanization of Labor Markets," in E. W. Bakke, ed., *Labor Mobility and Economic Opportunity* (Cambridge, Mass.: MIT Press, 1954); Walter Licht, *Working*

unionism—it can be termed "guild manorialism"—presaged the Congress of Industrial Organizations legalistic and bureaucratic approach.[15]

Still, guild manorialism was anathema to large employers. Small firms might tolerate craft controls as the price for local labor and product market stabilization. But because of the limited success of their organizing methods, unions were unable to offer a similar deal to large companies competing in national markets. In any event, large companies had sufficient resources to go it alone in a fight with a union rather than seek protection from a multiemployer bargaining group. Finally, although unionism helped small firms to secure a trained work force and maintain the quality of their skill-intensive products, large firms saw unionism as an impediment to their deskilled and technologically dynamic mode of production. Thus, while employer hostility caused American unionists to choose a conservative and decentralized form of unionism, their choice raised the incentive for large firms to avoid and resist unions and closed off the European option of getting employers to accept collective bargaining as a preferred alternative to more radical outcomes.

The same was true of Japan, where the early twentieth-century labor movement was dominated by ideas and techniques consciously borrowed from the AFL. Like their American counterparts, Japanese unionists found themselves in a country where radicalism had limited mass appeal and where large employers and the state were leery of union organization. Labor leaders like Suzuki Bunji therefore took a moderate stance in politics and at the workplace, and even more than Samuel Gompers or John Mitchell, stressed the need for orderly and peaceful resolution of disputes with employers.[16] Yet early Japanese unions faced considerable hostility despite their cooperative stance. During World War I, the unions became more aggressive, but their approach still largely was framed in terms of enterprise—rather than industrial or political—regulation.[17]

The largest Japanese labor federation was the Yuaikai, which, following a series of changes, emerged as Sodomei after the war. Like the AFL's

for the Railroad (Princeton: Princeton University Press, 1984); Robert Jackson, The Formation of Craft Labor Markets (New York: Academic Press, 1984).

[15] Hence it is a mistake to cast the Wagner Act and the War Labor Board as the harbingers of contractual unionism, as is done in Christopher L. Tomlins, The State and the Unions: Labor Relations, Law, and the Organized Labor Movement in America, 1880–1960 (Cambridge: Cambridge University Press, 1985).

[16] Stephen S. Large, The Yuaikai, 1912–1919: The Rise of Labor in Japan (Tokyo: Sophia University Press, 1972).

[17] Sheldon Garon, The State and Labor in Modern Japan (Berkeley: University of California Press, 1987), 18.

guild manorialism, the enterprise orientation of Sodomei's unions re-flected the size and stability of the companies in which Japanese unionism flourished. But the focus on the enterprise also stemmed from craft tra-ditions that were even weaker in Japan than in the United States. Japan's preindustrial guild system had collapsed during the nineteenth century under the combined pressure of rural migration, Meiji prohibitions, and technological change. By the time industrialization occurred, says Solo-mon Levine, "distinguishable crafts did not exist and there were few traditional craft labor markets."[18] Japanese workers therefore directed their struggles toward company-specific issues, seeking to become full-fledged members of their enterprise communities. Their vehicle for achiev-ing this was the enterprise union, a considerable number of which were created by workers acting on their own. These unions, to which roughly half of all Japanese union members belonged by 1928, characteristically were ambivalent, being alternately assertive and submissive toward management.[19]

Japanese employers were similarly ambivalent. During World War I, the government proposed legislation establishing works councils. Most employers were against the proposal, but after the war, when workers in some large firms began to organize their own factory unions, employers sought to preempt them by creating top-down company unions controlled by management. During the 1920s, employers boldly ousted the worker-controlled unions. At the same time, they began to implement bureau-cratic personnel policies—including internal promotion, seniority rules, and job security measures—that had the effect of tying workers more closely to the company and of reinforcing manorial tendencies in the labor movement.[20]

Enterprise unions were swept up by the Japanist labor movement of the early 1930s, which tried to "fuse" labor and capital in the pursuit of nationalist and militarist goals. Still later the army banned all forms of unionism in favor of official plant discussion councils or Sanpo units. Although most of these were ineffectual, they provided a nucleus around

[18] Gordon, *Labor Relations*, 49; Solomon B. Levine, "Japan's Labor Problems and Labor Movement, 1950–1955," in Okochi, *Labor in Modern Japan*, 109.
[19] Garon, *State and Labor*, 47–55; Gordon, *Labor Relations*, 235–46; Mikio Sumiya, "The Emergence of Modern Japan," in K. Okochi, B. Karsh, and S. B. Levine, eds., *Workers and Employers in Japan* (Tokyo: Tokyo University Press, 1973); Hiroshi Hazama, "Jap-anese Labor-Management Relations and Uno Riemon," *Journal of Japanese Studies* 5 (Winter 1976): 71–106.
[20] Gordon, *Labor Relations*, 126–61, 211–35; Garon, *State and Labor*, 47–55, 169–72.

which postwar labor relations were reconstructed. After the war, some Sanpo units were taken over by employers, while local labor activists turned others into relatively aggressive, Sodomei-affiliated enterprise unions.[21]

In short, prior to the emergence of mass unionism in Japan and the United States, each nation spawned a conservative and decentralized labor movement that was never sufficiently threatening to extract recognition from large employers. Yet the two nations did diverge in some important respects. In particular, craft traditions were much stronger in the United States than in Japan. Because of this, Japanese enterprise unionism lacked the job controls associated with the AFL's guild manorialism. Another consequence was the strong attraction of American employers to innovations like time study and incentive pay. These promised to weaken craft unionism along with less formal job controls, which, as Stanley Mathewson discovered in the 1920s, had penetrated even the ranks of unorganized workers. Not only did large American employers rely more on incentive pay and tight job structures than the Japanese, they had greater leeway to adopt those practices than European employers. A 1927 Conference Board survey found that in large American manufacturing plants (those employing more than fifteen hundred workers), 97 percent of the workers were on an incentive pay system such as a bonus plan or piecework. In this respect, American employment practices were truly exceptional.[22]

THE SECOND CRISIS, 1935–1950

The labor movement stood at the center of the turbulence that swept across America and Japan in the 1930s and 1940s. Mass unionism finally emerged in these nations and union density rates now rose to levels found in northern Europe. Organized labor acquired a power and legitimacy that it had never before enjoyed. Yet national bargaining and labor corporatism failed to appear in either country.

[21] Garon, *State and Labor*, 208–27; Joe Moore, *Japanese Workers and the Struggle for Power, 1945–1947* (Madison: University of Wisconsin Press, 1983), 31–42. Gordon, *Labor Relations*, 228–30, 299–325.

[22] Stanley B. Mathewson, *Restriction of Output Among Unorganized Workers* (New York: Viking, 1931); Wayne Lewchuk, *American Technology and the British Vehicle Industry* (Cambridge: Cambridge University Press, 1987); Daniel Nelson, "Scientific Management and the Workplace, 1920–1935," in Jacoby, ed., *Masters to Managers*, 74–89; Charles S. Maier, "Between Taylorism and Technocracy: European Ideologies and the Vision of Industrial Productivity in the 1920s," *Journal of Contemporary History* 5 (1970): 27–61.

This was not for lack of trying. Phil Murray, Walter Reuther, Clint Golden, and other CIO leaders attracted considerable attention during World War II with their plans for industry councils and tripartite "democratic planning bodies" that would give labor a voice equal to management's in return for cooperation on the shop floor.[23] Similarly, Japanese unions—both socialist (Sodomei) and communist (Sanbetsu)—demanded industrial bargaining and political influence after the war. But in each country these proposals were rejected by employers and by the state. American industrial relations remained highly decentralized, despite some pattern bargaining and despite labor's efforts on behalf of the Democratic party. In Japan, enterprise unionism remained the norm, only slightly moderated by industry-wide Shunto (annual pattern bargaining). Meanwhile, the unions remained shut out of political power, leading one scholar to describe postwar Japanese politics as "corporatism without labor."[24]

That events turned out this way has often been attributed to repression of radical CIO and Sanbetsu activists, especially communists, who were most devoted to the ideal of industrial and national bargaining.[25] In the United States, the Taft-Hartley Act of 1947 required union leaders to sign noncommunist affidavits and denied protection to unions whose leaders failed to comply. As a result, scores were blacklisted from the labor movement. Two years later, the CIO expelled ten unions with communist leaders and encouraged other unions to raid their membership. Congress nearly outlawed industry-wide bargaining (a ban had been proposed by the National Association of Manufacturers and included in the House version of the Taft-Hartley bill) and then passed provisions intended to weaken any such bargaining that developed.[26]

Not coincidentally, it was also around 1947 that the American oc-

---

[23] S. M. Jacoby, "Union-Management Cooperation in the United States During World War II," in M. Dubofsky, ed., *Technological Changes and Workers' Movements* (Beverly Hills: Sage, 1985).

[24] T. J. Pempel and Keiichi Taunekawa, "Corporatism Without Labor? The Japanese Anomaly," in P. C. Schmitter and G. Lehmbruch, eds., *Trends Toward Corporatist Intermediation* (Beverly Hills: Sage, 1979), 231–70. On labor's postwar political activities in the United States, see Derek Bok and John Dunlop, *Labor and the American Community* (New York: Simon and Schuster, 1970).

[25] Sisson, *The Management of Collective Bargaining*, 171–85; Bert Cochran, *Labor and Communism* (Princeton: Princeton University Press, 1977), 297–331; Nelson Lichtenstein, *Labor's War at Home* (Cambridge: Cambridge University Press, 1982), 240.

[26] Harry A. Millis and Emily Clark Brown, *From the Wagner Act to Taft-Hartley* (Chicago: University of Chicago Press, 1950), 386, 580; Howell J. Harris, *The Right to Manage* (Madison: University of Wisconsin Press, 1982), 121.

cupation forces in Japan (SCAP)—after a period of tolerating radical unionism—came to the conclusion that they would rather support a moderate federation like Sodomei, even if tainted by the old regime, than permit the Communist Sanbetsu to flourish. With support from SCAP and the deflationary Dodge Plan of 1948, employers began to fire radical activists and to replace Sanbetsu affiliates with more conservative and company-oriented "second" unions. By the early 1950s, Sanbetsu had largely been destroyed.[27]

Such repression was real, but in both countries it was facilitated by a relatively weak and divided Left. Much of the Left's strength in Sanbetsu and the CIO unions was concentrated among union staff and national level leadership. And even at the top, the Left was far from being in control. The American story—from internecine warfare in the UAW to the Wallace debacle of 1948—is well known. But the Japanese story is just now coming to light. As Andrew Gordon has shown, Sanbetsu in the late 1940s was filled with anticommunist dissidents who were dissatisfied with national leadership and ready to form new unions. At the local level, Sanbetsu's new industrial unions (and also Sodomei's) were rather weak. They were "little more than loose, coordinating bodies able to exercise little real power over their affiliates," the fickle factory unions that often belonged both to an enterprise federation and to an industrial union.[28] Hence it is an exaggeration to claim that postwar Japan was being swept by a workers' control movement that was ultimately expunged by SCAP. Even at its peak in 1946, only a tiny fraction of the labor force participated in so-called production control tactics. (Ironically, however, enterprise unionism got a boost from those communists who thought that factory councils were a first step toward workers' control.) In other words, if one were to imagine counterfactual situations—no Taft or McCarthy in America, no Red Purge in Japan—it is possible that the result would very likely still have been decentralized business unionism in the United States and enterprise unionism in Japan.[29]

Historians can go too far in emphasizing continuity. But American and Japanese mass unions appeared relatively late on the world industrial

---

[27]Garon, *State and Labor*, 229–48; Gordon, *Labor Relations* 335–36; Moore, *Japanese Workers*, 209–43; Michael A. Cusamano, *The Japanese Automobile Industry* (Cambridge, Mass.: Harvard University Press, 1985), 138–40; David Halberstam, *The Reckoning* (New York: Avon, 1986), 124.

[28]Levine, "Labor Problems," 101.

[29]Rodney Clark, *The Japanese Company* (New Haven: Yale University Press, 1979), 46; Moore, *Japanese Workers*, 120; Gordon, *Labor Relations*, 332.

scene, and so the past was a heavy hand shaping their response to the crises of the 1930s and 1940s. In the United States, organized labor was forced to adapt to a status quo established by management in large industrial firms. Taylorist wage incentives and job structures already were in place, along with bureaucratic personnel procedures. Although these often were only half-hearted attempts to provide security and fair treatment, enough was there to draw the new unions into joint administration and negotiated extension of the existing system. In so doing, they used earlier forms of unionism as their model, including guild manorialism and the industrial jurisprudence of the needle trades.[30] Out of this came increasingly bureaucratized employment relations, as unions wove their web of protective rules around existing job and employment structures. But the new unions also inherited from their predecessors a tradition of national unionism, which served to temper their single-firm focus with industrial solidarity. Given that solidarity, American employers might have tactically conceded industry or national bargaining. But they never offered and it never happened, in part because unions too quickly got caught up in the details of contractual job control.[31]

In postwar Japan, unions operating in the large-firm sector of the manufacturing economy also were confronted by policies that prefigured the present system, but which had not yet been fleshed out in a consistent or encompassing fashion. Those policies—lifetime employment, seniority wage and promotion plans, welfare benefits—shaped worker aspirations and made factory unionism a logical vehicle for realizing them. Given its long, though checkered, history, the factory union, says Gordon, "was naturally the relevant, comprehensible unit of action" for Japanese workers.[32]

Finally, it is important to remember that mass unionism emerged in Japan and America against a backdrop of enormous privation and insecurity. Had times been more prosperous, workers might have been less concerned with their own jobs and with enterprise-specific methods for improving them. The victories won by American and Japanese unions

---

[30] Howell Harris, "The Snares of Liberalism? Politicians, Bureaucrats, and the Shaping of Federal Labor Relations Policy in the United States, ca. 1915–47," in S. Tolliday and J. Zeitlin, eds., *Shop Floor Bargaining and the State* (Cambridge: Cambridge University Press, 1985); Steve Fraser, "Dress Rehearsal for the New Deal," in M. H. Frisch and D. J. Walkowitz, eds., *Working Class America* (Urbana: University of Illinois Press, 1983), 212–55.
[31] Jacoby, *Employing Bureaucracy*.
[32] Gordon, *Labor Relations*, 342.

were, therefore, for their members only, but they were real gains none-theless, even when measured by European standards. Unions in both countries reduced rankling status distinctions and raised employment security. Large firms now faced a host of moral and contractual con-straints on the way they treated and paid their employees. Although Japanese and American unions built their protective structures on top of a foundation laid by management, that foundation was itself a response to earlier pressures from unions and unorganized workers.

But even though the labor movements spawned in the United States and Japan were both relatively conservative and enterprise-oriented, they took different approaches to regulating employment at the enterprise level. American unions were more likely than those in Japan to pursue job controls and income (as opposed to employment) security policies. Large nonunion American firms, however, had employment systems that more closely resembled those found in Japan. The following sections examine the development of these enterprise-level employment systems in large American and Japanese firms, using the concept of an internal labor market to structure the discussion. Internal labor markets are en-terprise structures marked by hiring from within, job security, and the use of rules (rather than market forces) to guide administrative decisions. Large Japanese and American firms never entirely lacked these features, but considerably less "structure" existed prior to the 1930s and 1940s than subsequently.

EMPLOYMENT SYSTEMS: THE UNITED STATES

Between 1870 and 1915, employment for most American industrial workers was unstable and unpredictable. A worker's job depended on a personal relationship with his foreman, who had free rein to manage the hiring, payment, and supervision of labor. Foremen relied on a variety of methods to maintain or increase effort levels that collectively were known as the drive system, what Sumner Slichter called "the policy of obtaining efficiency not by rewarding merit, not by seeking to interest men in their work . . . but by putting pressure on them to turn out a large output. The dominating note of the drive policy is to inspire the worker with awe and fear of the management." The system depended on fear of job loss to ensure obedience, and discharges were liberally meted out. Dissatisfied workers had few alternatives than to quit. Quit and geographic mobility rates were high, making the labor market a market of movement.[33]

There were some exceptions, however. Salaried white-collar employees enjoyed a variety of privileges that were unavailable to manual workers—including paid vacations and the absence of night work—and had employment prospects that were substantially more stable and secure. Employers extended these perquisites both because staff were a fixed cost, and because employers entrusted their staffs with cash and company secrets (hence "secretary") and wanted this trust reciprocated. By giving a sense of attachment to the firm, job security fostered worker loyalty. So did deferred compensation plans (career ladders, pensions, anniversary checks) that paid off only if a worker avoided dismissal.[34]

Unionized craft workers also enjoyed better and more secure conditions. Union rules ensured that equitable procedures, rather than a foreman's whim, would govern pay and allocative decisions. Moreover, the closed shop undermined a key assumption of the drive system: that employment was a relationship of indefinite duration terminable at the employer's will. Instead, craft unions held that employment was a permanent relationship between the union—a set of workers—and the employer(s)—a set of jobs. The union behaved as if it owned a set of jobs continuing through time. Under the guild system, these jobs spanned employer boundaries; under manorialism they were restricted to a single firm.

Finally, some large nonunion companies devised relatively stable and structured employment systems for their skilled manual workers. The systems were a mixture of the incentives given to salaried employees and the policies pursued by craft unions. Companies like National Cash Register and International Harvester offered deferred compensation—including stock bonuses and pension plans—to their skilled workers along with job security and career ladders extending into the bottom ranks of management. Such practices raised the cost to skilled workers of union activity, although more was involved here than simple "union substitution," as modern economists term it. Taking over the skill transmission process (e.g., through corporation schools) and tying skilled workers to the firm gave employers more control of the labor process—by degrading

---

[33] Sumner Slichter, *The Turnover of Factory Labor* (New York: Appleton, 1919), 202.
[34] Jurgen Köcka, *White Collar Workers in America, 1890–1940* (Beverly Hills: Sage, 1980); S. M. Jacoby, "The Duration of Indefinite Employment Contracts in the U.S. and England: An Historical Analysis," *Comparative Labor Law* 5 (Winter 1982): 85–128.

or blending traditional crafts and by creating more stable and predictable effort norms. In effect, employers sought to take the guild out of guild manorialism.[35]

In spite of these exceptions, employers were reluctant to tamper with the drive system when it came to the great mass of unskilled and semi-skilled workers. Immigrant labor was abundant, which fostered an attitude of indifference to improving employment methods. Moreover, production managers thought that the drive system allowed for rapid adjustment of the work force to shifts in demand and was effective in holding down unit costs. They were reluctant to impose rules or to strengthen ties, fearing that this would raise costs and undermine discipline.

Salaried and industrial, 1915–1930. These attitudes began to shift around World War I, when career labor markets spread rapidly and became more elaborate. By 1920, personnel departments—one indicator of internalization—existed in 55 percent of firms employing over five thousand workers. Typically these departments fostered such practices as centralized hiring, dismissal, and wage determination; internal promotion and rationalized layoff plans; and deferred compensation and welfare programs. Most of these changes occurred during the five hectic years preceding the 1921 depression, when companies were confronted by an unprecedented combination of labor unrest, shortages, turnover, and reduced productivity. Facing a restive mass of unskilled and semiskilled workers, employers extended bureaucratic structures farther down the ranks than ever before in an attempt to preempt unionization, stabilize effort norms, and make labor costs more predictable.

In general, large firms were more likely to have internal labor markets than small firms, but differences were also caused by the values and attitudes of top management and the degree to which a firm was closely held. In tightly controlled firms, progressive employers such as Henry Dennison or William Hapgood could experiment at will. In addition,

[35] Edward P. Lazear, "Why Is There Mandatory Retirement?" *Journal of Political Economy* 87 (December 1979): 1261–84. Similar changes occurred outside of manufacturing. In retailing, a guild system existed in some large department stores, where salespeople were hired after acquiring broad experience by moving around from store to store. To reduce labor costs and create a cadre of loyal employees, firms set up programs to take relatively unskilled workers and turn them into salespeople by offering them training, internal promotion, and employment security. M. J. and S. B. Carter, "Internal Labor Markets in Retailing: The Early Years," *Industrial and Labor Relations Review* 38 (July 1985): 586–98.

advanced policies were more prevalent in the chemical, petroleum, electrical equipment, and public utility industries, where high and stable profit levels assured firms of sufficient funds to finance such personnel programs. Conversely, internal labor markets were less well developed in relatively low-profit industries like machinery, steel, textiles, and meat packing. Finally, the assurance of continuous product demand permitted firms to institute policies based on a presumption of a continuing employment relationship. Firms that had relatively stable employment—such as department stores and producers of consumer nondurables like soap and food products—were able to make commitments to their work force that would have been more costly for firms in less stable industries.[36]

Demand stability also influenced the type of employment system that firms adopted. Two variants were beginning to take shape during the 1920s. One was the *industrial model,* found in firms that relied on worker layoffs as their principal response to business downturns. When conditions improved, the firms would rehire former workers according to seniority, skill, and other factors. Industrial model firms produced cyclically sensitive goods like electrical machinery, autos, agricultural implements, and steel. They often had "chunky" capital-intensive technologies—such as blast furnaces—that did not permit gradual reductions in output or working hours during slack periods. The firms also used incentive pay schemes that reinforced the reliance on layoffs, because with incentive pay went a system of tying pay to specific jobs, thus inhibiting use of cross-training and transfers as alternatives to layoffs.[37]

Another type of internal labor market was the *salaried model,* found in firms that turned to work sharing (cutting hours), inventory production, and transfers before laying workers off. These firms faced demand that was relatively stable across seasons and cycles. Either they were in service industries like retailing or they manufactured consumer goods, especially those that could be produced for stock during slack times without risk of decay or obsolescence.[38] Packard Motor, known for its layoff avoidance policies during the 1920s, was the only major auto

[36] Jacoby, *Employing Bureaucracy,* 200–205.
[37] Seniority was already the primary factor at 40 percent of large firms surveyed in 1927. In some rare instances, industrial model firms provided income security during layoffs in the form of privately financed unemployment insurance, although these plans were most prevalent in the unionized apparel industry and should not be confused with the employment guarantee plans found in more stable firms and industries.
[38] A. D. H. Kaplan, *The Guarantee of Annual Wages* (Washington, D.C.: Brookings, 1947), 65.

producer in the 1920s that refused to adopt the new marketing strategy of annual model changes. Some salaried model firms made precision products that required highly skilled workers who were costly to recruit and replace. Others used production technologies that allowed output and hours to be reduced by degrees. Aside from these structural factors, layoff avoidance also reflected choices made by management. A 1927 study found that employers were drawn to layoff avoidance "in single-industry towns [where] the management may feel a certain obligation to provide at least some income for as many employees as possible." That was the case at Eastman Kodak, which consciously avoided layoffs during the 1920s and later adopted a private unemployment insurance plan because of management's perceived obligations to the city of Rochester in which Kodak was the largest employer.[39]

Managers at some salaried model firms made a virtue out of necessity and promoted layoff avoidance as a private solution to the unemployment problem. Under the rubric of "employment stabilization," they and their admirers asserted that any firm could reduce employment fluctuations through techniques such as production for inventory, sales planning, and training for transfers. The names of the few dozen companies that consciously pursued stabilization programs—Dennison Manufacturing, Dutchess Bleacheries, Leeds and Northrup, Procter and Gamble, Kodak, the Walworth Company—appeared and reappeared in literature on the subject, which was filled with case studies of successful programs.

Success often depended on having flexible job structures and a fluid internal labor market. For example, a firm that made various kinds of candy in different seasons cross-trained its workers to permit their employment throughout the year. More notable was a corset manufacturer whose workers were trained in a variety of operations to facilitate rapid transfers in response to style and product changes. This kind of flexibility required a central personnel department to coordinate transfers across departments; a low level of craft consciousness within the work force; and a limited reliance on incentive pay, which tightened the link between a worker's pay and his job.[40]

Employment stabilization combined business and social values, and so the firms practicing it attracted attention from management and social reformers during the 1920s. The firms also drew notice because they

[39] National Industrial Conference Board (NICB), *Layoff and Its Prevention* (New York, 1930), 26.
[40] Ibid., 16–17.

often pursued other progressive policies ranging from works councils to the "new" welfare work that included insurance, pensions, profit sharing, and stock ownership plans. In salaried model firms, then, career structures and welfare policies reinforced each other and promoted communitarian values. Layoffs were minimized because firms faced relatively mild demand fluctuations that could be absorbed through flexible compensation and job structures. Facing more variable demand, industrial model firms turned to layoffs, a choice that was reinforced by a relatively rigid labor process and compensation system. Consequently, neither workers nor managers held communitarian values in these firms.[41]

In *The Second Industrial Divide*, Michael Piore and Charles Sabel use the salaried model as the basis for their claim that the United States during the 1920s was developing an institutional nexus that would have become the norm in large industrial firms had it not been for the Great Depression, the rise of industrial unions, the Wagner Act's ban on company unions, and the consequent triumph of the industrial model.[42] This idea has received considerable attention, especially since it makes the ascendance of the industrial model appear as an accidental, rather than an inevitable, event—a critical "branching point," as they term it. But their argument exaggerates the potential of the salaried model. *Some* American firms were developing such employment policies but these were more common outside of goods-producing industries, and especially for white-collar employees. Employers were more willing to offer, and white-collar employees were more willing to accept, vague job definitions and some pay risk in exchange for substantial employment stability. Even here, however, few firms went so far as to offer formal employment guarantees.

Within goods-producing industry, the salaried model was hardly the dominant tendency during the 1920s, despite the considerable ink spilled on employment stabilization. Most large firms relied on either a layoff-rehire system for their workers or on more arbitrary methods that excluded rehiring commitments. Even when there was a rehiring policy, it

---

[41] Daniel Nelson, *Unemployment Insurance: The American Experience, 1915–1935* (Madison: University of Wisconsin Press, 1969); Jacoby, *Employing Bureaucracy,* 199. Both Procter and Gamble and Nunn-Bush, leaders in the stabilization movement, had company unions. Note that the terms "salaried" and "industrial" come from Paul Osterman, "Choice of Employment Systems in Internal Labor Markets," *Industrial Relations* 26 (Winter 1987): 46–67. In other words, each model traded off *flexibility* of response to market or technological shifts for *rigidity* in other dimensions such as wages, job structures, and the labor process.
[42] Piore and Sabel, *Second Industrial Divide,* 124–32.

often was limited to skilled or white-collar workers. As historian Ronald Schatz says of production workers at Westinghouse and General Electric, they "lived in a half-way house between arbitrary rule and systematic policy" during the 1920s.[43]

Layoff avoidance made only limited headway in American industry because it faced a formidable set of institutional barriers: craft traditions that inhibited internal flexibility and transfers; downwardly rigid pay rates; and the prevalence of incentive pay and other techniques that attached a worker's wage to his job. Among firms that had definite transfer pay policies in 1927—a rather select group—almost 85 percent tied a worker's pay to the job held after a transfer, which suggests, as do the data on incentive wages, that the pay/job link was the norm in most large industrial firms. Moreover, managers remained skeptical that productivity could be maintained unless workers were perpetually confronted by a risk of job loss. Although most managers recognized turnover and unstable effort norms as costly problems, they thought it cheaper to contain these problems through close supervision and incentive pay than by making labor a quasi-fixed cost. Thus, even before the Depression and the New Deal, the employment systems of most large industrial firms were developing along the lines of the industrial model.[44]

Union and nonunion systems, 1933–1950. Although the workplace reforms of the 1910s and 1920s were partial and uneven, they changed social norms regarding fair treatment at work. As the Depression eroded those reforms, American workers turned toward unionism to recover lost ground and to conquer new territory. In these years unionism, or the threat of it, brought a rapid expansion of policies intended to give workers more secure and predictable work lives, especially in firms that had never previously adopted much in the way of bureaucratic employment practices. Elsewhere the new unions took over the "half-way houses" that employers had earlier constructed and sought to make those structures more equitable and encompassing.

Unionism had a variety of effects. Deferred compensation was extended to blue-collar workers while other collar-linked status differences were reduced. There was a proliferation of negotiated rules—usually based on seniority—for allocating workers up (promotion), down (layoff

[43]Ronald W. Schatz, *The Electrical Workers: A History of Labor at General Electric and Westinghouse, 1923–1960* (Urbana: University of Illinois Press, 1983), 65–69.
[44]NICB, *Layoff*, 18, 21.

and rehire), and across job chains (transfers). Although jobs already had pay rates attached to them, unions equalized or narrowed rates on similar jobs. Employers defensively adopted job evaluation plans to rationalize their job/pay structures, though many unions eventually became proponents of the technique. As this suggests, the new unions became enmeshed in the logic of the internal labor market, although they were responsible for a considerable widening and deepening of its structures.[45]

Large firms that managed to avoid unionization during these years closely watched and often imitated union innovations. In response to the union threat, these firms bolstered their personnel departments, stripped foremen of many of their disciplinary powers and made employment security policies more explicit and encompassing. But differences remained between the employment policies of union and nonunion firms. Unionized firms responded to downturns through a layoff-rehire system that exposed workers to periodic joblessness but assured them of rehiring when demand picked up. This system—the old industrial model—became more acceptable to unionized workers as a result, first, of stricter seniority rules, and then of unemployment insurance (UI) and supplemental unemployment benefits (SUBs) negotiated in the 1950s.[46]

While the emphasis in the union sector was on income security, large nonunion firms tended to stress employment stability. These firms adjusted to downturns through work sharing along the lines of the salaried model. By the early 1950s, nonunion firms were twice as likely as unionized firms to rely on cuts in pay and hours as their policy of first choice in trimming labor costs; unionized firms were twice as likely to rely on layoffs. The gap widened during the 1950s and 1960s as UI benefit levels rose and SUB plans became more prevalent in the union sector. Whereas 5 percent of union contracts in 1954 called for layoffs when hours worked were below normal for four weeks or less, by 1971 that figure had risen to 43 percent. As a result, actual layoff rates were two to four times higher in the union than the nonunion sector in the early 1970s, and union workers were about 50 percent more likely to experience temporary layoffs.[47]

[45] Sar A. Levitan, "Union Attitudes toward Job Evaluation and Ingrade Progression," *Industrial and Labor Relations Review* 4 (January 1951): 268–74.

[46] Jacoby, *Employing Bureaucracy*, 232–39, 260; George P. Shultz, "A Nonunion Market for White Collar Labor," in National Bureau of Economic Research, *Aspects of Labor Economics* (Princeton: Princeton University Press, 1962), 122; Stephen Habbe, "How Not to Have Grievances," *Management Record* 11 (June 1949): 247–49.

[47] In 1962, over a third of large unionized firms were covered by SUB plans, as compared

Each of these security mechanisms was part of a larger ensemble of distinctive union and nonunion employment practices. Layoffs gave unionized firms a way to rapidly cut costs, but this flexibility was offset and often induced by rigidities in other areas, including practices that preceded unionism and protective structures that were the result of it. By and large, the new unions accepted the existing division of labor and used it as the basis for building job chains along which movement was governed by seniority.[48]

The seniority principle pervaded the union sector and so the financial returns to seniority were (and still are) larger for union members. Because it provided access to employment security, seniority gave workers a vested interest in the use of layoffs. And the interweaving of seniority with job structures legitimated and rigidified those structures in unionized firms. But that made it cumbersome to pursue cross-training, transfer, and other layoff avoidance practices.[49]

A third feature of unionized internal labor markets was the greater downward rigidity of nominal wages as compared to nonunion firms. After unionization (as well as other New Deal reforms discussed below), firms were less able than before the 1930s to rely on pay cuts during downturns. Hence the layoff system was forced to carry more of the load.[50]

In nonunion firms pay was less rigid due to the presence of various contingent pay plans not usually found in the union sector.[51] Survey data from the early 1950s and from the late 1970s show that these plans (bonuses, profit sharing, and stock purchase) were and still are rare in unionized settings. Unions have long been suspicious of the plans, seeing them as devices that substitute communitarian values for industrial sol-

to only about a tenth of comparable nonunion firms. Jacoby, *Employing Bureaucracy*, 246; H. E. Steele and H. Fisher, Jr., "A Study of the Effects of Unionism in Southern Plants," *Monthly Labor Review* 87 (March 1964): 269; James Medoff, "Layoffs and Alternatives Under Trade Unions in U.S. Manufacturing," *American Economic Review* (June 1979): 380–95.

[48] The large firms that were organized in the 1930s and 1940s had complex job structures with narrow job definitions linked to pay rates. In 1939, for example, a correlation existed (r = .43) across manufacturing industries between levels of CIO unionization and use of time and motion studies. J. N. Baron, F. R. Dobbin, and P. D. Jennings, "War and Peace: The Evolution of Modern Personnel Administration in U.S. Industry," *American Journal of Sociology* 92 (September 1986): 365.

[49] Richard Freeman and James Medoff, *What Do Unions Do?* (New York: Basic Books, 1984), 124–32.

[50] John T. Dunlop, *Wage Determination Under Trade Unions* (New York: Macmillan, 1944).

[51] D. J. B. Mitchell, *Unions, Wages, and Inflation* (Washington, D.C.: Brookings, 1980).

idarity and that permit employers to engage in financial legerdemain at the expense of worker pay. But contingent pay plans permitted nonunion payroll expenditures to be trimmed before hours or employment were cut, adding a degree of flexibility not present in unionized firms. At Kodak, for example, profit-sharing payments averaged about 7 percent of a worker's earnings in the 1940s and 1950s but the payments were cut sharply in the 1930s (down to zero in several years), thus cushioning the impact of the Depression on Kodak's employment levels.[52]

Large nonunion firms also featured more flexible job structures. Today nonunion establishments have only one-fourth the number of job classifications found in unionized workplaces of the same size. The situation forty years ago was very likely much the same, given the prevalence of time study and job control in the union sector. Also, pay in nonunion firms was less tightly tied to jobs. Nonunion employers were (and still are) more likely to use pay methods like performance appraisal and merit rating than standardized systems that link pay to job titles. Individualized pay methods increase wage inequality and can cause inequities in pay practices. But they also weaken the link between the reward structure and the job structure, making it easier for large nonunion firms to cross-train and transfer workers instead of having to lay them off, as was the case at Procter and Gamble during the 1930s or more recently occurred when IBM closed a plant at Greencastle, Indiana.[53]

Richard Freeman and James Medoff attribute many of these union-nonunion differences to the greater weight seniority is given in unionized settings. They argue that unions represent the interests of the average worker (the so-called median voter), whereas employers are more sensitive to the interests of recently hired employees (so-called marginal workers). Because the average employee has more tenure than the mar-

---

[52] Freeman and Medoff, *What Unions Do*, 65, 67; H. E. Steele, W. R. Myles, and S. C. McIntyre, "Personnel Practices in the South," *Industrial and Labor Relations Review* 9 (January 1956): 248; Steele and Fisher, "Effects of Unionism," 267.

[53] Freeman and Medoff, *What Unions Do*, 80–81; C. Ichniowski, J. T. Delaney, and D. Lewin, "The New Human Resource Management in U.S. Workplaces: Is It New and Is It Only Nonunion?" (Paper, Graduate School of Business, Columbia University, August 1988); Richard Freeman, "Union Wage Effects and Wage Dispersion Within Establishments," *Industrial and Labor Relations Review* 36 (October 1982): 3–21; Sumner Slichter, James Healy, and E. Robert Livernash, *The Impact of Collective Bargaining on Management* (Washington, D.C.: Brookings, 1960), 462–89; D. Quinn Mills, *The IBM Lesson: The Profitable Art of Full Employment* (New York: Times Books, 1988); Murray W. Latimer, *Guaranteed Wages: Report to the President by the Advisory Board, Office of Temporary Controls* (1947), 307–26. In the case of plant closures unionized firms prefer to liquidate their employees' income security rights by giving severance pay.

ginal one, seniority rules are more widespread in the union sector as are other policies that benefit senior workers such as pension and health insurance plans. The argument is logical and certainly fits the facts. But in trying to account for sectoral differences, Freeman and Medoff assign too much causal weight to the median voter and do so because an historical dimension is missing from their work.

The association between unionism and seniority that became so noticeable after the 1930s was, in fact, a historically contingent phenomenon. Prior to the 1930s, most unions were found in craft labor markets, where attachment to a given employer was weak and where firms tended to be small and short-lived. Hence seniority had less of a role to play (except under guild manorialism). Only 26 percent of a sample of union contracts collected by Slichter in the mid-1920s mentioned seniority as a factor in layoffs, whereas 40 percent of the large nonunion firms surveyed by the Conference Board in 1927 relied on seniority when making layoffs. In other words, contrary to Freeman and Medoff's argument, there is no automatic association between unionism and seniority. The link only became widespread after 1933, in part because the depression soured existing unions on work sharing, but more importantly because the new unions of the 1930s appeared in firms that already relied on seniority rules and layoff systems. By 1938, seniority determined layoffs in 95 percent of unionized firms, nearly double the ratio for the nonunion sector.[54]

These differences were as much a cause as a consequence of unionism. As we have seen, firms pursuing the industrial model during the 1920s were cyclically sensitive, capital-intensive, and relied on time study, incentive pay, and layoffs. When workers turned to unions during the 1930s, they did so, in part, out of insecurity and anger brought on by how firms operated the industrial model. These firms had high layoff rates during the Depression. Between 1929 and 1932, durable goods manufacturers—home to the industrial model and to industrial unionism—had much larger cuts in payrolls (70 percent versus 45 percent) and in employment (50 percent versus 25 percent) than manufacturers of nondurables. Anger came from the continuing prominence of the foreman, the use of incentive pay, and the inequities that resulted from the two combined. During the 1930s, managers were warned that inconsis-

---

[54]Sumner Slichter, *Union Policies and Industrial Management* (Washington, D.C.: Brookings, 1941), 105; Jacoby, *Employing Bureaucracy*, 245.

tent wage rates were "agitational dynamite," and indeed, there is a strong positive relationship between an industry's use of time and motion study in 1935 and its subsequent unionization rate. Finally, anger and insecurity were both touched off when foremen made layoff decisions without consistently applying criteria like seniority.[55]

In salaried model firms of the 1920s, largely in the nondurable manufacturing or service sectors, unionism made less headway. The depression had less of an effect on these companies and even when it did, layoffs typically were a last resort. Often the firms had production processes that permitted continuous hours reductions (unlike "chunky" blast furnaces). Thus, a corollary should be added to David Brody's hypothesis about the demise of welfare capitalism and the subsequent success of unionism: Unlike industrial model firms, salaried model firms avoided the worst ravages of the Depression and this, combined with the fact that many of them maintained their welfare programs during the early 1930s, helped them to avert unionization. For example, during the Depression Sears Roebuck and Kodak both kept intact their profit sharing, health insurance, and other welfare policies and also were able to avoid sizable layoffs. Subsequently neither firm was organized to any significant extent.[56]

In short, unions tended to appear during the 1930s and 1940s in firms with distinctive economic and technological features. Those features were associated with various pre-union employment practices, which unions then took over and codified during collective bargaining. That is one reason why contracts thickened so quickly in the 1940s. (For others, see the essay by Brody in this volume.) Still, unionism had many real consequences, and these widened existing differences between unionized and nonunion companies. The new unions not only took over existing seniority systems but made them more stringent. As early as 1938, one could see sectoral differences in this area. In firms that used seniority as a layoff criterion, it was the governing factor in 69 percent of unionized, but only 8 percent of nonunion, firms.[57]

[55] Ibid., 251; Baron et al., "War and Peace," 366; Kaplan, *Guarantee*, 104.
[56] A recent study found unions to prevail in workplaces that "require interdependent worker behavior in the production process." Interdependence leads to common rules governing the use of labor and technology, including rules on workshifts, seniority, and effort intensity. The authors hypothesize that unions arise in these settings because they provide a mechanism for influencing those rules. Greg Duncan and Frank Stafford, "Do Union Members Receive Compensating Differentials?" *American Economic Review* 70 (June 1980): 369.
[57] Jacoby, *Employing Bureaucracy*, 245. The same ratio existed in the early 1950s.

In accounting for this, there is something to be said for Freeman and Medoff's median voter model of unionism. Still, the stringency with which the new unions applied seniority is best seen not as a universal characteristic of unionism (as the median voter model would imply) but instead as a result of the decentralized kind of unionism found in the United States but not in most other nations. By making the firm and its rules the focus of their strategy for protecting worker rights, American unions magnified existing differences—in seniority and in job structure—between union and nonunion workplaces. Not surprisingly, this strategy incurred the wrath of managers threatened by the incursion of unionism into realms they considered sacrosanct. During the 1940s, the industrial relations literature was filled with material on "the union challenge to management control."[58] Unions backed up their strategy with strikes, or strike threats, which could impose significant costs on a single firm in a competitive market.

Ironically, the employer response to these challenges had the effect of widening sectoral differences even further. By taking a tough stand on the issue of their right to control production, employers discouraged unions from seeking employment security (output stabilization, guaranteed employment, etc.) because this would have taken labor deep into the details of plant management. Instead, postwar managements deflected unions to areas where resistance was weakest, in the realm of income security (layoffs mitigated by severance pay and SUBs). As Slichter and his colleagues said in 1960, "By choosing income security as the goal, unions avoid the necessity of bargaining over such essential management decisions as production schedules, capital improvement plans, and plant location. By and large, management has retained its freedom to make these decisions."[59] Absent a union, however, employment security policies posed none of those risks of codetermination, and large nonunion employers were more likely to pursue them. Thus, unions made it easier for their members to maintain their incomes during downturns, but their employment remained quite unstable. From 1958 to 1981, employment swings in highly unionized industries were about four times larger than in low-unionization industries.[60]

---

[58]Neil Chamberlain, *The Union Challenge to Management Control* (New York: Harper, 1948).

[59]Slichter, Healy, and Livernash, *Impact of Bargaining,* 448.

[60]Freeman and Medoff, *What Unions Do,* 113; John S. Heywood, "Do Union Members

Long-term contracts were another policy that unionized employers
initiated to contain the impact of unionism. By lengthening contracts,
firms could amortize over a longer period the fixed costs associated with
strikes or strike threats. Also, lengthy contracts facilitated multiyear projects by providing reasonable certainty that they would not be interrupted
by major work stoppages, a factor of some importance to capital-intensive
firms. Average contract durations steadily rose in the postwar years, with
most of the pressure to lengthen coming from management. But long-
term contracts had the effect of insulating union pay from business cycle
factors, raising the rigidity of union wages. Thus when unionized firms
had to trim payroll costs, they were even more likely than nonunion firms
to choose employment cuts instead of pay cuts.[61]

As in any analysis of an ideal type, here we have been taking existing
elements of reality and enhancing them so as to develop a standard against
which firms can be compared. Yet it should be emphasized that there
was considerable overlap between unionized and nonunion firms. Take
seniority, for example. Although more rigidly applied in the union sector,
it was, and still is, of great importance in nonunion settings, even in
promotion decisions. Nonunion does not by any means imply strict ad-
herence to merit.[62] Or take job security. Although unionized workers are
more exposed to layoffs, labor "hoarding" nevertheless occurs in unionized firms during downturns. Moreover, because older union workers
are protected from layoff except during a severe downturn or plant clo-
sure, they have considerable employment security. Because seniority and
employment security practices exist in both union and nonunion sectors,

Receive Compensating Differentials?: The Case of Employment Security," *Journal of
Labor Research* 10 (Summer 1989): 271–84.
[61] S. M. Jacoby and D. J. B. Mitchell, "Does Implicit Contracting Explain Explicit Contracting?" *Proceedings of the 35th Annual Meeting of the Industrial Relations Research
Association, 1982*, 319–28; Jacoby and Mitchell, "Development of Contractual Features
of the Union-Management Relationship," *Labor Law Journal* 33 (August 1982): 512–
18.
[62] K. G. Abraham and J. L. Medoff, "Length of Service and the Operation of Internal Labor
Markets," *Proceedings of the 35th Annual Meeting of the Industrial Relations Research
Association, New York, 1982*, 308–18. Between 1968 and 1980, the return on earnings
due to seniority was about 0.7 percent per year for union workers versus 0.3 percent for
comparable nonunion workers. Presently, seniority is substantially favored in promotion
decisions of 76 percent of hourly unionized employees but the figures for nonunion
workers are also quite high: 56 percent for hourly employees and 59 percent for salaried
nonexempt employees. K. G. Abraham and H. S. Farber, "Returns to Seniority in Union
and Nonunion Jobs," *Industrial and Labor Relations Review* 42 (October 1988): 13–
14.

a sizable segment of the American work force is shielded from job loss. In the 1980s, more than 40 percent of American workers over age forty-five held jobs that would last for the rest of their worklives.[63]

EMPLOYMENT SYSTEMS: JAPAN

As the preceding discussion suggests, Japanese and American employment systems also overlap considerably. As in the United States, the Japanese system developed in two stages: initially as a managerial response to economic imperatives and challenges from a refractory, but largely unorganized, work force; later as a result of more direct actions by organized labor. Skeptics are often doubtful of the role that unions played in the evolution of the Japanese system. But intense and significant struggles were waged by Japanese labor, although the outcomes were not quite the same as in the American union sector.

With relatively weak craft traditions in the work force, job control rarely was a pivotal strategy of Japanese unions, while employers were never so enamored of scientific management as their American counterparts. Take the steel industry, for example. Over half of American steelworkers in the 1920s and 1930s were on incentive pay, which caused the industry's wage structure to resemble a "maze," with one large wire mill reporting over one hundred thousand different rates in the 1930s. But at Nippon Kokkan, a major Japanese steel producer, only 10 percent of the work force received individual piecework wages in the mid-1920s. The Japanese steel industry, writes Robert E. Cole, was "not faced with strong craft unions. There was consequently no domestic model of job control available, and that meant there was none to be resurrected at a later date as unions developed their strength."

When Japanese unions were feeling their oats after World War II, they did much the same thing as American unions and based their demands

---

[63] Jerome Rosow and Robert Zager, *Employment Security in a Free Economy* (New York: Pergamon, 1984), 40; Jon A. Fay and James L. Medoff, "Labor and Output over the Business Cycle: Some Direct Evidence," *American Economic Review* 75 (September 1985): 638–55; Robert T. Hall, "The Importance of Lifetime Jobs in the U.S. Economy," *American Economic Review* 72 (September 1982): 718. In the 1970s, older union workers were less exposed to the risk of permanent job loss than were older nonunion workers, whereas younger unionized workers were more exposed to temporary *and* permanent job loss than were younger nonunion workers. When asked whether their job security was good, nonunion workers with fewer than twenty years of service expressed as much or more satisfaction than did unionized workers with comparable service, but the reverse was true for workers who had been on the job more than twenty years. Freeman and Medoff, 126–28.

on preexisting company policies. But while American unions pushed for seniority layoff systems built around a myriad of job/pay rates, the new Japanese unions "defined their role as [that of] protecting jobs in general." They demanded employment, rather than income, security. The absence of job control made it easier for Japanese employers to accommodate these demands through cross-training, transfers, and other stabilization methods.[64]

Yet the lack of American-style job control should not be taken to mean that Japanese employers had an easy time of it after the war. While employers may have defined the terrain of struggle, the outcome was neither necessary nor costless for them. As Gordon shows, successful strikes by Japanese workers led to a brief reign in the immediate postwar years of a "labor version" of Japanese employment practices, including a need-based wage system and guarantees of employment security "wrested from firms at the height of labor power." Then, in the late 1940s and early 1950s, Japanese employers "defeated radical labor and rejected the labor version of Japanese employment practices." But "the result was still a tremendous advance for workers when measured against the prewar or wartime systems. . . . The settlement of the 1950s was more complex than terms such as 'management victory' or 'labor defeat' convey."[65]

The terms of that settlement included substantial employment security for workers in large firms in exchange for which "unions continued to allow managers near total control over transfers and job definitions," a trade-off along salaried model lines. A relatively loose job/pay structure was retained so that, even today, the bulk of blue-collar workers in Japanese auto firms are grouped into only two job categories. In the wage arena, unions were forced to give up their need-based wage system but were able to redefine bonus pay as a matter for bargaining rather than something given out solely at management's discretion. Workers came to see bonuses as a regular part of their pay package, although that view changed during the 1970s recession, when bonus cuts occurred in re-

---

[64] National Industrial Conference Board, *Systems of Wage Payment* (New York, 1930); Katherine Stone, "The Origins of Job Structures in the Steel Industry," *Review of Radical Political Economics* (Summer 1974): 157; F. H. Harbison, "Steel," in Harry A. Millis, ed., *How Collective Bargaining Works* (New York: Twentieth Century Fund, 1945), 551–52; Cole, *Work and Participation,* 111; Gordon, *Labor Relations,* 165, 390–91; Thomas P. Rohlen, "Permanent Employment Faces Recession, Slow Growth, and an Aging Labor Force," *Journal of Japanese Studies* 5 (Summer 1979): 244–46.
[65] Gordon, *Labor Relations,* 330, 383, 386. Also see Shirai, "A Theory of Enterprise Unionism," in Shirai, ed., *Contemporary Industrial Relations in Japan,* 117–44.

sponse to oil price increases. Still, the cuts cushioned employment levels, again along the lines of the salaried model.[66]

Despite these parallels between Japanese and salaried model American firms, important differences remained. They suggest that the model did not operate according to any inherent or mechanical logic. As compared to large nonunion firms in the United States, large Japanese firms had policies that were (and are) more oriented to employment security as well as more communitarian. In part this is evidence of the impact of Japanese enterprise unions, whose continual concern with status equalization produced what one Japanese economist calls the "white-collarization of [Japanese] blue-collar workers." But to fully understand these differences, we must go beyond comparative labor dynamics and examine other institutions that shaped the Japanese workplace.[67]

Dualism and the state. The quest for employment security in Japan was affected by Japan's high degree of economic dualism, a consequence of the country's late and rapid development. Although dualism exists in most economies, it was especially pronounced in Japan. Late development meant that one segment of Japanese industry leapt into world markets using the large-scale, capital-intensive technologies of the day. Rapid growth, with domestic consumption patterns lagging behind changes in industrial structure, left another segment consisting of small, labor-intensive firms. Even as late as the 1960s, Japan—as compared to the United States—had a larger proportion of firms at both tails of the size distribution as well as lower concentration ratios in the bottom tail. That kept costs down in the peripheral sector and gave large Japanese firms an incentive to externalize risk and demand fluctuations by subcontracting with smaller firms. At the same time, externalization provided flexibility to offset the rigidity of job security practices in large firms.

State industrial policy provided additional incentives for the emergence

[66]Gordon, *Labor Relations,* 381; Rohlen, "Permanent Employment," 242; Cole, *Work and Participation,* 220. There is some disagreement about bonus wages. For contrasting appraisals, see Isao Ohasi, "On the Determinants of Bonuses and Basic Wages in Large Japanese Firms" (Paper, Economics Department, Nagoya University, January 1989); and Ronald Dore, *Flexible Rigidities: Industrial Policy and Structure Adjustment in the Japanese Economy* (Stanford: Stanford University Press, 1986), 103, versus Kazutoshi Koshiro, "Development of Collective Bargaining in Postwar Japan," in Shirai, ed., *Contemporary Industrial Relations in Japan,* 241; and Richard Freeman and Martin Weitzman, "Bonuses and Employment in Japan," *Journal of Japanese and International Economy* 1 (June 1987): 168–94.
[67]Koike, "Internal Labor Markets," 60.

of this system. By direct investment and by administrative actions (e.g., the allocation of military contracts) favoring industrial concentration and scale, the state fostered the emergence of large firms and cartelistic arrangements in heavy industry and finance. Not only did this encourage industrial dualism, but it gave large Japanese firms a way to prevent ruinous, deflationary competition. Firms and banks could openly coordinate policies to achieve price stability, whereas in the United States similar actions were stymied by a persistent threat of antitrust prosecution.[68]

Unlike Japan, the United States prior to the 1930s had a relatively small federal government and a citizenry suspicious of industrial concentration. While the Depression and the National Industrial Recovery Act changed some of those attitudes, New Deal policymakers still had to look beyond collusion to find price props, and wages were one place they looked, with the encouragement of underconsumption theorists. Putting a prop under prices by stabilizing wages was one of the rationales not only of the Recovery Act, but also of successive legislation like the Wagner Act, the Social Security Act, and the Fair Labor Standards Act. These laws had the effect of promoting a higher degree of rigidity in private wage setting than previously existed—by encouraging collective bargaining and fixed-term labor contracts, by linking pension and overtime benefits to a worker's nominal wage, and by minimum wage floors.[69] With incentives tilted toward wage rigidity, cyclical adjustment was more likely to occur via contractions in output and employment than wage and price cuts. No such incentives appeared in Japan. In fact, the Japanese government's main response to the depression was a 1936 law that "built upon existing employer practices" by requiring large firms to give severance pay to dismissed workers, thus providing a different incentive, namely, to avoid layoffs.[70]

Another consequence of Japan's *dirigiste* state was a rationalized and

[68] Richard E. Caves, "Industrial Organization," in Patrick and Rosovsky, *Asia's New Giant* (Washington, D.C.: Brookings Institution, 1976), 459–523; Joe S. Bain, *International Differences in Industrial Structure* (New Haven: Yale University Press, 1966); Seymour Broadbridge, *Industrial Dualism in Japan* (Chicago: Aldine, 1966); Robert Averitt, *The Dual Economy: The Dynamics of American Industry Structure* (New York: Norton, 1968); Suzanne Berger and Michael Piore, *Dualism and Discontinuity in Industrial Societies* (Cambridge: Cambridge University Press, 1980).

[69] Jacoby, *Employing Bureaucracy,* 216–17; D. J. B. Mitchell, "Explanations of Wage Inflexibility: Institutions and Incentives," in W. Beckerman, ed., *Wage Rigidity and Unemployment* (Baltimore: Johns Hopkins University Press, 1986).

[70] Andrew Gordon, "The Right to Work in Japan: Labor and the State in Depression," *Social Research* 54 (Summer 1987): 247–72.

highly meritocratic educational system, with national curricula, standardized tests, and high rates of school enrollment (higher in 1900 than
in some American states). Japanese schools performed an immense task
of quality control for the nation's employers, who could be reasonably
confident that "permanent" employment was being offered to the most
able graduates. This made it easier for large employers to adopt egalitarian and communitarian personnel ideologies and to put less stress on
performance as a reward criterion. Ever since the 1910s, meritocratic
efficiency movements have periodically swept American schools. But their
impact has always been fragmented by the country's decentralized and
relatively egalitarian public school system. As a result, American employers usually are reluctant to make employment commitments without
careful and lengthy screening of employees. Pervasive performance evaluation and relatively high dismissal rates in American firms function, in
part, as quality control mechanisms that make up for casual sorting by
the schools. Thus in Japan, the schools are the locus of competitive
meritocracy while the firm is relatively egalitarian; the reverse tends to
be true of the United States, which is one reason why Japanese firms with
U.S. facilities spend more time and money screening prospective employees than they do at home.[71]

Cultural factors. One should be wary of arguments based on differences
in national culture and attitudes because these can involve circular logic.
But an unnecessary burden is created if politics and economics are made
to carry the whole explanation. Anthropological studies show that a
desire for community and interdependence is part of Japanese culture,
and it is easy to see how it can reinforce a high degree of identification
with the work group and the firm. In Japan, communitarian values infuse
company unions, personnel policies, benefits, and leisure activities. By
contrast, American culture emphasizes individualism and economic
achievement; dependence is disparaged and rejected. As a former U.S.
union official said in 1917:

A job may be satisfactory in every respect, quite as good as they are likely to
find anywhere, and yet they will leave because they do not want to remain in

[71] "How Does Japan Inc. Pick Its American Workers?" *Business Week* 3 (October 1988):
84–88; William Landes and Lewis Solmon, "Compulsory Schooling Legislation in the
19th Century," *Journal of Economic History* 32 (March 1972): 54–91; Gary Allinson,
Japanese Urbanism: Industry and Politics in Kariya, 1872–1972 (Berkeley: University of
California Press, 1975); Raymond Callahan, *Education and the Cult of Efficiency* (Chicago: University of Chicago Press, 1962).

the shop for too long...this desire for change rests upon a fear of losing their independence, of getting into a frame of mind wherein they will come to attach disproportionate importance to the retention of a certain job.

Those attitudes are reflected in the weak ties and mobility-oriented emphasis of the industrial model. They also sustain the suspicion with which American workers and unions have greeted instances of corporate paternalism.[72]

Indeed, the imagery of laissez-faire contractualism has long pervaded commercial relations in the United States, including those of the workplace. As Philip Selznick puts it, the laissez-faire contract model is "infused with the spirit of restraint and delimitation; open-ended obligations are alien to its nature; arms-length negotiations is the keynote." With that model as the touchstone for an industrial relations system, it is hardly surprising that the parties—in both union and nonunion sectors—tend toward mutual suspicion, weak ties, and fear of opportunism.[73] While it would be hard to rank the United States and Britain on the average degree of trust in employment relations, Japan undoubtedly is the outlier on this dimension. Employment and other commercial transactions in Japan evince a different, more organic, approach to contracting, characterized by enduring obligations, harmonization of interests, and mutual trust.[74]

The implications of all this are readily apparent. For example, contingent pay systems are more difficult to administer when employees distrust their employers. Suspicious workers in a suspicious society will always wonder whether the employer really has experienced a reduction in demand that necessitates a pay cut. It is more rational for distrustful workers to insist on layoffs, which force the firm to cut back on output and to sell less. Were there more trust, however, workers might be less wary of income adjustments, especially if managers promised to cut their own pay first, as is often done in Japan. And that creates a virtuous

---

[72] Cole, *Work and Participation,* 224–50; Takeo Doi, *The Anatomy of Dependence* (Tokyo: Kodansha, 1973); T. P. Rohlen, *For Harmony and Strength: Japanese White-Collar Organization in Anthropological Perspective* (Berkeley: University of California Press, 1974), 34–61; Gordon, *Labor Relations,* 251–53; Koya Azumi, "Japanese Society: A Sociological View," in A. E. Tiedemann, ed., *An Introduction to Japanese Civilization* (New York: Columbia University Press, 1974), 515–35; Chie Nakane, *Japanese Society* (Berkeley: University of California Press, 1970); A. J. Portenar, "Centralized Labor Responsibility from a Trade Union Standpoint," *Annals of the American Academy of Social and Political Science* 71 (May 1917): 193.
[73] Philip Selznick, *Law, Society, and Industrial Justice* (New York: Russell Sage, 1969), 52.
[74] Ronald Dore, *Taking Japan Seriously: A Confucian Perspective on Leading Economic Issues* (Stanford: Stanford University Press, 1987); Oliver Williamson, *The Economic Institutions of Capitalism* (New York: Free Press, 1985).

SANFORD M. JACOBY

240

circle: worker loyalty to the firm deepens when the burden of adjustment is shared and when, if pay cuts are not enough, managers go to great lengths to avoid layoffs and to find alternate employment for employees. As British sociologist Alan Fox puts it, trust begets trust.[75]

Finally, Japanese employment security largely excludes women, who were and still are a "buffer" protecting the stable jobs extended to male workers in large firms. To some extent, the same has been true in the United States, where women are more likely to be found in peripheral jobs and to be excluded from the most secure or desirable jobs in large firms. Still, the use of women as a buffer labor force is more overt and extensive in Japan, the reasons for which undoubtedly are "cultural." As a result, although American women on average have less stable jobs than American men, the gender gap is smaller than in Japan.[76]

DEVELOPMENTS IN JAPAN AND THE UNITED STATES SINCE 1970

To sum up, a strong form of the salaried model developed in large Japanese companies, whereas large American firms bifurcated: unionized firms pursued the industrial model while nonunion firms had a weak form of the salaried model. These micro-level variations in employment practices are responsible for numerous macro-level differences in economic outcomes. Two examples: First, interfirm labor mobility rates in Japan are lower than in the United States, a condition that has existed from the late 1910s through the present. Second, nominal compensation in Japan is more sensitive to economic conditions, while industrial employment is less sensitive, than in the United States.[77]

Some might see these facts as proof that Japanese industrial relations

[75] Martin Weitzman, *The Share Economy* (Cambridge, Mass.: Harvard University Press, 1984); Arthur Okun, *Prices and Quantities: A Macroeconomic Analysis* (Washington, D.C.: Brookings Institution, 1981); Edgar Czarnecki, "Profit Sharing and Union Organizing," *Monthly Labor Review* 92 (December 1969): 61–63; Alan Fox, *Beyond Contract* (London: Faber and Faber, 1973).
[76] Hall, "Lifetime Jobs," 623; K. Abraham and S. Houseman, "Job Security and Work Force Adjustment: How Different Are U.S. and Japanese Practices?" (Paper, Economics Department, University of Maryland, December 1988). On women in Japan, see E. O. Reischauer, *The Japanese* (Cambridge Mass.: Harvard University Press, 1974), 204. Note that women workers constitute one of several buffers protecting the jobs of core employees. Other buffers include male temporary and part-time employees of core firms and employees of subcontractor firms in the periphery.
[77] Gordon, *Labor Relations*, 89; OECD 1965; Cole, *Work and Participation*, 83; Haruo Shimada, "The Japanese Labor Market After the Oil Crisis: Factual Report," *Keio Economic Studies* 14 (1977): 49–66; Robert J. Gordon, "Why U.S. Wage and Employment Behavior Differs From That in Japan," *Economic Journal* 92 (March 1982): 13–44.

are unique, the view held by modernization theorists in the 1950s and 1960s. But when outcomes in the United States, Japan, and Western Europe are compared along the above dimensions—labor mobility, wage rigidity, and employment volatility—it is the United States that takes the most extreme values in each case. In Europe, as we have seen, these results came about through a rather different process than in Japan: European unions used legislation and industry-wide bargaining to restrict employer discretion and to regulate other aspects of the employment relationship. Yet their activities at these levels, as well as their institutional security, made them less concerned with taking a job-control approach to regulating the workplace. Hence one finds in Europe less of this kind of regulation than in unionized American firms. A recent study reports that internal labor markets in Germany and Sweden, as compared to those in the United States, are "flexible and fluid [with] fewer job classifications . . . and a labor force more able and more willing to be assigned to a broad range of tasks." Thus, what makes the United States unique at the micro-level and skews its outcomes at the macro-level is the industrial model, which is a legacy of conservative craft unions, late-developing industrial unions, and powerful employers.[78]

Still, America shares with Japan limited public regulation of the workplace and, in the case of large nonunion U.S. companies, a common approach to organizing internal labor markets. And the overlap between Japanese and American employment systems is currently growing, as employers in each country back away from commitments negotiated during the crisis years of mass unionism. Behind this are recent changes in the economic environment, including intensified competition and slower growth rates. Competition is spurring employers to find ways of reducing labor costs, while sluggish growth rates are making internal labor market arrangements more costly. As new hiring slows, average employee tenure rises. With that comes an increase in average wage and salary levels as well as in the cost of labor hoarding, SUBs, and severance pay. The problem is compounded by each nation's aging labor force. Shortages of young workers first developed in Japan during the 1970s. Now they are appearing in the United States, as the small cohort behind

---

[78] Paul Osterman, *Employment Futures* (New York: Oxford University Press, 1988), 122; Michael J. Piore, "Perspective on Labor Market Flexibility," *Industrial Relations* 25 (Spring 1986): 146–66; K. G. Abraham and S. N. Houseman, "Employment Security and Employment Adjustment," *Proceedings of the 40th Meeting of the Industrial Relations Research Association, 1987*, 44–54.

the babyboomers enters the labor force. Shortages put pressure on entry-level wages and that pressure then is transmitted along the firm's wage structure.

To cut costs, employers in older industries are relocating to low-wage nations. Although the "rust belt" problem is more extensive in the United States, Japan has had its share of plant closures and capital flight in textiles, steel, coal mining, shipping, and other industries. Another cost-cutting measure favored by large firms is new technology, which reduces the demand for less skilled workers. Because security commitments are expensive and stand in the way of downsizing and restructuring, large Japanese and American firms have also been shrinking the number of workers employed in career labor markets while expanding the contingent work force.[79]

Economists in recent years have created various theories that seek to rationalize in efficiency terms the "sticky" employment relationships associated with internal labor markets. The theories demonstrate that various benefits accrue to employers from hiring workers on a quasi-permanent basis, including efficiencies in training, screening, and motivation. But the theories have a static quality, in part because they give insufficient attention to the costs of these arrangements.[80] As we have seen, neither Japanese nor American employers were unaware of those costs. Their reluctance to confer career status on less skilled workers reflected skepticism that doing so was a strict economic necessity. Hence Japanese and American workers had to struggle for nearly half a century to attain that status. By the 1950s many had succeeded, and for the next twenty years or so, employer skepticism was muted by various factors. The battles of the crisis years lingered in managers' minds, and so they were reluctant to tamper with career employment systems. Employment stability was thought to promote industrial relations stability, and no one wanted a return to the crisis years. Equally important was the fact that these were decades of steady economic growth. Japan was engaged in reconstruction followed by a successful export drive, while American firms faced only moderate competition at home and abroad.[81]

---

[79] Koshiro Kazutoshi, "Reality of Dualistic Labor Market in Japan," *East Asia* 2 (1984): 45

[80] For a recent literature review, see Michael Wachter and Randall Wright, "The Economics of Internal Labor Markets," *Industrial Relations* 29 (Spring 1990).

[81] T. A. Kochan and P. Cappelli, "The Transformation of the Industrial Relations and Personnel Function," in Paul Osterman, ed., *Internal Labor Markets* (Cambridge, Mass.: MIT Press, 1984), 133–63.

But things began to change during the 1970s and 1980s. First, competition and restructuring shrank the cushion of profits available to support labor hoarding and related policies. Second, slower growth rates removed a key justification for those policies: that they help firms respond in a timely fashion to cyclical upturns and other growth opportunities. Rather, companies today "are poised for contraction." Third, organized labor is declining and losing influence in both nations. In the United States, union density fell sharply after 1970, so that by 1990 only 12 percent of private-sector workers belonged to unions. In Japan, union density also fell between 1970 and 1990: from 35 percent to 25 percent, a drop that places it second to the United States among Western nations in its rate of union decline. Finally, memories of the crisis years are fading, particularly now that a new generation of managers is moving to the top. Thus employers perceive the cost of internal labor markets to be rising and their benefits declining. As earlier in the century, however, the balance is seen more favorably in the case of skilled and technical employees than of semiskilled service and production workers. It is the "implicit contracts" of this latter group that management most frequently seeks to renegotiate, though insecurity has grown throughout the ranks.[82]

In Japan, restructuring started during the recession that lasted from 1973 to 1978. Thousands of workers in large firms were fired—many of them women, who form the bulk of the temporary and part-time labor force—but the cuts extended to older male employees as well. In the ensuing recovery, large firms have been careful to keep a ceiling on the number of employees with quasi-permanent status. Whenever possible, they have been hiring temporary and part-time workers, while at the same time trying to cut back on overall employment levels. Since 1978, employment growth in Japan has been slowest in large firms. Based on an analysis of firms listed on the Tokyo stock exchange, a recent Japanese study finds a decrease in the relative share in total employment of jobs with secure employment opportunities, and predicts that this trend will continue.

The pressures on the Japanese employment system do not entirely stem from weak labor demand. Spot shortages exist in technical fields like

---

[82] Eileen Applebaum, "Restructuring Work: Temporary, Parttime, and At-Home Employment," in Heidi Hartman, ed., *Computer Chips and Paper Clips: Technology and Women's Employment* (Washington, D.C.: National Academy Press, 1987), 271. Unionization data are in Richard Freeman and Mark Rebick, "Crumbling Pillar? Declining Union Density in Japan" (Paper given at Tokyo Center of Economic Research, Conference on Labor Relations and the Firm, Tokyo, January 1989).

financial management and engineering. Here employees are being lured
from lifetime jobs by hefty pay offers, a phenomenon that has received
a lot of publicity. An article in *Tokyo Business Today* calls it a sign of
"the crumbling walls of lifetime employment." While that is hyperbole,
there is less stigma attached to midcareer job switching today than in
the past. Relatively few blue-collar workers in large firms are making
those moves, but in the future job switching may include them, thus
lending to the Japanese employment system some of the fluidity associated
with American labor markets.[83]

Internal labor markets in the United States have also been shrinking.
Since 1980, employment levels have been cut or held down in most large
industrial firms. At General Electric, more than a hundred thousand
jobs—over a quarter of the company's work force—were eliminated
between 1981 and 1986. As elsewhere, the cuts included salaried as well
as hourly employees, although the latter bore the brunt. But reductions
in core employment are only part of the story. Employers increasingly
rely on contingent workers—part-time, temporary, and leased—who are
granted neither employment nor income security, nor deferred compensation and other fringe benefits. The size of the contingent labor force is
not precisely known, but is estimated to include over a fifth of American
workers. The largest group consists of part-time workers, whose share
of the labor force grew from 15 percent in 1967 to 20 percent in 1987.
The number of temporary workers is more difficult to estimate because
some are hired directly by employers and not through a temporary help
agency. These agencies are one of the fastest growing industries, and the
demand for their services is widespread. Agency temps are used by 90
percent of U.S. firms surveyed in 1988. At some firms, temps account
for as much as 10 to 20 percent of the work force.[84]

[83] Masumi Tsuda, "The End of a Way of Life?" *Japan Economic Journal* (Summer 1988):
10–12; Dore, *Flexible Rigidities*, 81–96; Koike, "Internal Labor Markets," 48; Koshiro,
"Dualistic Labor Market," 49; Mutsuo Kawashima, "The Crumbling Walls of Lifetime
Employment," *Tokyo Business Today* (September 1988): 28–29; "Big Bucks vs. a Job
for Life: Why Top Talent Is Defecting," *Business Week* 9 (January 1989): 58; Rohlen,
"Permanent Employment," 237–39; Haruo Shimada, "Human Resource Strategies for
a Creative Society," *Japan Echo* 13 (1986): 40–46.

[84] Bennett Harrison and Barry Bluestone, *The Great U-Turn: Corporate Restructuring and
the Polarizing of America* (New York: Basic Books, 1988), 37, 45; Katharine Abraham,
"Flexible Staffing Arrangement and Employers' Strategies," National Bureau of Economic
Research, Working Paper No. 2617, November 1988; Applebaum, "Restructuring
Work," 267; Jeffrey Pfeffer and James Baron, "Taking the Workers Back Out: Recent
Trends in the Structuring of Employment," in Barry Staw and L. L. Cummings, eds.,
Research in Organizational Behavior, vol. 10 (Greenwich: JAI Press, 1988), 257–303;

Still, one should not get the impression that internal labor markets are vanishing or that contingent workers are simply a substitute for core employees. Instead, contingents are better viewed as a complement, buffering core employees from cyclical and technological shifts in demand. Although the core is a smaller portion of the work force than previously, it still exists, and contingents make it cheaper for firms to provide core workers with income or employment security. In that respect, U.S. developments resemble those occurring in Japan; American firms now even use Japanese categories like "permanent temporaries."[85]

But a development unique to the United States is the recomposition of core employment. In manufacturing and low-status white-collar jobs, the industrial model is gradually being displaced by a version of the salaried model. The terms of the shift are sometimes explicit, sometimes vague, but they usually involve some of the following items: Hourly workers are offered salaries, varying degrees of employment security, and contingent compensation like profit sharing. Invidious status distinctions—in uniforms, parking lots, and dining rooms—are eliminated. In return, workers are asked to accept lower base pay levels and less income security. Also, the job/pay system is loosened through the use of broader job definitions, teams, cross-training, and pay-for-learning systems. The shift to the salaried model means employment costs are becoming more fixed. That is, firms are giving up some of the rapid cost reductions that layoffs permitted under the industrial model. Flexible compensation for core workers is one way to offset this rigidity, although the heavy use of contingent workers also enables firms to cut costs without laying off core employees.[86]

Piore, Kochan, and others have emphasized the technological origins of this recomposition: Today, manufacturing and service products have shorter life cycles and are becoming more differentiated, both of which require a flexible division of labor and a work force with fungible skills. To ensure that workers stay put, employers provide them with more

Chris Tilly, "More Part-Time Jobs: Workers Don't Want Them so Why Are Firms Creating Them?" (paper, MIT Economics Department, 1987).

[85] "Permanent Temporaries Emerge," *Wall Street Journal,* 11 October 1988, 1; G. Mangum, D. Mayall, and K. Nelson, "The Temporary Help Industry," *Industrial and Labor Relations Review* 38 (July 1985): 599–611; S. M. Jacoby and D. Mitchell, "Sticky Stories: Economic Explanations of Employment and Wage Rigidity," *American Economic Review* 80 (May 1990).

[86] Douglas L. Kruse, "Profitsharing and Employment Variability: Evidence on the Weitzman Theory" (working paper, Institute of Management and Labor Relations, Rutgers University, 1988).

employment security, and that security promotes acceptance of change in technology and the division of labor. No doubt this is part of the story. But other elements need to be included.

First is union avoidance. As Mike Parker and other labor activists point out, because the salaried model promotes a high degree of identification with the firm and can reduce worker solidarity and union loyalty, it weakens existing unions and makes it harder to organize new ones. Second, the growing internationalization of competition means that large American firms benefit less from domestic stabilization of the sort that was facilitated by the industrial model's rigid wage system. Finally, unionized workers supported the industrial model because it provided a level of employment security for senior workers that was as good or better than that found in salaried model firms. But during the early 1980s, massive layoffs and plant closures threatened the jobs of those senior workers to an extent not felt since the late 1930s. In those circumstances, unions began to seek new policies. A former official of the Steelworkers said in 1983 that, "We may have backed ourselves into a corner by settling for income security rather than dealing with the immense complexities of fashioning job security arrangements."[87]

CONCLUSIONS

Consistent with the predictions of 1960s-style convergence theories, large Japanese firms today are moving in an American direction toward more market-oriented employment practices. But the theories never envisioned that change would be more radical and rapid on the other side of the Pacific, where U.S. firms are moving in a Japanese direction through the substitution of salaried for industrial internal labor markets and through greater employment dualism.

Similar developments are occurring in other countries, notably Britain, where the unfortunate term "Japanization" is being used to describe them. But it is important to realize that the United States, unlike Britain, has for several decades had a sizable, quasi-Japanese sector of nonunion, salaried model firms. And unions in large American firms have long had a stronger enterprise orientation than Britain's more market-oriented

---

[87]T. A. Kochan, H. Katz, and R. F. McKersie, *The Transformation of American Industrial Relations* (New York: Basic Books, 1986); Alan Arthurs, "Toward an Undivided Workforce: The Convergence of Blue- and White-Collar Employment Conditions" (Paper, School of Management, University of Bath); John Hoerr, "Why Job Security is More Important than Income Security," *Business Week* 21 (November 1983): 86.

unions. As a result, in the United States "Japanization" has had less distance to travel and is being accepted with greater equanimity and less friction than in Britain. For example, the UAW—a proponent of new work systems such as those contained in the Saturn agreement—remains in the vanguard of the AFL-CIO, while the British electricians' union (EETPU) was booted from the TUC for signing similar agreements.[88]

Still, American unions find themselves in crisis, with membership rates likely to drop below 10 percent by the end of the century. Even if that nadir is not reached, those concerned with preserving and expanding the realm of industrial democracy are now debating the question of how best to fill the regulatory and protective vacuum created by unionism's decline. Diehards within the labor movement think that unions can still fill the gap themselves. For example, rank-and-file groups such as the New Directions caucus within the UAW believe that the labor movement should revitalize itself by a combination of internal democratization and a more aggressively militant stance toward employers; while established leaders within the AFL-CIO stake their hopes on labor law reforms that would level the playing field between unions and employers and make it possible to organize new union members more rapidly. A different set of answers comes from skeptics within and outside the labor movement who doubt that any of this will happen in the foreseeable future. One group—including the American Civil Liberties Union, Democratic party strategists, and academics like David Ewing of the Harvard Business School—argues that unions and their supporters should accept the inevitable and push harder for a legislative and judicial approach to workplace regulation. To some extent, that already is happening in areas such as health care, safety, and dismissals, to name a few, although the idea is to push the approach further along in the direction of a national bill of employee rights. Another group, made up mostly of academic visionaries such as former Labor Secretary F. Ray Marshall, are casting about for entirely new models of employee representation and industrial democracy. While as yet there has been no gelling of consensus, there is considerable interest in some kind of legally mandated workplace representation, along the lines of European works councils and Japanese enterprise unions.

Although traditionalists in the house of labor's left and right wings react with horror at the prospect of "company unionism," others (e.g.,

---

[88]Leonard Rico, "The New Industrial Relations: British Electricians' New-Style Agreements," *Industrial and Labor Relations Review* 41 (October 1987): 63–78.

the AFL-CIO's secretary-treasurer Thomas Donahue) are interested in pursuing the idea, together with other reforms. Supporters of the idea recognize that the salaried model found in large nonunion companies doesn't leave much room for the traditional union approach to job regulation, and think that works councils and enterprise unions have succeeded reasonably well in Europe and Japan. Indeed, recent studies refute the claim that Japanese enterprise unions are simply pawns of management with little real power or influence.[89]

These findings confound simplistic stereotypes, but they also hold a warning for American advocates of workplace representation. Japanese unions may have declined so rapidly in recent years precisely because they reduce profits and induce employers to resist them. If so, proposals for mandated representation are likely to encounter similar resistance from U.S. employers. Nevertheless, if there is one thing to be learned from this comparative history of Japan and the United States, it is that efficiency incentives and employer objectives have never completely determined the evolution of their employment systems. Only in the minds of economists does the world work like that.

---

[89] Harry Bernstein, "Bid to Give Workers a Voice Runs into Opposition," *Los Angeles Times*, 28 February 1989. Based on attitude surveys, one study finds "no support for the 'strong corporatist' hypothesis that Japanese enterprise unions function directly to strengthen the bond between the employee and the firm." In fact, employee commitment is slightly lower in Japanese than American unionized firms. Another study finds that these unions have substantial positive effects on female wages, bonus pay, severance pay, and leisure time; newly organized Japanese unions raise wages about half the time. James Lincoln and Arne Kalleberg, "Work Organization and Workforce Commitment: A Study of Plants and Employees in the U.S. and Japan," *American Sociological Review* 50 (December 1985): 738–60; K. Nakamura, "The Effects of Labor Unions," cited in Freeman and Rebick, "Crumbling Pillar," 18. Also see D. Gallagher, J. Fiorito, P. Jarley, Y. Jeong, and M. Wakabayaski, "Dual Commitment in Japan: Preliminary Observations" (Paper presented at Industrial Relations Research Association, New York, December 1988). For a critical view, see Christoph Deutschmann, "Economic Restructuring and Company Unionism: The Japanese Model," *Economic and Industrial Democracy* 8 (November 1987): 463–88.

10

Industrial relations myth and shop-floor reality:
the "team concept" in the auto industry

MIKE PARKER

In the spring of 1987, General Motors (GM) ran a series of full-page advertisements declaring that it had developed a "new production method" rejecting the principles pioneered by Frederick Taylor and Henry Ford. General Motors, one advertisement claimed, was correcting the "great flaw in the assembly line concept [that] tends to exclude the creative and managerial skills of the people who work on the line." Citing an example from GM's Fort Wayne, Indiana, assembly plant, the next advertisement asserted that there are no longer workers and bosses in the plant, just "associates" and "advisors."[1]

Along with several other vanguard service and manufacturing firms, General Motors has spent nearly a decade in a corporation-wide effort to introduce the "team concept" into several of its facilities. The meaning of this new production relationship is not always easy to pin down. Often, as in the case of the Fort Wayne plant, it is described in terms of the new role of workers in assembly line production: replacing traditional management and the Taylorized work regime are teams of four to eight multiskilled workers who design their own jobs, rotate assignments, consult together to solve problems, and take over tasks once considered exclusively a management prerogative. The bureaucratic model, which once pushed decisions from the shop floor up, has been pruned and transformed into a decision-making system that sends authority down

I want to thank my collaborator, Jane Slaughter, and editor Nelson Lichtenstein for help in the preparation of this chapter.
[1] *Business Week,* 27 April 1987, 127; 4 May 1987, 115.

the chain of command. Indeed, assembly line pacing has been abolished, for workers now have a button or cord with which to stop the line.

What's going on here? For more than half a century, General Motors Corporation, the nation's largest, has jealously guarded management's right to run its factories and offices in the manner its executives have seen as correct. As several of the chapters in this volume have made clear, most notably those of David Brody and Nelson Lichtenstein, big companies like General Motors have structured their employment practices along lines that assume a sharp boundary between managers and workers and a long-standing and deeply ingrained resistance to employee and union participation in what management considers its vital supervisory functions. Are we to take the General Motors ad seriously? Has the company actually renounced the technology and organization of the assembly line most famously deployed by Henry Ford? And if its claims are spurious, why have such sophisticated manufacturers as GM felt compelled to make even such a rhetorical repudiation of classical Taylorism? And why have so many, including the corporation's traditional adversaries within the leadership of the union movement, welcomed GM's initiatives in such a cooperative and uncritical fashion?

Neither Fordism nor Taylorism has been abandoned by GM and other similarly situated corporations. Change, both organizational and ideological, has taken place, but the assembly line and traditional scientific management methods have actually found a new life in the team concept idea. We call this new production system "management by stress," in which a kind of worker empowerment takes place, but only insofar as it conforms to an even more carefully regimented shop-floor regime. Indeed, rather than taking a step toward a new era of industrial democracy, the new participatory management schemes constitute an intensification, not an abandonment, of the essence of classical Taylorism.

The team concept idea, and more generally the whole thrust of the new ideology of so-called non-adversarial labor relations, represents a substantial challenge to the industrial relations orthodoxy of the last half century. The notion that labor and management had fundamentally different interests in the workplace was central to this perspective and was hardly limited to those who viewed class struggle as a motive force in world history. Although American labor law carefully limits the extent to which workers can mount a collective challenge to the power of capital, the law nevertheless has continued to assume an adversarial relationship, which requires a legally regulated collective bargaining apparatus to ensure industrial peace and efficient production. It was the 1935 Wagner Act, after all, which declared that: "The denial by employers of the right of employees to organize and the refusal by employers to accept the procedure of collective bargaining lead to strikes and other forms of industrial strife or unrest." Industrial peace would be assured only when the state protected workers' rights to "full freedom of association, self-organization and designation of representatives of their own choosing, for the purpose of negotiating the terms and conditions of their employment or other mutual aid or protection."[2]

Writing nearly twenty years later, Clark Kerr spoke for an influential generation of industrial relations intellectuals whose own careers were premised on the notion that adroit mediation and administration could resolve social conflicts. Nevertheless, Kerr argued that "labor-management relations are a classic form of conflict" in any industrial society. Unlike Elton Mayo and others of the Harvard-based human relations school of industrial psychology, Kerr did not see irrationality or ill will at the core of this conflict. Rather, "organized labor and management are primarily engaged in sharing between themselves what is, at any one moment of time, a largely given amount of income and power. The more one gets or keeps, the less the other has." Concluded Kerr, "If management and labor are to retain their institutional identities, they must disagree and must act on the disagreement. Conflict is essential to survival. The union which is in constant and complete agreement with management has ceased to be a union."[3]

The industrial relations system described and defended by Clark Kerr and others seemed at the time one of inherent stability. For nearly two decades, beginning about 1948, the relations between capital and labor were conducted under ostensibly adversarial conditions, but clearly according to a set of political and economic guideposts that constrained and bureaucratized conflict. With hindsight, of course, we can now see that this postwar industrial order lasted for little more than a generation. It was based upon the near monopoly position enjoyed by many U.S. industries within the American market, and on the existence of a relatively

[2] As quoted in Eileen Boris and Nelson Lichtenstein, *Major Problems in the History of American Workers* (Lexington: D. C. Heath, 1991), 415–16.
[3] Clark Kerr, "Industrial Conflict and Its Mediation," in *Labor and Management in Industrial Society* (Garden City, N.Y.: Anchor, 1964), 169–70.

strong labor movement, in many instances still led by the radicals and
ex-radicals who had founded it in the 1930s.[4]

Despite its stability, neither labor nor capital fully accepted this postwar labor relations order; indeed, their discontent increased as the years
wore on. As James Atleson pointed out in Chapter 7, the evolution of
American labor law defined and defended essential management prerogatives that delimited the growth of worker and union participation in
many crucial decisions affecting shop-floor worklife. Moreover, in the
automobile industry—which has always been the pacesetting and arche-
typal arena of labor-management conflict in the twentieth-century United
States—shop-floor disputes, as measured by grievances processed, strikes
conducted (both authorized and unauthorized), and local election results,
did not decline after the Second World War but increased markedly,
especially during the boom years of the 1960s. United Automobile Workers president Walter Reuther denounced the industry's "gold plated
sweatshops" in 1964, while a few years later, the generation of young
workers energized by the black power and anti-Vietnam protests of the
late 1960s made worker empowerment and shop-floor democracy again
issues that had to be taken seriously by top union leaders and government
officials.[5] Protests and strikes at GM's Lordstown, Ohio, assembly plant
in the early 1970s, which won national attention, came to symbolize the
democratic aspirations of a new generation of workers.

The leadership of the UAW responded by incorporating and co-opting
these movements. They denied, quite correctly, that they had a specifically
generational content or that the issues raised by these well-publicized
insurgencies were fundamentally unique. Nat Weinberg, a longtime UAW
research aide, put it well in 1974: "The recent discovery of the job
satisfaction problem is, in one sense, much like Columbus' discovery of
America. The people most directly concerned—the Indians in one case
and the workers in the other—knew all along that it was there."[6] In
earlier years, UAW strategy for the amelioration of the tyranny of the
assembly line had involved a dual thrust: strengthen the shop steward
movement and grievance arbitration system at the base, while at the top,
campaign in Congress, within the federal government's regulatory ap-

[4]Kim Moody, *An Injury to All: The Decline of American Unionism* (London: Verso, 1988),
24–69.
[5]See, for example, the famous Department of Health, Education, and Welfare report *Work
in America* (Cambridge, Mass.: MIT Press, 1973).
[6]Speech at the 27th Annual Conference on Labor, New York, 14 June 1974 (in author's
possession).

paratus, and at the bargaining table to win for the union and the public some influence over auto industry health and safety policies, and in the UAW's more ambitious moments, over corporate pricing and investment decisions. But both of these avenues toward work reform had been blocked by the mid-1970s, the former as a result of the more hostile legal environment and the union's own stolid routinization of its grievance-handling apparatus; and the latter because of the decline of the New Deal-born labor-liberal political coalition and the resultant shift to a market-oriented orthodoxy in national economic and social policy.

But union weakness did not constitute a management victory. Despite their accommodation to collective bargaining in the years after World War II, American management never felt comfortable with even the limited power unionized workers held at the point of production. From the late 1950s onward, managers in heavy industry voiced a growing impatience with union work rules, the set of contractually defined guidelines and procedures, usually involving seniority, job definitions, and customary work loads, which together limited management flexibility and defined employee work rights. As early as the 1957–58 recession, American corporations, led by U.S. Steel, Chrysler, General Electric, and International Harvester, began a concerted effort to break or dilute such work rules and shift the shop-floor balance of power in their favor.[7]

This effort stalled during the prosperous 1960s, but by the end of the decade, managers in American manufacturing facilities faced an increasingly difficult and highly competitive economic environment that may well have cut return on investment by more than a third. In the automobile industry, German, and then Japanese and Korean imports took 20 to 25 percent of the domestic market. At first, managers blamed the lower wages paid foreign workers, but by the early 1980s, exchange rate adjusted European and Japanese wages were just about at par with those paid U.S. workers.

Thereafter, management-oriented explanations for the crisis turned increasingly desperate and faddish. A number of business-school analysts blamed U.S. industry difficulties on top management's fixation with corporate finance and short-term, bottom-line profits. This generated a failure to undertake the costly, long-term investments in plant, equipment, and new technology necessary to raise productivity and remain compet-

---

[7] Mike Davis, *Prisoners of the American Dream* (London: Verso, 1986), 141–46; George Strauss, "The Shifting Balance of Power in the Plant," *Industrial Relations* 1 (May 1962): 81–83.

itive in the world market. But when some high-profile manufacturing companies began a massive effort to automate and restructure their production facilities, the results seemed disappointing. General Motors alone spent $50 billion in a campaign to computerize and robotize its factories, but the company, which lost about 10 percent of its market share in the 1980s, found that this technological fix had failed to reduce substantially the Japanese advantage in production efficiency.[8]

The huge costs of such automation programs, and the inevitable first-round bugs, were soon ridiculed in the business press. The *Wall Street Journal*, for example, declared that GM's ultramodern Hamtramck assembly plant "instead of a show case looks more like a basket case."[9] Management's attitudes toward automation as a panacea for their productivity problems thereupon underwent a radical transformation. The *Journal* summarized this faddish shift, citing an Arthur Anderson and Company poll of December 1986. "In the five previous polls, 'automation got all the votes as the key to improving competitiveness. . . . But this year it got only 8%. That's good for only 12th place.' First place went to management practices."[10] Part of the reason for the rapid drop of automation as the strategy of choice was the difficulties inherent in implementing it. But far more important was the emergence of a model that actually seemed to produce results in the real world.

Management attention now shifted to the production frontier represented by several Japanese "transplants" in North America that were showing impressively high productivity and quality numbers and remarkably low unit costs. By the end of the 1980s, the new consensus was that superior Japanese productivity arose not so much from lower wages or extensive robotics, but from what seemed the willing consent of the work force, apparent in the more flexible work rules and the greater intensity of labor and utilization of total worktime characteristic of these factories, regardless of whether they were located in Japan or the United States.

American automobile executives understood this late twentieth-century version of "the labor problem" as well. Beginning in the late

[8]"The Right Stuff," *Time Magazine*, 29 October 1990, 74–84.
[9]Amal Nag, "Auto Makers Discover That 'Factory of the Future' Is Headache Just Now," *Wall Street Journal*, 13 May 1986. See also "GM's AGV Debacle," *Manufacturing Week*, 28 September 1987; Eileen Courter, "Chrysler Robotics Quality Test Results 'Disturbing,'" *Automotive News*, 2 September 1986; Charles Sykes, "HP Acknowledges Reappraisal of CIM Promise," *Automation News*, 11 August 1986.
[10]Paul Ingrassia, "Autos," *Wall Street Journal*, 12 June 1987.

1970s, both Ford and General Motors experimented with a variety of organizational reforms, some cooperatively with the United Automobile Workers. Quality circles and employee involvement schemes had been designed to generate qualitatively new levels of consent and commitment from their workers. These earlier programs were costly and had ambiguous results, but the relative failure of the new technology and the success of the Japanese transplants again made such so-called people strategies attractive. Thus GM Vice-President for Industrial Relations Alfred Warren explained at mid-decade:

For many years, we paid for hands and legs. . . . We were under the Frederick Taylor method of management; we told everyone what to do with their right hand and their left hand and so forth. We need more than that today, we need a great deal more than that. . . . There is no doubt that the employee knows more about the job than any member of management can ever know, and so the employee must be enrolled in this battle to try and become more and more competitive.[11]

According to GM, team concept was the only way to beat the competition and the only way out of the economic crisis. It was a win-win solution. The industry and its jobs are maintained, workers get dignity and empowerment, customers get high quality, communities and the United States retain their economic strength, and the companies return profits to shareholders.

This critical shift in management's reconceptualization of the labor problem has two essential elements. First is the idea that there is no real choice—new forms of work organization are socially and technologically determined. Modern production techniques require skilled, knowledgeable, flexible, involved workers. Any other approach simply amounts to economic suicide. Second, this new form of work organization is good for everyone involved: consumers, managers, owners, and particularly workers. From business-centered academics to labor leaders, even to socialist intellectuals, some variation of this formula seems to justify embracing the new system. If previous production regimes had driven management to exploit or dehumanize its workers, this new system impelled managers in the opposite direction. High productivity was now possible only when workers had reached their full potential. Logic and self-interest, therefore, consigned the old adversary relationship between labor and capital into the dustbin of history.

[11] As quoted in John Saunders, "Hacking Away at Job Titles," *Detroit Free Press*, 23 June 1986.

This perspective became nearly hegemonic in the 1980s. Early in the decade, the Harvard Business School-based team of William Abernathy, Kim Clark, and Alan Kantrow closely observed Japanese auto plants. They argued that "building a truly competitive organization also requires active enlistment of the best efforts of workers, especially line workers. Their skills, commitment, and enthusiasm are the means by which strategic goals get translated into practice.... Thus only when grafted onto a production system dedicated to on-going learning and communications, only when used in tandem with a skilled and responsible workforce, can new technologies realize their potential as competitive weapons."[12]

This reskilling imperative was most widely disseminated through the work of Michael Piore and Charles Sabel, whose *Second Industrial Divide: Possibilities for Prosperity* argued that the whole mass production epoch was something of a dead end, if not a giant historical mistake. The era of Fordism, with its mass-produced, standardized products and minute subdivision of labor, was coming to a close. Their book argued that the multiplicity of late twentieth-century markets, combined with a new generation of easily reprogrammable production tools, had already begun to replace mass production with a new era of flexible specialization, in which firms must master the art of small-batch production in order to respond quickly to the ever shifting variety of niche markets. Of course, flexible manufacturing requires a work force of craftlike workers, broadly skilled in many specialties and thus capable of shifting their talents from one job to another and knowledgeable enough to work with designers to overcome the inevitable bugs.[13]

Larry Hirschhorn, an influential commentator on computer technology in this era, emphasized the cooperative, team imperative in such new modes of production. Automatic controls on machines, he argued, solve many problems of machine failure. But they also increase the possibility for larger system failures and "create new modes of failure, or second-order errors." Hirschhorn continued:

The work group must become the new second-order control system. Work teams must import [responding to] error into their culture of work; they must learn and learn and learn.... Sociotechnical design ... permits coordination without

[12] William J. Abernathy, Kim B. Clark, and Alan M. Kantrow, *Industrial Renaissance: Producing a Competitive Future for America* (New York: Basic Books, 1983), 125.
[13] Michael J. Piore and Charles F. Sabel, *The Second Industrial Divide: Possibilities for Prosperity* (New York: Basic Books, 1984), 273.

hierarchy. It does all this by locating initiative in the teams, by providing cross-talk and rotation between the teams and by supporting a plant governance system that factory members use to monitor the team system and its relationship to the factory's environment.[14]

The three Massachusetts Institute of Technology directors of the highly touted "five-million-dollar, five-year study on the future of the automobile," James Womack, Daniel Jones, and Daniel Roos, also gushed with praise for this new "lean production system." They argued that rather than being rooted in Japanese history or culture, "the fundamental ideas of lean production are universal—applicable anywhere by anyone."[15] And the key is labor. "So in the end, it is the dynamic workteam that emerges as the heart of the lean factory. Building these efficient teams is not simple. First, workers need to be taught a variety of skills—in fact all the jobs in their work group so that tasks can be rotated and workers can fill in for each other. Workers then need to acquire many additional skills: simple machine repair, quality checking, housekeeping, and materials-ordering."[16]

High-ranking officials of the United Auto Workers, as well as many rank-and-file workers, welcomed management's new interest in the reorganization of the shop-floor work regime. The union motivation had two sources: first, a genuine hope that such cooperative, participatory schemes would in fact advance the union's historic interest in democratizing the workplace. By the 1970s, the generation of autoworkers who had known Depression-era nonunion conditions had largely passed from the scene, and for the work force that filled their shoes, the cumbersome shortcomings of the grievance procedure and local issue bargaining seemed all too apparent, the historic reasons for these institutions less clear. Participation schemes, even those clearly under management control, therefore appealed to many workers alienated from the UAW. Second, the UAW found itself in the midst of an industry-wide depression after 1979. Concession bargaining generated pay cuts and benefit givebacks for upward of a million workers. The union lost 400,000 members as scores of factories closed their doors. To many workers, therefore,

[14]Larry Hirschhorn, *Beyond Mechanization* (Cambridge, Mass.: MIT Press, 1984), 150–51.
[15]James P. Womack, Daniel T. Jones, and Daniel Roos, *The Machine That Changed the World* (Boston: Rawson Associates, 1990), 9.
[16]Ibid., 99.

any innovation that promised to save jobs and avoid a major conflict with the corporations seemed worth trying.[17]

In the 1970s, UAW Vice-President Irving Bluestone, then in charge of the union's dealings with General Motors, was one of the key labor leaders who first advocated "quality of work life" programs as the logical extension of unionism. Writing when the union still saw the incorporation of the Lordstown generation of rights-conscious workers as vital, Bluestone was emphatic in insisting that such worker-management cooperation schemes were not designed with increased productivity in mind, but rather would enable workers to "exercise the democratic right to participate in workplace decisions, including job structure and design, job layout, material flow, tools to be used, methods and processes of production, plant layout, work environment, etc. In the broadest sense it means decision-making as to how the work place will be managed and how the worker will effectively have a voice in being master of the job rather than being subservient to it."[18]

Over the next decade, the UAW continued to advance this perspective, not increased productivity, as the ideological justification on those occasions when it endorsed work reorganization schemes. A 1987 UAW convention resolution asserted that the team concept, when properly implemented, has the potential to reduce "some of the more adverse consequences of fragmented work assignments . . . and return some autonomy to workers, [allowing them] to make decisions on how—and by whom—work is to be performed."[19] Indeed, UAW vice-president Marc Stepp declared team concept agreements part of the "long time advocacy of trade unionists to institute industrial democracy. It's a concept where workers in-plant will have a say in their destiny."[20]

But facing desperate times, the union's actual operating principles clearly shifted, and it came to accept the view that U.S. industry could be saved only by a thorough reorganization that would make it competitive with foreign rivals. The union negotiated a series of "Modern Operating Agreements" at Chrysler factories and accepted team concept

[17] Nelson Lichtenstein, "UAW Bargaining Strategy and Shop Floor Conflict, 1946–1970," *Industrial Relations* (Fall 1985): 360–81; Moody, *An Injury to All*, 165–91.

[18] Irving Bluestone, "Human Dignity Is What It's All About," *Viewpoint*, AFL-CIO Industrial Union Department, 8 (1978).

[19] "Proposed Resolution: 1987 Collective Bargaining Program," *United Auto Worker*, 1987 Special Convention, 12–15 April 1987, p. 50.

[20] Quoted in Louise Kertesz, "Rift Brews in Chrysler-UAW Affair," *Automotive News*, 7 December 1987.

arrangements in General Motors and Ford plants. In most cases, these new contracts were a product not of demands from workers or local officials but were a product of management initiative. In many cases, worker acquiescence came only as a result of corporate threats, implied or actual, to close the factory and after repeated UAW local union votes until the rank and file "got it right."[21]

Deployment of this new form of work organization had its most dramatically influential test at the New United Motors Manufacturing Inc. (NUMMI) plant in Fremont, California, which started production in 1984. NUMMI, a joint venture of GM and Toyota, took over an existing plant GM had declared unprofitable and then proceeded to achieve remarkable productivity and quality records. Managed by Toyota, NUMMI built cars marketed by both companies under their own nameplates. NUMMI's low-tech success, evident in just two years from its start-up, proved particularly stunning, given the relative failure of GM's state-of-the-art technology deployed at its Poletown and Orion factories near Detroit. An internal GM comparison from a typical week in 1986 showed that NUMMI required 21.2 total labor hours per vehicle as compared with about 37 at other GM plants producing similar cars.[22] Announced one delighted GM official: "If GM were to be producing its current level of output at the NUMMI level of efficiency, we could . . . have two-thirds the number of people."[23]

Other Japanese transplants, including Honda in Ohio and Nissan in Tennessee, demonstrated similar levels of high productivity. But several factors made NUMMI a model for U.S. industry. NUMMI's technology was not particularly advanced; most NUMMI employees had worked in the same plant under GM and had the reputation of being militant, uncooperative, and prone to absenteeism. And perhaps most important, this factory, unlike almost all other Japanese transplants, was unionized: indeed, management bargained with the UAW before the plant hired its first worker.

The UAW saw NUMMI as a success story. Union president Owen Bieber cited the "worker centered environment" of NUMMI and the then still-to-be-completed GM Saturn plant in Tennessee as the two dramatic

---

[21] For a larger survey of this process, see Mike Parker and Jane Slaughter, *Choosing Sides: Unions and the Team Concept* (Detroit: Labor Notes, 1988), chapters 13–16, 22, 23.
[22] General Motors, *D–150 Labor Performance Report—Passenger Assembly,* week ending 5/11/86, No. 36.
[23] *Detroit Free Press,* 8 June 1987.

experiments that "should point to a bright future for the domestic auto industry."[24] The UAW's West Coast regional director was a good deal less restrained. In a 1988 *New York Times* essay, Bruce Lee declared, "The workers' revolution has finally come to the shop floor. The people who work on the assembly line have taken charge and have the power to make management do their jobs right."[25]

Even observers of American industry usually skeptical of management claims saw NUMMI as a nascent form of workers' control. Wrote UCLA sociology professor Ruth Milkman in 1989:

> On the surface, the plant seems like a worker's paradise. But a closer look reveals that it's actually the ultimate in capitalist efficiency—based, paradoxically, on giving workers what socialism alone once promised: real participation in managerial decision-making.... By embracing the team concept, management validates the left's traditional call for increasing workers' control and dignity and respect on the job. It's not easy to face the prospect that such a basic transformation can occur on the factory floor while leaving capitalist property relations intact, but that's what NUMMI is all about.[26]

Once NUMMI became a generally accepted success, other versions of the team concept with which management had been experimenting were shifted toward the new industrial relations model. Just as NUMMI provided GM managers access to Japanese expertise, newer transplants provided access for Ford and Chrysler. The Mazda assembly plant in Flat Rock, Michigan, began production in 1987 with special ties to Ford. The Illinois Diamond-Star plant began hiring in 1988 as a joint venture of Chrysler and Mitsubishi. And the $3.5 billion Saturn complex in Spring Hill, Tennessee, GM's first new carmaking division since the automaker acquired Chevrolet in 1918, was hailed as a "grand experiment in American manufacturing" that will answer one of the most pressing questions of the 1990s, "Can America compete with the Japanese?"[27]

---

[24] Owen Bieber, "Updating Labor-Management Relations Is Only Part of the Answer," *The Journal of State Government* (January–February 1987): 19; see also Jeff Stansbury, "NUMMI: A New Kind of Workplace," *Solidarity* (August 1985): 11–15.

[25] Bruce Lee, "Worker Harmony Makes NUMMI Work," *New York Times,* 25 December 1988.

[26] Ruth Milkman, "Team Dreams," *Voice Literary Supplement,* November 1988. In Europe, on the other hand, there is a lively debate on this issue. Two excellent pieces with analyses similar to that presented here are Knuth Dohse, Ulrich Jurgens, and Thomas Malsch, "From 'Fordism' to 'Toyotism'? The Social Organization of the Labor Process in the Japanese Automobile Industry," *Politics and Society* 14 (1985): 115–46; and Peter J. Turnbull, "The Limits of Japanization—Just-in-Time, Labor Relations and the UK Automobile Industry," *New Technology, Work and Employment* 3 (Autumn 1988).

[27] "The Right Stuff," *Time Magazine,* 29 October 1990, 74.

Some analysts view the adoption of Japanese methods as the Japanization of the U.S. auto industry. Yet, without denying the influence of Japanese industry, the term "Japanization" misses on several points. First, it contributes to the racism that already fogs the issues. Second, as the Japanese-managed plants around the world show, the system does not require some special Japanese culture for either management or workers to operate effectively. Third, although the system was highly refined in Japan, many of the techniques, especially in process control, were pioneered by Americans. The main point, however, is that the country of origin was not as relevant as the fact that these were management methods, adopted by employers of all nationalities for the purpose of squeezing unions and workers of all nationalities. Thus the production regimes at NUMMI and other similar team concept plants all had the same common themes. Whether called modern operating arrangements, synchronous manufacturing, world-class manufacturing, or lean production systems, they all had essentially the same reality for the workers in those newly reorganized factories.

And what was that reality? We call it management-by-stress because we believe it describes how the system actually works. Management-by-stress uses stress of all kinds—physical, social, and psychological—rather than management orders and decisions, to regulate and boost production. It is a system in that its features are interrelated and dependent upon each other. The remarkable productivity achieved by NUMMI is a function of a combination of these new policies. Among these are just-in-time (JIT) organization of inventory and production, stressing the system to force worker cooperation, extensive use of outside contracting, technology designed to minimize nonproductive labor, and design-for-manufacture products.[28]

Management-by-stress goes against many traditional U.S. management notions. It even seems to go against common sense. Isn't it logical to protect against possible breakdowns and glitches by stockpiling parts and hiring extra workers to fill in for absentees? But the operating principle of management-by-stress is to locate and remove systematically such protections. Stressing the system identifies the weak points and those that

---

[28] This interpretation is, of course, counterposed to that of most business-school observers, but it is remarkable how readily these commentators have accepted as simple truth management assertions that the new system does increase the actual skills of the work force and the level of group participation and individual autonomy. See, for example, Womack et al., *The Machine That Changed the World,* 101.

are too strong. The weak points will break down when the stress becomes too much, indicating that additional resources are needed. Just as important, production points that never break down are presumed to have too many resources, and are thus wasteful. They are targeted as well, and human or material resources are removed until the station can keep up, but just barely.

The "andon" board illustrates how management-by-stress works. At NUMMI a lighted board above the assembly line—called the andon board—shows the status of each workstation. When a worker falls behind or needs help, he or she pulls a cord; bells chime and the board lights up. If the cord is not pulled again within a set period of time (say a minute), the line stops. In one variation of the andon board, the status of each station is indicated with one of three lights: green—production is keeping up and there are no problems; yellow—operator is falling behind or needs help; red—problem requires stopping the line. In the traditional U.S. operation, management would want to see nothing but green lights and would design enough slack into the machinery and procedures so that an operation would almost always run in the green. Individual managers try to protect themselves with excess stock and excess workers to cover glitches or emergencies. CYA (cover your ass) is considered prudent operating procedure.

But in the management-by-stress production system, "all green" signals inefficiency. Workers are not working as hard as they might. If the system is stressed—by speeding up the line for example—the weakest points become evident and the yellow lights go on. A few jobs will go into the red and stop the line. Management can now focus on these few jobs and make necessary adjustments. Once the problems have been corrected, the system can then be further stressed (perhaps by reducing the number of workers) and then rebalanced. The ideal is for the system to run with all stations oscillating between green and yellow. Thus the system equilibrates or drives toward being evenly balanced as managers constantly readjust and rebalance to make production ever more efficient. After years of observing waste in traditional plants, some people, including many workers, are attracted to this vision of a smoothly functioning, rational management system. In engineering terms, it could be described as a tighter control system with "fast response inner loops." The only problem is that it is human beings that are under such rigid control, not machines.

The just-in-time production system is also an organic element in this new production regime. Just-in-time is best known because it allows (or requires) drastic cuts in inventories. Instead of stockpiling parts at various points in the production process, management attempts to reduce stockpiles as nearly as possible to zero and to organize production so that parts will arrive just as they are required. Thus a material handler does not replace stock until the line operation signals that it needs more. And a department does not produce until more is needed at the next stage of production.

There are several well-known savings with just-in-time: interest costs on the value of capital tied up in inventory, the cost of warehousing and storing the inventory, and easier quality control because there are fewer parts in the pipeline. By themselves, these are powerful reasons for management to adopt JIT. But what about the traditional reasons for inventory? By maintaining inventories or banks, one part of the production system is cushioned from problems in another part—the "just-in-case" method. There is time to fix a problem before it affects the next section of the plant. But consider an assembly operation under JIT. If a station in the middle stops, all work comes to a halt, downstream because the workers have no supply and upstream because they have no place to stockpile finished products.

These seemingly negative features of JIT become positive under a management-by-stress system. When a single workstation experiences trouble there is no hiding. It becomes instantly apparent and the crisis generates pressure upon the other production workers, team leaders, and lowest level management by making them solve the problem and catch up. There is no external assistance until management is satisfied that extraordinary efforts and all the resources available to the team have been deployed. And, as with the andon board, management can use JIT to identify those departments that never have a problem and then trim their resources.

Stress, rather than management directives, becomes the mechanism for coordinating different sections of the system. Ideally, this means that top management only needs to make a few key decisions about the output required and the system will automatically adjust to produce that output to specifications as efficiently and cheaply as possible. But this can only work if the material handler, supplier department, and supplier company are all firmly committed to deliver "just-in-time" despite any obstacles. In order to maintain this commitment over a long period of time there are penalties for failure. In the case of supplier companies, the penalties are financial. In the case of individual workers, the penalties include attention and pressure from one's peers and from management. That is why personal stress as well as system stress is required for MBS to keep running smoothly. A relaxed attitude—"I am just doing my job, I don't need to pay attention to anyone else's job"—makes the system inoperable.

That is also why management-by-stress relies so heavily on visual displays of the production system. When everyone can see who is responsible, peer pressure can be brought to bear on those who fail to respond to the demands of the system. As Toyota managers put it: "All processes and all shops are kept in the state where they have no surplus so that if trouble is left unattended, the line will immediately stop running and will affect the entire plant. The necessity for improvement can be easily understood by anyone."[29]

Thus the need for an ideological as well as a structural reorganization of the workplace. For more than a generation, individual local unions, or even particular work groups, could and did disrupt production despite the severe penalties that faced such workers. Indeed, much of the impulse for the decentralization of the American automobile industry in the immediate post–World War II era arose from management's effort to win greater leverage over such seemingly unpredictable workers. Ford's duplication and dispersal of so much of the giant River Rouge complex in the early 1950s is the key example of such a management strategy. But the return to the kind of highly integrated and recentralized production characteristic of the just-in-time system requires a cooperative and willing work force who will themselves enforce the high productivity standards implicit in this system. This is the ideological dimension necessary to the proper working of a team concept factory.

Contrary to his contemporary historical image, and to GM's ad campaign of the late 1980s, Frederick Taylor was not merely the man with the stopwatch. Among his most important insights was the realization that workers do have minds and valuable knowledge essential to efficient production. As he famously asserted in 1912, scientific management demands "the deliberate gathering in on the part of those on the management's side of all the great mass of traditional knowledge, which in the past has been in the heads of the workmen, and in the physical skill and

[29] Yasuhiro Monden, *Toyota Production System: Practical Approach to Production Management* (Tokyo: Industrial Engineering and Management Press, 1983), 65.

knack of the workmen, which [they have] acquired through years of experience."[30]

Management-by-stress systems seek to utilize a worker's sense of observation and shop knowledge, recognizing his or her understanding as a valuable resource that must not go to waste. And like Taylor, MBS seeks to harness that brain power. The super-Taylorism of management-by-stress correctly assumes that the people who actually do the work understand at least part of the process better than management observers, that workers have some knowledge of and therefore some power over production precisely because they are so close to it.

Like Taylor, these contemporary managers seek to gather this knowledge and decision making, but unlike the father of scientific management they want to concentrate it not among specialized management engineers, but instead in the lower ranks of factory supervision. The deliberate blurring of the line between foremen/women and the workers they supervise is central to this process, but the elaborate job charting of "standarized work," quality circles, and suggestion/reward systems are all components of this knowledge-gathering project.

Team leaders, who rotate through all jobs and are union members, are often effectively incorporated into management. Except for the fact that they lack formal powers of discipline, team leaders may have the full range of supervisory responsibilities and often come to think like supervisors. In many ways, such use of supervisors and team leaders represents a return to the use of the work group "straw bosses" that were eliminated by union demand fifty years ago. And like the straw bosses of that pre-union era, team leaders regularly work the line, a practice forbidden by the UAW in traditional auto plants.[31]

Within the limits of the basic process and the technology used, these supervisors have the main responsibility for designing jobs and adjusting them. At NUMMI there was no separate industrial engineering or time study department. While some jobs at that plant were designed by teams, most of the original members of these teams were engineers, supervisors, and management-selected team leaders, a number of whom had observed operations in Toyota's home plant in Japan. This original team charted

[30] Frederick Winslow Taylor, "Testimony Before the Special House Committee," in *Scientific Management* (Westport, Conn.: Greenwood Press, 1974), 40; see also, Daniel Nelson, *Frederick Taylor* (Madison: University of Wisconsin Press, 1980).

[31] Nelson Lichtenstein, "The Union's Early Days: Shop Stewards and Seniority Rights," in Mike Parker and Jane Slaughter, *Choosing Sides* (Boston: South End Press, 1988), 65–73.

the jobs, breaking each operation down into its component elements, studying and timing each motion, adjusting, and then shifting the work so that jobs were more or less equal. The end result was a detailed written specification of how each team member should do each job.[32]

As production increased and bugs worked out, there were fewer and fewer changes made in job operations. Workers brought onto the team were expected to follow the detailed procedures that had already been worked out. The team member was told exactly how many steps to take and what the left hand should be doing while the right hand is picking up the wrench. Of course, workers find ways to finish their jobs faster, but instead of "banking" this free time as in a traditional auto factory, workers at NUMMI and other such facilities *kaizen*, or continuously improve, their work. This means continuous rebalancing of the work so as to eliminate idle time and underused workers. Thus changes in a job can never result in more breathing space for team members. If team workers do have waiting time, they are to stand idle rather than help their teammates. As a Toyota production manual puts it: "In this way everyone will be able to see that he has free time and there will be less resistance if he is assigned one or two more jobs."[33]

As for claims of worker creativity and control, Becky Kiley, an assembler at NUMMI, voiced the sentiments of many:

I think its just the minute-by-minute doing your job, always working at somebody else's pace. You can't do the job any other way than the way it's supposed to be done because that's the most efficient way to do. Kaizening is supposed to be creative, but I mean how many times can you sit there and Kaizen a job after you've done it four and one-half years?...Just keep me in a job and I'll do it the way you want me to do it.[34]

Absenteeism cannot be tolerated under this taut system. At NUMMI and Mazda, no workers are hired and trained as regular replacements. An applicant's attendance record is one of management's most important

---

[32] Although the limited worker involvement in initial job design has often been the basis for the claim that team production equals a form of industrial democracy or workers' control, even this degree of participation is being eliminated in the most advanced plants. For example, the notion of "concurrent" or simultaneous engineering has become popular as a faster and better way to bring new products on line. The idea is to combine marketing, design, and process engineering. But such models, efficient as they may be, hardly involve production workers in the planning stage. Indeed, the goal is to eliminate slow start-ups, when workers actually do make practical contributions to job redesign. "Design-for-manufacture" thus seeks to eliminate such shop-floor tinkering and informal negotiation and discussion among workers and their supervisors.
[33] Monden, *Toyota Production System*, 122.
[34] As quoted in CBS News, *48 Hours*, "Fast Times," 8 March 1990.

considerations in hiring, and harsh penalties are applied to those who miss work with any regularity. Most importantly, the team system is designed to generate enormous peer pressure against absenteeism. If a team member is absent, either the team leader or other members of the team must take up the slack. Problems are not shifted upstairs by having the personnel department hire and maintain a redundant work force to cover for possible absences. As a result, team members tend to resent the missing worker who, given the assumptions of management-by-stress, seems to be the cause of their intensified labor. Indeed, several workers interviewed at NUMMI commented that they would like to have people who were absent too much removed from their group. And the system works: in 1988 GM claimed about 2 percent unscheduled absenteeism at NUMMI, compared to 8.8 percent for the corporation as a whole.[35]

Central to the notion of Fordism is that the pace of the assembly line controls the pace of its human attendants. Thus the claim that "Workers can stop the line" at NUMMI and at other similarly organized plants would seem nothing less than revolutionary. This right would turn Fordism inside out. Workers would now control the pace of their work. Exactly how a worker goes about stopping the line differs from plant to plant and even within the same workplace. At NUMMI and Mazda, on some jobs, "pulling the cord" results in distinctive chimes and flashing lights on the andon board. If the cord is not pulled again within a set time (usually one minute) then the line halts.

The ability to halt the line is powerfully attractive, and if genuine, a radical break from the entire history of automobile industry shop-floor practice. In the past, a worker did not stop the line unless someone were dying. It did not matter if a worker could not keep up or if scrap was going through. A worker tried to get his or her foreman's attention; only the latter could decide whether to stop the line or leave the problem to be picked up or repaired later on. Stopping the line without a really good cause courted a heavy punishment, for the decision to stop the line represented the boundary between the judgment of workers and the judgment of superiors.

Under management-by-stress, the right to stop the line is supposed to substitute for the cumbersome system that establishes work standards in a traditional automobile plant. Here a company industrial engineer or time study expert determines the particular operation and time allotment

[35] *Detroit Free Press,* 25 January 1988.

for each job. The union contract requires employees and union to be notified when a job is to be time-studied, and it prohibits management from setting standards under exceptional circumstances or by using workers who are unusually strong, nimble, or well trained. Work standards, once established, cannot be changed arbitrarily except by repeating the contractual procedure. Since World War II, UAW local unions have had the contractual right to grieve and strike over work standards they consider onerous.

UAW contracts have specified that when a tool, process, or part is changed, the old work standards did not apply. Consequently, many jobs were operated without formal production standards, but even then, workers had more protection than in a management-by-stress plant, because the contract language stated that supervision cannot discipline workers for failing to keep up as long as they were working at a "normal pace." Under these circumstances, management pressures to force higher production could be effectively resisted by the union as "harassment."[36]

But with the stop cord, why have all these bureaucratic procedures? Or so the argument goes. If a system exists that trusts workers and they make a genuine attempt but cannot keep up, they just pull the stop cord and with no penalty. At NUMMI, production standards are not grievable. Their resolution relied on a seemingly more direct approach, written into the contract:

If the problem in production or quality is such that they cannot complete their tasks in the proper manner, they are expected, without being subject to discipline, to pull the cord or push the button to sound the alarm, and ultimately stop the line, alerting a Group/Team Leader of the problem. If the problem is of a recurring nature, the employees will work together to *kaizen* (seek to improve) the operation.[37]

During trial-build and training periods, "the cord" seemed to work for everyone. It helped workers get assistance when problems came up, and it helped keep quality high even through all the problems of establishing a new line. It aided management in identifying problems so they could be quickly resolved.

However, once the job was well defined and most of the bugs worked out, the cord became oppressive. As the line speeds up and the whole

---

[36] See, for example, *Agreement Between Chrysler Corporation and the United Auto Workers*, Production and Maintenance, Section 44, 26 October 1985.

[37] *Agreement Between New United Motor Manufacturing Inc. and the UAW*, 1 July 1985, XXVII (1.2).

system becomes stressed, workers found it became harder and harder to keep up. Once the standardized work—so painstakingly charted, refined, and recharted—had been in operation for a while, management assumed any problem was the fault of the workers, who had the burden of proof to show otherwise. Stopping the line meant the chimes and lights of the andon board immediately identified who was not keeping up. As the NUMMI manual explains: "The role of the supervisor is to go to the trouble spot as soon as the *andon* displays the problem and find out what happened. If the line is stopped and there is no safety problem, the supervisor's first priority is to get the line back into operation as fast as possible. It is the supervisor's responsibility to find out the real cause of the problem, and take counter measures."[38]

There is good reason for this pressure. An idle assembly line represents enormous costs in equipment and labor. Just-in-time multiplies these costs many times over. Thus, once the line is up to full operating speed, supervisors do become "unglued" when the line actually stops. Such pressure translates into an extreme reluctance to pull the cord and a comparable desire to keep up with the job, whatever it takes. Indeed, some NUMMI workers have used part of their breaks or come in early to build stock or get ready for their work.[39]

Others just try to work harder. Some work "in the hole" in hopes of catching up later. A Mazda worker described the catch-22 situation in which a co-worker found herself:

She had a hard time one day and pulled the stop cord several times. The next day management literally focused attention on her. Several management officials observed and they set up a video camera to record her work.... She worked into the hole too far and fell off the end of the (two-foot) platform and injured her ankle. They told her it was her fault—she didn't pull the stop cord when she fell behind.

In Japan, Toyota has actually installed photoelectric cells in some stations to check for failure to complete all operations in the allotted time. Other checking devices include floor mat sensors that are triggered if an operator moves too far from the assigned position. These automatically shut down the line. According to a Toyota management report, workers did not appreciate this further refinement and "resisted such limited forms of automatic controls because they were forced to complete

[38] *Toyota Production System 2*, Toyota Motor Corporation, June 1984.
[39] Neil Chethik, "The Intercultural Honeymoon Ends," *San Jose Mercury News*, 8 February 1987.

their jobs within the assigned cycle time. [But after supervisors explained why these controls were necessary] the workers fully accepted the system, quality control improved, and the total time consumed by line stoppages was actually reduced."[40] Thus with a fairy tale explanation, management installs electronic supervisors and electric tethers and automates the very item—the cord—that was supposed to symbolize workers' power over production.

In their argument that modern work is being reskilled, Michael Piore and Charles Sabel correctly note the trend toward increasing flexibility in the production process, perhaps a result both of computer technology and of the growing fragmentation of markets in a world economy. But it hardly follows that flexible production necessarily requires greater skill in the work force or the wholesale elimination of union-negotiated work rules, as they insist in their highly influential work. Flexibility in manufacture does not require that every part of the production system also be flexible. The level of skill required to do a particular job and the rules that structure that work often involve a conscious social choice. To use a machine tool analogy, flexible machining does not require that a drill also double as a cutter. A flexible machine may use simple tools. The flexibility is in readily switching between them.

In their plea for a new flexibility, many commentators have simultaneously denounced union work rules and job classifications usually described as "rigid" or "antiquated." But in most plants, union reliance on work rules and the grievance procedure has reflected labor's weakness, not the strong system of job control implied by scholarly observers such as Harry Katz, Jonathan Zeitlin, and Steven Tolliday, as well as Piore and Sabel.[41] The emasculation of the shop steward system, the atrophy of the wildcat job action, and the defeat of labor efforts to unionize first-line supervision forced autoworkers into a defensive reliance on seniority-based job ownership, bidding rights, and layoffs. Together with the grievance procedure, these rights reduced management's latitude to discipline militants, intensify work, or expand the realm of management prerogatives. Such work rules and well-defined job classifications do not prevent a flexible approach to manufacturing, or the use of new methods, for

---

[40] Monden, *Toyota Production System*, 145.
[41] Harry Katz, *Shifting Gears* (Cambridge, Mass.: MIT Press, 1987), 40–47; Steven Tolliday and Jonathan Zeitlin, "Shop-Floor Bargaining, Contract Unionism and Job Control: An Anglo-American Comparison," in Steven Tolliday and Jonathan Zeitlin, *The Automobile Industry and Its Workers: Between Fordism and Flexibility* (Cambridge: Polity Press, 1986), 99–120.

workers routinely and voluntarily work out of classification, help each other out, and approach mutual problems as a team. But the existence of these shop rules does offer workers, individually and as a union, a certain level of power and discretion. In effect, they provide workers with a management-recognized set of shop-floor rights, which can be abridged and modified, but only with the consent of those who hold them. And when workers feel that managers are capricious or conditions decline, "work-to-rule" and other similar shop-floor tactics often prove a quasi-legal but highly useful weapon in labor's arsenal.[42]

Thus the attractiveness to managers of the team concept plant. Here flexibility is generated not by a true reskilling of each worker but by the deployment of a multifunctional work force in which each individual is able and willing to undertake any one of a series of tightly defined and closely monitored jobs, regardless of formal training, seniority, or shop tradition. Management calls it multiskilling, but this is a misleading term. In order for a worker to do every job, either he or she must be highly trained or the jobs must be made as simple as possible. The management-by-stress choice is to make the jobs simple and keep training time to a minimum. The "skills" required in performing several related jobs of very short duration are manual dexterity, physical stamina, and the ability to follow instructions precisely. They are not skills in the usual sense of requiring training and specialized knowledge.

For management, the essence of multiskilling is therefore the willingness, on the part of the union or the individual worker, to allow supervisors to reassign jobs whenever it wishes and for whatever reason. Thus, during hiring MBS plants have shown little interest in applicants' skills

---

[42] For a larger discussion of classifications, work rules, and union power, see Parker and Slaughter, *Choosing Sides*, 74–87. MIT's Womack, Jones, and Roos would seem to support the notion that the productivity issue is not the rules and classifications themselves, but the extent to which workers choose to exercise their rights on the job. In trying to account for the reason that U.S. Ford plants exhibited the same high level of productivity as that of the Japanese transplants, the MIT authors assert that because of the confidence Ford workers held in their operating management, these "workers were ignoring the technical details of the contract on a massive scale in order to get the job done."

Unfortunately there are few credible observers who believe that worker observation of contract details or the union response at Ford was significantly different from that at GM (although in both companies there were significant variations from plant to plant reflecting local conditions and local union politics). A more likely explanation for Ford's high productivity figures in this period is the combination of plant closures, massive production overtime, and postponed maintenance. Womack et al., *The Machine That Changed the World,* 100; Daniel Luria, "The Relations between Work Rules, Plant Performance, and Costs in Vehicle Assembly Plants and Parts Production" (Paper prepared for "The Future of Work in the Automobile Industry," WBZ Conference, Berlin, November 1987), 18.

acquired from previous work and much more interest in attendance records and general attitude toward management. Once hired, he or she learns how to carry out a large number of extremely plant-specific tasks. The issue of multiskilling thus becomes less an issue of training itself than of attitude and ideology: that is, of overcoming those institutional and psychological barriers that prevent workers from rapidly shifting their attention from one well-defined job to another.

Team concept plants like NUMMI do employ traditionally skilled electricians, millwrights, maintenance workers, and the like, but these classifications have come under unremitting attack in the factory of the future. MBS plants aim to reduce the in-house trades to preventative and programmed maintenance. The skilled components—construction and major maintenance—are taken out of the bargaining unit through outside contracting and transferring work, especially computer-related tasks, to lower levels of management. NUMMI and Mazda have roughly one-third the number of skilled trades workers as more traditional plants.

Unless reversed in some substantially dramatic fashion, the new industrial relations pioneered at NUMMI and other auto plants are generating a form of enterprise unionism in North America not dissimilar to that long associated with Japanese manufacturing. Once in place, jointness arrangements provide strong incentives for workers and their local officers to identify not simply with the company that employs them but with the individual plant in which they work. First, team concept plants have generated a whole new layer of company-paid union officials, who have a material interest in the success of these participatory labor relations schemes. These so-called cooperation cops or clipboarders, who comprise as much as 5 percent of the entire work force in some factories, patrol the production lines, enforce the "jointness" spirit, and play a major role in union affairs. Plant managers frequently draw from this ideologically reliable layer to staff lower level supervisory positions.[43]

Second, because of the responsibility unionized workers now take in sustaining productivity, their employment and a portion of their pay (through various profit-sharing arrangements) are now dependent upon the relative success of their efforts, thus putting local unions in a not so subtle competition with each other. This can lead to "whipsawing" by management over wages, work rules, and other concessions during pro-

---

[43] Tom Bramble, "Industry Restructuring and Union Organisation: A Case Study of the United Auto Workers of America, 1979–1989" (Discussion paper, School of Economics and Commerce, La Trobe University, Australia, March 1990).

duction slumps, and to further cooperation with management on political and economic issues relevant to corporate profitability.

And finally, this erosion of union solidarity is exacerbated by the generation of a Japanese-style dual labor force that almost always accompanies management guarantees of job security and worker participation. Led by the Japanese transplants, American automakers now outsource a large proportion of their parts and components to an increasingly nonunion, low-wage, and offshore base of supplier and parts companies. GM's new Saturn complex in Tennessee is surrounded by such a bodyguard of small supplier firms, mimicking Toyota City in Japan. And even within factories that operate on jointness principles, a contingent work force has begun to appear.

Of course the gap between the team concept's cooperative and democratic promise and its shop-floor reality has hardly been lost on all American autoworkers. These work reorganization schemes have been the focus of several bitterly contested local union elections, among them NUMMI, Mazda, and Van Nuys, California. At Fort Wayne Truck, which GM advertisements of the late 1980s had spotlighted as a successful example of nonadversarial labor-management relations, workers complained of broken promises and lack of input. "There is too much favoritism and too many games," asserted a unionist who chose to transfer from Fort Wayne to a more traditionally organized plant. "The Company, they get to call all the shots."[44] A 1990 survey of the local's membership seemed to confirm such dissatisfaction. Ninety percent who responded did not feel the truck plant was a "true joint operated plant," 83 percent opposed the team concept "as implemented," and by a vote of 59 to 41 percent, workers at Fort Wayne wanted more job classifications.[45] Similar levels of dissatisfaction were recorded at the Mazda transplant in Flat Rock, Michigan, where the fear that few workers could remain healthy enough to make it to retirement proved particularly pervasive.[46]

---

[44] David Heath, "Disillusioned Workers Eager to Leave GM Plant," *Columbus News Sentinel,* 27 March 1989.

[45] "Update No. 8," plant bulletin from Al Clark, Shop Chairman UAW Local 2209, GM Fort Wayne Truck Plant, 19 March 1990.

[46] In a survey (75 percent response) conducted by the Mazda local in preparation for the 1991 contract bargaining, 74 percent said that their program work sheet (step-by-step instructions for doing a job) had been changed without worker consultation; and 67 percent thought such changes made their jobs harder. UAW-MMUC UNIT Local 3000, *Negotiations Newsletter,* issues 1–3, December 1990, January 1991; Mike Parker, "New Mazda Contract Eases 'Management-by-Stress' System," *Labor Notes,* May 1991.

Such grievances in a variety of automobile factories helped fuel the growth of a larger industry-wide opposition to management's new system. The now-independent Canadian Auto Workers have fought joint-ness schemes, declaring in 1989 that "this 'partnership' and its promises are false.... The truth is that management's agenda is not about surrendering its power but of finding more sophisticated ways to extend it."[47] In the United States the UAW's New Directions caucus, the most broadly based opposition grouping in more than a generation, has made headway in a number of local union elections since the late 1980s. What impact these political developments may have on North American auto unionism and on the new industrial relations remains to be seen.[48] But one thing seems clear after a decade of management-oriented experimentation. There are no competitive, market, or technological imperatives driving management to offer workers dignity and democracy on the job. Workers who aspire to decent working conditions still need a union that can organize and fight for them.

[47] Herman Rosenfeld, "CAW and the Team Concept," *Canadian Dimension* (September 1989); see also Joseph J. Fucini and Suzy Fucini, *Working for the Japanese: Inside Mazda's American Auto Plant* (New York: Free Press, 1990).

[48] This political conflict within the union, combined with clear manifestations of rank-and-file disillusionment, and a continuing hard line from the major auto companies, have together forced top UAW officials to moderate their support for the team concept. A 1990 Bargaining Convention resolution referred to Employee Involvement and Quality of Worklife as "construed by many as loaded buzz words." The resolution did endorse new forms of work organization, including "work teams," but also provided many warnings of how employers had used such methods to "undermine the protections that workers have won." UAW, *Proposed Resolution, 1990 Collective Bargaining Program*, UAW Bargaining Convention, Kansas City, 21–23 May 1990, 73.

11

Epilogue: Toward a new century

NELSON LICHTENSTEIN

What are the prospects for a democratic reorganization of the workplace in the 1990s? What would it take for Americans again to put "industrial democracy," or another, updated phrase that carries elements of the old meaning, high on their social agenda? Does the history of this idea offer any guidance to those who seek its revival?

Several of the essays in this volume have demonstrated that a public recognition of the need to reorganize the work regime arises when two conditions are fulfilled. David Montgomery and Joseph McCartin have shown that an essential precondition lies in the vigor and imagination of a working-class movement, especially when its values and language hold a transcendent meaning for even broader sections of the body politic. In the era before and during the Great War, industrial democracy first achieved something of this definitional penumbra; in the 1930s, as Gary Gerstle has demonstrated in another context, the new unions gave to the once reactionary word "Americanism" a social-democratic and culturally pluralist meaning.[1] And in the 1960s, some heavily African-American unions successfully linked their struggle for recognition and power to that of a pervasive civil rights consciousness.[2]

Of course a powerful labor movement is not enough, for as Howell Harris has demonstrated, important sections of the business community must endure a sense of organizational and ideological crisis for individual capitalists or government policy makers to entertain, much less seek to implement, new ideas about the organization of work and authority in

[1] Gary Gerstle, *Working-Class Americanism: The Politics of Labor in a Textile City, 1914–1960* (Cambridge: Cambridge University Press, 1989), 153–95 passim.
[2] See especially Brian Greenberg and Leon Fink, *Upheaval in the Quiet Zone: A History of Hospital Workers' Union, Local 1199* (Urbana: University of Illinois Press, 1989).

shop, mill, mine, and office. Such managerial reformism emerged during the Great War and its aftermath, and then again in the first few years of the Great Depression and the New Deal.

Today, hardly a trace of the first condition applies—the union movement has never been weaker in the last half century—but there is considerable evidence that a large slice of the business community is aware that existing forms of work organization and social provision are inadequate to the competitive task at hand. America has a new "labor problem." A heterogeneous, poorly motivated, poorly educated work force, frustrated and distracted by the nation's faltering systems of transport and health care, may well be responsible for many of the ills that now plague American industry. Even among the burgeoning strata of semiprofessional knowledge workers, once seen as the hope of America's postindustrial future, productivity and income have hardly lived up to expectations.[3] The chapters by Howell Harris and Mike Parker have shown that in the 1990s as well as in 1919, management efforts to engender a willing and loyal work force necessarily stand near the top of its productivity agenda. Consent, participation, identity with the firm: all these have cash value at the bottom line.

In the 1920s and 1930s, progressives in business, labor, and reform circles saw the emergence of a so-called constitutionalized work regime as the key to this dilemma. The transposition to the workplace of those democratic values celebrated in the larger polity imposed genuine limits on the power of management and promised a more routinized amelioration of work-site conflicts. But a revival of workplace parliamentarianism is hardly on the agenda today, certainly not in its collective bargaining variant, nor even as an element of Japanese-style enterprise unionism. Schemes labeled "employee involvement," "team production," and "labor-management cooperation" proliferate, but virtually all the evidence leads to the conclusion that these programs have little in common with the autonomous expression of worker hopes and aspirations that were so vital to the experimentation of the interwar era.[4]

But despite such managerial objections to the formal structures of democratic participation, a remarkable rights consciousness has never-

[3]For a typical statement of the problem, see Robert B. Reich, "Training a Skilled Work Force: Why U.S. Corporations Neglect Their Workers," *Dissent* (Winter 1992): 42–46.
[4]There have been numerous critical surveys of these schemes. For the latest indictment see Jack Metzgar, " 'Employee Involvement' Plans and the Philosophy of Labor," *Dissent* (Winter 1992): 67–72.

theless unfolded within the American workplace. The trade union movement did little to engender this phenomenon; indeed, some labor leaders and many white male unionists have felt profoundly threatened by the work-rights idea when its beneficiaries have been black, brown, or female. Instead, a series of cross-class social movements have been responsible for engendering a new set of judicially enforceable rights over the last thirty years, entitlements in a system of state-mandated due process and antidiscriminatory rights that have curbed employer power and altered social norms and expectations to a remarkable degree.

First among the new rights were those that evolved out of the civil rights movement of the 1960s and the elaboration of Title VII of the Civil Rights Act of 1964. The hiring, pay, promotion, and layoff of employees are now subject to governmental review and private litigation to an extent the union movement could hardly match, even in the heyday of the Wagner Act. The women's movement has had a parallel impact. Indeed, the unfolding of a feminist consciousness within the workplace has helped generate laws covering areas of interpersonal relations and employer-employee contact once considered exclusively private.[5]

Other workplace rights have also been legitimized or at least put on the policy agenda. These encompass the safety, health, old age, sexual orientation, and parenthood of employees. Passage in 1990 of the sweeping Americans with Disabilities Act indicates that such rights-based employment guidelines continue to regulate employer behavior, even as the legislature and the courts turn their back on more traditional union-oriented employee protections. Indeed, in the last fifteen years employee rights protected by federal legislation have been reinforced by judicial rulings in state after state that have cut deeply into the old common law doctrine of "employment at will," which once gave managers total freedom to fire or demote their workers.[6]

Such rights-oriented employee protections fill a palpable need, for repeated surveys taken among both managers and workers have revealed a precipitous, decades-long drop in the proportion of those who rate company policies and rules favorably. Among clerical workers, those who labeled their employer "fair" dropped from 70 percent in the 1950s to 20 percent at the end of the 1970s. Altogether, such rights-oriented

---

[5] The most encyclopedic account is Hugh Davis Graham, *The Civil Rights Era: Origins and Development of National Policy* (New York: Oxford University Press, 1990).
[6] Aaron Bernstein, "More Dismissed Workers Are Telling It to the Judge," *Business Week,* October 17, 1988, 68–69.

protections have had a far greater effect on employer practices and work-place relations in recent years than any development arising out of the collective bargaining process.[7]

But such a rights-based movement to transform the workplace has clear limits. Individual workers have won a measure of protection, but a rights-based approach to a constitutionalization of the workplace fails to give collective voice to employees or confront capital with demands that cannot be defined as a judicially protected mandate. Indeed, as James Atleson has shown, at the very moment when employee rights to equal treatment were winning legislative and judicial protections, the same courts were ensuring that management's core of entrepreneurial control would remain untouched by either government regulation or union bargaining pressure. The rights-based effort to build a more democratic order at the work site has had remarkably little impact upon a whole range of management prerogatives: investment decisions, technological innovations, employment levels, wage structure, and the like.

Given the uncertainty and competitive pressures under which American firms now operate, such key aspects of the job seem increasingly capricious, often rendering the newly won work rights irrelevant. Thus in the mid-1970s, a long-fought legal battle—directed both at their union and their employer—finally won for African-American steelworkers equal seniority rights and promotion opportunities in their industry. But neither the influence of the government nor the United Steelworkers could ameliorate the collapse of domestic steel employment in the early 1980s, a debacle that rendered the steel industry civil rights breakthrough largely meaningless for its presumptive beneficiaries.[8] Likewise, the assault on the "employment at will" doctrine—sparked at first by middle-aged managers abruptly terminated by once-paternalistic employers—has had virtually no impact on the speculatively driven reorganization of so many firms in the last decade.

The U.S. pattern differs substantially from that of other similarly advanced industrial societies, especially those of Western Europe, which

[7] Charles Heckscher, "Crisis and Opportunity for Labor," *Labor Law Journal* 38 (August 1987): 465–70; see also Heckscher, *The New Unionism: Employee Involvement in the Changing Corporation* (New York: Basic Books, 1988), 85.

[8] William Gould, *Black Workers in White Unions: Job Discrimination in the United States* (Ithaca, N.Y.: Cornell University Press, 1977); Robert Norrell, "Caste in Steel: Jim Crow Careers in Birmingham, Alabama," *Journal of American History* 73 (December 1986): 669–701.

have now had two generations of experience with some form of corporatist industrial governance. In Europe, what Harold Wilensky has
called "democratic corporatism" has taken hold most firmly in the small,
cohesive, highly unionized countries: Austria, Sweden, the Netherlands,
but also Germany and France, if not so completely. U.S. social scientists
of a laborite bent have looked with increasing interest and envy toward
these northern European industrial relations systems because here even
the end of the postwar economic boom, the rise of intense competition
from Japan, and the election of conservative governments have done little
to weaken the unions, the welfare state, and the corporatist structure of
national economic bargaining.[9]

Indeed, such strong unions and politically entrenched capital-labor
accords have contributed materially to the elaboration of a system of
industrial governance that opens the door to a participative role for
workers in their shops and offices. The corporatist bargain struck at the
highest levels of the political economy supports a good social wage and
places clear limits on managerial authoritarianism. This combination
creates an institutional framework that tends toward a capital-intensive,
high-wage work regime in which the representation of worker interests
takes place on multiple levels: through works councils, trade unions, or
political parties.[10]

The situation in the United States is strikingly different. As Ronald
Schatz has shown, an American variant of such a corporatist schema has
not been entirely absent from the agenda of American policy intellectuals.
Indeed, during the heyday of the New Deal, a series of institutions,
ranging from the National Recovery Administration of the early 1930s
to the War Labor Board during World War II, were premised upon the
existence of a strong central state and the creation or maintenance of an
extensive, class-wide union movement. And even after the end of such
direct governmental intervention, it appeared that the consolidation of
industry-wide bargaining after the war might generate a kind of meso-
corporatism in the U.S. that would parallel that evolving in northern
Europe. Union leaders such as Philip Murray and Walter Reuther worked
toward this end: In the steel industry, tripartite bargaining proved the

---

[9]See most recently, Thomas Geoghegan, "Labor's Choice: Helmut Kohl for President,"
New York Times, 18 March 1992, A19.
[10]Lowell Turner, *Democracy at Work: Changing World Markets and the Future of Labor
Unions* (Ithaca, N.Y.: Cornell University Press, 1991), 1–27, 117–44, 153–71.

norm for a quarter century, with virtually all settlements ratified by the White House and the Council of Economic Advisors.[11]

But this quasi-corporatist arrangement began to erode almost as soon as it took effect. The racial oligarchs of the low-wage South were never reconciled to such a system, nor were the labor-intensive employers of the booming fast food and leisure industries, who made a denunciation of the "labor bosses" a cornerstone of the Taft-Goldwater-Reagan wing of the Republican party. Without a party of their own that could artic-ulate and aggregate a class-wide interest, American unions have clung to the decentralized system of firm-centered collective bargaining that has proved to be such a historical dead end in the face of both targeted competition from abroad and deregulatory Reaganism at home.[12]

Today, the regulation of capital, either by workers or the larger polity, remains a frontier of democratic control in this era of global financial turmoil. In the 1980s, even without government support, there was a good deal of experimentation, and it seemed just possible that some sort of worker/union penetration of the larger corporate decision-making pro-cess might prove feasible, if only as a quid pro quo for the wage, benefit, and work-rule concessions unionized employees offered—or were blud-geoned into relinquishing. The Chrysler Corporation put the UAW pres-ident on the company's board of directors. Unionized machinists at Eastern Airlines also won seats on their company's board and consid-erable influence over deployment of new technology and personnel in the shop. Employee stock ownership plans proliferated, as did union efforts to put pension fund financial clout at the service of corporate survival and job security.[13]

These efforts were almost all failures, as were the faintly heard calls for an industrial policy that emanated from Harvard's Kennedy School of Government and the AFL-CIO building across from the White House. Collapse of the debt-driven boom of the 1980s proved the proximate

---

[11] Ronald Schatz, "Battling over Government's Role," in Paul Clark, Peter Gottlieb, and Donald Kennedy, eds., *Forging a Union of Steel: Philip Murray, SWOC and the United Steelworkers* (Ithaca, N.Y.: ILR Press, 1987), 87–102.

[12] For an elaboration of this view, see Nelson Lichtenstein, "From Corporatism to Collective Bargaining: Organized Labor and the Eclipse of Social Democracy in the Postwar Era," in Steve Fraser and Gary Gerstle, eds., *The Rise and Fall of the New Deal Era* (Princeton: Princeton University Press, 1989), 122–52.

[13] Robert Reich and John D. Donahue, *New Deals: The Chrysler Revival and the American System* (New York: Times Books, 1985), 264–97; Kim Moody, *An Injury to All: The Decline of American Unionism* (New York: Verso, 1988), 288–301; George Strauss, "Industrial Relations: Time of Change," *Industrial Relations* 23 (Winter 1984): 1–15.

cause. But as Sanford Jacoby has most recently argued, in this volume and elsewhere, American managers have been quite exceptional in their hostility toward any effort that might limit their entrepreneurial freedom, even in periods of deep economic crisis. In contrast to the experience of virtually every other industrial nation, American managers had built large, autonomous business enterprises long before the rise of either a strong central state or a national union movement. By the time such counter institutions did arise in the New Deal era, the large business corporation effectively enjoyed a degree of political and institutional power without parallel in the capitalist world. The political party system, the courts, the civil service, local government, the federal regulatory tradition, all had been shaped by the early rise of these huge aggregations of capital and by the fiercely antiunion, antigovernment ideology that had sunk such deep roots within the American bourgeoisie.[14]

Thus even where workers and managers have sought to reorganize production and engender new forms of democratic participation, the attempt to do so in a single firm, factory, or office frequently degenerates into a form of employee manipulation. As Mike Parker has shown, workers are keenly aware that the economic and organizational penalties for failure to cooperate with management are all too often layoffs, work transfers, and plant closures. Without the protections offered by a dense welfare state, a broadly engaged union movement, and a relatively egalitarian wage structure, efforts to build industrial democracy in a single work site are virtually doomed, for the imbalance of power between workers and managers cannot be ignored no matter how sincere the collaboration or elaborate the participatory apparatus.[15]

The parochialism of the American union movement and the weakness of the U.S. welfare state have meant that managers in this country have found few obstacles to the progressive ghettoization of the unionized employment sector. Indeed, the weaker American labor has become, the more it is resented, and not only by those who hire fifty-dollar-an-hour plumbers and get their cars fixed at union garages. Confined to a few high-wage bastions, union labor seems a privileged elite, remote and

---

[14] Sanford Jacoby, "American Exceptionalism Revisited: The Importance of Management," in Jacoby, ed., *Masters to Managers* (New York: Columbia University Press, 1991), 180–95 passim.

[15] This point is well demonstrated through a comparison of the effort to introduce similar workplace participation schemes at Volvo and British Leyland. Jonas Pontusson, "The Politics of New Technology and Job Redesign: A Comparison of Volvo and British Leyland," *Economic and Industrial Democracy* 11 (1990): 311–36.

irrelevant to the working majority. Organized labor may therefore look arrogant, but it is in fact suffering from an isolation thrust upon it by its enemies.

Can this impasse be broken? Can the now shell-shocked trade unions reemerge as the organizational and ideological kernel of a revived industrial democracy? Nothing seems more problematic in this last decade of the twentieth century. Yet historians of social change know that when it comes, political and institutional democratization can be rapid indeed, as the unexpected events in Eastern Europe have so recently demonstrated. There communism collapsed, less because of its manifest inefficiency than because both workers and intellectuals found its ideology so utterly at variance with social and political reality.

To make the idea of industrial democracy concrete and relevant, three things have to happen. First, unions have to find some way to identify their organizational fate with the rights consciousness that remains so pervasive in American society. As David Brody has emphasized, whatever the fate of workplace contractualism, its origins lie in the quest for industrial justice that energized so many workers in the years between the Great War and the end of the Great Depression. During the battles over employee representation in the early New Deal, the terms of a just workplace system took shape and gained hegemonic assent. Empowered by the Wagner Act, the industrial unions then seized that system, gave it contractual form, and made themselves the institutional embodiment of the work rights newly claimed by basic industry workers.[16] This linkage must be revived, either in a reform version of contemporary unionism or in new organizations that nevertheless fulfill those same sociopolitical functions.

Second, fear and repression at work must decline. The American workplace today is not unlike that of Eastern Europe during the Brezhnev era. Men and women rely on custom, friendship, and ambition to carve out their own tolerable and autonomous worlds, but collective action in the workplace meets with legally sanctioned repression of a massive and sustained character. Yet when they can get away with it, workers flock to trade unions regardless of the color of their collar. In Canada and in most public sector workplaces, the danger of trying to organize a union is minimal: as a consequence, unionization rates are two or three times

[16] In addition to Brody's chapter, see Brody, "The Breakdown of Labor's Social Contract: Historical Reflections, Future Prospects," *Dissent* (Winter 1992): 40.

higher than in private American firms. And workers want democracy in the organizations that claim to represent their interests. This was most spectacularly demonstrated in the federally supervised Teamsters' Union election of 1991, which threw out a corrupt old guard and swept to power a slate of genuine reformists.[17]

Finally, advocates of industrial democracy must recognize that the workplace is not an isolated social laboratory; the potential for a reordering of work life there is linked by a hundred threads to the larger political economy. The feebleness of the American welfare state and the massive inequality of the nation's wage structure generate a serflike relation between even well-paid workers and their employers. When good jobs are scarce, workers see self-assertion as a threat to those jobs and to the vital health, vacation, and pension benefits to which such employment is linked.[18] Moreover, in even the most stable capitalist order, individual work sites are transitory institutions whose very existence is the product of economic forces far outside the control of workers or their immediate managers. A new industrial democracy must recognize this pressing reality and win some purchase upon the mobility of capital and the structure of the world economy. In short, the reemergence of democracy in the workplace requires more than ever the growth of a vigorous social and political democracy without.

[17] Paul Weiler, *Governing the Workplace: The Future of Labor and Employment Law* (Cambridge, Mass.: Harvard University Press, 1990); Craig Becker, "Democracy in the Workplace: Union Representation Elections and Federal Labor Law" (unpublished ms.); see also Thomas Geoghegan, *Which Side Are You On?: Trying to Be for Labor When It's Flat on Its Back* (New York: Farrar, Straus, and Giroux, 1991), for a wonderfully evocative portrayal of the union scene in contemporary Chicago.

[18] Defeat of the UAW Caterpillar workers is but the latest example. See Steven Greenhouse, "The Union Movement Loses Another Big One," *New York Times*, 19 April 1992, 1E; "Maybe Caterpillar Can Pick Up Where It Left Off," *Business Week*, 27 April 1992, 35.

About the authors

JAMES B. ATLESON is Professor of Law, State University of New York at Buffalo. He is the author of *Values and Assumptions in American Labor Law* (1983).

DAVID BRODY is Professor of History, University of California, Davis. His books include *Workers in Industrial America: Essays on the Twentieth Century Struggle* (1981), *Labor in Crisis: The Steel Strike of 1919* (1965), and *Steelworkers in America: The Nonunion Era* (1960).

HOWELL JOHN HARRIS is a Lecturer in History at the University of Durham. A Woodrow Wilson Center Fellow in 1986, he is the author of *The Right to Manage: Industrial Relations Policies of American Business in the 1940s* (1982).

SANFORD M. JACOBY is Professor of History and Industrial Relations at the University of California, Los Angeles. He is the author of *Employing Bureaucracy: Managers, Unions, and the Transformation of Work in American Industry* (1985) and editor of *Masters to Managers: Historical and Comparative Perspectives on American Employers* (1991).

MICHAEL J. LACEY, Director of the Division of United States Studies, Woodrow Wilson International Center for Scholars, is a coeditor of *A Culture of Rights: The Bill of Rights in Philosophy, Politics, and Law—1791 and 1991* (1992) and the editor of *Religion and Twentieth-Century American Intellectual Life* (1989) and *The Truman Presidency* (1989).

NELSON LICHTENSTEIN is Professor of History, University of Virginia. He is the editor of *On the Line: Essays in the History of Auto Work*

(1989) and the author of *Labor's War at Home: The CIO in World War II* (1983).

JOSEPH A. MCCARTIN is Assistant Professor of History, State University of New York at Geneseo. He received his doctorate at the State University of New York, Binghamton, and he is revising for publication his dissertation on workers, unions, and the state during World War I.

DAVID MONTGOMERY is Farnam Professor of History, Yale University. His books include *The Fall of the House of Labor: The Workplace, the State, and American Labor Activism, 1865–1925* (1987), *Workers' Control in America: Studies in the History of Work, Technology, and Labor Struggles* (1979), and *Beyond Equality: Labor and the Radical Republicans, 1862–1872* (1967).

MIKE PARKER is an industrial electrician in Detroit and a frequent lecturer on trade union issues. He is a coauthor, with Jane Slaughter, of *Choosing Sides: Unions and the Team Concept* (1988) and the author of *Inside the Circle: A Union Guide to Quality of Work Life* (1985).

RONALD W. SCHATZ is Associate Professor of History, Wesleyan University. He is the author of *The Electrical Workers: A History of Labor at General Electric and Westinghouse, 1923–60* (1983).

Index

287